Algorithms and Data Structures

Kurt Mehlhorn · Peter Sanders

Algorithms and Data Structures

The Basic Toolbox

 Springer

Prof. Dr. Kurt Mehlhorn
Max-Planck-Institut für Informatik
Saarbrücken
Germany
mehlhorn@mpi-inf.mpg.de

Prof. Dr. Peter Sanders
Universität Karlsruhe
Germany
sanders@ira.uka.de

ISBN 978-3-642-09682-2   e-ISBN 978-3-540-77978-0

DOI 10.1007/978-3-540-77978-0

ACM Computing Classification (1998): F.2, E.1, E.2, G.2, B.2, D.1, I.2.8

© 2010 Springer- Verlag Berlin Heidelberg

Cover design: KünkelLopka GmbH, Heidelberg

Printed on acid-free paper

9 8 7 6 5 4 3 2 1

springer.com

To all algorithmicists

Preface

Algorithms are at the heart of every nontrivial computer application. Therefore every computer scientist and every professional programmer should know about the basic algorithmic toolbox: structures that allow efficient organization and retrieval of data, frequently used algorithms, and generic techniques for modeling, understanding, and solving algorithmic problems.

This book is a concise introduction to this basic toolbox, intended for students and professionals familiar with programming and basic mathematical language. We have used the book in undergraduate courses on algorithmics. In our graduate-level courses, we make most of the book a prerequisite, and concentrate on the starred sections and the more advanced material. We believe that, even for undergraduates, a concise yet clear and simple presentation makes material more accessible, as long as it includes examples, pictures, informal explanations, exercises, and some linkage to the real world.

Most chapters have the same basic structure. We begin by discussing a problem as it occurs in a real-life situation. We illustrate the most important applications and then introduce simple solutions *as informally as possible and as formally as necessary* to really understand the issues at hand. When we move to more advanced and optional issues, this approach gradually leads to a more mathematical treatment, including theorems and proofs. This way, the book should work for readers with a wide range of mathematical expertise. There are also advanced sections (marked with a *) where we *recommend* that readers should skip them on first reading. Exercises provide additional examples, alternative approaches and opportunities to think about the problems. It is highly recommended to take a look at the exercises even if there is no time to solve them during the first reading. In order to be able to concentrate on ideas rather than programming details, we use pictures, words, and high-level pseudocode to explain our algorithms. A section "implementation notes" links these abstract ideas to clean, efficient implementations in real programming languages such as C++ and Java. Each chapter ends with a section on further findings that provides a glimpse at the state of the art, generalizations, and advanced solutions.

Algorithmics is a modern and active area of computer science, even at the level of the basic toolbox. We have made sure that we present algorithms in a modern way, including explicitly formulated invariants. We also discuss recent trends, such as algorithm engineering, memory hierarchies, algorithm libraries, and certifying algorithms.

We have chosen to organize most of the material by problem domain and not by solution technique. The final chapter on optimization techniques is an exception. We find that presentation by problem domain allows a more concise presentation. However, it is also important that readers and students obtain a good grasp of the available techniques. Therefore, we have structured the final chapter by techniques, and an extensive index provides cross-references between different applications of the same technique. Bold page numbers in the Index indicate the pages where concepts are defined.

Karlsruhe, Saarbrücken,   *Kurt Mehlhorn*
February, 2008   *Peter Sanders*

Contents

1

Appetizer: Integer Arithmetics

An appetizer is supposed to stimulate the appetite at the beginning of a meal. This is exactly the purpose of this chapter. We want to stimulate your interest in algorithmic[1] techniques by showing you a surprising result. The school method for multiplying integers is not the best multiplication algorithm; there are much faster ways to multiply large integers, i.e., integers with thousands or even millions of digits, and we shall teach you one of them.

Arithmetic on long integers is needed in areas such as cryptography, geometric computing, and computer algebra and so an improved multiplication algorithm is not just an intellectual gem but also useful for applications. On the way, we shall learn basic analysis and basic algorithm engineering techniques in a simple setting. We shall also see the interplay of theory and experiment.

We assume that integers are represented as digit strings. In the base B number system, where B is an integer larger than one, there are digits 0, 1, to $B - 1$ and a digit string $a_{n-1}a_{n-2}\ldots a_1 a_0$ represents the number $\sum_{0 \leq i < n} a_i B^i$. The most important systems with a small value of B are base 2, with digits 0 and 1, base 10, with digits 0 to 9, and base 16, with digits 0 to 15 (frequently written as 0 to 9, A, B, C, D, E, and F). Larger bases, such as 2^8, 2^{16}, 2^{32}, and 2^{64}, are also useful. For example,

$$\text{``10101'' in base 2 represents} \quad 1 \cdot 2^4 + 0 \cdot 2^3 + 1 \cdot 2^2 + 0 \cdot 2^1 + 1 \cdot 2^0 = \quad 21,$$

$$\text{``924'' in base 10 represents} \quad 9 \cdot 10^2 + 2 \cdot 10^1 + 4 \cdot 10^0 = \quad 924\,.$$

We assume that we have two primitive operations at our disposal: the addition of three digits with a two-digit result (this is sometimes called a full adder), and the

---

[1] The Soviet stamp on this page shows *Muhammad ibn Musa al-Khwarizmi* (born approximately 780; died between 835 and 850), Persian mathematician and astronomer from the Khorasan province of present-day Uzbekistan. The word "algorithm" is derived from his name.

multiplication of two digits with a two-digit result.[2] For example, in base 10, we have

$$\begin{array}{r} 3 \\ 5 \\ \underline{5} \\ 13 \end{array} \qquad \text{and} \qquad 6 \cdot 7 = 42 \,.$$

We shall measure the efficiency of our algorithms by the number of primitive operations executed.

We can artificially turn any n-digit integer into an m-digit integer for any $m \geq n$ by adding additional leading zeros. Concretely, "425" and "000425" represent the same integer. We shall use a and b for the two operands of an addition or multiplication and assume throughout this section that a and b are n-digit integers. The assumption that both operands have the same length simplifies the presentation without changing the key message of the chapter. We shall come back to this remark at the end of the chapter. We refer to the digits of a as a_{n-1} to a_0, with a_{n-1} being the most significant digit (also called leading digit) and a_0 being the least significant digit, and write $a = (a_{n-1} \ldots a_0)$. The leading digit may be zero. Similarly, we use b_{n-1} to b_0 to denote the digits of b, and write $b = (b_{n-1} \ldots b_0)$.

1.1 Addition

We all know how to add two integers $a = (a_{n-1} \ldots a_0)$ and $b = (b_{n-1} \ldots b_0)$. We simply write one under the other with the least significant digits aligned, and sum the integers digitwise, carrying a single digit from one position to the next. This digit is called a *carry*. The result will be an $n+1$-digit integer $s = (s_n \ldots s_0)$. Graphically,

a_{n-1}	$\ldots$	a_1	a_0	first operand
b_{n-1}	$\ldots$	b_1	b_0	second operand
$c_n \; c_{n-1}$	$\ldots$	c_1	0	carries
$s_n \; s_{n-1}$	$\ldots$	s_1	s_0	sum

where c_n to c_0 is the sequence of carries and $s = (s_n \ldots s_0)$ is the sum. We have $c_0 = 0$, $c_{i+1} \cdot B + s_i = a_i + b_i + c_i$ for $0 \leq i < n$ and $s_n = c_n$. As a program, this is written as

$c = 0 : Digit$ // Variable for the carry digit
for $i := 0$ **to** $n-1$ **do** add a_i, b_i, and c to form s_i and a new carry c
$s_n := c$

We need one primitive operation for each position, and hence a total of n primitive operations.

Theorem 1.1. *The addition of two n-digit integers requires exactly n primitive operations. The result is an $n+1$-digit integer.*

---

[2] Observe that the sum of three digits is at most $3(B-1)$ and the product of two digits is at most $(B-1)^2$, and that both expressions are bounded by $(B-1) \cdot B^1 + (B-1) \cdot B^0 = B^2 - 1$, the largest integer that can be written with two digits.

1.2 Multiplication: The School Method

We all know how to multiply two integers. In this section, we shall review the "school method". In a later section, we shall get to know a method which is significantly faster for large integers.

We shall proceed slowly. We first review how to multiply an n-digit integer a by a one-digit integer b_j. We use b_j for the one-digit integer, since this is how we need it below. For any digit a_i of a, we form the product $a_i \cdot b_j$. The result is a two-digit integer $(c_i d_i)$, i.e.,

$$a_i \cdot b_j = c_i \cdot B + d_i .$$

We form two integers, $c = (c_{n-1} \ldots c_0\, 0)$ and $d = (d_{n-1} \ldots d_0)$, from the c's and d's, respectively. Since the c's are the higher-order digits in the products, we add a zero digit at the end. We add c and d to obtain the product $p_j = a \cdot b_j$. Graphically,

$$(a_{n-1} \ldots a_i \ldots a_0) \cdot b_j \quad \longrightarrow \quad \frac{\begin{array}{ccccccc} c_{n-1} & c_{n-2} & \ldots & c_i & c_{i-1} & \ldots & c_0 & 0 \\ d_{n-1} & \ldots & d_{i+1} & d_i & & \ldots & d_1 & d_0 \end{array}}{\text{sum of } c \text{ and } d}$$

Let us determine the number of primitive operations. For each i, we need one primitive operation to form the product $a_i \cdot b_j$, for a total of n primitive operations. Then we add two $n+1$-digit numbers. This requires $n+1$ primitive operations. So the total number of primitive operations is $2n+1$.

Lemma 1.2. *We can multiply an n-digit number by a one-digit number with $2n+1$ primitive operations. The result is an $n+1$-digit number.*

When you multiply an n-digit number by a one-digit number, you will probably proceed slightly differently. You combine[3] the generation of the products $a_i \cdot b_j$ with the summation of c and d into a single phase, i.e., you create the digits of c and d when they are needed in the final addition. We have chosen to generate them in a separate phase because this simplifies the description of the algorithm.

Exercise 1.1. Give a program for the multiplication of a and b_j that operates in a single phase.

We can now turn to the multiplication of two n-digit integers. The school method for integer multiplication works as follows: we first form partial products p_j by multiplying a by the j-th digit b_j of b, and then sum the suitably aligned products $p_j \cdot B^j$ to obtain the product of a and b. Graphically,

$$\frac{\begin{array}{cccccccc} p_{0,n} & p_{0,n-1} & \cdots & p_{0,2} & p_{0,1} & p_{0,0} \\ p_{1,n} & p_{1,n-1} & p_{1,n-2} & \cdots & p_{1,1} & p_{1,0} \\ p_{2,n} & p_{2,n-1} & p_{2,n-2} & p_{2,n-3} & \cdots & p_{2,0} \\ & & \cdots & & & \\ p_{n-1,n} & \cdots & p_{n-1,3} & p_{n-1,2} & p_{n-1,1} & p_{n-1,0} \end{array}}{\text{sum of the } n \text{ partial products}}$$

---

[3] In the literature on compiler construction and performance optimization, this transformation is known as *loop fusion*.

The description in pseudocode is more compact. We initialize the product p to zero and then add to it the partial products $a \cdot b_j \cdot B^j$ one by one:

$$p = 0 \; : \mathbb{N}$$
$$\textbf{for } j := 0 \textbf{ to } n-1 \textbf{ do } \; p := p + a \cdot b_j \cdot B^j$$

Let us analyze the number of primitive operations required by the school method. Each partial product p_j requires $2n+1$ primitive operations, and hence all partial products together require $2n^2 + n$ primitive operations. The product $a \cdot b$ is a $2n$-digit number, and hence all summations $p + a \cdot b_j \cdot B^j$ are summations of $2n$-digit integers. Each such addition requires at most $2n$ primitive operations, and hence all additions together require at most $2n^2$ primitive operations. Thus, we need no more than $4n^2 + n$ primitive operations in total.

A simple observation allows us to improve this bound. The number $a \cdot b_j \cdot B^j$ has $n+1+j$ digits, the last j of which are zero. We can therefore start the addition in the $j+1$-th position. Also, when we add $a \cdot b_j \cdot B^j$ to p, we have $p = a \cdot (b_{j-1} \cdots b_0)$, i.e., p has $n+j$ digits. Thus, the addition of p and $a \cdot b_j \cdot B^j$ amounts to the addition of two $n+1$-digit numbers and requires only $n+1$ primitive operations. Therefore, all additions together require only $n^2 + n$ primitive operations. We have thus shown the following result.

Theorem 1.3. *The school method multiplies two n-digit integers with $3n^2 + 2n$ primitive operations.*

We have now analyzed the numbers of primitive operations required by the school methods for integer addition and integer multiplication. The number M_n of primitive operations for the school method for integer multiplication is $3n^2 + 2n$. Observe that $3n^2 + 2n = n^2(3 + 2/n)$, and hence $3n^2 + 2n$ is essentially the same as $3n^2$ for large n. We say that M_n *grows quadratically*. Observe also that

$$M_n / M_{n/2} = \frac{3n^2 + 2n}{3(n/2)^2 + 2(n/2)} = \frac{n^2(3 + 2/n)}{(n/2)^2(3 + 4/n)} = 4 \cdot \frac{3n+2}{3n+4} \approx 4 \,,$$

i.e., quadratic growth has the consequence of essentially quadrupling the number of primitive operations when the size of the instance is doubled.

Assume now that we actually implement the multiplication algorithm in our favorite programming language (we shall do so later in the chapter), and then time the program on our favorite machine for various n-digit integers a and b and various n. What should we expect? We want to argue that we shall see quadratic growth. The reason is that *primitive operations are representative of the running time of the algorithm*. Consider the addition of two n-digit integers first. What happens when the program is executed? For each position i, the digits a_i and b_i have to be moved to the processing unit, the sum $a_i + b_i + c$ has to be formed, the digit s_i of the result needs to be stored in memory, the carry c is updated, the index i is incremented, and a test for loop exit needs to be performed. Thus, for each i, the same number of machine cycles is executed. We have counted one primitive operation for each i, and hence the number of primitive operations is representative of the number of machine cycles executed. Of course, there are additional effects, for example pipelining and the

n	T_n (sec)	$T_n/T_{n/2}$
8	0.00000469	
16	0.0000154	3.28527
32	0.0000567	3.67967
64	0.000222	3.91413
128	0.000860	3.87532
256	0.00347	4.03819
512	0.0138	3.98466
1024	0.0547	3.95623
2048	0.220	4.01923
4096	0.880	4
8192	3.53	4.01136
16384	14.2	4.01416
32768	56.7	4.00212
65536	227	4.00635
131072	910	4.00449

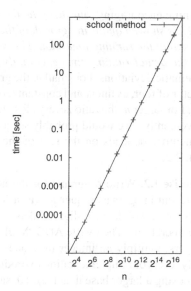

Fig. 1.1. The running time of the school method for the multiplication of n-digit integers. The three columns of the table on the *left* give n, the running time T_n of the C++ implementation given in Sect. 1.7, and the ratio $T_n/T_{n/2}$. The plot on the *right* shows $\log T_n$ versus $\log n$, and we see essentially a line. Observe that if $T_n = \alpha n^\beta$ for some constants α and β, then $T_n/T_{n/2} = 2^\beta$ and $\log T_n = \beta \log n + \log \alpha$, i.e., $\log T_n$ depends linearly on $\log n$ with slope β. In our case, the slope is two. Please, use a ruler to check

complex transport mechanism for data between memory and the processing unit, but they will have a similar effect for all i, and hence the number of primitive operations is also representative of the running time of an actual implementation on an actual machine. The argument extends to multiplication, since multiplication of a number by a one-digit number is a process similar to addition and the second phase of the school method for multiplication amounts to a series of additions.

Let us confirm the above argument by an experiment. Figure 1.1 shows execution times of a C++ implementation of the school method; the program can be found in Sect. 1.7. For each n, we performed a large number[4] of multiplications of n-digit random integers and then determined the average running time T_n; T_n is listed in the second column. We also show the ratio $T_n/T_{n/2}$. Figure 1.1 also shows a plot of the data points[5] $(\log n, \log T_n)$. The data exhibits approximately quadratic growth, as we can deduce in various ways. The ratio $T_n/T_{n/2}$ is always close to four, and the double logarithmic plot shows essentially a line of slope two. The experiments

---

[4] The internal clock that measures CPU time returns its timings in some units, say milliseconds, and hence the rounding required introduces an error of up to one-half of this unit. It is therefore important that the experiment timed takes much longer than this unit, in order to reduce the effect of rounding.

[5] Throughout this book, we use $\log x$ to denote the logarithm to base 2, $\log_2 x$.

are quite encouraging: *our theoretical analysis has predictive value. Our theoretical analysis showed quadratic growth of the number of primitive operations, we argued above that the running time should be related to the number of primitive operations, and the actual running time essentially grows quadratically.* However, we also see systematic deviations. For small n, the growth from one row to the next is less than by a factor of four, as linear and constant terms in the running time still play a substantial role. For larger n, the ratio is very close to four. For very large n (too large to be timed conveniently), we would probably see a factor larger than four, since the access time to memory depends on the size of the data. We shall come back to this point in Sect. 2.2.

Exercise 1.2. Write programs for the addition and multiplication of long integers. Represent integers as sequences (arrays or lists or whatever your programming language offers) of decimal digits and use the built-in arithmetic to implement the primitive operations. Then write ADD, MULTIPLY1, and MULTIPLY functions that add integers, multiply an integer by a one-digit number, and multiply integers, respectively. Use your implementation to produce your own version of Fig. 1.1. Experiment with using a larger base than base 10, say base 2^{16}.

Exercise 1.3. Describe and analyze the school method for division.

1.3 Result Checking

Our algorithms for addition and multiplication are quite simple, and hence it is fair to assume that we can implement them correctly in the programming language of our choice. However, writing software[6] is an error-prone activity, and hence we should always ask ourselves whether we can check the results of a computation. For multiplication, the authors were taught the following technique in elementary school. The method is known as *Neunerprobe* in German, "casting out nines" in English, and *preuve par neuf* in French.

Add the digits of a. If the sum is a number with more than one digit, sum its digits. Repeat until you arrive at a one-digit number, called the checksum of a. We use s_a to denote this checksum. Here is an example:

$$4528 \to 19 \to 10 \to 1 .$$

Do the same for b and the result c of the computation. This gives the checksums s_b and s_c. All checksums are single-digit numbers. Compute $s_a \cdot s_b$ and form its checksum s. If s differs from s_c, c is not equal to $a \cdot b$. This test was described by al-Khwarizmi in his book on algebra.

Let us go through a simple example. Let $a = 429$, $b = 357$, and $c = 154153$. Then $s_a = 6$, $s_b = 6$, and $s_c = 1$. Also, $s_a \cdot s_b = 36$ and hence $s = 9$. So $s_c \neq s$ and

---

[6] The bug in the division algorithm of the floating-point unit of the original Pentium chip became infamous. It was caused by a few missing entries in a lookup table used by the algorithm.

hence s_c is not the product of a and b. Indeed, the correct product is $c = 153153$. Its checksum is 9, and hence the correct product passes the test. The test is not foolproof, as $c = 135153$ also passes the test. However, the test is quite useful and detects many mistakes.

What is the mathematics behind this test? We shall explain a more general method. Let q be any positive integer; in the method described above, $q = 9$. Let s_a be the remainder, or residue, in the integer division of a by q, i.e., $s_a = a - \lfloor a/q \rfloor \cdot q$. Then $0 \leq s_a < q$. In mathematical notation, $s_a = a \bmod q$.[7] Similarly, $s_b = b \bmod q$ and $s_c = c \bmod q$. Finally, $s = (s_a \cdot s_b) \bmod q$. If $c = a \cdot b$, then it must be the case that $s = s_c$. Thus $s \neq s_c$ proves $c \neq a \cdot b$ and uncovers a mistake in the multiplication. What do we know if $s = s_c$? We know that q divides the difference of c and $a \cdot b$. If this difference is nonzero, the mistake will be detected by any q which does not divide the difference.

Let us continue with our example and take $q = 7$. Then $a \bmod 7 = 2$, $b \bmod 7 = 0$ and hence $s = (2 \cdot 0) \bmod 7 = 0$. But $135153 \bmod 7 = 4$, and we have uncovered that $135153 \neq 429 \cdot 357$.

Exercise 1.4. Explain why the method learned by the authors in school corresponds to the case $q = 9$. Hint: $10^k \bmod 9 = 1$ for all $k \geq 0$.

Exercise 1.5 (*Elferprobe*, casting out elevens). Powers of ten have very simple remainders modulo 11, namely $10^k \bmod 11 = (-1)^k$ for all $k \geq 0$, i.e., $1 \bmod 11 = 1$, $10 \bmod 11 = -1$, $100 \bmod 11 = +1$, $1\,000 \bmod 11 = -1$, etc. Describe a simple test to check the correctness of a multiplication modulo 11.

1.4 A Recursive Version of the School Method

We shall now derive a recursive version of the school method. This will be our first encounter with the *divide-and-conquer* paradigm, one of the fundamental paradigms in algorithm design.

Let a and b be our two n-digit integers which we want to multiply. Let $k = \lfloor n/2 \rfloor$. We split a into two numbers a_1 and a_0; a_0 consists of the k least significant digits and a_1 consists of the $n - k$ most significant digits.[8] We split b analogously. Then

$$a = a_1 \cdot B^k + a_0 \quad \text{and} \quad b = b_1 \cdot B^k + b_0 ,$$

and hence

$$a \cdot b = a_1 \cdot b_1 \cdot B^{2k} + (a_1 \cdot b_0 + a_0 \cdot b_1) \cdot B^k + a_0 \cdot b_0 .$$

This formula suggests the following algorithm for computing $a \cdot b$:

---

[7] The method taught in school uses residues in the range 1 to 9 instead of 0 to 8 according to the definition $s_a = a - (\lceil a/q \rceil - 1) \cdot q$.

[8] Observe that we have changed notation; a_0 and a_1 now denote the two parts of a and are no longer single digits.

(a) Split a and b into a_1, a_0, b_1, and b_0.
(b) Compute the four products $a_1 \cdot b_1$, $a_1 \cdot b_0$, $a_0 \cdot b_1$, and $a_0 \cdot b_0$.
(c) Add the suitably aligned products to obtain $a \cdot b$.

Observe that the numbers a_1, a_0, b_1, and b_0 are $\lceil n/2 \rceil$-digit numbers and hence the multiplications in step (b) are simpler than the original multiplication if $\lceil n/2 \rceil < n$, i.e., $n > 1$. The complete algorithm is now as follows. To multiply one-digit numbers, use the multiplication primitive. To multiply n-digit numbers for $n \geq 2$, use the three-step approach above.

It is clear why this approach is called *divide-and-conquer*. We reduce the problem of multiplying a and b to some number of *simpler* problems of the same kind. A divide-and-conquer algorithm always consists of three parts: in the first part, we split the original problem into simpler problems of the same kind (our step (a)); in the second part we solve the simpler problems using the same method (our step (b)); and, in the third part, we obtain the solution to the original problem from the solutions to the subproblems (our step (c)).

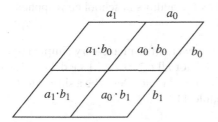

Fig. 1.2. Visualization of the school method and its recursive variant. The rhombus-shaped area indicates the partial products in the multiplication $a \cdot b$. The four subareas correspond to the partial products $a_1 \cdot b_1$, $a_1 \cdot b_0$, $a_0 \cdot b_1$, and $a_0 \cdot b_0$. In the recursive scheme, we first sum the partial products in the four subareas and then, in a second step, add the four resulting sums

What is the connection of our recursive integer multiplication to the school method? It is really the same method. Figure 1.2 shows that the products $a_1 \cdot b_1$, $a_1 \cdot b_0$, $a_0 \cdot b_1$, and $a_0 \cdot b_0$ are also computed in the school method. Knowing that our recursive integer multiplication is just the school method in disguise tells us that the recursive algorithm uses a quadratic number of primitive operations. Let us also derive this from first principles. This will allow us to introduce recurrence relations, a powerful concept for the analysis of recursive algorithms.

Lemma 1.4. *Let $T(n)$ be the maximal number of primitive operations required by our recursive multiplication algorithm when applied to n-digit integers. Then*

$$T(n) \leq \begin{cases} 1 & \text{if } n = 1, \\ 4 \cdot T(\lceil n/2 \rceil) + 3 \cdot 2 \cdot n & \text{if } n \geq 2. \end{cases}$$

Proof. Multiplying two one-digit numbers requires one primitive multiplication. This justifies the case $n = 1$. So, assume $n \geq 2$. Splitting a and b into the four pieces a_1, a_0, b_1, and b_0 requires no primitive operations.[9] Each piece has at most $\lceil n/2 \rceil$

---

[9] It will require work, but it is work that we do not account for in our analysis.

digits and hence the four recursive multiplications require at most $4 \cdot T(\lceil n/2 \rceil)$ primitive operations. Finally, we need three additions to assemble the final result. Each addition involves two numbers of at most $2n$ digits and hence requires at most $2n$ primitive operations. This justifies the inequality for $n \geq 2$. $\square$

In Sect. 2.6, we shall learn that such recurrences are easy to solve and yield the already conjectured quadratic execution time of the recursive algorithm.

Lemma 1.5. *Let $T(n)$ be the maximal number of primitive operations required by our recursive multiplication algorithm when applied to n-digit integers. Then $T(n) \leq 7n^2$ if n is a power of two, and $T(n) \leq 28n^2$ for all n.*

Proof. We refer the reader to Sect. 1.8 for a proof. $\square$

1.5 Karatsuba Multiplication

In 1962, the Soviet mathematician Karatsuba [104] discovered a faster way of multiplying large integers. The running time of his algorithm grows like $n^{\log 3} \approx n^{1.58}$. The method is surprisingly simple. Karatsuba observed that a simple algebraic identity allows one multiplication to be eliminated in the divide-and-conquer implementation, i.e., one can multiply n-bit numbers using only *three* multiplications of integers half the size.

The details are as follows. Let a and b be our two n-digit integers which we want to multiply. Let $k = \lfloor n/2 \rfloor$. As above, we split a into two numbers a_1 and a_0; a_0 consists of the k least significant digits and a_1 consists of the $n - k$ most significant digits. We split b in the same way. Then

$$a = a_1 \cdot B^k + a_0 \quad \text{and} \quad b = b_1 \cdot B^k + b_0$$

and hence (the magic is in the second equality)

$$a \cdot b = a_1 \cdot b_1 \cdot B^{2k} + (a_1 \cdot b_0 + a_0 \cdot b_1) \cdot B^k + a_0 \cdot b_0$$
$$= a_1 \cdot b_1 \cdot B^{2k} + ((a_1 + a_0) \cdot (b_1 + b_0) - (a_1 \cdot b_1 + a_0 \cdot b_0)) \cdot B^k + a_0 \cdot b_0 .$$

At first sight, we have only made things more complicated. A second look, however, shows that the last formula can be evaluated with only three multiplications, namely, $a_1 \cdot b_1$, $a_1 \cdot b_0$, and $(a_1 + a_0) \cdot (b_1 + b_0)$. We also need six additions.[10] That is three more than in the recursive implementation of the school method. The key is that additions are cheap compared with multiplications, and hence saving a multiplication more than outweighs three additional additions. We obtain the following algorithm for computing $a \cdot b$:

---

[10] Actually, five additions and one subtraction. We leave it to readers to convince themselves that subtractions are no harder than additions.

(a) Split a and b into a_1, a_0, b_1, and b_0.

(b) Compute the three products

$$p_2 = a_1 \cdot b_1, \quad p_0 = a_0 \cdot b_0, \quad p_1 = (a_1 + a_0) \cdot (b_1 + b_0).$$

(c) Add the suitably aligned products to obtain $a \cdot b$, i.e., compute $a \cdot b$ according to the formula

$$a \cdot b = p_2 \cdot B^{2k} + (p_1 - (p_2 + p_0)) \cdot B^k + p_0.$$

The numbers a_1, a_0, b_1, b_0, $a_1 + a_0$, and $b_1 + b_0$ are $\lceil n/2 \rceil + 1$-digit numbers and hence the multiplications in step (b) are simpler than the original multiplication if $\lceil n/2 \rceil + 1 < n$, i.e., $n \geq 4$. The complete algorithm is now as follows: to multiply three-digit numbers, use the school method, and to multiply n-digit numbers for $n \geq 4$, use the three-step approach above.

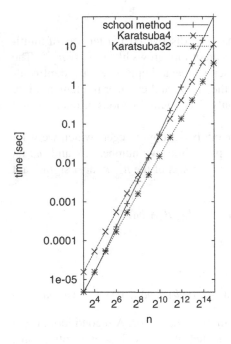

Fig. 1.3. The running times of implementations of the Karatsuba and school methods for integer multiplication. The running times for two versions of Karatsuba's method are shown: Karatsuba4 switches to the school method for integers with fewer than four digits, and Karatsuba32 switches to the school method for integers with fewer than 32 digits. The slopes of the lines for the Karatsuba variants are approximately 1.58. The running time of Karatsuba32 is approximately one-third the running time of Karatsuba4.

Figure 1.3 shows the running times $T_K(n)$ and $T_S(n)$ of C++ implementations of the Karatsuba method and the school method for n-digit integers. The scales on both axes are logarithmic. We see, essentially, straight lines of different slope. The running time of the school method grows like n^2, and hence the slope is 2 in the case of the school method. The slope is smaller in the case of the Karatsuba method and this suggests that its running time grows like n^β with $\beta < 2$. In fact, the ratio[11] $T_K(n)/T_K(n/2)$ is close to three, and this suggests that β is such that $2^\beta = 3$ or

---

[11] $T_K(1024) = 0.0455$, $T_K(2048) = 0.1375$, and $T_K(4096) = 0.41$.

$\beta = \log 3 \approx 1.58$. Alternatively, you may determine the slope from Fig. 1.3. We shall prove below that $T_K(n)$ grows like $n^{\log 3}$. We say that the *Karatsuba method has better asymptotic behavior*. We also see that the inputs have to be quite big before the superior asymptotic behavior of the Karatsuba method actually results in a smaller running time. Observe that for $n = 2^8$, the school method is still faster, that for $n = 2^9$, the two methods have about the same running time, and that the Karatsuba method wins for $n = 2^{10}$. The lessons to remember are:

- Better asymptotic behavior ultimately wins.
- An asymptotically slower algorithm can be faster on small inputs.

In the next section, we shall learn how to improve the behavior of the Karatsuba method for small inputs. The resulting algorithm will always be at least as good as the school method. It is time to derive the asymptotics of the Karatsuba method.

Lemma 1.6. *Let $T_K(n)$ be the maximal number of primitive operations required by the Karatsuba algorithm when applied to n-digit integers. Then*

$$T_K(n) \leq \begin{cases} 3n^2 + 2n & \text{if } n \leq 3, \\ 3 \cdot T_K(\lceil n/2 \rceil + 1) + 6 \cdot 2 \cdot n & \text{if } n \geq 4. \end{cases}$$

Proof. Multiplying two n-bit numbers using the school method requires no more than $3n^2 + 2n$ primitive operations, by Lemma 1.3. This justifies the first line. So, assume $n \geq 4$. Splitting a and b into the four pieces a_1, a_0, b_1, and b_0 requires no primitive operations.[12] Each piece and the sums $a_0 + a_1$ and $b_0 + b_1$ have at most $\lceil n/2 \rceil + 1$ digits, and hence the three recursive multiplications require at most $3 \cdot T_K(\lceil n/2 \rceil + 1)$ primitive operations. Finally, we need two additions to form $a_0 + a_1$ and $b_0 + b_1$, and four additions to assemble the final result. Each addition involves two numbers of at most $2n$ digits and hence requires at most $2n$ primitive operations. This justifies the inequality for $n \geq 4$.   □

In Sect. 2.6, we shall learn some general techniques for solving recurrences of this kind.

Theorem 1.7. *Let $T_K(n)$ be the maximal number of primitive operations required by the Karatsuba algorithm when applied to n-digit integers. Then $T_K(n) \leq 99n^{\log 3} + 48 \cdot n + 48 \cdot \log n$ for all n.*

Proof. We refer the reader to Sect. 1.8 for a proof.   □

1.6 Algorithm Engineering

Karatsuba integer multiplication is superior to the school method for large inputs. In our implementation, the superiority only shows for integers with more than 1 000

---

[12] It will require work, but it is work that we do not account for in our analysis.

digits. However, a simple refinement improves the performance significantly. Since the school method is superior to the Karatsuba method for short integers, we should stop the recursion earlier and switch to the school method for numbers which have fewer than n_0 digits for some yet to be determined n_0. We call this approach the *refined Karatsuba method*. It is never worse than either the school method or the original Karatsuba algorithm.

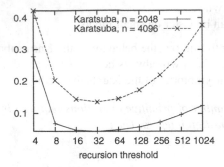

Fig. 1.4. The running time of the Karatsuba method as a function of the recursion threshold n_0. The times consumed for multiplying 2048-digit and 4096-digit integers are shown. The minimum is at $n_0 = 32$

What is a good choice for n_0? We shall answer this question both experimentally and analytically. Let us discuss the experimental approach first. We simply time the refined Karatsuba algorithm for different values of n_0 and then adopt the value giving the smallest running time. For our implementation, the best results were obtained for $n_0 = 32$ (see Fig. 1.4). The asymptotic behavior of the refined Karatsuba method is shown in Fig. 1.3. We see that the running time of the refined method still grows like $n^{\log 3}$, that the refined method is about three times faster than the basic Karatsuba method and hence the refinement is highly effective, and that the refined method is never slower than the school method.

Exercise 1.6. Derive a recurrence for the worst-case number $T_R(n)$ of primitive operations performed by the refined Karatsuba method.

We can also approach the question analytically. If we use the school method to multiply n-digit numbers, we need $3n^2 + 2n$ primitive operations. If we use one Karatsuba step and then multiply the resulting numbers of length $\lceil n/2 \rceil + 1$ using the school method, we need about $3(3(n/2 + 1)^2 + 2(n/2 + 1)) + 12n$ primitive operations. The latter is smaller for $n \geq 28$ and hence a recursive step saves primitive operations as long as the number of digits is more than 28. You should not take this as an indication that an actual implementation should switch at integers of approximately 28 digits, as the argument concentrates solely on primitive operations. You should take it as an argument that it is wise to have a nontrivial recursion threshold n_0 and then determine the threshold experimentally.

Exercise 1.7. Throughout this chapter, we have assumed that both arguments of a multiplication are n-digit integers. What can you say about the complexity of multiplying n-digit and m-digit integers? (a) Show that the school method requires no more than $\alpha \cdot nm$ primitive operations for some constant α. (b) Assume $n \geq m$ and divide a into $\lceil n/m \rceil$ numbers of m digits each. Multiply each of the fragments by b using Karatsuba's method and combine the results. What is the running time of this approach?

1.7 The Programs

We give C++ programs for the school and Karatsuba methods below. These programs were used for the timing experiments described in this chapter. The programs were executed on a machine with a 2 GHz dual-core Intel T7200 processor with 4 Mbyte of cache memory and 2 Gbyte of main memory. The programs were compiled with GNU C++ version 3.3.5 using optimization level -O2.

A digit is simply an unsigned int and an integer is a vector of digits; here, "vector" is the vector type of the standard template library. A declaration *integer* $a(n)$ declares an integer with n digits, $a.size()$ returns the size of a, and $a[i]$ returns a reference to the i-th digit of a. Digits are numbered starting at zero. The global variable B stores the base. The functions *fullAdder* and *digitMult* implement the primitive operations on digits. We sometimes need to access digits beyond the size of an integer; the function *getDigit*(a, i) returns $a[i]$ if i is a legal index for a and returns zero otherwise:

```
typedef unsigned int digit;
typedef vector<digit> integer;
unsigned int B = 10;                    // Base, 2 <= B <= 2^16

void fullAdder(digit a, digit b, digit c, digit& s, digit& carry)
{ unsigned int sum = a + b + c; carry = sum/B; s = sum - carry*B; }

void digitMult(digit a, digit b, digit& s, digit& carry)
{ unsigned int prod = a*b; carry = prod/B; s = prod - carry*B; }

digit getDigit(const integer& a, int i)
{ return ( i < a.size()? a[i] : 0 ); }
```

We want to run our programs on random integers: *randDigit* is a simple random generator for digits, and *randInteger* fills its argument with random digits.

```
unsigned int X = 542351;
digit randDigit() { X = 443143*X + 6412431; return X % B ; }
void randInteger(integer& a)
{ int n = a.size(); for (int i=0; i<n; i++) a[i] = randDigit();}
```

We come to the school method of multiplication. We start with a routine that multiplies an integer a by a digit b and returns the result in *atimesb*. In each iteration, we compute d and c such that $c * B + d = a[i] * b$. We then add d, the c from the previous iteration, and the *carry* from the previous iteration, store the result in *atimesb*$[i]$, and remember the *carry*. The school method (the function *mult*) multiplies a by each digit of b and then adds it at the appropriate position to the result (the function *addAt*).

```
void mult(const integer& a, const digit& b, integer& atimesb)
{ int n = a.size(); assert(atimesb.size() == n+1);
  digit carry = 0, c, d, cprev = 0;

  for (int i = 0; i < n; i++)
    { digitMult(a[i],b,d,c);
    fullAdder(d, cprev, carry, atimesb[i], carry); cprev = c;
    }
  d = 0;
  fullAdder(d, cprev, carry, atimesb[n], carry);  assert(carry == 0);
}
void addAt(integer& p, const integer& atimesbj, int j)
{ // p has length n+m,
  digit carry = 0; int L = p.size();
  for (int i = j; i < L; i++)
    fullAdder(p[i], getDigit(atimesbj,i-j), carry, p[i], carry);
  assert(carry == 0);
}
integer mult(const integer& a, const integer& b)
{ int n = a.size(); int m = b.size();
  integer p(n + m,0);  integer atimesbj(n+1);
  for (int j = 0; j < m; j++)
    { mult(a, b[j], atimesbj); addAt(p, atimesbj, j); }
  return p;
}
```

For Karatsuba's method, we also need algorithms for general addition and subtraction. The subtraction method may assume that the first argument is no smaller than the second. It computes its result in the first argument:

```
integer add(const integer& a, const integer& b)
{ int n = max(a.size(),b.size());
  integer s(n+1); digit carry = 0;
  for (int i = 0; i < n; i++)
    fullAdder(getDigit(a,i), getDigit(b,i), carry, s[i], carry);
  s[n] = carry;
  return s;
}
void sub(integer& a, const integer& b) // requires a >= b
{ digit carry = 0;

  for (int i = 0; i < a.size(); i++)
    if ( a[i] >= ( getDigit(b,i) + carry ))
    { a[i] = a[i] - getDigit(b,i) - carry; carry = 0; }
    else { a[i] = a[i] + B - getDigit(b,i) - carry; carry = 1;}
  assert(carry == 0);
}
```

The function *split* splits an integer into two integers of half the size:

```
void split(const integer& a,integer& a1,  integer& a0)
{ int n = a.size(); int k = n/2;
  for (int i = 0; i < k; i++) a0[i] = a[i];
  for (int i = 0; i < n - k; i++) a1[i] = a[k+ i];
}
```

The function *Karatsuba* works exactly as described in the text. If the inputs have fewer than *n0* digits, the school method is employed. Otherwise, the inputs are split into numbers of half the size and the products *p0*, *p1*, and *p2* are formed. Then *p0* and *p2* are written into the output vector and subtracted from *p1*. Finally, the modified *p1* is added to the result:

```
integer Karatsuba(const integer& a, const integer& b, int n0)
{ int n = a.size(); int m = b.size(); assert(n == m); assert(n0 >= 4);
  integer p(2*n);

  if (n < n0) return mult(a,b);

  int k = n/2; integer a0(k), a1(n - k), b0(k), b1(n - k);

  split(a,a1,a0); split(b,b1,b0);

  integer p2 = Karatsuba(a1,b1,n0),
          p1 = Karatsuba(add(a1,a0),add(b1,b0),n0),
          p0 = Karatsuba(a0,b0,n0);

  for (int i = 0; i < 2*k; i++) p[i] = p0[i];
  for (int i = 2*k; i < n+m; i++) p[i] = p2[i - 2*k];

  sub(p1,p0); sub(p1,p2); addAt(p,p1,k);

  return p;
}
```

The following program generated the data for Fig. 1.3:

```
inline double cpuTime() { return double(clock())/CLOCKS_PER_SEC; }

int main(){

for (int n = 8; n <= 131072; n *= 2)
{ integer a(n),  b(n); randInteger(a); randInteger(b);

  double T = cpuTime();   int k = 0;
  while (cpuTime() - T < 1) {  mult(a,b); k++; }
  cout << "\n" << n << " school = " << (cpuTime() - T)/k;

  T = cpuTime(); k = 0;
  while (cpuTime() - T < 1) {  Karatsuba(a,b,4); k++; }
  cout << " Karatsuba4 = " << (cpuTime() - T) /k; cout.flush();

  T = cpuTime(); k = 0;
  while (cpuTime() - T < 1) {  Karatsuba(a,b,32); k++; }
  cout << " Karatsuba32 = " << (cpuTime() - T) /k; cout.flush();
}
return 0;
}
```

1.8 Proofs of Lemma 1.5 and Theorem 1.7

To make this chapter self-contained, we include proofs of Lemma 1.5 and Theorem 1.7. We start with an analysis of the recursive version of the school method. Recall that $T(n)$, the maximal number of primitive operations required by our recursive multiplication algorithm when applied to n-digit integers, satisfies

$$T(n) \leq \begin{cases} 1 & \text{if } n = 1, \\ 4 \cdot T(\lceil n/2 \rceil) + 3 \cdot 2 \cdot n & \text{if } n \geq 2. \end{cases}$$

We use induction on n to show that $T(n) \leq 7n^2 - 6n$ when n is a power of two. For $n = 1$, we have $T(1) \leq 1 = 7n^2 - 6n$. For $n > 1$, we have

$$T(n) \leq 4T(n/2) + 6n \leq 4(7(n/2)^2 - 6n/2) + 6n = 7n^2 - 6n ,$$

where the second inequality follows from the induction hypothesis. For general n, we observe that multiplying n-digit integers is certainly no more costly than multiplying $2^{\lceil \log n \rceil}$-digit integers and hence $T(n) \leq T(2^{\lceil \log n \rceil})$. Since $2^{\lceil \log n \rceil} \leq 2n$, we conclude that $T(n) \leq 28n^2$ for all n.

Exercise 1.8. Prove a bound on the recurrence $T(1) \leq 1$ and $T(n) \leq 4T(n/2) + 9n$ when n is a power of two.

How did we know that "$7n^2 - 6n$" was the bound to be proved? There is no magic here. For $n = 2^k$, repeated substitution yields

$$T(2^k) \leq 4 \cdot T(2^{k-1}) + 6 \cdot 2^k \leq 4^2 T(2^{k-2}) + 6 \cdot (4^1 \cdot 2^{k-1} + 2^k)$$
$$\leq 4^3 T(2^{k-3}) + 6 \cdot (4^2 \cdot 2^{k-2} + 4^1 \cdot 2^{k-1} + 2^k) \leq \cdots$$
$$\leq 4^k T(1) + 6 \sum_{0 \leq i \leq k-1} 4^i 2^{k-i} \leq 4^k + 6 \cdot 2^k \sum_{0 \leq i \leq k-1} 2^i$$
$$\leq 4^k + 6 \cdot 2^k (2^k - 1) = n^2 + 6n(n - 1) = 7n^2 - 6n .$$

We turn now to the proof of Theorem 1.7. Recall that T_K satisfies the recurrence

$$T_K(n) \leq \begin{cases} 3n^2 + 2n & \text{if } n \leq 3, \\ 3 \cdot T_K(\lceil n/2 \rceil + 1) + 12n & \text{if } n \geq 4. \end{cases}$$

The recurrence for the school method has the nice property that if n is a power of two, the arguments of T on the right-hand side are again powers of two. This is not true for T_K. However, if $n = 2^k + 2$ and $k \geq 1$, then $\lceil n/2 \rceil + 1 = 2^{k-1} + 2$, and hence we should now use numbers of the form $n = 2^k + 2$, $k \geq 0$, as the basis of the inductive argument. We shall show that

$$T_K(2^k + 2) \leq 33 \cdot 3^k + 12 \cdot (2^{k+1} + 2k - 2)$$

for $k \geq 0$. For $k = 0$, we have

$$T_K(2^0+2) = T_K(3) \le 3 \cdot 3^2 + 2 \cdot 3 = 33 = 33 \cdot 2^0 + 12 \cdot (2^1 + 2 \cdot 0 - 2).$$

For $k \ge 1$, we have

$$T_K(2^k+2) \le 3T_K(2^{k-1}+2) + 12 \cdot (2^k+2)$$
$$\le 3 \cdot \left(33 \cdot 3^{k-1} + 12 \cdot (2^k + 2(k-1) - 2) \right) + 12 \cdot (2^k+2)$$
$$= 33 \cdot 3^k + 12 \cdot (2^{k+1} + 2k - 2).$$

Again, there is no magic in coming up with the right induction hypothesis. It is obtained by repeated substitution. Namely,

$$T_K(2^k+2) \le 3T_K(2^{k-1}+2) + 12 \cdot (2^k+2)$$
$$\le 3^k T_K(2^0+2) + 12 \cdot (2^k + 2 + 2^{k-1} + 2 + \ldots + 2^1 + 2)$$
$$\le 33 \cdot 3^k + 12 \cdot (2^{k+1} - 2 + 2k).$$

It remains to extend the bound to all n. Let k be the minimal integer such that $n \le 2^k + 2$. Then $k \le 1 + \log n$. Also, multiplying n-digit numbers is no more costly than multiplying (2^k+2)-digit numbers, and hence

$$T_K(n) \le 33 \cdot 3^k + 12 \cdot (2^{k+1} - 2 + 2k)$$
$$\le 99 \cdot 3^{\log n} + 48 \cdot (2^{\log n} - 2 + 2(1 + \log n))$$
$$\le 99 \cdot n^{\log 3} + 48 \cdot n + 48 \cdot \log n,$$

where the equality $3^{\log n} = 2^{(\log 3) \cdot (\log n)} = n^{\log 3}$ has been used.

Exercise 1.9. Solve the recurrence

$$T_R(n) \le \begin{cases} 3n^2 + 2n & \text{if } n < 32, \\ 3 \cdot T_R(\lceil n/2 \rceil + 1) + 12n & \text{if } n \ge 4. \end{cases}$$

1.9 Implementation Notes

The programs given in Sect. 1.7 are not optimized. The base of the number system should be a power of two so that sums and carries can be extracted by bit operations. Also, the size of a digit should agree with the word size of the machine and a little more work should be invested in implementing primitive operations on digits.

1.9.1 C++

GMP [74] and LEDA [118] offer high-precision integer, rational, and floating-point arithmetic. Highly optimized implementations of Karatsuba's method are used for multiplication.

1.9.2 Java

java.math implements arbitrary-precision integers and floating-point numbers.

1.10 Historical Notes and Further Findings

Is the Karatsuba method the fastest known method for integer multiplication? No, much faster methods are known. Karatsuba's method splits an integer into two parts and requires three multiplications of integers of half the length. The natural extension is to split integers into k parts of length n/k each. If the recursive step requires ℓ multiplications of numbers of length n/k, the running time of the resulting algorithm grows like $n^{\log_k \ell}$. In this way, Toom [196] and Cook [43] reduced the running time to[13] $O(n^{1+\varepsilon})$ for arbitrary positive ε. The asymptotically most efficient algorithms are the work of Schönhage and Strassen [171] and Schönhage [170]. The former multiplies n-bit integers with $O(n \log n \log \log n)$ bit operations, and it can be implemented to run in this time bound on a Turing machine. The latter runs in linear time $O(n)$ and requires the machine model discussed in Sect. 2.2. In this model, integers with $\log n$ bits can be multiplied in constant time.

---

[13] The $O(\cdot)$ notation is defined in Sect. 2.1.

2

Introduction

When you want to become a sculptor[1] you have to learn some basic techniques: where to get the right stones, how to move them, how to handle the chisel, how to erect scaffolding, ... Knowing these techniques will not make you a famous artist, but even if you have a really exceptional talent, it will be very difficult to develop into a successful artist without knowing them. It is not necessary to master all of the basic techniques before sculpting the first piece. But you always have to be willing to go back to improve your basic techniques.

This introductory chapter plays a similar role in this book. We introduce basic concepts that make it simpler to discuss and analyze algorithms in the subsequent chapters. There is no need for you to read this chapter from beginning to end before you proceed to later chapters. On first reading, we recommend that you should read carefully to the end of Sect. 2.3 and skim through the remaining sections. We begin in Sect. 2.1 by introducing some notation and terminology that allow us to argue about the complexity of algorithms in a concise way. We then introduce a simple machine model in Sect. 2.2 that allows us to abstract from the highly variable complications introduced by real hardware. The model is concrete enough to have predictive value and abstract enough to allow elegant arguments. Section 2.3 then introduces a high-level pseudocode notation for algorithms that is much more convenient for expressing algorithms than the machine code of our abstract machine. Pseudocode is also more convenient than actual programming languages, since we can use high-level concepts borrowed from mathematics without having to worry about exactly how they can be compiled to run on actual hardware. We frequently annotate programs to make algorithms more readable and easier to prove correct. This is the subject of Sect. 2.4. Section 2.5 gives the first comprehensive example: binary search in a sorted array. In Sect. 2.6, we introduce mathematical techniques for analyzing the complexity of programs, in particular, for analyzing nested loops and recursive pro-

---

[1] The above illustration of Stonehenge is from [156].

cedure calls. Additional analysis techniques are needed for average-case analysis; these are covered in Sect. 2.7. Randomized algorithms, discussed in Sect. 2.8, use coin tosses in their execution. Section 2.9 is devoted to graphs, a concept that will play an important role throughout the book. In Sect. 2.10, we discuss the question of when an algorithm should be called efficient, and introduce the complexity classes **P** and **NP**. Finally, as in every chapter of this book, there are sections containing implementation notes (Sect. 2.11) and historical notes and further findings (Sect. 2.12).

2.1 Asymptotic Notation

The main purpose of algorithm analysis is to give performance guarantees, for example bounds on running time, that are at the same time accurate, concise, general, and easy to understand. It is difficult to meet all these criteria simultaneously. For example, the most accurate way to characterize the running time T of an algorithm is to view T as a mapping from the set I of all inputs to the set of nonnegative numbers $\mathbb{R}_+$. For any problem instance i, $T(i)$ is the running time on i. This level of detail is so overwhelming that we could not possibly derive a theory about it. A useful theory needs a more global view of the performance of an algorithm.

We group the set of all inputs into classes of "similar" inputs and summarize the performance on all instances in the same class into a single number. The most useful grouping is by *size*. Usually, there is a natural way to assign a size to each problem instance. The size of an integer is the number of digits in its representation, and the size of a set is the number of elements in the set. The size of an instance is always a natural number. Sometimes we use more than one parameter to measure the size of an instance; for example, it is customary to measure the size of a graph by its number of nodes and its number of edges. We ignore this complication for now. We use $size(i)$ to denote the size of instance i, and I_n to denote the instances of size n for $n \in \mathbb{N}$. For the inputs of size n, we are interested in the maximum, minimum, and average execution times:[2]

$$\begin{aligned}
\textbf{worst case:} \quad & T(n) = \max\{T(i) : i \in I_n\} \\
\textbf{best case:} \quad & T(n) = \min\{T(i) : i \in I_n\} \\
\textbf{average case:} \quad & T(n) = \frac{1}{|I_n|}\sum_{i \in I_n} T(i) \,.
\end{aligned}$$

We are interested most in the worst-case execution time, since it gives us the strongest performance guarantee. A comparison of the best case and the worst case tells us how much the execution time varies for different inputs in the same class. If the discrepancy is big, the average case may give more insight into the true performance of the algorithm. Section 2.7 gives an example.

We shall perform one more step of data reduction: we shall concentrate on *growth rate* or *asymptotic analysis*. Functions $f(n)$ and $g(n)$ have the *same growth rate* if

---

[2] We shall make sure that $\{T(i) : i \in I_n\}$ always has a proper minimum and maximum, and that I_n is finite when we consider averages.

there are positive constants c and d such that $c \leq f(n)/g(n) \leq d$ for all sufficiently large n, and $f(n)$ *grows faster* than $g(n)$ if, for all positive constants c, we have $f(n) \geq c \cdot g(n)$ for all sufficiently large n. For example, the functions n^2, $n^2 + 7n$, $5n^2 - 7n$, and $n^2/10 + 10^6 n$ all have the same growth rate. Also, they grow faster than $n^{3/2}$, which in turn grows faster than $n \log n$. The growth rate talks about the behavior for large n. The word "asymptotic" in "asymptotic analysis" also stresses the fact that we are interested in the behavior for large n.

Why are we interested only in growth rates and the behavior for large n? We are interested in the behavior for large n because the whole purpose of designing efficient algorithms is to be able to solve large instances. For large n, an algorithm whose running time has a smaller growth rate than the running time of another algorithm will be superior. Also, our machine model is an abstraction of real machines and hence can predict actual running times only up to a constant factor, and this suggests that we should not distinguish between algorithms whose running times have the same growth rate. A pleasing side effect of concentrating on growth rate is that we can characterize the running times of algorithms by simple functions. However, in the sections on implementation, we shall frequently take a closer look and go beyond asymptotic analysis. Also, when using one of the algorithms described in this book, you should always ask yourself whether the asymptotic view is justified.

The following definitions allow us to argue precisely about *asymptotic behavior*. Let $f(n)$ and $g(n)$ denote functions that map nonnegative integers to nonnegative real numbers:

$$O(f(n)) = \{g(n) : \exists c > 0 : \exists n_0 \in \mathbb{N}_+ : \forall n \geq n_0 : g(n) \leq c \cdot f(n)\},$$
$$\Omega(f(n)) = \{g(n) : \exists c > 0 : \exists n_0 \in \mathbb{N}_+ : \forall n \geq n_0 : g(n) \geq c \cdot f(n)\},$$
$$\Theta(f(n)) = O(f(n)) \cap \Omega(f(n)),$$
$$o(f(n)) = \{g(n) : \forall c > 0 : \exists n_0 \in \mathbb{N}_+ : \forall n \geq n_0 : g(n) \leq c \cdot f(n)\},$$
$$\omega(f(n)) = \{g(n) : \forall c > 0 : \exists n_0 \in \mathbb{N}_+ : \forall n \geq n_0 : g(n) \geq c \cdot f(n)\}.$$

The left-hand sides should be read as "big O of f", "big omega of f", "theta of f", "little o of f", and "little omega of f", respectively.

Let us see some examples. $O(n^2)$ is the set of all functions that grow at most quadratically, $o(n^2)$ is the set of functions that grow less than quadratically, and $o(1)$ is the set of functions that go to zero as n goes to infinity. Here "1" stands for the function $n \mapsto 1$, which is one everywhere, and hence $f \in o(1)$ if $f(n) \leq c \cdot 1$ for any positive c and sufficiently large n, i.e., $f(n)$ goes to zero as n goes to infinity. Generally, $O(f(n))$ is the set of all functions that "grow no faster than" $f(n)$. Similarly, $\Omega(f(n))$ is the set of all functions that "grow at least as fast as" $f(n)$. For example, the Karatsuba algorithm for integer multiplication has a worst-case running time in $O(n^{1.58})$, whereas the school algorithm has a worst-case running time in $\Omega(n^2)$, so that we can say that the Karatsuba algorithm is asymptotically faster than the school algorithm. The "little o" notation $o(f(n))$ denotes the set of all functions that "grow strictly more slowly than" $f(n)$. Its twin $\omega(f(n))$ is rarely used, and is only shown for completeness.

The growth rate of most algorithms discussed in this book is either a polynomial or a logarithmic function, or the product of a polynomial and a logarithmic function. We use polynomials to introduce our readers to some basic manipulations of asymptotic notation.

Lemma 2.1. *Let* $p(n) = \sum_{i=0}^{k} a_i n^i$ *denote any polynomial and assume* $a_k > 0$. *Then* $p(n) \in \Theta(n^k)$.

Proof. It suffices to show that $p(n) \in O(n^k)$ and $p(n) \in \Omega(n^k)$. First observe that for $n > 0$,

$$p(n) \le \sum_{i=0}^{k} |a_i| n^i \le n^k \sum_{i=0}^{k} |a_i| ,$$

and hence $p(n) \le (\sum_{i=0}^{k} |a_i|) n^k$ for all positive n. Thus $p(n) \in O(n^k)$.

Let $A = \sum_{i=0}^{k-1} |a_i|$. For positive n we have

$$p(n) \ge a_k n^k - A n^{k-1} = \frac{a_k}{2} n^k + n^{k-1} \left(\frac{a_k}{2} n - A \right)$$

and hence $p(n) \ge (a_k/2) n^k$ for $n > 2A/a_k$. We choose $c = a_k/2$ and $n_0 = 2A/a_k$ in the definition of $\Omega(n^k)$, and obtain $p(n) \in \Omega(n^k)$.   □

Exercise 2.1. Right or wrong? (a) $n^2 + 10^6 n \in O(n^2)$, (b) $n \log n \in O(n)$, (c) $n \log n \in \Omega(n)$, (d) $\log n \in o(n)$.

Asymptotic notation is used a lot in algorithm analysis, and it is convenient to stretch mathematical notation a little in order to allow sets of functions (such as $O(n^2)$) to be treated similarly to ordinary functions. In particular, we shall always write $h = O(f)$ instead of $h \in O(f)$, and $O(h) = O(f)$ instead of $O(h) \subseteq O(f)$. For example,

$$3n^2 + 7n = O(n^2) = O(n^3) .$$

Be warned that sequences of equalities involving O-notation should only be read from left to right.

If h is a function, F and G are sets of functions, and $\circ$ is an operator such as $+$, $\cdot$, or $/$, then $F \circ G$ is a shorthand for $\{f \circ g : f \in F, g \in G\}$, and $h \circ F$ stands for $\{h\} \circ F$. So $f(n) + o(f(n))$ denotes the set of all functions $f(n) + g(n)$ where $g(n)$ grows strictly more slowly than $f(n)$, i.e., the ratio $(f(n) + g(n))/f(n)$ goes to one as n goes to infinity. Equivalently, we can write $(1 + o(1)) f(n)$. We use this notation whenever we care about the constant in the leading term but want to ignore *lower-order terms*.

Lemma 2.2. *The following rules hold for O-notation:*

$$c f(n) = \Theta(f(n)) \text{ for any positive constant,}$$
$$f(n) + g(n) = \Omega(f(n)),$$
$$f(n) + g(n) = O(f(n)) \text{ if } g(n) = O(f(n)),$$
$$O(f(n)) \cdot O(g(n)) = O(f(n) \cdot g(n)).$$

Exercise 2.2. Prove Lemma 2.2.

Exercise 2.3. Sharpen Lemma 2.1 and show that $p(n) = a_k n^k + o(n^k)$.

Exercise 2.4. Prove that $n^k = o(c^n)$ for any integer k and any $c > 1$. How does $n^{\log \log n}$ compare with n^k and c^n?

2.2 The Machine Model

In 1945, John von Neumann (Fig. 2.1) introduced a computer architecture [201] which was simple, yet powerful. The limited hardware technology of the time forced him to come up with an elegant design that concentrated on the essentials; otherwise, realization would have been impossible. Hardware technology has developed tremendously since 1945. However, the programming model resulting from von Neumann's design is so elegant and powerful that it is still the basis for most of modern programming. Usually, programs written with von Neumann's model in mind also work well on the vastly more complex hardware of today's machines.

The variant of von Neumann's model used in algorithmic analysis is called the *RAM* (random access machine) model. It was introduced by Sheperdson and Sturgis [179]. It is a *sequential* machine with uniform memory, i.e., there is a single processing unit, and all memory accesses take the same amount of

Fig. 2.1. John von Neumann born Dec. 28, 1903 in Budapest, died Feb. 8, 1957 in Washington, DC

time. The memory or *store*, consists of infinitely many cells $S[0]$, $S[1]$, $S[2]$, …; at any point in time, only a finite number of them will be in use.

The memory cells store "small" integers, also called *words*. In our discussion of integer arithmetic in Chap. 1, we assumed that "small" meant one-digit. It is more reasonable and convenient to assume that the interpretation of "small" depends on the size of the input. Our default assumption is that integers bounded by a polynomial in the size of the data being processed can be stored in a single cell. Such integers can be represented by a number of bits that is logarithmic in the size of the input. This assumption is reasonable because we could always spread out the contents of a single cell over logarithmically many cells with a logarithmic overhead in time and space and obtain constant size cells. The assumption is convenient because we want to be able to store array indices in a single cell. The assumption is necessary because allowing cells to store arbitrary numbers would lead to absurdly overoptimistic algorithms. For example, by repeated squaring, we could generate a number with 2^n bits in n steps. Namely, if we start with the number $2 = 2^1$, squaring it once gives $4 = 2^2 = 2^{2^1}$, squaring it twice gives $16 = 2^4 = 2^{2^2}$, and squaring it n times gives 2^{2^n}.

Our model supports a limited form of parallelism. We can perform simple operations on a logarithmic number of bits in constant time.

In addition to the main memory, there are a small number of *registers* $R_1, \ldots, R_k$. Our RAM can execute the following *machine instructions*:

- $R_i := S[R_j]$ *loads* the contents of the memory cell indexed by the contents of R_j into register R_i.
- $S[R_j] := R_i$ *stores* register R_i into the memory cell indexed by the contents of R_j.
- $R_i := R_j \odot R_\ell$ is a *binary* register operation where "$\odot$" is a placeholder for a variety of operations. The *arithmetic* operations are the usual $+$, $-$, and $*$ but also the bitwise operations $|$ (OR), $\&$ (AND), $>>$ (shift right), $<<$ (shift left), and $\oplus$ (exclusive OR, XOR). The operations **div** and **mod** stand for integer division and the remainder, respectively. The *comparison* operations $\leq$, $<$, $>$, and $\geq$ yield *true* ($= 1$) or *false* ($= 0$). The *logical* operations $\wedge$ and $\vee$ manipulate the *truth values* 0 and 1. We may also assume that there are operations which interpret the bits stored in a register as a floating-point number, i.e., a finite-precision approximation of a real number.
- $R_i := \odot R_j$ is a *unary* operation using the operators $-$, $\neg$ (logical NOT), or $\sim$ (bitwise NOT).
- $R_i := C$ assigns a *constant* value to R_i.
- JZ j, R_i continues execution at memory address j if register R_i is zero.
- J j continues execution at memory address j.

Each instruction takes one time step to execute. The total execution time of a program is the number of instructions executed. A program is a list of instructions numbered starting at one. The addresses in jump-instructions refer to this numbering. The input for a computation is stored in memory cells $S[1]$ to $S[R_1]$.

It is important to remember that the RAM model is an abstraction. One should not confuse it with physically existing machines. In particular, real machines have a finite memory and a fixed number of bits per register (e.g., 32 or 64). In contrast, the word size and memory of a RAM scale with input size. This can be viewed as an abstraction of the historical development. Microprocessors have had words of 4, 8, 16, and 32 bits in succession, and now often have 64-bit words. Words of 64 bits can index a memory of size 2^{64}. Thus, at current prices, memory size is limited by cost and not by physical limitations. Observe that this statement was also true when 32-bit words were introduced.

Our complexity model is also a gross oversimplification: modern processors attempt to execute many instructions in parallel. How well they succeed depends on factors such as data dependencies between successive operations. As a consequence, an operation does not have a fixed cost. This effect is particularly pronounced for memory accesses. The worst-case time for a memory access to the main memory can be hundreds of times higher than the best-case time. The reason is that modern processors attempt to keep frequently used data in *caches* – small, fast memories close to the processors. How well caches work depends a lot on their architecture, the program, and the particular input.

We could attempt to introduce a very accurate cost model, but this would miss the point. We would end up with a complex model that would be difficult to handle. Even a successful complexity analysis would lead to a monstrous formula depending on many parameters that change with every new processor generation. Although such a formula would contain detailed information, the very complexity of the formula would make it useless. We therefore go to the other extreme and eliminate all model parameters by assuming that each instruction takes exactly one unit of time. The result is that constant factors in our model are quite meaningless – one more reason to stick to asymptotic analysis most of the time. We compensate for this drawback by providing implementation notes, in which we discuss implementation choices and trade-offs.

2.2.1 External Memory

The biggest difference between a RAM and a real machine is in the memory: a uniform memory in a RAM and a complex memory hierarchy in a real machine. In Sects. 5.7, 6.3, and 7.6, we shall discuss algorithms that have been specifically designed for huge data sets which have to be stored on slow memory, such as disks. We shall use the *external-memory model* to study these algorithms.

The external-memory model is like the RAM model except that the fast memory S is limited in size to M words. Additionally, there is an external memory with unlimited size. There are special *I/O operations*, which transfer B consecutive words between slow and fast memory. For example, the external memory could be a hard disk, M would then be the size of the main memory, and B would be a block size that is a good compromise between low latency and high bandwidth. With current technology, $M = 2$ Gbyte and $B = 2$ Mbyte are realistic values. One I/O step would then take around 10 ms which is $2 \cdot 10^7$ clock cycles of a 2 GHz machine. With another setting of the parameters M and B, we could model the smaller access time difference between a hardware cache and main memory.

2.2.2 Parallel Processing

On modern machines, we are confronted with many forms of parallel processing. Many processors have 128–512-bit-wide *SIMD* registers that allow the parallel execution of a single instruction on multiple data objects. *Simultaneous multithreading* allows processors to better utilize their resources by running multiple threads of activity on a single processor core. Even mobile devices often have multiple processor cores that can independently execute programs, and most servers have several such *multicore* processors accessing the same *shared memory*. Coprocessors, in particular those used for graphics processing, have even more parallelism on a single chip. High-performance computers consist of multiple server-type systems interconnected by a fast, dedicated network. Finally, more loosely connected computers of all types interact through various kinds of network (the Internet, radio networks, ...) in *distributed systems* that may consist of millions of nodes. As you can imagine, no single simple model can be used to describe parallel programs running on these many levels of parallelism. We shall therefore restrict ourselves to occasional informal arguments as to why a certain sequential algorithm may be more or less easy to adapt to parallel processing. For example, the algorithms for high-precision arithmetic in Chap. 1 could make use of SIMD instructions.

2.3 Pseudocode

Our RAM model is an abstraction and simplification of the machine programs executed on microprocessors. The purpose of the model is to provide a precise definition of running time. However, the model is much too low-level for formulating complex algorithms. Our programs would become too long and too hard to read. Instead, we formulate our algorithms in *pseudocode*, which is an abstraction and simplification of imperative programming languages such as C, C++, Java, C#, and Pascal, combined with liberal use of mathematical notation. We now describe the conventions used in this book, and derive a timing model for pseudocode programs. The timing model is quite simple: *basic pseudocode instructions take constant time, and procedure and function calls take constant time plus the time to execute their body.* We justify the timing model by outlining how pseudocode can be translated into equivalent RAM code. We do this only to the extent necessary to understand the timing model. There is no need to worry about compiler optimization techniques, since constant factors are outside our theory. The reader may decide to skip the paragraphs describing the translation and adopt the timing model as an axiom. The syntax of our pseudocode is akin to that of Pascal [99], because we find this notation typographically nicer for a book than the more widely known syntax of C and its descendants C++ and Java.

2.3.1 Variables and Elementary Data Types

A *variable declaration* "$v = x : T$" introduces a variable v of type T, and initializes it with the value x. For example, "*answer* $= 42 : \mathbb{N}$" introduces a variable *answer* assuming integer values and initializes it to the value 42. When the type of a variable is clear from the context, we shall sometimes omit it from the declaration. A type is either a basic type (e.g., integer, Boolean value, or pointer) or a composite type. We have predefined composite types such as arrays, and application-specific classes (see below). When the type of a variable is irrelevant to the discussion, we use the unspecified type *Element* as a placeholder for an arbitrary type. We take the liberty of extending numeric types by the values $-\infty$ and ∞ whenever this is convenient. Similarly, we sometimes extend types by an undefined value (denoted by the symbol $\perp$), which we assume to be distinguishable from any "proper" element of the type T. In particular, for pointer types it is useful to have an undefined value. The values of the pointer type "**Pointer to** T" are handles of objects of type T. In the RAM model, this is the index of the first cell in a region of storage holding an object of type T.

A declaration "$a : Array\ [i..j]$ **of** T" introduces an *array* a consisting of $j - i + 1$ *elements* of type T, stored in $a[i], a[i+1], \ldots, a[j]$. Arrays are implemented as contiguous pieces of memory. To find an element $a[k]$, it suffices to know the starting address of a and the size of an object of type T. For example, if register R_a stores the starting address of array $a[0..k]$ and the elements have unit size, the instruction sequence "$R_1 := R_a + 42; R_2 := S[R_1]$" loads $a[42]$ into register R_2. The size of an array is fixed at the time of declaration; such arrays are called *static*. In Sect. 3.2, we show how to implement *unbounded arrays* that can grow and shrink during execution.

A declaration "c : **Class** *age* : $\mathbb{N}$, *income* : $\mathbb{N}$ **end**" introduces a variable c whose values are pairs of integers. The components of c are denoted by $c.age$ and $c.income$. For a variable c, **addressof** c returns the address of c. We also say that it returns a handle to c. If p is an appropriate pointer type, $p :=$ **addressof** c stores a handle to c in p and $*p$ gives us back c. The fields of c can then also be accessed through $p \rightarrow age$ and $p \rightarrow income$. Alternatively, one may write (but nobody ever does) $(*p).age$ and $(*p).income$.

Arrays and objects referenced by pointers can be allocated and deallocated by the commands **allocate** and **dispose**. For example, $p :=$ **allocate** *Array* $[1..n]$ **of** T allocates an array of n objects of type T. That is, the statement allocates a contiguous chunk of memory of size n times the size of an object of type T, and assigns a handle of this chunk (= the starting address of the chunk) to p. The statement **dispose** p frees this memory and makes it available for reuse. With **allocate** and **dispose**, we can cut our memory array S into disjoint pieces that can be referred to separately. These functions can be implemented to run in constant time. The simplest implementation is as follows. We keep track of the used portion of S by storing the index of the first free cell of S in a special variable, say *free*. A call of **allocate** reserves a chunk of memory starting at *free* and increases *free* by the size of the allocated chunk. A call of **dispose** does nothing. This implementation is time-efficient, but not space-efficient. Any call of **allocate** or **dispose** takes constant time. However, the total space consumption is the total space that has ever been allocated and not the maximal space simultaneously used, i.e., allocated but not yet freed, at any one time. It is not known whether an arbitrary sequence of **allocate** and **dispose** operations can be realized space-efficiently and with constant time per operation. However, for all algorithms presented in this book, **allocate** and **dispose** can be realized in a time- and space-efficient way.

We borrow some composite data structures from mathematics. In particular, we use tuples, sequences, and sets. *Pairs*, *triples*, and other *tuples* are written in round brackets, for example $(3, 1)$, $(3, 1, 4)$, and $(3, 1, 4, 1, 5)$. Since tuples only contain a constant number of elements, operations on them can be broken into operations on their constituents in an obvious way. *Sequences* store elements in a specified order; for example "$s = \langle 3, 1, 4, 1 \rangle$: *Sequence* **of** $\mathbb{Z}$" declares a sequence s of integers and initializes it to contain the numbers 3, 1, 4, and 1 in that order. Sequences are a natural abstraction of many data structures, such as files, strings, lists, stacks, and queues. In Chap. 3, we shall study many ways to represent sequences. In later chapters, we shall make extensive use of sequences as a mathematical abstraction with little further reference to implementation details. The empty sequence is written as $\langle \rangle$.

Sets play an important role in mathematical arguments and we shall also use them in our pseudocode. In particular, you shall see declarations such as "$M = \{3, 1, 4\}$

: *Set* **of** $\mathbb{N}$" that are analogous to declarations of arrays or sequences. Sets are usually implemented as sequences.

2.3.2 Statements

The simplest statement is an assignment $x := E$, where x is a variable and E is an expression. An assignment is easily transformed into a constant number of RAM instructions. For example, the statement $a := a + bc$ is translated into "$R_1 := R_b * R_c$; $R_a := R_a + R_1$", where R_a, R_b, and R_c stand for the registers storing a, b, and c, respectively. From C, we borrow the shorthands $++$ and $--$ for incrementing and decrementing variables. We also use parallel assignment to several variables. For example, if a and b are variables of the same type, "$(a,b) := (b,a)$" swaps the contents of a and b.

The conditional statement "**if** C **then** I **else** J", where C is a Boolean expression and I and J are statements, translates into the instruction sequence

$$eval(C); \ JZ \ sElse, \ R_c; \ trans(I); \ J \ sEnd; \ trans(J) \ ,$$

where $eval(C)$ is a sequence of instructions that evaluate the expression C and leave its value in register R_c, $trans(I)$ is a sequence of instructions that implement statement I, $trans(J)$ implements J, $sElse$ is the address of the first instruction in $trans(J)$, and $sEnd$ is the address of the first instruction after $trans(J)$. The sequence above first evaluates C. If C evaluates to false ($= 0$), the program jumps to the first instruction of the translation of J. If C evaluates to true ($= 1$), the program continues with the translation of I and then jumps to the instruction after the translation of J. The statement "**if** C **then** I" is a shorthand for "**if** C **then** I **else** ;", i.e., an if–then–else with an empty "else" part.

Our written representation of programs is intended for humans and uses less strict syntax than do programming languages. In particular, we usually group statements by indentation and in this way avoid the proliferation of brackets observed in programming languages such as C that are designed as a compromise between readability for humans and for computers. We use brackets only if the program would be ambiguous otherwise. For the same reason, a line break can replace a semicolon for the purpose of separating statements.

The loop "**repeat** I **until** C" translates into $trans(I); \ eval(C); \ JZ \ sI, \ R_c$, where sI is the address of the first instruction in $trans(I)$. We shall also use many other types of loop that can be viewed as shorthands for repeat loops. In the following list, the shorthand on the left expands into the statements on the right:

while C **do** I	**if** C **then repeat** I **until** $\neg C$
for $i := a$ **to** b **do** I	$i := a$; **while** $i \leq b$ **do** I; $i{+}{+}$
for $i := a$ **to** ∞ **while** C **do** I	$i := a$; **while** C **do** I; $i{+}{+}$
foreach $e \in s$ **do** I	**for** $i := 1$ **to** $|s|$ **do** $e := s[i]$; I

Many low-level optimizations are possible when loops are translated into RAM code. These optimizations are of no concern for us. For us, it is only important that the execution time of a loop can be bounded by summing the execution times of each of its iterations, including the time needed for evaluating conditions.

2.3.3 Procedures and Functions

A subroutine with the name *foo* is declared in the form "**Procedure** *foo*(*D*) *I*", where *I* is the body of the procedure and *D* is a sequence of variable declarations specifying the parameters of *foo*. A call of *foo* has the form *foo*(*P*), where *P* is a parameter list. The parameter list has the same length as the variable declaration list. Parameter passing is either "by value" or "by reference". Our default assumption is that basic objects such as integers and Booleans are passed by value and that complex objects such as arrays are passed by reference. These conventions are similar to the conventions used by C and guarantee that parameter passing takes constant time. The semantics of parameter passing is defined as follows. For a value parameter *x* of type *T*, the actual parameter must be an expression *E* of the same type. Parameter passing is equivalent to the declaration of a local variable *x* of type *T* initialized to *E*. For a reference parameter *x* of type *T*, the actual parameter must be a variable of the same type and the formal parameter is simply an alternative name for the actual parameter.

As with variable declarations, we sometimes omit type declarations for parameters if they are unimportant or clear from the context. Sometimes we also declare parameters implicitly using mathematical notation. For example, the declaration **Procedure** *bar*($\langle a_1, \ldots, a_n \rangle$) introduces a procedure whose argument is a sequence of *n* elements of unspecified type.

Most procedure calls can be compiled into machine code by simply substituting the procedure body for the procedure call and making provisions for parameter passing; this is called *inlining*. Value passing is implemented by making appropriate assignments to copy the parameter values into the local variables of the procedure. Reference passing to a formal parameter *x* : *T* is implemented by changing the type of *x* to **Pointer to** *T*, replacing all occurrences of *x* in the body of the procedure by ($*x$) and initializing *x* by the assignment *x* := **addressof** *y*, where *y* is the actual parameter. Inlining gives the compiler many opportunities for optimization, so that inlining is the most efficient approach for small procedures and for procedures that are called from only a single place.

Functions are similar to procedures, except that they allow the return statement to return a value. Figure 2.2 shows the declaration of a recursive function that returns *n*! and its translation into RAM code. The substitution approach fails for *recursive* procedures and functions that directly or indirectly call themselves – substitution would never terminate. Realizing recursive procedures in RAM code requires the concept of a *recursion stack*. Explicit subroutine calls over a stack are also used for large procedures that are called multiple times where inlining would unduly increase the code size. The recursion stack is a reserved part of the memory; we use *RS* to denote it. *RS* contains a sequence of *activation records*, one for each active procedure call. A special register R_r always points to the first free entry in this stack. The activation record for a procedure with *k* parameters and ℓ local variables has size $1 + k + \ell$. The first location contains the return address, i.e., the address of the instruction where execution is to be continued after the call has terminated, the next *k* locations are reserved for the parameters, and the final ℓ locations are for the local variables. A procedure call is now implemented as follows. First, the calling procedure *caller*

Function *factorial(n)* : $\mathbb{Z}$
   if $n = 1$ **then return** 1 **else return** $n \cdot factorial(n - 1)$

factorial:	// the first instruction of *factorial*
$R_n := RS[R_r - 1]$	// load n into register R_n
JZ thenCase, R_n	// jump to then case, if n is zero
$RS[R_r] =$ aRecCall	// else case; return address for recursive call
$RS[R_r + 1] := R_n - 1$	// parameter is $n - 1$
$R_r := R_r + 2$	// increase stack pointer
J factorial	// start recursive call
aRecCall:	// return address for recursive call
$R_{result} := RS[R_r - 1] * R_{result}$	// store $n * factorial(n - 1)$ in result register
J return	// goto return
thenCase:	// code for then case
$R_{result} := 1$	// put 1 into result register
return:	// code for return
$R_r := R_r - 2$	// free activation record
J $RS[R_r]$	// jump to return address

Fig. 2.2. A recursive function *factorial* and the corresponding RAM code. The RAM code returns the function value in register R_{result}

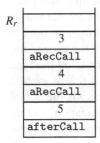

Fig. 2.3. The recursion stack of a call *factorial*(5) when the recursion has reached *factorial*(3)

pushes the return address and the actual parameters onto the stack, increases R_r accordingly, and jumps to the first instruction of the called routine *called*. The called routine reserves space for its local variables by increasing R_r appropriately. Then the body of *called* is executed. During execution of the body, any access to the i-th formal parameter ($0 \leq i < k$) is an access to $RS[R_r - \ell - k + i]$ and any access to the i-th local variable ($0 \leq i < \ell$) is an access to $RS[R_r - \ell + i]$. When *called* executes a **return** statement, it decreases R_r by $1 + k + \ell$ (observe that *called* knows k and ℓ) and execution continues at the return address (which can be found at $RS[R_r]$). Thus control is returned to *caller*. Note that recursion is no problem with this scheme, since each incarnation of a routine will have its own stack area for its parameters and local variables. Figure 2.3 shows the contents of the recursion stack of a call *factorial*(5) when the recursion has reached *factorial*(3). The label afterCall is the address of the instruction following the call *factorial*(5), and aRecCall is defined in Fig. 2.2.

Exercise 2.5 (sieve of Eratosthenes). Translate the following pseudocode for finding all prime numbers up to n into RAM machine code. Argue correctness first.

$a = \langle 1, \dots, 1 \rangle$: *Array* $[2..n]$ **of** $\{0, 1\}$ // if $a[i]$ is false, i is known to be nonprime
for $i := 2$ **to** $\lfloor \sqrt{n} \rfloor$ **do**
    if $a[i]$ **then for** $j := 2i$ **to** n **step** i **do** $a[j] := 0$
           // if $a[i]$ is true, i is prime and all multiples of i are nonprime
for $i := 2$ **to** n **do if** $a[i]$ **then** output "i is prime"

2.3.4 Object Orientation

We also need a simple form of object-oriented programming so that we can separate the interface and the implementation of the data structures. We shall introduce our notation by way of example. The definition

Class *Complex*$(x, y : Element)$ **of** *Number*
    Number $r := x$
    Number $i := y$
    Function *abs* : *Number* **return** $\sqrt{r^2 + i^2}$
    Function *add*$(c'$: *Complex*$)$: *Complex*   **return** *Complex*$(r + c'.r, i + c'.i)$

gives a (partial) implementation of a complex number type that can use arbitrary numeric types for the real and imaginary parts. Very often, our class names will begin with capital letters. The real and imaginary parts are stored in the *member variables* r and i, respectively. Now, the declaration "c : *Complex*$(2, 3)$ **of** $\mathbb{R}$" declares a complex number c initialized to $2 + 3i$; $c.i$ is the imaginary part, and $c.abs$ returns the absolute value of c.

The type after the **of** allows us to parameterize classes with types in a way similar to the template mechanism of C++ or the generic types of Java. Note that in the light of this notation, the types "*Set* **of** *Element*" and "*Sequence* **of** *Element*" mentioned earlier are ordinary classes. Objects of a class are initialized by setting the member variables as specified in the class definition.

2.4 Designing Correct Algorithms and Programs

An algorithm is a general method for solving problems of a certain kind. We describe algorithms using natural language and mathematical notation. Algorithms, as such, cannot be executed by a computer. The formulation of an algorithm in a programming language is called a program. Designing correct algorithms and translating a correct algorithm into a correct program are nontrivial and error prone tasks. In this section, we learn about assertions and invariants, two useful concepts for the design of correct algorithms and programs.

2.4.1 Assertions and Invariants

Assertions and *invariants* describe properties of the program state, i.e., properties of single variables and relations between the values of several variables. Typical properties are that a pointer has a defined value, an integer is nonnegative, a list is nonempty, or the value of an integer variable *length* is equal to the length of a certain list L. Figure 2.4 shows an example of the use of assertions and invariants in a function $power(a, n_0)$ that computes a^{n_0} for a real number a and a nonnegative integer n_0.

We start with the assertion **assert** $n_0 \geq 0$ and $\neg(a = 0 \wedge n_0 = 0)$. This states that the program expects a nonnegative integer n_0 and that not both a and n_0 are allowed to be zero. We make no claim about the behavior of our program for inputs that violate this assertion. This assertion is therefore called the *precondition* of the program. It is good programming practice to check the precondition of a program, i.e., to write code which checks the precondition and signals an error if it is violated. When the precondition holds (and the program is correct), a *postcondition* holds at the termination of the program. In our example, we assert that $r = a^{n_0}$. It is also good programming practice to verify the postcondition before returning from a program. We shall come back to this point at the end of this section.

One can view preconditions and postconditions as a *contract* between the caller and the called routine: if the caller passes parameters satisfying the precondition, the routine produces a result satisfying the postcondition.

For conciseness, we shall use assertions sparingly, assuming that certain "obvious" conditions are implicit from the textual description of the algorithm. Much more elaborate assertions may be required for safety-critical programs or for formal verification.

Preconditions and postconditions are assertions that describe the initial and the final state of a program or function. We also need to describe properties of intermediate states. Some particularly important consistency properties should hold at many places in a program. These properties are called *invariants*. Loop invariants and data structure invariants are of particular importance.

Function $power(a : \mathbb{R}; \; n_0 : \mathbb{N}) : \mathbb{R}$
　　　assert $n_0 \geq 0$ *and* $\neg(a = 0 \wedge n_0 = 0)$　　　　　// It is not so clear what 0^0 should be
　　　$p = a : \mathbb{R}; \quad r = 1 : \mathbb{R}; \quad n = n_0 : \mathbb{N}$　　　　　// we have: $p^n r = a^{n_0}$
　　　while $n > 0$ **do**
　　　　　invariant $p^n r = a^{n_0}$
　　　　　if n *is odd* **then** $n{-}{-}; \; r := r \cdot p$　　　　// invariant violated between assignments
　　　　　else $(n, p) := (n/2, p \cdot p)$　　　　// parallel assignment maintains invariant
　　　assert $r = a^{n_0}$　　　　// This is a consequence of the invariant and $n = 0$
　　　return r

Fig. 2.4. An algorithm that computes integer powers of real numbers

2.4.2 Loop Invariants

A *loop invariant* holds before and after each loop iteration. In our example, we claim that $p^n r = a^{n_0}$ before each iteration. This is true before the first iteration. The initialization of the program variables takes care of this. In fact, an invariant frequently tells us how to initialize the variables. Assume that the invariant holds before execution of the loop body, and $n > 0$. If n is odd, we decrement n and multiply r by p. This reestablishes the invariant (note that the invariant is violated between the assignments). If n is even, we halve n and square p, and again reestablish the invariant. When the loop terminates, we have $p^n r = a^{n_0}$ by the invariant, and $n = 0$ by the condition of the loop. Thus $r = a^{n_0}$ and we have established the postcondition.

The algorithm in Fig. 2.4 and many more algorithms described in this book have a quite simple structure. A few variables are declared and initialized to establish the loop invariant. Then, a main loop manipulates the state of the program. When the loop terminates, the loop invariant together with the termination condition of the loop implies that the correct result has been computed. The loop invariant therefore plays a pivotal role in understanding why a program works correctly. Once we understand the loop invariant, it suffices to check that the loop invariant is true initially and after each loop iteration. This is particularly easy if the loop body consists of only a small number of statements, as in the example above.

2.4.3 Data Structure Invariants

More complex programs encapsulate their state in objects whose consistent representation is also governed by invariants. Such *data structure invariants* are declared together with the data type. They are true after an object is constructed, and they are preconditions and postconditions of all methods of a class. For example, we shall discuss the representation of sets by sorted arrays. The data structure invariant will state that the data structure uses an array a and an integer n, that n is the size of a, that the set S stored in the data structure is equal to $\{a[1], \ldots, a[n]\}$, and that $a[1] < a[2] < \ldots < a[n]$. The methods of the class have to maintain this invariant and they are allowed to leverage the invariant; for example, the search method may make use of the fact that the array is sorted.

2.4.4 Certifying Algorithms

We mentioned above that it is good programming practice to check assertions. It is not always clear how to do this efficiently; in our example program, it is easy to check the precondition, but there seems to be no easy way to check the postcondition. In many situations, however, *the task of checking assertions can be simplified by computing additional information*. This additional information is called a *certificate* or *witness*, and its purpose is to simplify the check of an assertion. When an algorithm computes a certificate for the postcondition, we call it a *certifying algorithm*. We shall illustrate the idea by an example. Consider a function whose input is a graph $G = (V, E)$. Graphs are defined in Sect. 2.9. The task is to test whether the graph is bipartite, i.e., whether there is a labeling of the nodes of G with the colors blue and red such that any edge of G connects nodes of different colors. As specified so far, the function returns true or false – true if G is bipartite, and false otherwise. With this rudimentary output, the postcondition cannot be checked. However, we may augment the program as follows. When the program declares G bipartite, it also returns a two-coloring of the graph. When the program declares G nonbipartite, it also returns a cycle of odd length in the graph. For the augmented program, the postcondition is easy to check. In the first case, we simply check whether all edges connect nodes of different colors, and in the second case, we do nothing. An odd-length cycle proves that the graph is nonbipartite. Most algorithms in this book can be made certifying without increasing the asymptotic running time.

2.5 An Example – Binary Search

Binary search is a very useful technique for searching in an ordered set of items. We shall use it over and over again in later chapters.

The simplest scenario is as follows. We are given a sorted array $a[1..n]$ of pairwise distinct elements, i.e., $a[1] < a[2] < \ldots < a[n]$, and an element x. Now we are required to find the index i with $a[i-1] < x \le a[i]$; here, $a[0]$ and $a[n+1]$ should be interpreted as fictitious elements with values $-\infty$ and $+\infty$, respectively. We can use these fictitious elements in the invariants and the proofs, but cannot access them in the program.

Binary search is based on the principle of divide-and-conquer. We choose an index $m \in [1..n]$ and compare x with $a[m]$. If $x = a[m]$, we are done and return $i = m$. If $x < a[m]$, we restrict the search to the part of the array before $a[m]$, and if $x > a[m]$, we restrict the search to the part of the array after $a[m]$. We need to say more clearly what it means to restrict the search to a subinterval. We have two indices ℓ and r, and maintain the invariant

$$(I) \qquad 0 \le \ell < r \le n+1 \quad \text{and} \quad a[\ell] < x < a[r] .$$

This is true initially with $\ell = 0$ and $r = n+1$. If ℓ and r are consecutive indices, x is not contained in the array. Figure 2.5 shows the complete program.

The comments in the program show that the second part of the invariant is maintained. With respect to the first part, we observe that the loop is entered with $\ell < r$. If $\ell + 1 = r$, we stop and return. Otherwise, $\ell + 2 \le r$ and hence $\ell < m < r$. Thus m is a legal array index, and we can access $a[m]$. If $x = a[m]$, we stop. Otherwise, we set either $r = m$ or $\ell = m$ and hence have $\ell < r$ at the end of the loop. Thus the invariant is maintained.

Let us argue for termination next. We observe first that if an iteration is not the last one, then we either increase ℓ or decrease r, and hence $r - \ell$ decreases. Thus the search terminates. We want to show more. We want to show that the search terminates in a logarithmic number of steps. To do this, we study the quantity $r - \ell - 1$. Note that this is the number of indices i with $\ell < i < r$, and hence a natural measure of the size of the current subproblem. We shall show that each iteration except the last at least halves the size of the problem. If an iteration is not the last, $r - \ell - 1$ decreases to something less than or equal to

$$\max\{r - \lfloor (r+\ell)/2 \rfloor - 1, \lfloor (r+\ell)/2 \rfloor - \ell - 1\}$$
$$\leq \max\{r - ((r+\ell)/2 - 1/2) - 1, (r+\ell)/2 - \ell - 1\}$$
$$= \max\{(r-\ell-1)/2, (r-\ell)/2 - 1\} = (r-\ell-1)/2,$$

and hence it is at least halved. We start with $r - \ell - 1 = n + 1 - 0 - 1 = n$, and hence have $r - \ell - 1 \leq \lfloor n/2^k \rfloor$ after k iterations. The $(k+1)$-th iteration is certainly the last if we enter it with $r = \ell + 1$. This is guaranteed if $n/2^k < 1$ or $k > \log n$. We conclude that, at most, $2 + \log n$ iterations are performed. Since the number of comparisons is a natural number, we can sharpen the bound to $2 + \lfloor \log n \rfloor$.

Theorem 2.3. *Binary search finds an element in a sorted array of size n in $2 + \lfloor \log n \rfloor$ comparisons between elements.*

Exercise 2.6. Show that the above bound is sharp, i.e., for every n there are instances where exactly $2 + \lfloor \log n \rfloor$ comparisons are needed.

Exercise 2.7. Formulate binary search with two-way comparisons, i.e., distinguish between the cases $x < a[m]$, and $x \geq a[m]$.

We next discuss two important extensions of binary search. First, there is no need for the values $a[i]$ to be stored in an array. We only need the capability to compute $a[i]$, given i. For example, if we have a strictly monotonic function f and arguments i and j with $f(i) < x < f(j)$, we can use binary search to find m such that $f(m) \leq x < f(m+1)$. In this context, binary search is often referred to as the *bisection method*.

Second, we can extend binary search to the case where the array is infinite. Assume we have an infinite array $a[1..\infty]$ with $a[1] \leq x$ and want to find m such that $a[m] \leq x < a[m+1]$. If x is larger than all elements in the array, the procedure is allowed to diverge. We proceed as follows. We compare x with $a[2^1]$, $a[2^2]$, $a[2^3]$, ..., until the first i with $x < a[2^i]$ is found. This is called an *exponential search*. Then we complete the search by binary search on the array $a[2^{i-1}..2^i]$.

```
(ℓ,r) := (0, n+1)
while true do
    invariant I                                    // i.e., invariant (I) holds here
    if ℓ+1 = r then return "a[ℓ] < x < a[ℓ+1]"
    m := ⌊(r+ℓ)/2⌋                                  // ℓ < m < r
    s := compare(x, a[m])        // −1 if x < a[m], 0 if x = a[m], +1 if x > a[m]
    if s = 0 then return "x is equal to a[m]";
    if s < 0
        then r := m                                 // a[ℓ] < x < a[m] = a[r]
        else ℓ := m                                 // a[ℓ] = a[m] < x < a[r]
```

Fig. 2.5. Binary search for x in a sorted array $a[1..n]$

Theorem 2.4. *The combination of exponential and binary search finds x in an unbounded sorted array in at most $2\log m + 3$ comparisons, where $a[m] \leq x < a[m+1]$.*

Proof. We need i comparisons to find the first i such that $x < a[2^i]$, followed by $\log(2^i - 2^{i-1}) + 2$ comparisons for the binary search. This gives a total of $2i + 1$ comparisons. Since $m \geq 2^{i-1}$, we have $i \leq 1 + \log m$ and the claim follows.   □

Binary search is certifying. It returns an index m with $a[m] \leq x < a[m+1]$. If $x = a[m]$, the index proves that x is stored in the array. If $a[m] < x < a[m+1]$ and the array is sorted, the index proves that x is not stored in the array. Of course, if the array violates the precondition and is not sorted, we know nothing. There is no way to check the precondition in logarithmic time.

2.6 Basic Algorithm Analysis

Let us summarize the principles of algorithm analysis. We abstract from the complications of a real machine to the simplified RAM model. In the RAM model, running time is measured by the number of instructions executed. We simplify the analysis further by grouping inputs by size and focusing on the worst case. The use of asymptotic notation allows us to ignore constant factors and lower-order terms. This coarsening of our view also allows us to look at upper bounds on the execution time rather than the exact worst case, as long as the asymptotic result remains unchanged. The total effect of these simplifications is that the running time of pseudocode can be analyzed directly. There is no need to translate the program into machine code first.

We shall next introduce a set of simple rules for analyzing pseudocode. Let $T(I)$ denote the worst-case execution time of a piece of program I. The following rules then tell us how to estimate the running time for larger programs, given that we know the running times of their constituents:

- $T(I; I') = T(I) + T(I')$.
- $T(\textbf{if } C \textbf{ then } I \textbf{ else } I') = O(T(C) + \max(T(I), T(I')))$.
- $T(\textbf{repeat } I \textbf{ until } C) = O\left(\sum_{i=1}^{k} T(i)\right)$, where k is the number of loop iterations, and $T(i)$ is the time needed in the i-th iteration of the loop, including the test C.

We postpone the treatment of subroutine calls to Sect. 2.6.2. Of the rules above, only the rule for loops is nontrivial to apply; it requires evaluating sums.

2.6.1 "Doing Sums"

We now introduce some basic techniques for evaluating sums. Sums arise in the analysis of loops, in average-case analysis, and also in the analysis of randomized algorithms.

For example, the insertion sort algorithm introduced in Sect. 5.1 has two nested loops. The outer loop counts i, from 2 to n. The inner loop performs at most $i - 1$ iterations. Hence, the total number of iterations of the inner loop is at most

$$\sum_{i=2}^{n}(i-1) = \sum_{i=1}^{n-1} i = \frac{n(n-1)}{2} = O(n^2) \ ,$$

where the second equality comes from (A.11). Since the time for one execution of the inner loop is $O(1)$, we get a worst-case execution time of $\Theta(n^2)$. All nested loops with an easily predictable number of iterations can be analyzed in an analogous fashion: work your way outwards by repeatedly finding a closed-form expression for the innermost loop. Using simple manipulations such as $\sum_i ca_i = c\sum_i a_i$, $\sum_i (a_i + b_i) = \sum_i a_i + \sum_i b_i$, or $\sum_{i=2}^n a_i = -a_1 + \sum_{i=1}^n a_i$, one can often reduce the sums to simple forms that can be looked up in a catalog of sums. A small sample of such formulae can be found in Appendix A. Since we are usually interested only in the asymptotic behavior, we can frequently avoid doing sums exactly and resort to estimates. For example, instead of evaluating the sum above exactly, we may argue more simply as follows:

$$\sum_{i=2}^{n}(i-1) \le \sum_{i=1}^{n} n = n^2 = O(n^2) \ ,$$

$$\sum_{i=2}^{n}(i-1) \ge \sum_{i=\lceil n/2 \rceil}^{n} n/2 = \lfloor n/2 \rfloor \cdot n/2 = \Omega(n^2) \ .$$

2.6.2 Recurrences

In our rules for analyzing programs, we have so far neglected subroutine calls. Non-recursive subroutines are easy to handle, since we can analyze the subroutine separately and then substitute the bound obtained into the expression for the running time of the calling routine. For recursive programs, however, this approach does not lead to a closed formula, but to a recurrence relation.

For example, for the recursive variant of the school method of multiplication, we obtained $T(1) = 1$ and $T(n) = 6n + 4T(\lceil n/2 \rceil)$ for the number of primitive operations. For the Karatsuba algorithm, the corresponding expression was $T(n) = 3n^2 + 2n$ for $n \le 3$ and $T(n) = 12n + 3T(\lceil n/2 \rceil + 1)$ otherwise. In general, a *recurrence relation* defines a function in terms of the same function using smaller arguments. Explicit definitions for small parameter values make the function well defined. Solving recurrences, i.e., finding nonrecursive, closed-form expressions for them, is an interesting subject in mathematics. Here we focus on the recurrence relations that typically emerge from divide-and-conquer algorithms. We begin with a simple case that will suffice for the purpose of understanding the main ideas. We have a problem of size $n = b^k$ for some integer k. If $k > 1$, we invest linear work cn in dividing the problem into d subproblems of size n/b and combining the results. If $k = 0$, there are no recursive calls, we invest work a, and are done.

Theorem 2.5 (master theorem (simple form)). *For positive constants a, b, c, and d, and $n = b^k$ for some integer k, consider the recurrence*

$$r(n) = \begin{cases} a & \text{if } n = 1 \ , \\ cn + d \cdot r(n/b) & \text{if } n > 1 \ . \end{cases}$$

Then

$$r(n) = \begin{cases} \Theta(n) & \text{if } d < b, \\ \Theta(n \log n) & \text{if } d = b, \\ \Theta(n^{\log_b d}) & \text{if } d > b. \end{cases}$$

Figure 2.6 illustrates the main insight behind Theorem 2.5. We consider the amount of work done at each level of recursion. We start with a problem of size n. At the i-th level of the recursion, we have d^i problems, each of size n/b^i. Thus the total size of the problems at the i-th level is equal to

$$d^i \frac{n}{b^i} = n \left(\frac{d}{b} \right)^i.$$

The work performed for a problem is c times the problem size, and hence the work performed at any level of the recursion is proportional to the total problem size at that level. Depending on whether d/b is less than, equal to, or larger than 1, we have different kinds of behavior.

If $d < b$, the work *decreases geometrically* with the level of recursion and the *first* level of recursion accounts for a constant fraction of the total execution time.

If $d = b$, we have the same amount of work at *every* level of recursion. Since there are logarithmically many levels, the total amount of work is $\Theta(n \log n)$.

Finally, if $d > b$, we have a geometrically *growing* amount of work at each level of recursion so that the *last* level accounts for a constant fraction of the total running time. We formalize this reasoning next.

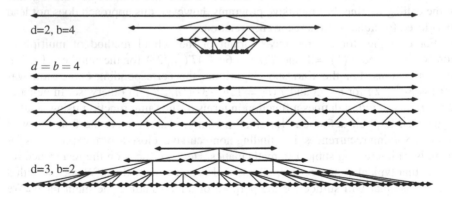

Fig. 2.6. Examples of the three cases of the master theorem. Problems are indicated by horizontal line segments with arrows at both ends. The length of a segment represents the size of the problem, and the subproblems resulting from a problem are shown in the line below it. The topmost part of figure corresponds to the case $d = 2$ and $b = 4$, i.e., each problem generates two subproblems of one-fourth the size. Thus the total size of the subproblems is only half of the original size. The middle part of the figure illustrates the case $d = b = 2$, and the bottommost part illustrates the case $d = 3$ and $b = 2$

Proof. We start with a single problem of size $n = b^k$. W call this level zero of the recursion.[3] At level 1, we have d problems, each of size $n/b = b^{k-1}$. At level 2, we have d^2 problems, each of size $n/b^2 = b^{k-2}$. At level i, we have d^i problems, each of size $n/b^i = b^{k-i}$. At level k, we have d^k problems, each of size $n/b^k = b^{k-k} = 1$. Each such problem has a cost a, and hence the total cost at level k is ad^k.

Let us next compute the total cost of the divide-and-conquer steps at levels 1 to $k - 1$. At level i, we have d^i recursive calls each for subproblems of size b^{k-i}. Each call contributes a cost of $c \cdot b^{k-i}$, and hence the cost at level i is $d^i \cdot c \cdot b^{k-i}$. Thus the combined cost over all levels is

$$\sum_{i=0}^{k-1} d^i \cdot c \cdot b^{k-i} = c \cdot b^k \cdot \sum_{i=0}^{k-1} \left(\frac{d}{b}\right)^i = cn \cdot \sum_{i=0}^{k-1} \left(\frac{d}{b}\right)^i .$$

We now distinguish cases according to the relative sizes of d and b.

Case $d = b$. We have a cost $ad^k = ab^k = an = \Theta(n)$ for the bottom of the recursion and $cnk = cn\log_b n = \Theta(n\log n)$ for the divide-and-conquer steps.

Case $d < b$. We have a cost $ad^k < ab^k = an = O(n)$ for the bottom of the recursion. For the cost of the divide-and-conquer steps, we use (A.13) for a geometric series, namely $\sum_{0 \le i < k} x^i = (1 - x^k)/(1 - x)$ for $x > 0$ and $x \neq 1$, and obtain

$$cn \cdot \sum_{i=0}^{k-1} \left(\frac{d}{b}\right)^i = cn \cdot \frac{1 - (d/b)^k}{1 - d/b} < cn \cdot \frac{1}{1 - d/b} = O(n)$$

and

$$cn \cdot \sum_{i=0}^{k-1} \left(\frac{d}{b}\right)^i = cn \cdot \frac{1 - (d/b)^k}{1 - d/b} > cn = \Omega(n) .$$

Case $d > b$. First, note that

$$d^k = 2^{k\log d} = 2^{k\frac{\log b}{\log b}\log d} = b^{k\frac{\log d}{\log b}} = b^{k\log_b d} = n^{\log_b d} .$$

Hence the bottom of the recursion has a cost of $an^{\log_b d} = \Theta(n^{\log_b d})$. For the divide-and-conquer steps we use the geometric series again and obtain

$$cb^k \frac{(d/b)^k - 1}{d/b - 1} = c\frac{d^k - b^k}{d/b - 1} = cd^k \frac{1 - (b/d)^k}{d/b - 1} = \Theta(d^k) = \Theta(n^{\log_b d}) .$$

□

We shall use the master theorem many times in this book. Unfortunately, the recurrence $T(n) = 3n^2 + 2n$ for $n \le 3$ and $T(n) \le 12n + 3T(\lceil n/2 \rceil + 1)$, governing

---

[3] In this proof, we use the terminology of recursive programs in order to give an intuitive idea of what we are doing. However, our mathematical arguments apply to any recurrence relation of the right form, even if it does not stem from a recursive program.

Karatsuba's algorithm, is not covered by our master theorem, which neglects rounding issues. We shall now show how to extend the master theorem to the following recurrence:

$$r(n) \leq \begin{cases} a & \text{if } n \leq n_0, \\ cn + d \cdot r(\lceil n/b \rceil + e) & \text{if } n > n_0, \end{cases}$$

where a, b, c, d, and e are constants, and n_0 is such that $\lceil n/b \rceil + e < n$ for $n > n_0$. We proceed in two steps. We first concentrate on n of the form $b^k + z$, where z is such that $\lceil z/b \rceil + e = z$. For example, for $b = 2$ and $e = 3$, we would choose $z = 6$. Note that for n of this form, we have $\lceil n/b \rceil + e = \lceil (b^k + z)/b \rceil + e = b^{k-1} + \lceil z/b \rceil + e = b^{k-1} + z$, i.e., the reduced problem size has the same form. For the n's in this special form, we then argue exactly as in Theorem 2.5.

How do we generalize to arbitrary n? The simplest way is semantic reasoning. It is clear[4] that the cost grows with the problem size, and hence the cost for an input of size n will be no larger than the cost for an input whose size is equal to the next input size of special form. Since this input is at most b times larger and b is a constant, the bound derived for special n is affected only by a constant factor.

The formal reasoning is as follows (you may want to skip this paragraph and come back to it when the need arises). We define a function $R(n)$ by the same recurrence, with $\leq$ replaced by equality: $R(n) = a$ for $n \leq n_0$ and $R(n) = cn + dR(\lceil n/b \rceil + e)$ for $n > n_0$. Obviously, $r(n) \leq R(n)$. We derive a bound for $R(n)$ and n of special form as described above. Finally, we argue by induction that $R(n) \leq R(s(n))$, where $s(n)$ is the smallest number of the form $b^k + z$ with $b^k + z \geq n$. The induction step is as follows:

$$R(n) = cn + dR(\lceil n/b \rceil + e) \leq cs(n) + dR(s(\lceil n/b \rceil + e)) = R(s(n)),$$

where the inequality uses the induction hypothesis and $n \leq s(n)$. The last equality uses the fact that for $s(n) = b^k + z$ (and hence $b^{k-1} + z < n$), we have $b^{k-2} + z < \lceil n/b \rceil + e \leq b^{k-1} + z$ and hence $s(\lceil n/b \rceil + e) = b^{k-1} + z = \lceil s(n)/b \rceil + e$.

There are many generalizations of the master theorem: we might break the recursion earlier, the cost for dividing and conquering may be nonlinear, the size of the subproblems might vary within certain bounds, the number of subproblems may depend on the input size, etc. We refer the reader to the books [81, 175] for further information.

Exercise 2.8. Consider the recurrence

$$C(n) = \begin{cases} 1 & \text{if } n = 1, \\ C(\lfloor n/2 \rfloor) + C(\lceil n/2 \rceil) + cn & \text{if } n > 1. \end{cases}$$

Show that $C(n) = O(n \log n)$.

---

[4] Be aware that most errors in mathematical arguments are near occurrences of the word "clearly".

Exercise 2.9. Suppose you have a divide-and-conquer algorithm whose running time is governed by the recurrence $T(1) = a$, $T(n) = cn + \lceil \sqrt{n} \rceil T(\lceil n/\lceil \sqrt{n} \rceil \rceil)$. Show that the running time of the program is $O(n \log \log n)$.

Exercise 2.10. Access to data structures is often governed by the following recurrence: $T(1) = a$, $T(n) = c + T(n/2)$. Show that $T(n) = O(\log n)$.

2.6.3 Global Arguments

The algorithm analysis techniques introduced so far are syntax-oriented in the following sense: in order to analyze a large program, we first analyze its parts and then combine the analyses of the parts into an analysis of the large program. The combination step involves sums and recurrences.

We shall also use a completely different approach which one might call semantics-oriented. In this approach we associate parts of the execution with parts of a combinatorial structure and then argue about the combinatorial structure. For example, we might argue that a certain piece of program is executed at most once for each edge of a graph or that the execution of a certain piece of program at least doubles the size of a certain structure, that the size is one initially, and at most n at termination, and hence the number of executions is bounded logarithmically.

2.7 Average-Case Analysis

In this section we shall introduce you to average-case analysis. We shall do so by way of three examples of increasing complexity. We assume that you are familiar with basic concepts of probability theory such as discrete probability distributions, expected values, indicator variables, and the linearity of expectations. Section A.3 reviews the basics.

2.7.1 Incrementing a Counter

We begin with a very simple example. Our input is an array $a[0..n-1]$ filled with digits zero and one. We want to increment the number represented by the array by one.

```
i:=0
while (i < n and a[i] = 1) do a[i] = 0; i++;
if i < n then a[i] = 1
```

How often is the body of the while loop executed? Clearly, n times in the worst case and 0 times in the best case. What is the average case? The first step in an average-case analysis is always to define the model of randomness, i.e., to define the underlying probability space. We postulate the following model of randomness: each digit is zero or one with probability $1/2$, and different digits are independent. The loop body is executed k times, $0 \le k \le n$, iff the last $k+1$ digits of a are 01^k or k

is equal to n and all digits of a are equal to one. The former event has probability $2^{-(k+1)}$, and the latter event has probability 2^{-n}. Therefore, the average number of executions is equal to

$$\sum_{0 \leq k < n} k2^{-(k+1)} + n2^{-n} \leq \sum_{k \geq 0} k2^{-k} = 2 ,$$

where the last equality is the same as (A.14).

2.7.2 Left-to-Right Maxima

Our second example is slightly more demanding. Consider the following simple program that determines the maximum element in an array $a[1..n]$:

$m := a[1];$ **for** $i := 2$ **to** n **do if** $a[i] > m$ **then** $m := a[i]$

How often is the assignment $m := a[i]$ executed? In the worst case, it is executed in every iteration of the loop and hence $n - 1$ times. In the best case, it is not executed at all. What is the average case? Again, we start by defining the probability space. We assume that the array contains n distinct elements and that any order of these elements is equally likely. In other words, our probability space consists of the $n!$ permutations of the array elements. Each permutation is equally likely and therefore has probability $1/n!$. Since the exact nature of the array elements is unimportant, we may assume that the array contains the numbers 1 to n in some order. We are interested in the average number of *left-to-right maxima*. A left-to-right maximum in a sequence is an element which is larger than all preceding elements. So, $(1,2,4,3)$ has three left-to-right-maxima and $(3,1,2,4)$ has two left-to-right-maxima. For a permutation π of the integers 1 to n, let $M_n(\pi)$ be the number of left-to-right-maxima. What is $E[M_n]$? We shall describe two ways to determine the expectation. For small n, it is easy to determine $E[M_n]$ by direct calculation. For $n = 1$, there is only one permutation, namely (1), and it has one maximum. So $E[M_1] = 1$. For $n = 2$, there are two permutations, namely $(1,2)$ and $(2,1)$. The former has two maxima and the latter has one maximum. So $E[M_2] = 1.5$. For larger n, we argue as follows.

We write M_n as a sum of indicator variables I_1 to I_n, i.e., $M_n = I_1 + \ldots + I_n$, where I_k is equal to one for a permutation π if the k-th element of π is a left-to-right maximum. For example, $I_3((3,1,2,4)) = 0$ and $I_4((3,1,2,4)) = 1$. We have

$$E[M_n] = E[I_1 + I_2 + \ldots + I_n]$$
$$= E[I_1] + E[I_2] + \ldots + E[I_n]$$
$$= \text{prob}(I_1 = 1) + \text{prob}(I_2 = 1) + \ldots + \text{prob}(I_n = 1) ,$$

where the second equality is the linearity of expectations (A.2) and the third equality follows from the I_k's being indicator variables. It remains to determine the probability that $I_k = 1$. The k-th element of a random permutation is a left-to-right maximum if and only if the k-th element is the largest of the first k elements. In a random permutation, any position is equally likely to hold the maximum, so that the probability we are looking for is $\text{prob}(I_k = 1) = 1/k$ and hence

$$E[M_n] = \sum_{1 \leq k < n} \text{prob}(I_k = 1) = \sum_{1 \leq k \leq n} \frac{1}{k}.$$

So, $E[M_4] = 1 + 1/2 + 1/3 + 1/4 = (12 + 6 + 4 + 3)/12 = 25/12$. The sum $\sum_{1 \leq k \leq n} 1/k$ will appear several times in this book. It is known under the name "n-th harmonic number" and is denoted by H_n. It is known that $\ln n \leq H_n \leq 1 + \ln n$, i.e., $H_n \approx \ln n$; see (A.12). We conclude that the average number of left-to-right maxima is much smaller than in the worst case.

Exercise 2.11. Show that $\sum_{k=1}^{n} \frac{1}{k} \leq \ln n + 1$. Hint: show first that $\sum_{k=2}^{n} \frac{1}{k} \leq \int_{1}^{n} \frac{1}{x} \, dx$.

We now describe an alternative analysis. We introduce A_n as a shorthand for $E[M_n]$ and set $A_0 = 0$. The first element is always a left-to-right maximum, and each number is equally likely as the first element. If the first element is equal to i, then only the numbers $i + 1$ to n can be further left-to-right maxima. They appear in random order in the remaining sequence, and hence we shall see an expected number of A_{n-i} further maxima. Thus

$$A_n = 1 + \left(\sum_{1 \leq i \leq n} A_{n-i} \right) / n \qquad \text{or} \qquad nA_n = n + \sum_{0 \leq i \leq n-1} A_i.$$

A simple trick simplifies this recurrence. The corresponding equation for $n - 1$ instead of n is $(n - 1)A_{n-1} = n - 1 + \sum_{1 \leq i \leq n-2} A_i$. Subtracting the equation for $n - 1$ from the equation for n yields

$$nA_n - (n - 1)A_{n-1} = 1 + A_{n-1} \qquad \text{or} \qquad A_n = 1/n + A_{n-1},$$

and hence $A_n = H_n$.

2.7.3 Linear Search

We come now to our third example; this example is even more demanding. Consider the following search problem. We have items 1 to n, which we are required to arrange linearly in some order; say, we put item i in position ℓ_i. Once we have arranged the items, we perform searches. In order to search for an item x, we go through the sequence from left to right until we encounter x. In this way, it will take ℓ_i steps to access item i.

Suppose now that we also know that we shall access the items with different probabilities; say, we search for item i with probability p_i, where $p_i \geq 0$ for all i, $1 \leq i \leq n$, and $\sum_i p_i = 1$. In this situation, the *expected* or *average* cost of a search is equal to $\sum_i p_i \ell_i$, since we search for item i with probability p_i and the cost of the search is ℓ_i.

What is the best way of arranging the items? Intuition tells us that we should arrange the items in order of decreasing probability. Let us prove this.

Lemma 2.6. *An arrangement is optimal with respect to the expected search cost if it has the property that $p_i > p_j$ implies $\ell_i < \ell_j$. If $p_1 \geq p_2 \geq \ldots \geq p_n$, the placement $\ell_i = i$ results in the optimal expected search cost $Opt = \sum_i p_i i$.*

Proof. Consider an arrangement in which, for some i and j, we have $p_i > p_j$ and $\ell_i > \ell_j$, i.e., item i is more probable than item j and yet placed after it. Interchanging items i and j changes the search cost by

$$-(p_i\ell_i + p_j\ell_j) + (p_i\ell_j + p_j\ell_i) = (p_i - p_j)(\ell_i - \ell_j) < 0,$$

i.e., the new arrangement is better and hence the old arrangement is not optimal.

Let us now consider the case $p_1 > p_2 > \ldots > p_n$. Since there are only $n!$ possible arrangements, there is an optimal arrangement. Also, if $i < j$ and i is placed after j, the arrangement is not optimal by the argument in the preceding paragraph. Thus the optimal arrangement puts item i in position $\ell_i = i$ and its expected search cost is $\sum_i p_i i$.

If $p_1 \geq p_2 \geq \ldots \geq p_n$, the arrangement $\ell_i = i$ for all i is still optimal. However, if some probabilities are equal, we have more than one optimal arrangement. Within blocks of equal probabilities, the order is irrelevant.   □

Can we still do something intelligent if the probabilities p_i are not known to us? The answer is yes, and a very simple heuristic does the job. It is called the *move-to-front heuristic*. Suppose we access item i and find it in position ℓ_i. If $\ell_i = 1$, we are happy and do nothing. Otherwise, we place it in position 1 and move the items in positions 1 to $\ell_i - 1$ one position to the rear. The hope is that, in this way, frequently accessed items tend to stay near the front of the arrangement and infrequently accessed items move to the rear. We shall now analyze the expected behavior of the move-to-front heuristic.

Consider two items i and j and suppose that both of them were accessed in the past. Item i will be accessed before item j if the last access to item i occurred after the last access to item j. Thus the probability that item i is before item j is $p_i/(p_i + p_j)$. With probability $p_j/(p_i + p_j)$, item j stands before item i.

Now, ℓ_i is simply one plus the number of elements before i in the list. Thus the expected value of ℓ_i is equal to $1 + \sum_{j;\ j\neq i} p_j/(p_i + p_j)$, and hence the expected search cost in the move-to-front heuristic is

$$C_{MTF} = \sum_i p_i \left(1 + \sum_{j;\ j\neq i} \frac{p_j}{p_i + p_j}\right) = \sum_i p_i + \sum_{i,j;\ i\neq j} \frac{p_i p_j}{p_i + p_j}.$$

Observe that for each i and j with $i \neq j$, the term $p_i p_j/(p_i + p_j)$ appears twice in the sum above. In order to proceed with the analysis, we assume $p_1 \geq p_2 \geq \ldots \geq p_n$. This is an assumption used in the analysis, the algorithm has no knowledge of this. Then

$$C_{MTF} = \sum_i p_i + 2 \sum_{j;\ j<i} \frac{p_i p_j}{p_l + p_j} = \sum_i p_i \left(1 + 2 \sum_{j;\ j<i} \frac{p_j}{p_i + p_j} \right)$$

$$\leq \sum_i p_i \left(1 + 2 \sum_{j;\ j<i} 1 \right) < \sum_i p_i 2i = 2 \sum_i p_i i = 2Opt .$$

Theorem 2.7. *The move-to-front heuristic achieves an expected search time which is at most twice the optimum.*

2.8 Randomized Algorithms

Suppose you are offered the chance to participate in a TV game show. There are 100 boxes that you can open in an order of your choice. Box i contains an amount m_i of money. This amount is unknown to you but becomes known once the box is opened. No two boxes contain the same amount of money. The rules of the game are very simple:

- At the beginning of the game, the presenter gives you 10 tokens.
- When you open a box and the contents of the box are larger than the contents of all previously opened boxes, you have to hand back a token.[5]
- When you have to hand back a token but have no tokens, the game ends and you lose.
- When you manage to open all of the boxes, you win and can keep all the money.

There are strange pictures on the boxes, and the presenter gives hints by suggesting the box to be opened next. Your aunt, who is addicted to this show, tells you that only a few candidates win. Now, you ask yourself whether it is worth participating in this game. Is there a strategy that gives you a good chance of winning? Are the presenter's hints useful?

Let us first analyze the obvious algorithm – you always follow the presenter. The worst case is that he makes you open the boxes in order of increasing value. Whenever you open a box, you have to hand back a token, and when you open the 11th box you are dead. The candidates and viewers would hate the presenter and he would soon be fired. Worst-case analysis does not give us the right information in this situation. The best case is that the presenter immediately tells you the best box. You would be happy, but there would be no time to place advertisements, so that the presenter would again be fired. Best-case analysis also does not give us the right information in this situation. We next observe that the game is really the left-to-right maxima question of the preceding section in disguise. You have to hand back a token whenever a new maximum shows up. We saw in the preceding section that the expected number of left-to-right maxima in a random permutation is H_n, the n-th

---

[5] The contents of the first box opened are larger than the contents of all previously opened boxes, and hence the first token goes back to the presenter in the first round.

harmonic number. For $n = 100$, $H_n < 6$. So if the presenter were to point to the boxes in random order, you would have to hand back only 6 tokens on average. But why should the presenter offer you the boxes in random order? He has no incentive to have too many winners.

The solution is to take your fate into your own hands: *open the boxes in random order*. You select one of the boxes at random, open it, then choose a random box from the remaining ones, and so on. How do you choose a random box? When there are k boxes left, you choose a random box by tossing a die with k sides or by choosing a random number in the range 1 to k. In this way, you generate a random permutation of the boxes and hence the analysis in the previous section still applies. On average you will have to return fewer than 6 tokens and hence your 10 tokens suffice. You have just seen a *randomized algorithm*. We want to stress that, although the mathematical analysis is the same, the conclusions are very different. In the average-case scenario, you are at the mercy of the presenter. If he opens the boxes in random order, the analysis applies; if he does not, it does not. You have no way to tell, except after many shows and with hindsight. In other words, the presenter controls the dice and it is up to him whether he uses fair dice. The situation is completely different in the randomized-algorithms scenario. You control the dice, and you generate the random permutation. The analysis is valid no matter what the presenter does.

2.8.1 The Formal Model

Formally, we equip our RAM with an additional instruction: $R_i := randInt(C)$ assigns a *random* integer between 0 and $C - 1$ to R_i. In pseudocode, we write $v := randInt(C)$, where v is an integer variable. The cost of making a random choice is one time unit. Algorithms *not* using randomization are called *deterministic*.

The running time of a randomized algorithm will generally depend on the random choices made by the algorithm. So the running time on an instance i is no longer a number, but a random variable depending on the random choices. We may eliminate the dependency of the running time on random choices by equipping our machine with a timer. At the beginning of the execution, we set the timer to a value $T(n)$, which may depend on the size n of the problem instance, and stop the machine once the timer goes off. In this way, we can guarantee that the running time is bounded by $T(n)$. However, if the algorithm runs out of time, it does not deliver an answer.

The output of a randomized algorithm may also depend on the random choices made. How can an algorithm be useful if the answer on an instance i may depend on the random choices made by the algorithm – if the answer may be "Yes" today and "No" tomorrow? If the two cases are equally probable, the answer given by the algorithm has no value. However, if the correct answer is much more likely than the incorrect answer, the answer does have value. Let us see an example.

Alice and Bob are connected over a slow telephone line. Alice has an integer x_A and Bob has an integer x_B, each with n bits. They want to determine whether they have the same number. As communication is slow, their goal is to minimize the amount of information exchanged. Local computation is not an issue.

In the obvious solution, Alice sends her number to Bob, and Bob checks whether the numbers are equal and announces the result. This requires them to transmit n digits. Alternatively, Alice could send the number digit by digit, and Bob would check for equality as the digits arrived and announce the result as soon as he knew it, i.e., as soon as corresponding digits differed or all digits had been transmitted. In the worst case, all n digits have to be transmitted. We shall now show that randomization leads to a dramatic improvement. After transmission of only $O(\log n)$ bits, equality and inequality can be decided with high probability.

Alice and Bob follow the following protocol. Each of them prepares an ordered list of prime numbers. The list consists of the smallest L primes with k or more bits and leading bit 1. Each such prime has a value of at least 2^k. We shall say more about the choice of L and k below. In this way, it is guaranteed that both Alice and Bob generate the same list. Then Alice chooses an index i, $1 \leq i \leq L$, at random and sends i and $x_A \bmod p_i$ to Bob. Bob computes $x_B \bmod p_i$. If $x_A \bmod p_i \neq x_B \bmod p_i$, he declares that the numbers are different. Otherwise, he declares the numbers the same. Clearly, if the numbers are the same, Bob will say so. If the numbers are different and $x_A \bmod p_i \neq x_B \bmod p_i$, he will declare them different. However, if $x_A \neq x_B$ and yet $x_A \bmod p_i = x_B \bmod p_i$, he will erroneously declare the numbers equal. What is the probability of an error?

An error occurs if $x_A \neq x_B$ but $x_A \equiv x_B (\bmod\, p_i)$. The latter condition is equivalent to p_i dividing the difference $D = x_A - x_B$. This difference is at most 2^n in absolute value. Since each prime p_i has a value of at least 2^k, our list contains at most n/k primes that divide[6] the difference, and hence the probability of error is at most $(n/k)/L$. We can make this probability arbitrarily small by choosing L large enough. If, say, we want to make the probability less than $0.000001 = 10^{-6}$, we choose $L = 10^6(n/k)$.

What is the appropriate choice of k? Out of the numbers with k bits, approximately $2^k/k$ are primes.[7] Hence, if $2^k/k \geq 10^6 n/k$, the list will contain only k-bit integers. The condition $2^k \geq 10^6 n$ is tantamount to $k \geq \log n + 6 \log 10$. With this choice of k, the protocol transmits $\log L + k = \log n + 12 \log 10$ bits. *This is exponentially better than the naive protocol.*

What can we do if we want an error probability less than 10^{-12}? We could redo the calculations above with $L = 10^{12} n$. Alternatively, we could run the protocol twice and declare the numbers different if at least one run declares them different. This two-stage protocol errs only if both runs err, and hence the probability of error is at most $10^{-6} \cdot 10^{-6} = 10^{-12}$.

Exercise 2.12. Compare the efficiency of the two approaches for obtaining an error probability of 10^{-12}.

---

[6] Let d be the number of primes on our list that divide D. Then $2^n \geq |D| \geq (2^k)^d = 2^{kd}$ and hence $d \leq n/k$.

[7] For any integer x, let $\pi(x)$ be the number of primes less than or equal to x. For example, $\pi(10) = 4$ because there are four prime numbers (2, 3, 5 and 7) less than or equal to 10. Then $x/(\ln x + 2) < \pi(x) < x/(\ln x - 4)$ for $x \geq 55$. See the Wikipedia entry on "prime numbers" for more information.

Exercise 2.13. In the protocol described above, Alice and Bob have to prepare ridiculously long lists of prime numbers. Discuss the following modified protocol. Alice chooses a random k-bit integer p (with leading bit 1) and tests it for primality. If p is not prime, she repeats the process. If p is prime, she sends p and $x_A \bmod p$ to Bob.

Exercise 2.14. Assume you have an algorithm which errs with a probability of at most $1/4$ and that you run the algorithm k times and output the majority output. Derive a bound on the error probability as a function of k. Do a precise calculation for $k = 2$ and $k = 3$, and give a bound for large k. Finally, determine k such that the error probability is less than a given ε.

2.8.2 Las Vegas and Monte Carlo Algorithms

Randomized algorithms come in two main varieties, the Las Vegas and the Monte Carlo variety. A *Las Vegas algorithm* always computes the correct answer but its running time is a random variable. Our solution for the game show is a Las Vegas algorithm; it always finds the box containing the maximum; however, the number of left-to-right maxima is a random variable. A *Monte Carlo* algorithm always has the same run time, but there is a nonzero probability that it gives an incorrect answer. The probability that the answer is incorrect is at most 1/4. Our algorithm for comparing two numbers over a telephone line is a Monte Carlo algorithm. In Exercise 2.14, it is shown that the error probability can be made arbitrarily small.

Exercise 2.15. Suppose you have a Las Vegas algorithm with an expected execution time $t(n)$, and that you run it for $4t(n)$ steps. If it returns an answer within the alloted time, this answer is returned, otherwise an arbitrary answer is returned. Show that the resulting algorithm is a Monte Carlo algorithm.

Exercise 2.16. Suppose you have a Monte Carlo algorithm with an execution time $m(n)$ that gives a correct answer with probability p and a deterministic algorithm that verifies in time $v(n)$ whether the Monte Carlo algorithm has given the correct answer. Explain how to use these two algorithms to obtain a Las Vegas algorithm with expected execution time $(m(n) + v(n))/(1 - p)$.

We come back to our game show example. You have 10 tokens available to you. The expected number of tokens required is less than 6. How sure should you be that you will go home a winner? We need to bound the probability that M_n is larger than 11, because you lose exactly if the sequence in which you order the boxes has 11 or more left-to-right maxima. *Markov's inequality* allows you to bound this probability. It states that, for a nonnegative random variable X and any constant $c \geq 1$, $\mathrm{prob}(X \geq c \cdot \mathrm{E}[X]) \leq 1/c$; see (A.4) for additional information. We apply the inequality with $X = M_n$ and $c = 11/6$. We obtain

$$\mathrm{prob}(M_n \geq 11) \leq \mathrm{prob}\left(M_n \geq \frac{11}{6}\mathrm{E}[M_n]\right) \leq \frac{6}{11},$$

and hence the probability of winning is more than 5/11.

2.9 Graphs

Graphs are an extremely useful concept in algorithmics. We use them whenever we want to model objects and relations between them; in graph terminology, the objects are called *nodes*, and the relations between nodes are called *edges*. Some obvious applications are road maps and communication networks, but there are also more abstract applications. For example, nodes could be tasks to be completed when building a house, such as "build the walls" or "put in the windows", and edges could model precedence relations such as "the walls have to be built before the windows can be put in". We shall also see many examples of data structures where it is natural to view objects as nodes and pointers as edges between the object storing the pointer and the object pointed to.

When humans think about graphs, they usually find it convenient to work with pictures showing nodes as bullets and edges as lines and arrows. To treat graphs algorithmically, a more mathematical notation is needed: a *directed graph* $G = (V, E)$ is a pair consisting of a *node set* (or *vertex set*) V and an *edge set* (or *arc set*) $E \subseteq V \times V$. We sometimes abbreviate "directed graph" to *digraph*. For example, Fig. 2.7 shows the graph $G = (\{s, t, u, v, w, x, y, z\}, \{(s,t), (t,u), (u,v), (v,w), (w,x), (x,y), (y,z), (z,s), (s,v), (z,w), (y,t), (x,u)\})$. Throughout this book, we use the convention $n = |V|$ and $m = |E|$ if no other definitions for n or m are given. An edge $e = (u,v) \in E$ represents a connection from u to v. We call u and v the *source* and *target*, respectively, of e. We say that e is *incident* on u and v and that v and u are *adjacent*. The special case of a *self-loop* (v,v) is disallowed unless specifically mentioned.

The *outdegree* of a node v is the number of edges leaving it, and its *indegree* is the number of edges ending at it, formally, $outdegree(v) = |\{(v,u) \in E\}|$ and $indegree(v) = |\{(u,v) \in E\}|$. For example, node w in graph G in Fig. 2.7 has indegree two and outdegree one.

A *bidirected graph* is a digraph where, for any edge (u,v), the reverse edge (v,u) is also present. An *undirected graph* can be viewed as a streamlined representation of a bidirected graph, where we write a pair of edges (u,v), (v,u) as the two-element set $\{u,v\}$. Figure 2.7 shows a three-node undirected graph and its bidirected counterpart. Most graph-theoretic terms for undirected graphs have the same definition as for

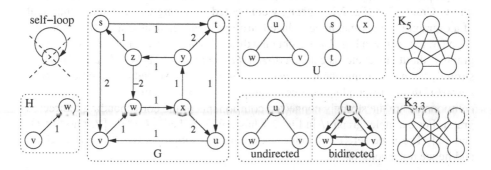

Fig. 2.7. Some graphs

their bidirected counterparts, and so this section will concentrate on directed graphs and only mention undirected graphs when there is something special about them. For example, the number of edges of an undirected graph is only half the number of edges of its bidirected counterpart. Nodes of an undirected graph have identical indegree and outdegree, and so we simply talk about their *degree*. Undirected graphs are important because directions often do not matter and because many problems are easier to solve (or even to define) for undirected graphs than for general digraphs.

A graph $G' = (V', E')$ is a *subgraph* of G if $V' \subseteq V$ and $E' \subseteq E$. Given $G = (V, E)$ and a subset $V' \subseteq V$, the subgraph *induced* by V' is defined as $G' = (V', E \cap (V' \times V'))$. In Fig. 2.7, the node set $\{v, w\}$ in G induces the subgraph $H = (\{v, w\}, \{(v, w)\})$. A subset $E' \subseteq E$ of edges induces the subgraph (V, E').

Often, additional information is associated with nodes or edges. In particular, we shall often need *edge weights* or *costs* $c : E \to \mathbb{R}$ that map edges to some numeric value. For example, the edge (z, w) in graph G in Fig. 2.7 has a weight $c((z, w)) = -2$. Note that an edge $\{u, v\}$ of an undirected graph has a unique edge weight, whereas, in a bidirected graph, we can have $c((u, v)) \neq c((v, u))$.

We have now seen quite many definitions on one page of text. If you want to see them at work, you may jump to Chap. 8 to see algorithms operating on graphs. But things are also becoming more interesting here.

An important higher-level graph-theoretic concept is the notion of a path. A *path* $p = \langle v_0, \ldots, v_k \rangle$ is a sequence of nodes in which consecutive nodes are connected by edges in E, i.e., $(v_0, v_1) \in E$, $(v_1, v_2) \in E$, $\ldots$, $(v_{k-1}, v_k) \in E$; p has length k and runs from v_0 to v_k. Sometimes a path is also represented by its sequence of edges. For example, $\langle u, v, w \rangle = \langle (u, v), (v, w) \rangle$ is a path of length 2 in Fig. 2.7. A path is *simple* if its nodes, except maybe for v_0 and v_k, are pairwise distinct. In Fig. 2.7, $\langle z, w, x, u, v, w, x, y \rangle$ is a nonsimple path.

Cycles are paths with a common first and last node. A simple cycle visiting all nodes of a graph is called a *Hamiltonian* cycle. For example, the cycle $\langle s, t, u, v, w, x, y, z, s \rangle$ in graph G in Fig. 2.7 is Hamiltonian. A simple undirected cycle contains at least three nodes, since we also do not allow edges to be used twice in simple undirected cycles.

The concepts of paths and cycles help us to define even higher-level concepts. A digraph is *strongly connected* if for any two nodes u and v there is a path from u to v. Graph G in Fig. 2.7 is strongly connected. A strongly connected component of a digraph is a maximal node-induced strongly connected subgraph. If we remove edge (w, x) from G in Fig. 2.7, we obtain a digraph without any directed cycles. A digraph without any cycles is called a *directed acyclic graph* (DAG). In a DAG, every strongly connected component consists of a single node. An undirected graph is *connected* if the corresponding bidirected graph is strongly connected. The connected components are the strongly connected components of the corresponding bidirected graph. For example, graph U in Fig. 2.7 has connected components $\{u, v, w\}$, $\{s, t\}$, and $\{x\}$. The node set $\{u, w\}$ induces a connected subgraph, but it is not maximal and hence not a component.

Exercise 2.17. Describe 10 substantially different applications that can be modeled using graphs; car and bicycle networks are not considered substantially different. At least five should be applications not mentioned in this book.

Exercise 2.18. A *planar graph* is a graph that can be drawn on a sheet of paper such that no two edges cross each other. Argue that street networks are *not* necessarily planar. Show that the graphs K_5 and K_{33} in Fig. 2.7 are not planar.

2.9.1 A First Graph Algorithm

It is time for an example algorithm. We shall describe an algorithm for testing whether a directed graph is acyclic. We use the simple observation that a node v with outdegree zero cannot appear in any cycle. Hence, by deleting v (and its incoming edges) from the graph, we obtain a new graph G' that is acyclic if and only if G is acyclic. By iterating this transformation, we either arrive at the empty graph, which is certainly acyclic, or obtain a graph G^* where every node has an outdegree of at least one. In the latter case, it is easy to find a cycle: start at any node v and construct a path by repeatedly choosing an arbitrary outgoing edge until you reach a node v' that you have seen before. The constructed path will have the form $(v, \ldots, v', \ldots, v')$, i.e., the part $(v', \ldots, v')$ forms a cycle. For example, in Fig. 2.7, graph G has no node with outdegree zero. To find a cycle, we might start at node z and follow the path $\langle z, w, x, u, v, w \rangle$ until we encounter w a second time. Hence, we have identified the cycle $\langle w, x, u, v, w \rangle$. In contrast, if the edge (w, x) is removed, there is no cycle. Indeed, our algorithm will remove all nodes in the order w, v, u, t, s, z, y, x. In Chap. 8, we shall see how to represent graphs such that this algorithm can be implemented to run in linear time. See also Exercise 8.3. We can easily make our algorithm certifying. If the algorithm finds a cycle, the graph is certainly cyclic. If the algorithm reduces the graph to the empty graph, we number the nodes in the order in which they are removed from G. Since we always remove a node v of outdegree zero from the current graph, any edge out of v in the original graph must go to a node that was removed previously and hence has received a smaller number. Thus the ordering proves acyclicity: along any edge, the node numbers decrease.

Exercise 2.19. Show an n-node DAG that has $n(n-1)/2$ edges.

2.9.2 Trees

An undirected graph is a *tree* if there is *exactly* one path between any pair of nodes; see Fig. 2.8 for an example. An undirected graph is a *forest* if there is *at most* one path between any pair of nodes. Note that each component of a forest is a tree.

Lemma 2.8. *The following properties of an undirected graph G are equivalent:*

1. *G is a tree.*
2. *G is connected and has exactly $n-1$ edges.*
3. *G is connected and contains no cycles.*

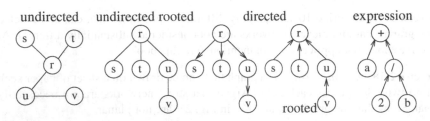

Fig. 2.8. Different kinds of trees. From *left* to *right*, we see an undirected tree, an undirected rooted tree, a directed out-tree, a directed in-tree, and an arithmetic expression

Proof. In a tree, there is a unique path between any two nodes. Hence the graph is connected and contains no cycles. Conversely, if there are two nodes that are connected by more than one path, the graph contains a cycle. Thus (1) and (3) are equivalent. We next show the equivalence of (2) and (3). Assume that $G = (V, E)$ is connected, and let $m = |E|$. We perform the following experiment: we start with the empty graph and add the edges in E one by one. Addition of an edge can reduce the number of connected components by at most one. We start with n components and must end up with one component. Thus $m \geq n - 1$. Assume now that there is an edge $e = \{u, v\}$ whose addition does not reduce the number of connected components. Then u and v are already connected by a path, and hence addition of e creates a cycle. If G is cycle-free, this case cannot occur, and hence $m = n - 1$. Thus (3) implies (2). Assume next that G is connected and has exactly $n - 1$ edges. Again, add the edges one by one and assume that adding $e = \{u, v\}$ creates a cycle. Then u and v are already connected, and hence e does not reduce the number of connected components. Thus (2) implies (3). □

Lemma 2.8 does not carry over to digraphs. For example, a DAG may have many more than $n - 1$ edges. A directed graph is an *out-tree* with a *root* node r, if there is exactly one path from r to any other node. It is an *in-tree* with a root node r if there is exactly one path from any other node to r. Figure 2.8 shows examples. The *depth* of a node in a rooted tree is the length of the path to the root. The *height* of a rooted tree is the maximum over the depths of its nodes.

We can also make an undirected tree rooted by declaring one of its nodes to be the root. Computer scientists have the peculiar habit of drawing rooted trees with the root at the top and all edges going downwards. For rooted trees, it is customary to denote relations between nodes by terms borrowed from family relations. Edges go between a unique *parent* and its *children*. Nodes with the same parent are *siblings*. Nodes without children are *leaves*. Nonroot, nonleaf nodes are *interior* nodes. Consider a path such that u is between the root and another node v. Then u is an *ancestor* of v, and v is a *descendant* of u. A node u and its descendants form a *subtree* rooted at u. For example, in Fig. 2.8, r is the root; s, t, and v are leaves; s, t, and u are siblings because they are children of the same parent r; u is an interior node; r and u are ancestors of v; s, t, u, and v are descendants of r; and v and u form a subtree rooted at u.

Function *eval*(*r*) : $\mathbb{R}$
   if *r is a leaf* **then return** *the number stored in r*
   else   // *r* is an operator node
      $v_1 := eval$(*first child of r*)
      $v_2 := eval$(*second child of r*)
      return $v_1 operator(r) v_2$ // apply the operator stored in *r*

Fig. 2.9. Recursive evaluation of an expression tree rooted at *r*

2.9.3 Ordered Trees

Trees are ideally suited to representing hierarchies. For example, consider the expression $a + 2/b$. We have learned that this expression means that a and $2/b$ are added. But deriving this from the sequence of characters $\langle a, +, 2, /, b \rangle$ is difficult. For example, it requires knowledge of the rule that division binds more tightly than addition. Therefore compilers isolate this syntactical knowledge in *parsers* that produce a more structured representation based on trees. Our example would be transformed into the expression tree given in Fig. 2.8. Such trees are directed and, in contrast to graph-theoretic trees, they are *ordered*. In our example, a is the first, or left, child of the root, and / is the right, or second, child of the root.

Expression trees are easy to evaluate by a simple recursive algorithm. Figure 2.9 shows an algorithm for evaluating expression trees whose leaves are numbers and whose interior nodes are binary operators (say $+, -, \cdot, /$).

We shall see many more examples of ordered trees in this book. Chapters 6 and 7 use them to represent fundamental data structures, and Chapter 12 uses them to systematically explore solution spaces.

2.10 P and NP

When should we call an algorithm efficient? Are there problems for which there is no efficient algorithm? Of course, drawing the line between "efficient" and "inefficient" is a somewhat arbitrary business. The following distinction has proved useful: an algorithm $\mathscr{A}$ runs in *polynomial time*, or is a *polynomial-time algorithm*, if there is a polynomial $p(n)$ such that its execution time on inputs of size n is $O(p(n))$. If not otherwise mentioned, the size of the input will be measured in bits. A problem can be solved in *polynomial time* if there is a polynomial-time algorithm that solves it. We equate "efficiently solvable" with "polynomial-time solvable". A big advantage of this definition is that implementation details are usually not important. For example, it does not matter whether a clever data structure can accelerate an $O(n^3)$ algorithm by a factor of n. All chapters of this book, except for Chap. 12, are about efficient algorithms.

There are many problems for which no efficient algorithm is known. Here, we mention only six examples:

- The Hamiltonian cycle problem: given an undirected graph, decide whether it contains a Hamiltonian cycle.
- The Boolean satisfiability problem: given a Boolean expression in conjunctive form, decide whether it has a satisfying assignment. A Boolean expression in conjunctive form is a conjunction $C_1 \wedge C_2 \wedge \ldots \wedge C_k$ of clauses. A clause is a disjunction $\ell_1 \vee \ell_2 \vee \ldots \vee \ell_h$ of literals, and a literal is a variable or a negated variable. For example, $v_1 \vee \neg v_3 \vee \neg v_9$ is a clause.
- The clique problem: given an undirected graph and an integer k, decide whether the graph contains a complete subgraph (= a clique) on k nodes.
- The knapsack problem: given n pairs of integers (w_i, p_i) and integers M and P, decide whether there is a subset $I \subseteq [1..n]$ such that $\sum_{i \in I} w_i \leq M$ and $\sum_{i \in I} p_i \geq P$.
- The traveling salesman problem: given an edge-weighted undirected graph and an integer C, decide whether the graph contains a Hamiltonian cycle of length at most C. See Sect. 11.6.2 for more details.
- The graph coloring problem: given an undirected graph and an integer k, decide whether there is a coloring of the nodes with k colors such that any two adjacent nodes are colored differently.

The fact that we know no efficient algorithms for these problems does not imply that none exists. It is simply not known whether an efficient algorithm exists or not. In particular, we have no proof that such algorithms do not exist. In general, it is very hard to prove that a problem cannot be solved in a given time bound. We shall see some simple lower bounds in Sect. 5.3. Most algorithmicists believe that the six problems above have no efficient solution.

Complexity theory has found an interesting surrogate for the absence of lower-bound proofs. It clusters algorithmic problems into large groups that are equivalent with respect to some complexity measure. In particular, there is a large class of equivalent problems known as **NP**-*complete* problems. Here, **NP** is an abbreviation for "nondeterministic polynomial time". If the term "nondeterministic polynomial time" does not mean anything to you, ignore it and carry on. The six problems mentioned above are **NP**-complete, and so are many other natural problems. It is widely believed that **P** is a proper subset of **NP**. This would imply, in particular, that **NP**-complete problems have no efficient algorithm. In the remainder of this section, we shall give a formal definition of the class **NP**. We refer the reader to books about theory of computation and complexity theory [14, 72, 181, 205] for a thorough treatment.

We assume, as is customary in complexity theory, that inputs are encoded in some fixed finite alphabet Σ. A *decision problem* is a subset $L \subseteq \Sigma^*$. We use χ_L to denote the characteristic function of L, i.e., $\chi_L(x) = 1$ if $x \in L$ and $\chi_L(x) = 0$ if $x \notin L$. A decision problem is polynomial-time solvable iff its characteristic function is polynomial-time computable. We use **P** to denote the class of polynomial-time-solvable decision problems.

A decision problem L is in **NP** iff there is a predicate $Q(x, y)$ and a polynomial p such that

(1) for any $x \in \Sigma^*$, $x \in L$ iff there is a $y \in \Sigma^*$ with $|y| \leq p(|x|)$ and $Q(x, y)$, and

(2) Q is computable in polynomial time.

We call y a *witness* or *proof* of membership. For our example problems, it is easy to show that they belong to **NP**. In the case of the Hamiltonian cycle problem, the witness is a Hamiltonian cycle in the input graph. A witness for a Boolean formula is an assignment of truth values to variables that make the formula true. The solvability of an instance of the knapsack problem is witnessed by a subset of elements that fit into the knapsack and achieve the profit bound P.

Exercise 2.9. Prove that the clique problem, the traveling salesman problem, and the graph coloring problem are in **NP**.

A decision problem L is *polynomial-time reducible* (or simply *reducible*) to a decision problem L' if there is a polynomial-time-computable function g such that for all $x \in \Sigma^*$, we have $x \in L$ iff $g(x) \in L'$. Clearly, if L is reducible to L' and $L' \in \textbf{P}$, then $L \in \textbf{P}$. Also, reducibility is transitive. A decision problem L is **NP**-*hard* if every problem in **NP** is polynomial-time reducible to it. A problem is **NP**-*complete* if it is **NP**-hard and in **NP**. At first glance, it might seem prohibitively difficult to prove any problem **NP**-complete – one would have to show that *every* problem in **NP** was polynomial-time reducible to it. However, in 1971, Cook and Levin independently managed to do this for the Boolean satisfiability problem [44, 120]. From that time on, it was "easy". Assume you want to show that a problem L is **NP**-complete. You need to show two things: (1) $L \in \textbf{NP}$, and (2) there is *some* known **NP**-complete problem L' that can be reduced to it. Transitivity of the reducibility relation then implies that all problems in **NP** are reducible to L. With every new complete problem, it becomes easier to show that other problems are **NP**-complete. The website http://www.nada.kth.se/~viggo/wwwcompendium/wwwcompendium.html maintains a compendium of **NP**-complete problems. We give one example of a reduction.

Lemma 2.10. *The Boolean satisfiability problem is polynomial-time reducible to the clique problem.*

Proof. Let $F = C_1 \wedge \ldots \wedge C_k$, where $C_i = \ell_{i1} \vee \ldots \vee \ell_{ih_i}$ and $\ell_{ij} = x_{ij}^{\beta_{ij}}$, be a formula in conjunctive form. Here, x_{ij} is a variable and $\beta_{ij} \in \{0, 1\}$. A superscript 0 indicates a negated variable. Consider the following graph G. Its nodes V represent the literals in our formula, i.e., $V = \{r_{ij} : 1 \le i \le k \text{ and } 1 \le j \le h_i\}$. Two nodes r_{ij} and $r_{i'j'}$ are connected by an edge iff $i \ne i'$ and either $x_{ij} \ne x_{i'j'}$ or $\beta_{ij} = \beta_{i'j'}$. In words, the representatives of two literals are connected by an edge if they belong to different clauses and an assignment can satisfy them simultaneously. We claim that F is satisfiable iff G has a clique of size k.

Assume first that there is a satisfying assignment α. The assignment must satisfy at least one literal in every clause, say literal ℓ_{ij_i} in clause C_i. Consider the subgraph of G spanned by the r_{ij_i}, $1 \le i \le k$. This is a clique of size k. Assume otherwise; say, r_{ij_i} and $r_{i'j_{i'}}$ are not connected by an edge. Then, $x_{ij_i} = x_{i'j_{i'}}$ and $\beta_{ij_i} \ne \beta_{i'j_{i'}}$. But then the literals ℓ_{ij_i} and $\ell_{i'j_{i'}}$ are complements of each other, and α cannot satisfy them both.

Conversely, assume that there is a clique K of size k in G. We can construct a satisfying assignment α. For each i, $1 \leq i \leq k$, K contains exactly one node r_{ij_i}. We construct a satisfying assignment α by setting $\alpha(x_{ij_i}) = \beta_{ij_i}$. Note that α is well defined because $x_{ij_i} = x_{i'j_{i'}}$ implies $\beta_{ij_i} = \beta_{i'j_{i'}}$; otherwise, r_{ij_i} and $r_{i'j_{i'}}$ would not be connected by an edge. α clearly satisfies F.   □

Exercise 2.20. Show that the Hamiltonian cycle problem is polynomial-time reducible to the traveling salesman problem.

Exercise 2.21. Show that the clique problem is polynomial-time reducible to the graph-coloring problem.

All **NP**-complete problems have a common destiny. If anybody should find a polynomial time algorithm for *one* of them, then **NP** = **P**. Since so many people have tried to find such solutions, it is becoming less and less likely that this will ever happen: The **NP**-complete problems are mutual witnesses of their hardness.

Does the theory of **NP**-completeness also apply to optimization problems? Optimization problems are easily turned into decision problems. Instead of asking for an optimal solution, we ask whether there is a solution with an objective value greater than or equal to k, where k is an additional input. Conversely, if we have an algorithm to decide whether there is a solution with a value greater than or equal to k, we can use a combination of exponential and binary search (see Sect. 2.5) to find the optimal objective value.

An algorithm for a decision problem returns yes or no, depending on whether the instance belongs to the problem or not. It does not return a witness. Frequently, witnesses can be constructed by applying the decision algorithm repeatedly. Assume we want to find a clique of size k, but have only an algorithm that decides whether a clique of size k exists. We select an arbitrary node v and ask whether $G' = G \setminus v$ has a clique of size k. If so, we recursively search for a clique in G'. If not, we know that v must be part of the clique. Let V' be the set of neighbors of v. We recursively search for a clique C_{k-1} of size $k-1$ in the subgraph spanned by V'. Then $v \cup C_{k-1}$ is a clique of size k in G.

2.11 Implementation Notes

Our pseudocode is easily converted into actual programs in any imperative programming language. We shall give more detailed comments for C++ and Java below. The Eiffel programming language [138] has extensive support for assertions, invariants, preconditions, and postconditions.

Our special values $\bot$, $-\infty$, and ∞ are available for floating-point numbers. For other data types, we have to emulate these values. For example, one could use the smallest and largest representable integers for $-\infty$ and ∞, respectively. Undefined pointers are often represented by a null pointer **null**. Sometimes we use special values for convenience only, and a robust implementation should avoid using them. You will find examples in later chapters.

Randomized algorithms need access to a random source. You have a choice between a hardware generator that generates true random numbers and an algorithmic generator that generates pseudo-random numbers. We refer the reader to the Wikipedia page on "random numbers" for more information.

2.11.1 C++

Our pseudocode can be viewed as a concise notation for a subset of C++. The memory management operations **allocate** and **dispose** are similar to the C++ operations *new* and *delete*. C++ calls the default constructor for each element of an array, i.e., allocating an array of n objects takes time $\Omega(n)$ whereas allocating an array n of *ints* takes constant time. In contrast, we assume that *all* arrays which are not explicitly initialized contain garbage. In C++, you can obtain this effect using the C functions *malloc* and *free*. However, this is a deprecated practice and should only be used when array initialization would be a severe performance bottleneck. If memory management of many small objects is performance-critical, you can customize it using the *allocator* class of the C++ standard library.

Our parameterizations of classes using **of** is a special case of the C++-template mechanism. The parameters added in brackets after a class name correspond to the parameters of a C++ constructor.

Assertions are implemented as C macros in the include file `assert.h`. By default, violated assertions trigger a runtime error and print their position in the program text. If the macro *NDEBUG* is defined, assertion checking is disabled.

For many of the data structures and algorithms discussed in this book, excellent implementations are available in software libraries. Good sources are the standard template library STL [157], the Boost [27] C++ libraries, and the LEDA [131, 118] library of efficient algorithms and data structures.

2.11.2 Java

Java has no explicit memory management. Rather, a *garbage collector* periodically recycles pieces of memory that are no longer referenced. While this simplifies programming enormously, it can be a performance problem. Remedies are beyond the scope of this book. Generic types provide parameterization of classes. Assertions are implemented with the *assert* statement.

Excellent implementations for many data structures and algorithms are available in the package *java.util* and in the JDSL [78] data structure library.

2.12 Historical Notes and Further Findings

Sheperdson and Sturgis [179] defined the RAM model for use in algorithmic analysis. The RAM model restricts cells to holding a logarithmic number of bits. Dropping this assumption has undesirable consequences; for example, the complexity classes

P and **PSPACE** collapse [87]. Knuth [113] has described a more detailed abstract machine model.

Floyd [62] introduced the method of invariants to assign meaning to programs and Hoare [91, 92] systemized their use. The book [81] is a compendium on sums and recurrences and, more generally, discrete mathematics.

Books on compiler construction (e.g., [144, 207]) tell you more about the compilation of high-level programming languages into machine code.

3

Representing Sequences by Arrays and Linked Lists

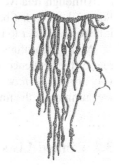

Perhaps the world's oldest data structures were the tablets in cuneiform script[1] used more than 5 000 years ago by custodians in Sumerian temples. These custodians kept lists of goods, and their quantities, owners, and buyers. The picture on the left shows an example. This was possibly the first application of written language. The operations performed on such lists have remained the same – adding entries, storing them for later, searching entries and changing them, going through a list to compile summaries, etc. The Peruvian quipu [137] that you see in the picture on the right served a similar purpose in the Inca empire, using knots in colored strings arranged sequentially on a master string. It is probably easier to maintain and use data on tablets than to use knotted string, but one would not want to haul stone tablets over Andean mountain trails. It is apparent that different representations make sense for the same kind of data.

The abstract notion of a sequence, list, or table is very simple and is independent of its representation in a computer. Mathematically, the only important property is that the elements of a sequence $s = \langle e_0, \ldots, e_{n-1} \rangle$ are arranged in a linear order – in contrast to the trees and graphs discussed in Chaps. 7 and 8, or the unordered hash tables discussed in Chap. 4. There are two basic ways of referring to the elements of a sequence.

One is to specify the index of an element. This is the way we usually think about arrays, where $s[i]$ returns the i-th element of a sequence s. Our pseudocode supports *static* arrays. In a *static* data structure, the size is known in advance, and the data structure is not modifiable by insertions and deletions. In a *bounded* data structure, the maximal size is known in advance. In Sect. 3.2, we introduce *dynamic* or *un-*

---

[1] The 4 600 year old tablet at the top left is a list of gifts to the high priestess of Adab (see
commons.wikimedia.org/wiki/Image:Sumerian_26th_c_Adab.jpg).

bounded arrays, which can grow and shrink as elements are inserted and removed. The analysis of unbounded arrays introduces the concept of *amortized analysis*.

The second way of referring to the elements of a sequence is relative to other elements. For example, one could ask for the successor of an element e, the predecessor of an element e', or for the subsequence $\langle e, \dots, e' \rangle$ of elements between e and e'. Although relative access can be simulated using array indexing, we shall see in Sect. 3.1 that a list-based representation of sequences is more flexible. In particular, it becomes easier to insert or remove arbitrary pieces of a sequence.

Many algorithms use sequences in a quite limited way. Only the front and/or the rear of the sequence are read and modified. Sequences that are used in this restricted way are called *stacks*, *queues*, and *deques*. We discuss them in Sect. 3.4. In Sect. 3.5, we summarize the findings of the chapter.

3.1 Linked Lists

In this section, we study the representation of sequences by linked lists. In a doubly linked list, each item points to its successor and to its predecessor. In a singly linked list, each item points to its successor. We shall see that linked lists are easily modified in many ways: we may insert or delete items or sublists, and we may concatenate lists. The drawback is that random access (the operator $[\cdot]$) is not supported. We study doubly linked lists in Sect. 3.1.1, and singly linked lists in Sect. 3.1.2. Singly linked lists are more space-efficient, and somewhat faster, and should therefore be preferred whenever their functionality suffices. A good way to think of a linked list is to imagine a chain, where one element is written on each link. Once we get hold of one link of the chain, we can retrieve all elements.

3.1.1 Doubly Linked Lists

Figure 3.1 shows the basic building blocks of a linked list. A list *item* stores an element, and pointers to its successor and predecessor. We call a pointer to a list item a *handle*. This sounds simple enough, but pointers are so powerful that we can make a big mess if we are not careful. What makes a consistent list data structure? We

Class *Handle* = **Pointer to** *Item*

Class *Item* **of** *Element*   // one link in a doubly linked list
    e : *Element*
    next : *Handle*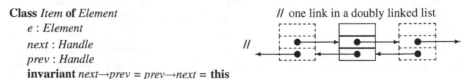
    prev : *Handle*
    invariant *next*→*prev* = *prev*→*next* = **this**

Fig. 3.1. The items of a doubly linked list

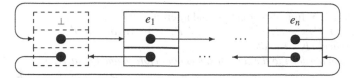

Fig. 3.2. The representation of a sequence $\langle e_1, \ldots, e_n \rangle$ by a doubly linked list. There are $n+1$ items arranged in a ring, a special dummy item h containing no element, and one item for each element of the sequence. The item containing e_i is the successor of the item containing e_{i-1} and the predecessor of the item containing e_{i+1}. The dummy item is between the item containing e_n and the item containing e_1

require that for each item *it*, the successor of its predecessor is equal to *it* and the predecessor of its successor is also equal to *it*.

A sequence of n elements is represented by a ring of $n+1$ items. There is a special dummy item h, which stores no element. The successor h_1 of h stores the first element of the sequence, the successor of h_1 stores the second element of the sequence, and so on. The predecessor of h stores the last element of the sequence; see Fig. 3.2. The empty sequence is represented by a ring consisting only of h. Since there are no elements in that sequence, h is its own successor and predecessor. Figure 3.4 defines a representation of sequences by lists. An object of class *List* contains a single list item h. The constructor of the class initializes the header h to an item containing $\perp$ and having itself as successor and predecessor. In this way, the list is initialized to the empty sequence.

We implement all basic list operations in terms of the single operation *splice* shown in Fig. 3.3. *splice* cuts out a sublist from one list and inserts it after some target item. The sublist is specified by handles a and b to its first and its last element, respectively. In other words, b must be reachable from a by following zero or more next pointers but without going through the dummy item. The target item t can be either in the same list or in a different list; in the former case, it must not be inside the sublist starting at a and ending at b.

splice does not change the number of items in the system. We assume that there is one special list, *freeList*, that keeps a supply of unused elements. When inserting new elements into a list, we take the necessary items from *freeList*, and when removing elements, we return the corresponding items to *freeList*. The function *checkFreeList* allocates memory for new items when necessary. We defer its implementation to Exercise 3.3 and a short discussion in Sect. 3.6.

With these conventions in place, a large number of useful operations can be implemented as one-line functions that all run in constant-time. Thanks to the power of *splice*, we can even manipulate arbitrarily long sublists in constant-time. Figures 3.4 and 3.5 show many examples. In order to test whether a list is empty, we simply check whether h is its own successor. If a sequence is nonempty, its first and its last element are the successor and predecessor, respectively, of h. In order to move an item b to the positions after an item a', we simply cut out the sublist starting and ending at b and insert it after a'. This is exactly what $splice(b, b, a')$ does. We move

// Remove $\langle a,\ldots,b \rangle$ from its current list and insert it after t
// $\ldots, d', a, \ldots, b, b', \ldots + \ldots, t, t', \ldots \mapsto \ldots, d', b', \ldots + \ldots, t, a, \ldots, b, t', \ldots$
Procedure $splice(a,b,t : Handle)$
　　assert a and b belong to the same list, b is not before a, and $t \notin \langle a,\ldots,b \rangle$

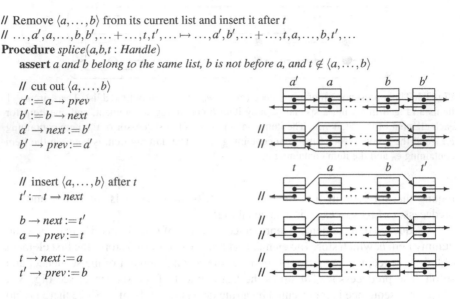

　　// cut out $\langle a,\ldots,b \rangle$
　　$d' := a \to prev$
　　$b' := b \to next$
　　$d' \to next := b'$　　　　　　//
　　$b' \to prev := d'$　　　　　　//

　　// insert $\langle a,\ldots,b \rangle$ after t
　　$t' := t \to next$　　　　　　//

　　$b \to next := t'$　　　　　　//
　　$a \to prev := t$　　　　　　//

　　$t \to next := a$　　　　　　//
　　$t' \to prev := b$　　　　　　//

Fig. 3.3. Splicing lists

Class *List* **of** *Element*
　　// Item h is the predecessor of the first element and the successor of the last element.

$h = \begin{pmatrix} \bot \\ \textbf{this} \\ \textbf{this} \end{pmatrix} : Item$　　　　　　// init to empty sequence

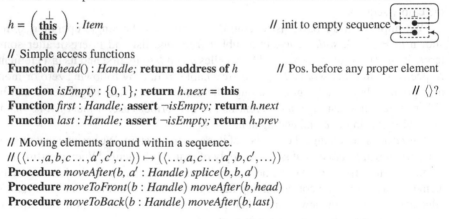

　　// Simple access functions
　　Function $head()$: $Handle$; **return address of** h　　　// Pos. before any proper element

　　Function $isEmpty$: $\{0,1\}$; **return** $h.next = $ **this**　　　　　　　　　　　// $\langle \rangle$?
　　Function $first$: $Handle$; **assert** $\neg isEmpty$; **return** $h.next$
　　Function $last$: $Handle$; **assert** $\neg isEmpty$; **return** $h.prev$

　　// Moving elements around within a sequence.
　　// $(\langle \ldots, a, b, c \ldots, a', c', \ldots \rangle) \mapsto (\langle \ldots, a, c \ldots, a', b, c', \ldots \rangle)$
　　Procedure $moveAfter(b, a' : Handle)$ $splice(b,b,a')$
　　Procedure $moveToFront(b : Handle)$ $moveAfter(b,head)$
　　Procedure $moveToBack(b : Handle)$ $moveAfter(b,last)$

Fig. 3.4. Some constant-time operations on doubly linked lists

an element to the first or last position of a sequence by moving it after the head
or after the last element, respectively. In order to delete an element b, we move it to
freeList. To insert a new element e, we take the first item of *freeList*, store the element
in it, and move it to the place of insertion.

// Deleting and inserting elements.
// $\langle\ldots,a,b,c,\ldots\rangle \mapsto \langle\ldots,a,c,\ldots\rangle$
Procedure *remove(b : Handle) moveAfter(b, freeList.head)*
Procedure *popFront remove(first)*
Procedure *popBack remove(last)*

// $\langle\ldots,a,b,\ldots\rangle \mapsto \langle\ldots,a,e,b,\ldots\rangle$
Function *insertAfter(x : Element; a : Handle) : Handle*
    checkFreeList   // make sure *freeList* is nonempty. See also Exercise 3.3
    $a' := freeList.first$ // Obtain an item a' to hold x,
    moveAfter(a', a)   // put it at the right place.
    $a' \to e := x$ // and fill it with the right content.
    return a'

Function *insertBefore(x : Element; b : Handle) : Handle* **return** *insertAfter(e, pred(b))*
Procedure *pushFront(x : Element) insertAfter(x, head)*
Procedure *pushBack(x : Element) insertAfter(x, last)*

// Manipulations of entire lists
// $(\langle a,\ldots,b\rangle, \langle c,\ldots,d\rangle) \mapsto (\langle a,\ldots,b,c,\ldots,d\rangle, \langle\rangle)$
Procedure *concat(L' : List)*
    splice(L'.first, L'.last, last)

// $\langle a,\ldots,b\rangle \mapsto \langle\rangle$
Procedure *makeEmpty*
    *freeList.concat(***this** *)*   //

Fig. 3.5. More constant-time operations on doubly linked lists

Exercise 3.1 (alternative list implementation). Discuss an alternative implementation of *List* that does not need the dummy item *h*. Instead, this representation stores a pointer to the first list item in the list object. The position before the first list element is encoded as a null pointer. The interface and the asymptotic execution times of all operations should remain the same. Give at least one advantage and one disadvantage of this implementation compared with the one given in the text.

The dummy item is also useful for other operations. For example, consider the problem of finding the next occurrence of an element *x* starting at an item *from*. If *x* is not present, *head* should be returned. We use the dummy element as a *sentinel*. A sentinel is an element in a data structure that makes sure that some loop will terminate. In the case of a list, we store the key we are looking for in the dummy element. This ensures that *x* is present in the list structure and hence a search for it will always terminate. The search will terminate in a proper list item or the dummy item, depending on whether *x* was present in the list originally. It is no longer necessary, to test whether the end of the list has been reached. In this way, the trick of using the dummy item *h* as a sentinel saves one test in each iteration and significantly improves the efficiency of the search:

Function *findNext*(*x* : *Element; from* : *Handle*) : *Handle*
    h.e = *x*   *// Sentinel*
    while *from* → *e* ≠ *x* **do**
        from := *from* → *next*
    return *from*

Exercise 3.2. Implement a procedure *swap* that swaps two sublists in constant time, i.e., sequences $(\langle\ldots,a',a,\ldots,b,b',\ldots\rangle,\langle\ldots,c',c,\ldots,d,d',\ldots\rangle)$ are transformed into $(\langle\ldots,a',c,\ldots,d,b',\ldots\rangle,\langle\ldots,c',a,\ldots,b,d',\ldots\rangle)$. Is *splice* a special case of *swap*?

Exercise 3.3 (memory management). Implement the function *checkFreelist* called by *insertAfter* in Fig. 3.5. Since an individual call of the programming-language primitive **allocate** for every single item might be too slow, your function should allocate space for items in large batches. The worst-case execution time of *checkFreeList* should be independent of the batch size. Hint: in addition to *freeList*, use a small array of free items.

Exercise 3.4. Give a constant-time implementation of an algorithm for rotating a list to the right: $\langle a,\ldots,b,c\rangle \mapsto \langle c,a,\ldots,b\rangle$. Generalize your algorithm to rotate $\langle a,\ldots,b,c,\ldots,d\rangle$ to $\langle c,\ldots,d,a,\ldots,b\rangle$ in constant time.

Exercise 3.5. *findNext* using sentinels is faster than an implementation that checks for the end of the list in each iteration. But how much faster? What speed difference do you predict for many searches in a short list with 100 elements, and in a long list with 10 000 000 elements, respectively? Why is the relative speed difference dependent on the size of the list?

Maintaining the Size of a List

In our simple list data type, it is not possible to determine the length of a list in constant time. This can be fixed by introducing a member variable *size* that is updated whenever the number of elements changes. Operations that affect several lists now need to know about the lists involved, even if low-level functions such as *splice* only need handles to the items involved. For example, consider the following code for moving an element *a* from a list *L* to the position after *a'* in a list *L'*:

    Procedure *moveAfter*(*a, a'* : *Handle; L, L'* : *List*)
        splice(*a,a,a'*);   *L.size*--;   *L'.size*++

Maintaining the size of lists interferes with other list operations. When we move elements as above, we need to know the sequences containing them and, more seriously, operations that move sublists between lists cannot be implemented in constant time anymore. The next exercise offers a compromise.

Exercise 3.6. Design a list data type that allows sublists to be moved between lists in constant time and allows constant-time access to *size* whenever sublist operations have not been used since the last access to the list size. When sublist operations have been used, *size* is recomputed only when needed.

Exercise 3.7. Explain how the operations *remove*, *insertAfter*, and *concat* have to be modified to keep track of the length of a *List*.

3.1.2 Singly Linked Lists

The two pointers per item of a doubly linked list make programming quite easy. Singly linked lists are the lean sisters of doubly linked lists. We use *SItem* to refer to an item in a singly linked list. *SItem*s scrap the predecessor pointer and store only a pointer to the successor. This makes singly linked lists more space-efficient and often faster than their doubly linked brothers. The downside is that some operations can no longer be performed in constant time or can no longer be supported in full generality. For example, we can remove an *SItem* only if we know its predecessor.

We adopt the implementation approach used with doubly linked lists. *SItem*s form collections of cycles, and an *SList* has a dummy *SItem* h that precedes the first proper element and is the successor of the last proper element. Many operations on *List*s can still be performed if we change the interface slightly. For example, the following implementation of *splice* needs the *predecessor* of the first element of the sublist to be moved:

$$ \mathbin{/\!/} (\langle \ldots, a', a, \ldots, b, b' \ldots \rangle, \langle \ldots, t, t', \ldots \rangle) \mapsto (\langle \ldots, a', b' \ldots \rangle, \langle \ldots, t, a, \ldots, b, t', \ldots \rangle) $$

Procedure *splice*(*a'*,*b*,*t* : *SHandle*)

$$ \begin{pmatrix} a' \to next \\ t \to next \\ b \to next \end{pmatrix} := \begin{pmatrix} b \to next \\ a' \to next \\ t \to next \end{pmatrix} $$

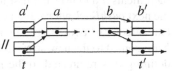

Similarly, *findNext* should not return the handle of the *SItem* with the next hit but its *predecessor*, so that it remains possible to remove the element found. Consequently, *findNext* can only start searching at the item *after* the item given to it. A useful addition to *SList* is a pointer to the last element because it allows us to support *pushBack* in constant time.

Exercise 3.8. Implement classes *SHandle*, *SItem*, and *SList* for singly linked lists in analogy to *Handle*, *Item*, and *List*. Show that the following functions can be implemented to run in constant time. The operations *head*, *first*, *last*, *isEmpty*, *popFront*, *pushFront*, *pushBack*, *insertAfter*, *concat*, and *makeEmpty* should have the same interface as before. The operations *moveAfter*, *moveToFront*, *moveToBack*, *remove*, *popFront*, and *findNext* need different interfaces.

We shall see several applications of singly linked lists in later chapters, for example in hash tables in Sect. 4.1 and in mergesort in Sect. 5.2. We may also use singly linked lists to implement free lists of memory managers – even for items in doubly linked lists.

3.2 Unbounded Arrays

Consider an array data structure that, besides the indexing operation $[\cdot]$, supports the following operations *pushBack*, *popBack*, and *size*:

$$\langle e_0, \ldots, e_n \rangle.pushBack(e) = \langle e_0, \ldots, e_n, e \rangle ,$$
$$\langle e_0, \ldots, e_n \rangle.popBack = \langle e_0, \ldots, e_{n-1} \rangle ,$$
$$size(\langle e_0, \ldots, e_{n-1} \rangle) = n .$$

Why are unbounded arrays important? Because in many situations we do not know in advance how large an array should be. Here is a typical example: suppose you want to implement the Unix command `sort` for sorting the lines of a file. You decide to read the file into an array of lines, sort the array internally, and finally output the sorted array. With unbounded arrays, this is easy. With bounded arrays, you would have to read the file twice: once to find the number of lines it contains, and once again to actually load it into the array.

We come now to the implementation of unbounded arrays. We emulate an unbounded array u with n elements by use of a dynamically allocated bounded array b with w entries, where $w \geq n$. The first n entries of b are used to store the elements of u. The last $w - n$ entries of b are unused. As long as $w > n$, *pushBack* simply increments n and uses the first unused entry of b for the new element. When $w = n$, the next *pushBack* allocates a new bounded array b' that is larger by a constant factor (say a factor of two). To reestablish the invariant that u is stored in b, the contents of b are copied to the new array so that the old b can be deallocated. Finally, the pointer defining b is redirected to the new array. Deleting the last element with *popBack* is even easier, since there is no danger that b may become too small. However, we might waste a lot of space if we allow b to be much larger than needed. The wasted space can be kept small by shrinking b when n becomes too small. Figure 3.6 gives the complete pseudocode for an unbounded-array class. Growing and shrinking are performed using the same utility procedure *reallocate*. Our implementation uses constants α and β, with $\beta = 2$ and $\alpha = 4$. Whenever the current bounded array becomes too small, we replace it by an array of β times the old size. Whenever the size of the current array becomes α times as large as its used part, we replace it by an array of size βn. The reasons for the choice of α and β shall become clear later.

3.2.1 Amortized Analysis of Unbounded Arrays: The Global Argument

Our implementation of unbounded arrays follows the algorithm design principle "make the common case fast". Array access with $[\cdot]$ is as fast as for bounded arrays. Intuitively, *pushBack* and *popBack* should "usually" be fast – we just have to update n. However, some insertions and deletions incur a cost of $\Theta(n)$. We shall show that such expensive operations are rare and that any sequence of m operations starting with an empty array can be executed in time $O(m)$.

Lemma 3.1. *Consider an unbounded array u that is initially empty. Any sequence $\sigma = \langle \sigma_1, \ldots, \sigma_m \rangle$ of pushBack or popBack operations on u is executed in time $O(m)$.*

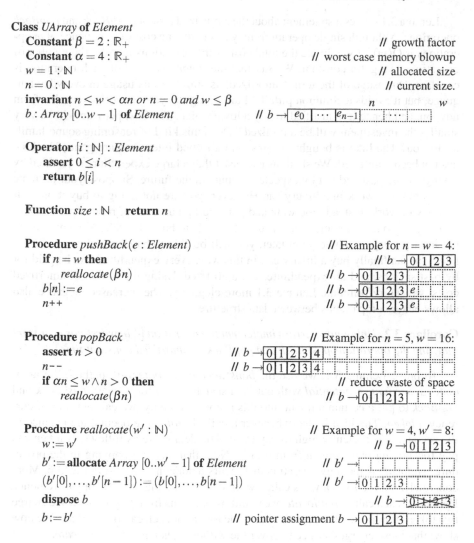

Class *UArray* **of** *Element*
    Constant $\beta = 2 : \mathbb{R}_+$ // growth factor
    Constant $\alpha = 4 : \mathbb{R}_+$ // worst case memory blowup
    $w = 1 : \mathbb{N}$ // allocated size
    $n = 0 : \mathbb{N}$ // current size.
    invariant $n \leq w < \alpha n$ *or* $n = 0$ *and* $w \leq \beta$
    $b :$ *Array* $[0..w-1]$ **of** *Element*   // $b \to$ [e_0 | $\cdots$ | e_{n-1} | $\cdots$]

    Operator $[i : \mathbb{N}] :$ *Element*
      assert $0 \leq i < n$
      return $b[i]$

    Function *size* : $\mathbb{N}$ **return** n

    Procedure *pushBack*$(e :$ *Element*$)$ // Example for $n = w = 4$:
      if $n = w$ **then**   // $b \to$ [0|1|2|3]
        reallocate(βn) // $b \to$ [0|1|2|3| | | |]
      $b[n] := e$ // $b \to$ [0|1|2|3|e| | |]
      $n{+}{+}$ // $b \to$ [0|1|2|3|e| | |]

    Procedure *popBack*   // Example for $n = 5, w = 16$:
      assert $n > 0$ // $b \to$ [0|1|2|3|4| ...]
      $n{-}{-}$ // $b \to$ [0|1|2|3|4| ...]
      if $\alpha n \leq w \wedge n > 0$ **then**   // reduce waste of space
        reallocate(βn) // $b \to$ [0|1|2|3| | | |]

    Procedure *reallocate*$(w' : \mathbb{N})$ // Example for $w = 4, w' = 8$:
      $w := w'$ // $b \to$ [0|1|2|3]
      $b' :=$ **allocate** *Array* $[0..w'-1]$ **of** *Element*   // $b' \to$ [| | | | | | |]
      $(b'[0], \ldots, b'[n-1]) := (b[0], \ldots, b[n-1])$ // $b' \to$ [0|1|2|3| | | |]
      dispose b // $b \to$ [0̶|1̶|2̶|3̶]
      $b := b'$ // pointer assignment $b \to$ [0|1|2|3| | | |]

Fig. 3.6. Pseudocode for unbounded arrays

Lemma 3.1 is a nontrivial statement. A small and innocent-looking change to the program invalidates it.

Exercise 3.9. Your manager asks you to change the initialization of α to $\alpha = 2$. He argues that it is wasteful to shrink an array only when three-fourths of it are unused. He proposes to shrink it when $n \leq w/2$. Convince him that this is a bad idea by giving a sequence of m *pushBack* and *popBack* operations that would need time $\Theta(m^2)$ if his proposal was implemented.

Lemma 3.1 makes a statement about the amortized cost of *pushBack* and *popBack* operations. Although single operations may be costly, the cost of a sequence of m operations is $O(m)$. If we divide the total cost of the operations in σ by the number of operations, we get a constant. We say that the *amortized cost* of each operation is constant. Our usage of the term "amortized" is similar to its usage in everyday language, but it avoids a common pitfall. "I am going to cycle to work every day from now on, and hence it is justified to buy a luxury bike. The cost per ride will be very small – the investment will be amortized." Does this kind of reasoning sound familiar to you? The bike is bought, it rains, and all good intentions are gone. The bike has not been amortized. We shall instead insist that a large expenditure is justified by savings in the past and not by expected savings in the future. Suppose your ultimate goal is to go to work in a luxury car. However, you are not going to buy it on your first day of work. Instead, you walk and put a certain amount of money per day into a savings account. At some point, you will be able to buy a bicycle. You continue to put money away. At some point later, you will be able to buy a small car, and even later you can finally buy a luxury car. In this way, every expenditure can be paid for by past savings, and all expenditures are amortized. Using the notion of amortized costs, we can reformulate Lemma 3.1 more elegantly. The increased elegance also allows better comparisons between data structures.

Corollary 3.2. *Unbounded arrays implement the operation* $[\cdot]$ *in worst-case constant time and the operations pushBack and popBack in amortized constant time.*

To prove Lemma 3.1, we use the *bank account* or *potential* method. We associate an *account* or *potential* with our data structure and force every *pushBack* and *popBack* to put a certain amount into this account. Usually, we call our unit of currency a *token*. The idea is that whenever a call of *reallocate* occurs, the balance in the account is sufficiently high to pay for it. The details are as follows. A token can pay for moving one element from b to b'. Note that element copying in the procedure *reallocate* is the only operation that incurs a nonconstant cost in Fig. 3.6. More concretely, *reallocate* is always called with $w' = 2n$ and thus has to copy n elements. Hence, for each call of *reallocate*, we withdraw n tokens from the account. We charge two tokens for each call of *pushBack* and one token for each call of *popBack*. We now show that these charges suffice to cover the withdrawals made by *reallocate*.

The first call of *reallocate* occurs when there is one element already in the array and a new element is to be inserted. The element already in the array has deposited two tokens in the account, and this more than covers the one token withdrawn by *reallocate*. The new element provides its tokens for the next call of *reallocate*.

After a call of *reallocate*, we have an array of w elements: $n = w/2$ slots are occupied and $w/2$ are free. The next call of *reallocate* occurs when either $n = w$ or $4n \le w$. In the first case, at least $w/2$ elements have been added to the array since the last call of *reallocate*, and each one of them has deposited two tokens. So we have at least w tokens available and can cover the withdrawal made by the next call of *reallocate*. In the second case, at least $w/2 - w/4 = w/4$ elements have been removed from the array since the last call of *reallocate*, and each one of them has deposited one token. So we have at least $w/4$ tokens available. The call of *reallocate* needs at most $w/4$ tokens, and hence the cost of the call is covered. This completes the proof of Lemma 3.1.   □

Exercise 3.10. Redo the argument above for general values of α and β, and charge $\beta/(\beta-1)$ tokens for each call of *pushBack* and $\beta/(\alpha-\beta)$ tokens for each call of *popBack*. Let n' be such that $w = \beta n'$. Then, after a *reallocate*, n' elements are occupied and $(\beta-1)n' = ((\beta-1)/\beta)w$ are free. The next call of *reallocate* occurs when either $n = w$ or $\alpha n \le w$. Argue that in both cases there are enough tokens.

Amortized analysis is an extremely versatile tool, and so we think that it is worthwhile to know some alternative proof methods. We shall now give two variants of the proof above.

Above, we charged two tokens for each *pushBack* and one token for each *popBack*. Alternatively, we could charge three tokens for each *pushBack* and not charge *popBack* at all. The accounting is simple. The first two tokens pay for the insertion as above, and the third token is used when the element is deleted.

Exercise 3.11 (continuation of Exercise 3.10). Show that a charge of $\beta/(\beta-1)+$ $\beta/(\alpha-\beta)$ tokens for each *pushBack* is enough. Determine values of α such that $\beta/(\alpha-\beta) \le 1/(\beta-1)$ and $\beta/(\alpha-\beta) \le \beta/(\beta-1)$, respectively.

3.2.2 Amortized Analysis of Unbounded Arrays: The Local Argument

We now describe our second modification of the proof. In the argument above, we used a global argument in order to show that there are enough tokens in the account before each call of *reallocate*. We now show how to replace the global argument by a local argument. Recall that, immediately after a call of *reallocate*, we have an array of w elements, out of which $w/2$ are filled and $w/2$ are free. We argue that at any time after the first call of *reallocate*, the following token invariant holds:

the account contains at least $\max(2(n-w/2), w/2-n)$ tokens.

Observe that this number is always nonnegative. We use induction on the number of operations. Immediately after the first *reallocate*, there is one token in the account and the invariant requires none. A *pushBack* increases n by one and adds two tokens. So the invariant is maintained. A *popBack* removes one element and adds one token. So the invariant is again maintained. When a call of *reallocate* occurs, we have either $n = w$ or $4n \le w$. In the former case, the account contains at least n tokens, and n tokens are required for the reallocation. In the latter case, the account contains at least $w/4$ tokens, and n are required. So, in either case, the number of tokens suffices. Also, after the reallocation, $n = w/2$ and hence no tokens are required.

Exercise 3.12. Charge three tokens for a *pushBack* and no tokens for a *popBack*. Argue that the account contains always at least $n + \max(2(n-w/2), w/2-n) = \max(3n-w, w/2)$ tokens.

Exercise 3.13 (popping many elements). Implement an operation $popBack(k)$ that removes the last k elements in amortized constant time independent of k.

Exercise 3.14 (worst-case constant access time). Suppose, for a real-time application, you need an unbounded array data structure with a *worst-case* constant execution time for all operations. Design such a data structure. Hint: store the elements in up to two arrays. Start moving elements to a larger array well before a small array is completely exhausted.

Exercise 3.15 (implicitly growing arrays). Implement unbounded arrays where the operation $[i]$ allows any positive index. When $i \geq n$, the array is implicitly grown to size $n = i + 1$. When $n \geq w$, the array is reallocated as for *UArray*. Initialize entries that have never been written with some default value $\bot$.

Exercise 3.16 (sparse arrays). Implement bounded arrays with constant time for allocating arrays and constant time for the operation $[\cdot]$. All array elements should be (implicitly) initialized to $\bot$. You are not allowed to make any assumptions about the contents of a freshly allocated array. Hint: use an extra array of the same size, and store the number t of array elements to which a value has already been assigned. Therefore $t = 0$ initially. An array entry i to which a value has been assigned stores that value and an index j, $1 \leq j \leq t$, of the extra array, and i is stored in that index of the extra array.

3.2.3 Amortized Analysis of Binary Counters

In order to demonstrate that our techniques for amortized analysis are also useful for other applications, we shall now give a second example. We look at the amortized cost of incrementing a binary counter. The value n of the counter is represented by a sequence $\ldots \beta_i \ldots \beta_1 \beta_0$ of binary digits, i.e., $\beta_i \in \{0, 1\}$ and $n = \sum_{i \geq 0} \beta_i 2^i$. The initial value is zero. Its representation is a string of zeros. We define the cost of incrementing the counter as one plus the number of trailing ones in the binary representation, i.e., the transition

$$\ldots 01^k \to \ldots 10^k$$

has a cost $k + 1$. What is the total cost of m increments? We shall show that the cost is $O(m)$. Again, we give a global argument first and then a local argument.

If the counter is incremented m times, the final value is m. The representation of the number m requires $L = 1 + \lceil \log m \rceil$ bits. Among the numbers 0 to $m - 1$, there are at most 2^{L-k-1} numbers whose binary representation ends with a zero followed by k ones. For each one of them, an increment costs $1 + k$. Thus the total cost of the m increments is bounded by

$$\sum_{0 \leq k < L} (k+1)2^{L-k-1} = 2^L \sum_{1 \leq k \leq L} k/2^k \leq 2^L \sum_{k \geq 1} k/2^k = 2 \cdot 2^L \leq 4m \,,$$

where the last equality uses (A.14). Hence, the amortized cost of an increment is $O(1)$.

The argument above is global, in the sense that it requires an estimate of the number of representations ending in a zero followed by k ones. We now give a local argument which does not need such a bound. We associate a bank account with the counter. Its balance is the number of ones in the binary representation of the counter. So the balance is initially zero. Consider an increment of cost $k + 1$. Before the increment, the representation ends in a zero followed by k ones, and after the increment, the representation ends in a one followed by $k - 1$ zeros. So the number of ones in the representation decreases by $k - 1$, i.e., the operation releases $k - 1$ tokens from the account. The cost of the increment is $k + 1$. We cover a cost of $k - 1$ by the tokens released from the account, and charge a cost of two for the operation. Thus the total cost of m operations is at most $2m$.

3.3 *Amortized Analysis

We give here a general definition of amortized time bounds and amortized analysis. We recommend that one should read this section quickly and come back to it when needed. We consider an arbitrary data structure. The values of all program variables comprise the state of the data structure; we use S to denote the set of states. In the first example in the previous section, the state of our data structure is formed by the values of n, w, and b. Let s_0 be the initial state. In our example, we have $n = 0$, $w = 1$, and b is an array of size one in the initial state. We have operations to transform the data structure. In our example, we had the operations *pushBack*, *popBack*, and *reallocate*. The application of an operation X in a state s transforms the data structure to a new state s' and has a cost $T_X(s)$. In our example, the cost of a *pushBack* or *popBack* is 1, excluding the cost of the possible call to *reallocate*. The cost of a call *reallocate*(βn) is $\Theta(n)$.

Let F be a sequence of operations $Op_1, Op_2, Op_3, \ldots, Op_n$. Starting at the initial state s_0, F takes us through a sequence of states to a final state s_n:

$$s_0 \xrightarrow{Op_1} s_1 \xrightarrow{Op_2} s_2 \xrightarrow{Op_3} \cdots \xrightarrow{Op_n} s_n \; .$$

The cost $T(F)$ of F is given by

$$T(F) = \sum_{1 \leq i \leq n} T_{Op_i}(s_{i-1}) \; .$$

A family of functions $A_X(s)$, one for each operation X, is called a *family of amortized time bounds* if, for every sequence F of operations,

$$T(F) \leq A(F) := c + \sum_{1 \leq i \leq n} A_{Op_i}(s_{i-1})$$

for some constant c not depending on F, i.e., up to an additive constant, the total actual execution time is bounded by the total amortized execution time.

There is always a trivial way to define a family of amortized time bounds, namely $A_X(s) := T_X(s)$ for all s. The challenge is to find a family of simple functions $A_X(s)$ that form a family of amortized time bounds. In our example, the functions $A_{pushBack}(s) = A_{popBack}(s) = A_{[\cdot]}(s) = O(1)$ and $A_{reallocate}(s) = 0$ for all s form a family of amortized time bounds.

3.3.1 The Potential or Bank Account Method for Amortized Analysis

We now formalize the technique used in the previous section. We have a function *pot* that associates a nonnegative potential with every state of the data structure, i.e., $pot : S \longrightarrow \mathbb{R}_{\geq 0}$. We call $pot(s)$ the potential of the state s, or the balance of the savings account when the data structure is in the state s. It requires ingenuity to come up with an appropriate function *pot*. For an operation X that transforms a state s into a state s' and has cost $T_X(s)$, we define the amortized cost $A_X(s)$ as the sum of the potential change and the actual cost, i.e., $A_X(s) = pot(s') - pot(s) + T_X(s)$. The functions obtained in this way form a family of amortized time bounds.

Theorem 3.3 (potential method). *Let S be the set of states of a data structure, let s_0 be the initial state, and let $pot : S \longrightarrow \mathbb{R}_{\geq 0}$ be a nonnegative function. For an operation X and a state s with $s \xrightarrow{X} s'$, we define*

$$A_X(s) = pot(s') - pot(s) + T_X(s).$$

The functions $A_X(s)$ are then a family of amortized time bounds.

Proof. A short computation suffices. Consider a sequence $F = \langle Op_1, \ldots, Op_n \rangle$ of operations. We have

$$\sum_{1 \leq i \leq n} A_{Op_i}(s_{i-1}) = \sum_{1 \leq i \leq n} (pot(s_i) - pot(s_{i-1}) + T_{Op_i}(s_{i-1}))$$
$$= pot(s_n) - pot(s_0) + \sum_{1 \leq i \leq n} T_{Op_i}(s_{i-1})$$
$$\geq \sum_{1 \leq i \leq n} T_{Op_i}(s_{i-1}) - pot(s_0),$$

since $pot(s_n) \geq 0$. Thus $T(F) \leq A(F) + pot(s_0)$. □

Let us formulate the analysis of unbounded arrays in the language above. The state of an unbounded array is characterized by the values of n and w. Following Exercise 3.12, the potential in state (n, w) is $\max(3n - w, w/2)$. The actual costs T of *pushBack* and *popBack* are 1 and the actual cost of *reallocate*(βn) is n. The potential of the initial state $(n, w) = (0, 1)$ is $1/2$. A *pushBack* increases n by 1 and hence increases the potential by at most 3. Thus its amortized cost is bounded by 4. A *popBack* decreases n by 1 and hence does not increase the potential. Its amortized cost is therefore at most 1. The first *reallocate* occurs when the data structure is in the state $(n, w) = (1, 1)$. The potential of this state is $\max(3 - 1, 1/2) = 2$, and the actual cost of the *reallocate* is 1. After the *reallocate*, the data structure is in the state $(n,w) = (1,2)$ and has a potential $\max(3-2,1) = 1$. Therefore the amortized cost of the first *reallocate* is $1-2+1 = 0$. Consider any other call of *reallocate*. We have either $n = w$ or $4n \leq w$. In the former case, the potential before the *reallocate* is $2n$, the actual cost is n, and the new state is $(n,2n)$ and has a potential n. Thus the amortized cost is $n - 2n + n = 0$. In the latter case, the potential before the operation is $w/2$, the actual cost is n, which is at most $w/4$, and the new state is $(n,w/2)$ and has a potential $w/4$. Thus the amortized cost is at most $w/4 - w/2 + w/4 = 0$. We conclude that the amortized costs of *pushBack* and *popBack* are $O(1)$ and the amortized cost of *reallocate* is zero or less. Thus a sequence of m operations on an unbounded array has cost $O(m)$.

Exercise 3.17 (amortized analysis of binary counters). Consider a nonnegative integer c represented by an array of binary digits, and a sequence of m increment and decrement operations. Initially, $c = 0$. This exercise continues the discussion at the end of Sect. 3.2.

(a) What is the worst-case execution time of an increment or a decrement as a function of m? Assume that you can work with only one bit per step.
(b) Prove that the amortized cost of the increments is constant if there are no decrements. Hint: define the potential of c as the number of ones in the binary representation of c.
(c) Give a sequence of m increment and decrement operations with cost $\Theta(m \log m)$.
(d) Give a representation of counters such that you can achieve worst-case constant time for increments and decrements.
(e) Allow each digit d_i to take values from $\{-1,0,1\}$. The value of the counter is $c = \sum_i d_i 2^i$. Show that in this *redundant ternary* number system, increments and decrements have constant amortized cost. Is there an easy way to tell whether the value of the counter is zero?

3.3.2 Universality of Potential Method

We argue here that the potential-function technique is strong enough to obtain any family of amortized time bounds.

Theorem 3.4. *Let $B_X(s)$ be a family of amortized time bounds. There is then a potential function pot such that $A_X(s) \leq B_X(s)$ for all states s and all operations X, where $A_X(s)$ is defined according to Theorem 3.3.*

Proof. Let c be such that $T(F) \leq B(F) + c$ for any sequence of operations F starting at the initial state. For any state s, we define its potential $pot(s)$ by

$$pot(s) = \inf\{B(F) + c - T(F) : F \text{ is a sequence of operations with final state } s\} \ .$$

We need to write inf instead of min, since there might be infinitely many sequences leading to s. We have $pot(s) \geq 0$ for any s, since $T(F) \leq B(F) + c$ for any sequence F. Thus *pot* is a potential function, and the functions $A_X(s)$ form a family of amortized time bounds. We need to show that $A_X(s) \leq B_X(s)$ for all X and s. Let $\varepsilon > 0$ be arbitrary. We shall show that $A_X(s) \leq B_X(s) + \varepsilon$. Since ε is arbitrary, this proves that $A_X(s) \leq B_X(s)$.

Let F be a sequence with final state s and $B(F) + c - T(F) \leq pot(s) + \varepsilon$. Let F' be F followed by X, i.e.,

$$s_0 \xrightarrow{F} s \xrightarrow{X} s' .$$

Then $pot(s') \leq B(F') + c - T(F')$ by the definition of $pot(s')$, $pot(s) \geq B(F) + c - T(F) - \varepsilon$ by the choice of F, $B(F') = B(F) + B_X(s)$ and $T(F') = T(F) + T_X(s)$ since $F' = F \circ X$, and $A_X(s) = pot(s') - pot(s) + T_X(s)$ by the definition of $A_X(s)$. Combining these inequalities, we obtain

$$A_X(s) \leq (B(F') + c - T(F')) - (B(F) + c - T(F) - \varepsilon) + T_X(s)$$
$$= (B(F') - B(F)) - (T(F') - T(F) - T_X(s)) + \varepsilon$$
$$= B_X(s) + \varepsilon .$$

$\square$

3.4 Stacks and Queues

Sequences are often used in a rather limited way. Let us start with some examples from precomputer days. Sometimes a clerk will work in the following way: the clerk keeps a *stack* of unprocessed files on her desk. New files are placed on the top of the stack. When the clerk processes the next file, she also takes it from the top of the stack. The easy handling of this "data structure" justifies its use; of course, files may stay in the stack for a long time. In the terminology of the preceding sections, a stack is a sequence that supports only the operations *pushBack*, *popBack*, and *last*. We shall use the simplified names *push*, *pop*, and *top* for the three stack operations.

The behavior is different when people stand in line waiting for service at a post office: customers join the line at one end and leave it at the other end. Such sequences are called *FIFO (first in, first out) queues* or simply *queues*. In the terminology of the *List* class, FIFO queues use only the operations *first*, *pushBack*, and *popFront*.

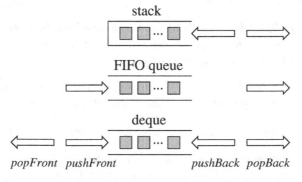

popFront pushFront   pushBack popBack

Fig. 3.7. Operations on stacks, queues, and double-ended queues (deques)

The more general *deque* (pronounced "deck"), or *double-ended queue*, allows the operations *first, last, pushFront, pushBack, popFront,* and *popBack* and can also be observed at a post office when some not so nice individual jumps the line, or when the clerk at the counter gives priority to a pregnant woman at the end of the line. Figure 3.7 illustrates the access patterns of stacks, queues, and deques.

Exercise 3.18 (the Tower of Hanoi). *In the great temple of Brahma in Benares, on a brass plate under the dome that marks the center of the world, there are 64 disks of pure gold that the priests carry one at a time between three diamond needles according to Brahma's immutable law: no disk may be placed on a smaller disk. At the beginning of the world, all 64 disks formed the Tower of Brahma on one needle. Now, however, the process of transfer of the tower from one needle to another is in mid-course. When the last disk is finally in place, once again forming the Tower of Brahma but on a different needle, then the end of the world will come and all will turn to dust,* [93].[2]

Describe the problem formally for any number k of disks. Write a program that uses three stacks for the piles and produces a sequence of stack operations that transform the state $(\langle k, \ldots, 1 \rangle, \langle \rangle, \langle \rangle)$ into the state $(\langle \rangle, \langle \rangle, \langle k, \ldots, 1 \rangle)$.

Exercise 3.19. Explain how to implement a FIFO queue using two stacks so that each FIFO operation takes amortized constant time.

Why should we care about these specialized types of sequence if we already know a list data structure which supports all of the operations above and more in constant time? There are at least three reasons. First, programs become more readable and are easier to debug if special usage patterns of data structures are made explicit. Second, simple interfaces also allow a wider range of implementations. In particular, the simplicity of stacks and queues allows specialized implementations that are more space-efficient than general *Lists*. We shall elaborate on this algorithmic aspect in the remainder of this section. In particular, we shall strive for implementations based on arrays rather than lists. Third, lists are not suited for external-memory use because any access to a list item may cause an I/O operation. The sequential access patterns to stacks and queues translate into good reuse of cache blocks when stacks and queues are represented by arrays.

Bounded stacks, where we know the maximal size in advance, are readily implemented with bounded arrays. For unbounded stacks, we can use unbounded arrays. Stacks can also be represented by singly linked lists: the top of the stack corresponds to the front of the list. FIFO queues are easy to realize with singly linked lists with a pointer to the last element. However, deques cannot be represented efficiently by singly linked lists.

We discuss next an implementation of bounded FIFO queues by use of arrays; see Fig. 3.8. We view an array as a cyclic structure where entry zero follows the last entry. In other words, we have array indices 0 to n, and view the indices modulo $n + 1$. We

---

[2] In fact, this mathematical puzzle was invented by the French mathematician Edouard Lucas in 1883.

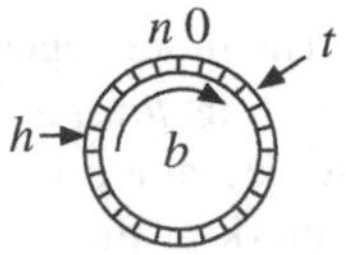

Class *BoundedFIFO(n* : ℕ*)* **of** *Element*
   b : *Array* [0*..n*] **of** *Element*
   h = 0 : ℕ   // index of first element
   t = 0 : ℕ   // index of first free entry

   Function *isEmpty* : {0,1}; **return** $h = t$

   Function *first* : *Element;* **assert** ¬*isEmpty;* **return** $b[h]$

   Function *size* : ℕ; **return** $(t - h + n + 1) \bmod (n + 1)$

   Procedure *pushBack*(*x* : *Element*)
      assert *size*< *n*
      $b[t] := x$
      $t := (t + 1) \bmod (n + 1)$

   Procedure *popFront* **assert** ¬*isEmpty;* $h := (h + 1) \bmod (n + 1)$

Fig. 3.8. An array-based bounded FIFO queue implementation

maintain two indices h and t that delimit the range of valid queue entries; the queue comprises the array elements indexed by $h..t - 1$. The indices travel around the cycle as elements are queued and dequeued. The cyclic semantics of the indices can be implemented using arithmetics modulo the array size.[3] We always leave at least one entry of the array empty, because otherwise it would be difficult to distinguish a full queue from an empty queue. The implementation is readily generalized to bounded deques. Circular arrays also support the random access operator [·]:

   Operator $[i : ℕ]$: *Element;* **return** $b[i + h \bmod n]$

Bounded queues and deques can be made unbounded using techniques similar to those used for unbounded arrays in Sect. 3.2.

   We have now seen the major techniques for implementing stacks, queues, and deques. These techniques may be combined to obtain solutions that are particularly suited for very large sequences or for external-memory computations.

Exercise 3.20 (lists of arrays). Here we aim to develop a simple data structure for stacks, FIFO queues, and deques that combines all the advantages of lists and unbounded arrays and is more space-efficient than either lists or unbounded arrays. Use a list (doubly linked for deques) where each item stores an array of K elements for some large constant K. Implement such a data structure in your favorite programming language. Compare the space consumption and execution time with those for linked lists and unbounded arrays in the case of large stacks.

Exercise 3.21 (external-memory stacks and queues). Design a stack data structure that needs $O(1/B)$ I/Os per operation in the I/O model described in Sect. 2.2. It

---

[3] On some machines, one might obtain significant speedups by choosing the array size to be a power of two and replacing **mod** by bit operations.

suffices to keep two blocks in internal memory. What can happen in a naive implementation with only one block in memory? Adapt your data structure to implement
FIFO queues, again using two blocks of internal buffer memory. Implement deques
using four buffer blocks.

3.5 Lists Versus Arrays

Table 3.1 summarizes the findings of this chapter. Arrays are better at indexed access, whereas linked lists have their strength in manipulations of sequences at arbitrary positions. Both of these approaches realize the operations needed for stacks
and queues efficiently. However, arrays are more cache-efficient here, whereas lists
provide worst-case performance guarantees.

Table 3.1. Running times of operations on sequences with n elements. The entries have an
implicit $O(\cdot)$ around them. *List* stands for doubly linked lists, *SList* stands for singly linked
lists, *UArray* stands for unbounded arrays, and *CArray* stands for circular arrays

Operation	List	SList	UArray	CArray	Explanation of "*"
[·]	n	n	1	1	
size	1*	1*	1	1	Not with interlist *splice*
first	1	1	1	1	
last	1	1	1	1	
insert	1	1*	n	n	*insertAfter* only
remove	1	1*	n	n	*removeAfter* only
pushBack	1	1	1*	1*	Amortized
pushFront	1	1	n	1*	Amortized
popBack	1	n	1*	1*	Amortized
popFront	1	1	n	1*	Amortized
concat	1	1	n	n	
splice	1	1	n	n	
findNext,...	n	n	n*	n*	Cache-efficient

Singly linked lists can compete with doubly linked lists in most but not all re-
spects. The only advantage of cyclic arrays over unbounded arrays is that they can
implement *pushFront* and *popFront* efficiently.

Space efficiency is also a nontrivial issue. Linked lists are very compact if the
elements are much larger than the pointers. For small *Element* types, arrays are usually more compact because there is no overhead for pointers. This is certainly true
if the sizes of the arrays are known in advance so that bounded arrays can be used.
Unbounded arrays have a trade-off between space efficiency and copying overhead
during reallocation.

3.6 Implementation Notes

Every decent programming language supports bounded arrays. In addition, un-bounded arrays, lists, stacks, queues, and deques are provided in libraries that are available for the major imperative languages. Nevertheless, you will often have to implement listlike data structures yourself, for example when your objects are members of several linked lists. In such implementations, memory management is often a major challenge.

3.6.1 C++

The class *vector⟨Element⟩* in the STL realizes unbounded arrays. However, most implementations never shrink the array. There is functionality for manually setting the allocated size. Usually, you will give some initial estimate for the sequence size n when the *vector* is constructed. This can save you many grow operations. Often, you also know when the array will stop changing size, and you can then force $w = n$. With these refinements, there is little reason to use the built-in C-style arrays. An added benefit of *vector*s is that they are automatically destroyed when the variable goes out of scope. Furthermore, during debugging, you may switch to implementations with bound checking.

There are some additional issues that you might want to address if you need very high performance for arrays that grow or shrink a lot. During reallocation, *vector* has to move array elements using the copy constructor of *Element*. In most cases, a call to the low-level byte copy operation *memcpy* would be much faster. Another low-level optimization is to implement *reallocate* using the standard C function *realloc*. The memory manager might be able to avoid copying the data entirely.

A stumbling block with unbounded arrays is that pointers to array elements become invalid when the array is reallocated. You should make sure that the array does not change size while such pointers are being used. If reallocations cannot be ruled out, you can use array indices rather than pointers.

The STL and LEDA [118] offer doubly linked lists in the class *list⟨Element⟩*, and singly linked lists in the class *slist⟨Element⟩*. Their memory management uses free lists for all objects of (roughly) the same size, rather than only for objects of the same class.

If you need to implement a listlike data structure, note that the operator *new* can be redefined for each class. The standard library class *allocator* offers an interface that allows you to use your own memory management while cooperating with the memory managers of other classes.

The STL provides the classes *stack⟨Element⟩* and *deque⟨Element⟩* for stacks and double-ended queues, respectively. *Deque*s also allow constant-time indexed access using [·]. LEDA offers the classes *stack⟨Element⟩* and *queue⟨Element⟩* for unbounded stacks, and FIFO queues implemented via linked lists. It also offers bounded variants that are implemented as arrays.

Iterators are a central concept of the STL; they implement our abstract view of sequences independent of the particular representation.

3.6.2 Java

The *util* package of the Java 6 platform provides *ArrayList* for unbounded arrays and *LinkedList* for doubly linked lists. There is a *Deque* interface, with implementations by use of *ArrayDeque* and *LinkedList*. A *Stack* is implemented as an extension to *Vector*.

Many Java books proudly announce that Java has no pointers so that you might wonder how to implement linked lists. The solution is that object references in Java are essentially pointers. In a sense, Java has *only* pointers, because members of non-simple type are always references, and are never stored in the parent object itself.

Explicit memory management is optional in Java, since it provides garbage collections of all objects that are not referenced any more.

3.7 Historical Notes and Further Findings

All of the algorithms described in this chapter are "folklore", i.e., they have been around for a long time and nobody claims to be their inventor. Indeed, we have seen that many of the underlying concepts predate computers.

Amortization is as old as the analysis of algorithms. The *bank account* and *potential* methods were introduced at the beginning of the 1980s by R. E. Brown, S. Huddlestone, K. Mehlhorn, D. D. Sleator, and R. E. Tarjan [32, 95, 182, 183]. The overview article [188] popularized the term *amortized analysis*, and Theorem 3.4 first appeared in [127].

There is an arraylike data structure that supports indexed access in constant time and arbitrary element insertion and deletion in amortized time $O(\sqrt{n})$. The trick is relatively simple. The array is split into subarrays of size $n' = \Theta(\sqrt{n})$. Only the last subarray may contain fewer elements. The subarrays are maintained as cyclic arrays, as described in Sect. 3.4. Element i can be found in entry i **mod** n' of subarray $\lfloor i/n' \rfloor$. A new element is inserted into its subarray in time $O(\sqrt{n})$. To repair the invariant that subarrays have the same size, the last element of this subarray is inserted as the first element of the next subarray in constant time. This process of shifting the extra element is repeated $O(n/n') = O(\sqrt{n})$ times until the last subarray is reached. Deletion works similarly. Occasionally, one has to start a new last subarray or change n' and reallocate everything. The amortized cost of these additional operations can be kept small. With some additional modifications, all deque operations can be performed in constant time. We refer the reader to [107] for more sophisticated implementations of deques and an implementation study.

4

Hash Tables and Associative Arrays

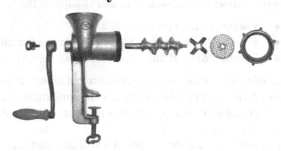

If you want to get a book from the central library of the University of Karlsruhe, you have to order the book in advance. The library personnel fetch the book from the stacks and deliver it to a room with 100 shelves. You find your book on a shelf numbered with the last *two digits of your library card. Why the last digits and not the leading digits? Probably because this distributes the books more evenly among the shelves. The library cards are numbered consecutively as students sign up, and the University of Karlsruhe was founded in 1825. Therefore, the students enrolled at the same time are likely to have the same leading digits in their card number, and only a few shelves would be in use if the leading digits were used.*

The subject of this chapter is the robust and efficient implementation of the above "delivery shelf data structure". In computer science, this data structure is known as a *hash*[1] *table*. Hash tables are one implementation of *associative arrays*, or *dictionaries*. The other implementation is the tree data structures which we shall study in Chap. 7. An associative array is an array with a potentially infinite or at least very large index set, out of which only a small number of indices are actually in use. For example, the potential indices may be all strings, and the indices in use may be all identifiers used in a particular C++ program. Or the potential indices may be all ways of placing chess pieces on a chess board, and the indices in use may be the placements required in the analysis of a particular game. Associative arrays are versatile data structures. Compilers use them for their *symbol table*, which associates identifiers with information about them. Combinatorial search programs often use them for detecting whether a situation has already been looked at. For example, chess programs have to deal with the fact that board positions can be reached by different sequences of moves. However, each position needs to be evaluated only once. The solution is to store positions in an associative array. One of the most widely used implementations of the *join* operation in relational databases temporarily stores one of the participating relations in an associative array. Scripting languages such as AWK

---

[1] Photograph of the mincer above by Kku, Rainer Zenz (Wikipedia), Licence CC-by-SA 2.5.

[7] and `Perl` [203] use associative arrays as their *main* data structure. In all of the examples above, the associative array is usually implemented as a hash table. The exercises in this section ask you to develop some further uses of associative arrays.

Formally, an associative array S stores a set of elements. Each element e has an associated key $key(e) \in Key$. We assume keys to be unique, i.e., distinct elements have distinct keys. Associative arrays support the following operations:

- $S.insert(e : Element)$: $S := S \cup \{e\}$.
- $S.remove(k : Key)$: $S := S \setminus \{e\}$, where e is the unique element with $key(e) = k$.
- $S.find(k : Key)$: If there is an $e \in S$ with $key(e) = k$, return e; otherwise, return $\bot$.

In addition, we assume a mechanism that allows us to retrieve all elements in S. Since this *forall* operation is usually easy to implement, we discuss it only in the exercises. Observe that the *find* operation is essentially the random access operator for an array; hence the name "associative array". *Key* is the set of potential array indices, and the elements of S are the indices in use at any particular time. Throughout this chapter, we use n to denote the size of S, and N to denote the size of *Key*. In a typical application of associative arrays, N is humongous and hence the use of an array of size N is out of the question. We are aiming for solutions which use space $O(n)$.

In the library example, *Key* is the set of all library card numbers, and elements are the book orders. Another precomputer example is provided by an English–German dictionary. The keys are English words, and an element is an English word together with its German translations.

The basic idea behind the hash table implementation of associative arrays is simple. We use a *hash function* h to map the set *Key* of potential array indices to a small range $0..m - 1$ of integers. We also have an array t with index set $0..m - 1$, the *hash table*. In order to keep the space requirement low, we want m to be about the number of elements in S. The hash function associates with each element e a *hash value* $h(key(e))$. In order to simplify the notation, we write $h(e)$ instead of $h(key(e))$ for the hash value of e. In the library example, h maps each library card number to its last two digits. Ideally, we would like to store element e in the table entry $t[h(e)]$. If this works, we obtain constant execution time[2] for our three operations *insert*, *remove*, and *find*.

Unfortunately, storing e in $t[h(e)]$ will not always work, as several elements might *collide*, i.e., map to the same table entry. The library example suggests a fix: allow several book orders to go to the same shelf. The entire shelf then has to be searched to find a particular order. A generalization of this fix leads to *hashing with chaining*. We store a set of elements in each table entry, and implement the set using singly linked lists. Section 4.1 analyzes hashing with chaining using some rather optimistic (and hence unrealistic) assumptions about the properties of the hash function. In this model, we achieve constant expected time for all three dictionary operations.

In Sect. 4.2, we drop the unrealistic assumptions and construct hash functions that come with (probabilistic) performance guarantees. Even our simple examples show

---

[2] Strictly speaking, we have to add additional terms for evaluating the hash function and for moving elements around. To simplify the notation, we assume in this chapter that all of this takes constant time.

that finding good hash functions is nontrivial. For example, if we apply the least-significant-digit idea from the library example to an English–German dictionary, we might come up with a hash function based on the last four letters of a word. But then we would have many collisions for words ending in "tion", "able", etc.

We can simplify hash tables (but not their analysis) by returning to the original idea of storing all elements in the table itself. When a newly inserted element e finds the entry $t[h(x)]$ occupied, it scans the table until a free entry is found. In the library example, assume that shelves can hold exactly one book. The librarians would then use adjacent shelves to store books that map to the same delivery shelf. Section 4.3 elaborates on this idea, which is known as *hashing with open addressing and linear probing*.

Why are hash tables called hash tables? The dictionary defines "to hash" as "to chop up, as of potatoes". This is exactly what hash functions usually do. For example, if keys are strings, the hash function may chop up the string into pieces of fixed size, interpret each fixed-size piece as a number, and then compute a single number from the sequence of numbers. A good hash function creates disorder and, in this way, avoids collisions.

Exercise 4.1. Assume you are given a set M of pairs of integers. M defines a binary relation R_M. Use an associative array to check whether R_M is symmetric. A relation is symmetric if $\forall (a,b) \in M : (b,a) \in M$.

Exercise 4.2. Write a program that reads a text file and outputs the 100 most frequent words in the text.

Exercise 4.3 (a billing system). Assume you have a large file consisting of triples (transaction, price, customer ID). Explain how to compute the total payment due for each customer. Your algorithm should run in linear time.

Exercise 4.4 (scanning a hash table). Show how to realize the *forall* operation for hashing with chaining and for hashing with open addressing and linear probing. What is the running time of your solution?

4.1 Hashing with Chaining

Hashing with chaining maintains an array t of linear lists (see Fig. 4.1). The associative-array operations are easy to implement. To insert an element e, we insert it somewhere in the sequence $t[h(e)]$. To remove an element with key k, we scan through $t[h(k)]$. If an element e with $h(e) = k$ is encountered, we remove it and return. To find the element with key k, we also scan through $t[h(k)]$. If an element e with $h(e) = k$ is encountered, we return it. Otherwise, we return $\perp$.

Insertions take constant time. The space consumption is $O(n+m)$. To remove or find a key k, we have to scan the sequence $t[h(k)]$. In the worst case, for example if *find* looks for an element that is not there, the entire list has to be scanned. If we are

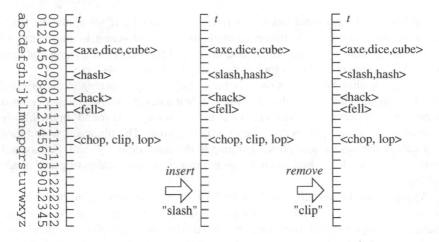

Fig. 4.1. Hashing with chaining. We have a table t of sequences. The figure shows an example where a set of words (short synonyms of "hash") is stored using a hash function that maps the last character to the integers $0..25$. We see that this hash function is not very good

unlucky, all elements are mapped to the same table entry and the execution time is $\Theta(n)$. So, in the worst case, hashing with chaining is no better than linear lists.

Are there hash functions that guarantee that all sequences are short? The answer is clearly no. A hash function maps the set of keys to the range $0..m-1$, and hence for every hash function there is always a set of N/m keys that all map to the same table entry. In most applications, $n < N/m$ and hence hashing can always deteriorate to a linear search. We shall study three approaches to dealing with the worst-case behavior. The first approach is average-case analysis. We shall study this approach in this section. The second approach is to use randomization, and to choose the hash function at random from a collection of hash functions. We shall study this approach in this section and the next. The third approach is to change the algorithm. For example, we could make the hash function depend on the set of keys in actual use. We shall investigate this approach in Sect. 4.5 and shall show that it leads to good worst-case behavior.

Let H be the set of all functions from *Key* to $0..m-1$. We assume that the hash function h is chosen randomly[3] from H and shall show that for any fixed set S of n keys, the expected execution time of *remove* or *find* will be $O(1+n/m)$.

Theorem 4.1. *If n elements are stored in a hash table with m entries and a random hash function is used, the expected execution time of remove or find is $O(1+n/m)$.*

---

[3] This assumption is completely unrealistic. There are m^N functions in H, and hence it requires $N\log m$ bits to specify a function in H. This defeats the goal of reducing the space requirement from N to n.

Proof. The proof requires the probabilistic concepts of random variables, their expectation, and the linearity of expectations as described in Sect. A.3. Consider the execution time of *remove* or *find* for a fixed key k. Both need constant time plus the time for scanning the sequence $t[h(k)]$. Hence the expected execution time is $O(1+E[X])$, where the random variable X stands for the length of the sequence $t[h(k)]$. Let S be the set of n elements stored in the hash table. For each $e \in S$, let X_e be the *indicator* variable which tells us whether e hashes to the same location as k, i.e., $X_e = 1$ if $h(e) = h(k)$ and $X_e = 0$ otherwise. In shorthand, $X_e = [h(e) = h(k)]$. We have $X = \sum_{e \in S} X_e$. Using the linearity of expectations, we obtain

$$E[X] = E[\sum_{e \in S} X_e] = \sum_{e \in S} E[X_e] = \sum_{e \in S} \text{prob}(X_i = 1) .$$

A random hash function maps e to all m table entries with the same probability, independent of $h(k)$. Hence, $\text{prob}(X_e = 1) = 1/m$ and therefore $E[X] = n/m$. Thus, the expected execution time of *find* and *remove* is $O(1+n/m)$.   □

We can achieve a linear space requirement and a constant expected execution time of all three operations by guaranteeing that $m = \Theta(n)$ at all times. Adaptive reallocation, as described for unbounded arrays in Sect. 3.2, is the appropriate technique.

Exercise 4.5 (unbounded hash tables). Explain how to guarantee $m = \Theta(n)$ in hashing with chaining. You may assume the existence of a hash function $h' : Key \rightarrow \mathbb{N}$. Set $h(k) = h'(k)$ mod m and use adaptive reallocation.

Exercise 4.6 (waste of space). The waste of space in hashing with chaining is due to empty table entries. Assuming a random hash function, compute the expected number of empty table entries as a function of m and n. Hint: define indicator random variables $Y_0, \ldots, Y_{m-1}$, where $Y_i = 1$ if $t[i]$ is empty.

Exercise 4.7 (average-case behavior). Assume that the hash function distributes the set of potential keys evenly over the table, i.e., for each i, $0 \le i \le m-1$, we have $|\{k \in Key : h(k) = i\}| \le \lceil N/m \rceil$. Assume also that a random set S of n keys is stored in the table, i.e., S is a random subset of Key of size n. Show that for any table position i, the expected number of elements in S that hash to i is at most $\lceil N/m \rceil \cdot n/N \approx n/m$.

4.2 Universal Hashing

Theorem 4.1 is unsatisfactory, as it presupposes that the hash function is chosen randomly from the set of all functions[4] from keys to table positions. The class of all such functions is much too big to be useful. We shall show in this section that the same performance can be obtained with much smaller classes of hash functions. The families presented in this section are so small that a member can be specified in constant space. Moreover, the functions are easy to evaluate.

---

[4] We shall usually talk about a *class* of functions or a *family* of functions in this chapter, and reserve the word "set" for the set of keys stored in the hash table.

Definition 4.2. *Let c be a positive constant. A family H of functions from Key to* $0..m-1$ *is called c-universal if any two distinct keys collide with a probability of at most* c/m, *i.e., for all x, y in Key with* $x \neq y$,

$$|\{h \in H : h(x) = h(y)\}| \leq \frac{c}{m}|H| .$$

In other words, for random $h \in H$,

$$\text{prob}(h(x) = h(y)) \leq \frac{c}{m} .$$

This definition has been constructed such that the proof of Theorem 4.1 can be extended.

Theorem 4.3. *If n elements are stored in a hash table with m entries using hashing with chaining and a random hash function from a c-universal family is used, the expected execution time of remove or find is* $O(1 + cn/m)$.

Proof. We can reuse the proof of Theorem 4.1 almost word for word. Consider the execution time of *remove* or *find* for a fixed key k. Both need constant time plus the time for scanning the sequence $t[h(k)]$. Hence the expected execution time is $O(1 + E[X])$, where the random variable X stands for the length of the sequence $t[h(k)]$. Let S be the set of n elements stored in the hash table. For each $e \in S$, let X_e be the indicator variable which tells us whether e hashes to the same location as k, i.e., $X_e = 1$ if $h(e) = h(k)$ and $X_e = 0$ otherwise. In shorthand, $X_e = [h(e) = h(k)]$. We have $X = \sum_{e \in S} X_e$. Using the linearity of expectations, we obtain

$$E[X] = E[\sum_{e \in S} X_e] = \sum_{e \in S} E[X_e] = \sum_{e \in S} \text{prob}(X_i = 1) .$$

Since h is chosen uniformly from a c-universal class, we have $\text{prob}(X_e = 1) \leq c/m$, and hence $E[X] = cn/m$. Thus, the expected execution time of *find* and *remove* is $O(1 + cn/m)$. □

Now it remains to find c-universal families of hash functions that are easy to construct and easy to evaluate. We shall describe a simple and quite practical 1-universal family in detail and give further examples in the exercises. We assume that our keys are bit strings of a certain fixed length; in the exercises, we discuss how the fixed-length assumption can be overcome. We also assume that the table size m is a prime number. Why a prime number? Because arithmetic modulo a prime is particularly nice; in particular, the set $\mathbb{Z}_m = \{0, \ldots, m-1\}$ of numbers modulo m form a field.[5] Let $w = \lfloor \log m \rfloor$. We subdivide the keys into pieces of w bits each, say k pieces. We interpret each piece as an integer in the range $0..2^w - 1$ and keys as k-tuples of such integers. For a key $\mathbf{x}$, we write $\mathbf{x} = (x_1, \ldots, x_k)$ to denote its partition

---

[5] A field is a set with special elements 0 and 1 and with addition and multiplication operations. Addition and multiplication satisfy the usual laws known for the field of rational numbers.

into pieces. Each x_i lies in $0..2^w - 1$. We can now define our class of hash functions. For each $\mathbf{a} = (a_1, \ldots, a_k) \in \{0..m-1\}^k$, we define a function $h_\mathbf{a}$ from *Key* to $0..m-1$ as follows. Let $\mathbf{x} = (x_1, \ldots, x_k)$ be a key and let $\mathbf{a} \cdot \mathbf{x} = \sum_{i=1}^{k} a_i x_i$ denote the scalar product of $\mathbf{a}$ and $\mathbf{x}$. Then

$$h_\mathbf{a}(x) = \mathbf{a} \cdot \mathbf{x} \bmod m .$$

It is time for an example. Let $m = 17$ and $k = 4$. Then $w = 4$ and we view keys as 4-tuples of integers in the range $0..15$, for example $\mathbf{x} = (11, 7, 4, 3)$. A hash function is specified by a 4-tuple of integers in the range $0..16$, for example $\mathbf{a} = (2, 4, 7, 16)$. Then $h_\mathbf{a}(\mathbf{x}) = (2 \cdot 11 + 4 \cdot 7 + 7 \cdot 4 + 16 \cdot 3) \bmod 17 = 7$.

Theorem 4.4.

$$H = \left\{ h_\mathbf{a} : \mathbf{a} \in \{0..m-1\}^k \right\}$$

is a 1-universal family of hash functions if m is prime.

In other words, the scalar product between a tuple representation of a key and a random vector modulo m defines a good hash function.

Proof. Consider two distinct keys $\mathbf{x} = (x_1, \ldots, x_k)$ and $\mathbf{y} = (y_1, \ldots, y_k)$. To determine $\text{prob}(h_\mathbf{a}(x) = h_\mathbf{a}(y))$, we count the number of choices for $\mathbf{a}$ such that $h_\mathbf{a}(\mathbf{x}) = h_\mathbf{a}(\mathbf{y})$. Fix an index j such that $x_j \neq y_j$. Then $(x_j - y_j) \not\equiv 0 \pmod{m}$, and hence any equation of the form $a_j(x_j - y_j) \equiv b \pmod{m}$, where $b \in \mathbb{Z}_m$, has a unique solution in a_j, namely $a_j \equiv (x_j - y_j)^{-1} b \pmod{m}$. Here $(x_j - y_j)^{-1}$ denotes the *multiplicative inverse*[6] of $(x_j - y_j)$.

We claim that for each choice of the a_i's with $i \neq j$, there is exactly one choice of a_j such that $h_\mathbf{a}(\mathbf{x}) = h_\mathbf{a}(\mathbf{y})$. Indeed,

$$h_\mathbf{a}(\mathbf{x}) = h_\mathbf{a}(\mathbf{y}) \Leftrightarrow \sum_{1 \leq i \leq k} a_i x_i \equiv \sum_{1 \leq i \leq k} a_i y_i \qquad (\bmod\ m)$$

$$\Leftrightarrow a_j(x_j - y_j) \equiv \sum_{i \neq j} a_i(y_i - x_i) \qquad (\bmod\ m)$$

$$\Leftrightarrow a_j \equiv (y_j - x_j)^{-1} \sum_{i \neq j} a_i(x_i - y_i) \ (\bmod\ m) .$$

There are m^{k-1} ways to choose the a_i with $i \neq j$, and for each such choice there is a unique choice for a_j. Since the total number of choices for $\mathbf{a}$ is m^k, we obtain

$$\text{prob}(h_\mathbf{a}(x) = h_\mathbf{a}(y)) = \frac{m^{k-1}}{m^k} = \frac{1}{m} . \qquad \square$$

Is it a serious restriction that we need prime table sizes? At first glance, yes. We certainly cannot burden users with the task of providing appropriate primes. Also, when we adaptively grow or shrink an array, it is not clear how to obtain prime

---

[6] In a field, any element $z \neq 0$ has a unique multiplicative inverse, i.e., there is a unique element z^{-1} such that $z^{-1} \cdot z = 1$. Multiplicative inverses allow one to solve linear equations of the form $zx = b$, where $z \neq 0$. The solution is $x = z^{-1}b$.

numbers for the new value of m. A closer look shows that the problem is easy to resolve. The easiest solution is to consult a table of primes. An analytical solution is not much harder to obtain. First, number theory [82] tells us that primes are abundant. More precisely, for any integer k there is a prime in the interval $[k^3, (k+1)^3]$. So, if we are aiming for a table size of about m, we determine k such that $k^3 \leq m \leq (k+1)^3$ and then search for a prime in this interval. How does this search work? Any nonprime in the interval must have a divisor which is at most $\sqrt{(k+1)^3} = (k+1)^{3/2}$. We therefore iterate over the numbers from 1 to $(k+1)^{3/2}$, and for each such j remove its multiples in $[k^3, (k+1)^3]$. For each fixed j, this takes time $((k+1)^3 - k^3)/j = O(k^2/j)$. The total time required is

$$\sum_{j \leq (k+1)^{3/2}} O\left(\frac{k^2}{j}\right) = k^2 \sum_{j \leq (k+1)^{3/2}} O\left(\frac{1}{j}\right)$$

$$= O\left(k^2 \ln\left((k+1)^{3/2}\right)\right) = O(k^2 \ln k) = o(m)$$

and hence is negligible compared with the cost of initializing a table of size m. The second equality in the equation above uses the harmonic sum (A.12).

Exercise 4.8 (strings as keys). Implement the universal family $H^\cdot$ for strings. Assume that each character requires eight bits (= a byte). You may assume that the table size is at least $m = 257$. The time for evaluating a hash function should be proportional to the length of the string being processed. Input strings may have arbitrary lengths not known in advance. Hint: compute the random vector $\mathbf{a}$ lazily, extending it only when needed.

Exercise 4.9 (hashing using bit matrix multiplication). For this exercise, keys are bit strings of length k, i.e., $Key = \{0, 1\}^k$, and the table size m is a power of two, say $m = 2^w$. Each $w \times k$ matrix M with entries in $\{0, 1\}$ defines a hash function h_M. For $x \in \{0, 1\}^k$, let $h_M(x) = Mx \bmod 2$, i.e., $h_M(x)$ is a matrix–vector product computed modulo 2. The resulting w-bit vector is interpreted as a number in $[0 \ldots m-1]$. Let

$$H^{\text{lin}} = \left\{ h_M : M \in \{0, 1\}^{w \times k} \right\} .$$

For $M = \begin{pmatrix} 1 & 0 & 1 & 1 \\ 0 & 1 & 1 & 1 \end{pmatrix}$ and $x = (1, 0, 0, 1)^T$, we have $Mx \bmod 2 = (0, 1)^T$. Note that multiplication modulo two is the logical AND operation, and that addition modulo two is the logical exclusive-OR operation $\oplus$.

(a) Explain how $h_M(x)$ can be evaluated using k bit-parallel exclusive-OR operations. Hint: the ones in x select columns of M. Add the selected columns.

(b) Explain how $h_M(x)$ can be evaluated using w bit-parallel AND operations and w parity operations. Many machines provide an instruction $parity(y)$ that returns one if the number of ones in y is odd, and zero otherwise. Hint: multiply each row of M by x.

(c) We now want to show that H^{lin} is 1-universal. (1) Show that for any two keys $x \neq y$, any bit position j, where x and y differ, and any choice of the columns M_i of the matrix with $i \neq j$, there is exactly one choice of a column M_j such that $h_M(x) = h_M(y)$. (2) Count the number of ways to choose $k - 1$ columns of M. (3) Count the total number of ways to choose M. (4) Compute the probability $\text{prob}(h_M(x) = h_M(y))$ for $x \neq y$ if M is chosen randomly.

*Exercise 4.10 (more matrix multiplication). Define a class of hash functions

$$H^\times = \left\{ h_M : M \in \{0..p-1\}^{w \times k} \right\}$$

that generalizes the class H^{lin} by using arithmetic modulo p for some prime number p. Show that $H^\times$ is 1-universal. Explain how $H^\cdot$ is a special case of $H^\times$.

Exercise 4.11 (simple linear hash functions). Assume that $Key = 0..p - 1 = \mathbb{Z}_p$ for some prime number p. For $a, b \in \mathbb{Z}_p$, let $h_{(a,b)}(x) = ((ax + b) \bmod p) \bmod m$, and $m \leq p$. For example, if $p = 97$ and $m = 8$, we have $h_{(23,73)}(2) = ((23 \cdot 2 + 73) \bmod 97) \bmod 8 = 22 \bmod 8 = 6$. Let

$$H^* = \left\{ h_{(a,b)} : a, b \in 0..p-1 \right\} .$$

Show that this family is $(\lceil p/m \rceil / (p/m))^2$-universal.

Exercise 4.12 (continuation). Show that the following holds for the class H^* defined in the previous exercise. For any pair of distinct keys x and y and any i and j in $0..m - 1$, $\text{prob}(h_{(a,b)}(x) = i \text{ and } h_{(a,b)}(y) = j) \leq c/m^2$ for some constant c.

Exercise 4.13 (a counterexample). Let $Key = 0..p - 1$, and consider the set of hash functions

$$H^{\text{fool}} = \left\{ h_{(a,b)} : a, b \in 0..p-1 \right\}$$

with $h_{(a,b)}(x) = (ax + b) \bmod m$. Show that there is a set S of $\lceil p/m \rceil$ keys such that for any two keys x and y in S, all functions in H^{fool} map x and y to the same value. Hint: let $S = \{0, m, 2m, \ldots, \lfloor p/m \rfloor m\}$.

Exercise 4.14 (table size 2^ℓ). Let $Key = 0..2^k - 1$. Show that the family of hash functions

$$H^\gg = \left\{ h_a : 0 < a < 2^k \wedge a \text{ is odd} \right\}$$

with $h_a(x) = (ax \bmod 2^k) \operatorname{div} 2^{k-\ell}$ is 2-universal. Hint: see [53].

Exercise 4.15 (table lookup). Let $m = 2^w$, and view keys as $k + 1$-tuples, where the zeroth element is a w-bit number and the remaining elements are a-bit numbers for some small constant a. A hash function is defined by tables t_1 to t_k, each having a size $s = 2^a$ and storing bit strings of length w. We then have

$$h_{\oplus(t_1,\ldots,t_k)}((x_0,x_1,\ldots,x_k)) = x_0 \oplus \bigoplus_{i=1}^{k} t_i[x_i] \ ,$$

i.e., x_i selects an element in table t_i, and then the bitwise exclusive-OR of x_0 and the $t_i[x_i]$ is formed. Show that

$$H^{\oplus[]} = \left\{ h_{(t_1,\ldots,t_k)} : t_i \in \{0..m-1\}^s \right\}$$

is 1-universal.

4.3 Hashing with Linear Probing

Hashing with chaining is categorized as a *closed* hashing approach because each table entry has to cope with all elements hashing to it. In contrast, *open* hashing schemes open up other table entries to take the overflow from overloaded fellow entries. This added flexibility allows us to do away with secondary data structures such as linked lists – all elements are stored directly in table entries. Many ways of organizing open hashing have been investigated [153]. We shall explore only the simplest scheme. Unused entries are filled with a special element $\bot$. An element e is stored in the entry $t[h(e)]$ or further to the right. But we only go away from the index $h(e)$ with good reason: if e is stored in $t[i]$ with $i > h(e)$, then the positions $h(e)$ to $i-1$ are occupied by other elements.

The implementations of *insert* and *find* are trivial. To insert an element e, we linearly scan the table starting at $t[h(e)]$, until a free entry is found, where e is then stored. Figure 4.2 gives an example. Similarly, to find an element e, we scan the table, starting at $t[h(e)]$, until the element is found. The search is aborted when an empty table entry is encountered. So far, this sounds easy enough, but we have to deal with one complication. What happens if we reach the end of the table during an insertion? We choose a very simple fix by allocating m' table entries to the right of the largest index produced by the hash function h. For "benign" hash functions, it should be sufficient to choose m' much smaller than m in order to avoid table overflows. Alternatively, one may treat the table as a cyclic array; see Exercise 4.16 and Sect. 3.4. This alternative is more robust but slightly slower.

The implementation of *remove* is nontrivial. Simply overwriting the element with $\bot$ does not suffice, as it may destroy the invariant. Assume that $h(x) = h(z)$, $h(y) = h(x) + 1$, and x, y, and z are inserted in this order. Then z is stored at position $h(x) + 2$. Overwriting y with $\bot$ will make z inaccessible. There are three solutions. First, we can disallow removals. Second, we can mark y but not actually remove it. Searches are allowed to stop at $\bot$, but not at marked elements. The problem with this approach is that the number of nonempty cells (occupied or marked) keeps increasing, so that searches eventually become slow. This can be mitigated only by introducing the additional complication of periodic reorganizations of the table. Third, we can actively restore the invariant. Assume that we want to remove the element at i. We overwrite it with $\bot$ leaving a "hole". We then scan the entries to the right

insert : axe, chop, clip, cube, dice, fell, hack, hash, lop, slash

an	bo	cp	dq	er	fs	gt	hu	iv	jw	kx	ly	mz
t 0	1	2	3	4	5	6	7	8	9	10	11	12
⊥	⊥	⊥	⊥	axe	⊥	⊥	⊥	⊥	⊥	⊥	⊥	⊥
⊥	⊥	chop	⊥	axe	⊥	⊥	⊥	⊥	⊥	⊥	⊥	⊥
⊥	⊥	chop	clip	axe	⊥	⊥	⊥	⊥	⊥	⊥	⊥	⊥
⊥	⊥	chop	clip	axe	cube	⊥	⊥	⊥	⊥	⊥	⊥	⊥
⊥	⊥	chop	clip	axe	cube	dice	⊥	⊥	⊥	⊥	⊥	⊥
⊥	⊥	chop	clip	axe	cube	dice	⊥	⊥	⊥	⊥	fell	⊥
⊥	⊥	chop	clip	axe	cube	dice	⊥	⊥	⊥	hack	fell	⊥
⊥	⊥	chop	clip	axe	cube	dice	hash	⊥	⊥	⊥	fell	⊥
⊥	⊥	chop	clip	axe	cube	dice	hash	lop	⊥	hack	fell	⊥
⊥	⊥	chop	clip	axe	cube	dice	hash	lop	slash	hack	fell	⊥

remove ⇓ clip

an	bo	cp	dq	er	fs	gt	hu	iv	jw	kx	ly	mz
⊥	⊥	chop	~~clip~~	axe	cube	dice	hash	lop	slash	hack	fell	⊥
⊥	⊥	chop	lop	axe	cube	dice	hash	~~lop~~	slash	hack	fell	⊥
⊥	⊥	chop	lop	axe	cube	dice	hash	slash	~~slash~~	hack	fell	⊥
⊥	⊥	chop	lop	axe	cube	dice	hash	slash	⊥	hack	fell	⊥

Fig. 4.2. Hashing with linear probing. We have a table *t* with 13 entries storing synonyms of "(to) hash". The hash function maps the last character of the word to the integers 0..12 as indicated above the table: a and n are mapped to 0, b and o are mapped to 1, and so on. First, the words are inserted in alphabetical order. Then "clip" is removed. The figure shows the state changes of the table. Gray areas show the range that is scanned between the state changes

of i to check for violations of the invariant. We set j to $i+1$. If $t[j] = \bot$, we are finished. Otherwise, let f be the element stored in $t[j]$. If $h(f) > i$, there is nothing to do and we increment j. If $h(f) \leq i$, leaving the hole would violate the invariant, and f would not be found anymore. We therefore move f to $t[i]$ and write $\bot$ into $t[j]$. In other words, we swap f and the hole. We set the hole position i to its new position j and continue with $j := j + 1$. Figure 4.2 gives an example.

Exercise 4.16 (cyclic linear probing). Implement a variant of linear probing, where the table size is m rather than $m + m'$. To avoid overflow at the right-hand end of the array, make probing wrap around. (1) Adapt *insert* and *remove* by replacing increments with $i := i + 1 \bmod m$. (2) Specify a predicate *between*(i, j, k) that is true if and only if i is cyclically between j and k. (3) Reformulate the invariant using *between*. (4) Adapt *remove*.

Exercise 4.17 (unbounded linear probing). Implement unbounded hash tables using linear probing and universal hash functions. Pick a new random hash function whenever the table is reallocated. Let α, β, and γ denote constants with $1 < \gamma < \beta <$

α that we are free to choose. Keep track of the number of stored elements n. Expand the table to $m = \beta n$ if $n > m/\gamma$. Shrink the table to $m = \beta n$ if $n < m/\alpha$. If you do not use cyclic probing as in Exercise 4.16, set $m' = \delta m$ for some $\delta < 1$ and reallocate the table if the right-hand end should overflow.

4.4 Chaining Versus Linear Probing

We have seen two different approaches to hash tables, chaining and linear probing. Which one is better? This question is beyond theoretical analysis, as the answer depends on the intended use and many technical parameters. We shall therefore discuss some qualitative issues and report on some experiments performed by us.

An advantage of chaining is referential integrity. Subsequent find operations for the same element will return the same location in memory, and hence references to the results of find operations can be established. In contrast, linear probing moves elements during element removal and hence invalidates references to them.

An advantage of linear probing is that each table access touches a contiguous piece of memory. The memory subsystems of modern processors are optimized for this kind of access pattern, whereas they are quite slow at chasing pointers when the data does not fit into cache memory. A disadvantage of linear probing is that search times become high when the number of elements approaches the table size. For chaining, the expected access time remains small. On the other hand, chaining wastes space on pointers that linear probing could use for a larger table. A fair comparison must be based on space consumption and not just on table size.

We have implemented both approaches and performed extensive experiments. The outcome was that both techniques performed almost equally well when they were given the same amount of memory. The differences were so small that details of the implementation, compiler, operating system, and machine used could reverse the picture. Hence we do not report exact figures.

However, we found chaining harder to implement. Only the optimizations discussed in Sect. 4.6 made it competitive with linear probing. Chaining is much slower if the implementation is sloppy or memory management is not implemented well.

4.5 *Perfect Hashing

The hashing schemes discussed so far guarantee only *expected* constant time for the operations *find*, *insert*, and *remove*. This makes them unsuitable for real-time applications that require a worst-case guarantee. In this section, we shall study *perfect hashing*, which guarantees constant worst-case time for *find*. To keep things simple, we shall restrict ourselves to the *static* case, where we consider a fixed set S of n elements with keys k_1 to k_n.

In this section, we use H_m to denote a family of c-universal hash functions with range $0..m-1$. In Exercise 4.11, it is shown that 2-universal classes exist for every

m. For $h \in H_m$, we use $C(h)$ to denote the number of collisions produced by h, i.e., the number of pairs of distinct keys in S which are mapped to the same position:

$$C(h) = \{(x,y) : x,y \in S, \ x \neq y \text{ and } h(x) = h(y)\} \ .$$

As a first step, we derive a bound on the expectation of $C(h)$.

Lemma 4.5. $E[C(h)] \leq cn(n-1)/m$. *Also, for at least half of the functions $h \in H_m$, we have $C(h) \leq 2cn(n-1)/m$.*

Proof. We define $n(n-1)$ indicator random variables $X_{ij}(h)$. For $i \neq j$, let $X_{ij}(h) = 1$ iff $h(k_i) = h(k_j)$. Then $C(h) = \sum_{ij} X_{ij}(h)$, and hence

$$E[C] = E[\sum_{ij} X_{ij}] = \sum_{ij} E[X_{ij}] = \sum_{ij} \text{prob}(X_{ij} = 1) \leq n(n-1) \cdot c/m \ ,$$

where the second equality follows from the linearity of expectations (see (A.2)) and the last equality follows from the universality of H_m. The second claim follows from Markov's inequality (A.4). $\qquad\square$

If we are willing to work with a quadratic-size table, our problem is solved.

Lemma 4.6. *If $m \geq cn(n-1)+1$, at least half of the functions $h \in H_m$ operate injectively on S.*

Proof. By Lemma 4.5, we have $C(h) < 2$ for half of the functions in H_m. Since $C(h)$ is even, $C(h) < 2$ implies $C(h) = 0$, and so h operates injectively on S. $\qquad\square$

So we choose a random $h \in H_m$ with $m \geq cn(n-1)+1$ and check whether it is injective on S. If not, we repeat the exercise. After an average of two trials, we are successful.

In the remainder of this section, we show how to bring the table size down to linear. The idea is to use a two-stage mapping of keys (see Fig. 4.3). The first stage maps keys to buckets of constant average size. The second stage uses a quadratic amount of space for each bucket. We use the information about $C(h)$ to bound the number of keys hashing to any table location. For $\ell \in 0..m-1$ and $h \in H_m$, let B_ℓ^h be the elements in S that are mapped to ℓ by h and let b_ℓ^h be the cardinality of B_ℓ^h.

Lemma 4.7. $C(h) = \sum_\ell b_\ell^h(b_\ell^h - 1)$.

Proof. For any ℓ, the keys in B_ℓ^h give rise to $b_\ell^h(b_\ell^h - 1)$ pairs of keys mapping to the same location. Summation over ℓ completes the proof. $\qquad\square$

The construction of the perfect hash function is now as follows. Let α be a constant, which we shall fix later. We choose a hash function $h \in H_{\lceil \alpha n \rceil}$ to split S into subsets B_ℓ. Of course, we choose h to be in the good half of $H_{\lceil \alpha n \rceil}$, i.e., we choose $h \in H_{\lceil \alpha n \rceil}$ with $C(h) \leq 2cn(n-1)/\lceil \alpha n \rceil \leq 2cn/\alpha$. For each ℓ, let B_ℓ be the elements in S mapped to ℓ and let $b_\ell = |B_\ell|$.

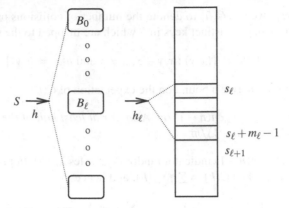

Fig. 4.3. Perfect hashing. The top-level hash function h splits S into subsets $B_0, \dots, B_\ell, \dots$. Let $b_\ell = |B_\ell|$ and $m_\ell = cb_\ell(b_\ell - 1) + 1$. The function h_ℓ maps B_ℓ injectively into a table of size m_ℓ. We arrange the subtables into a single table. The subtable for B_ℓ then starts at position $s_\ell = m_0 + \dots + m_{\ell-1}$ and ends at position $s_\ell + m_\ell - 1$

Now consider any B_ℓ. Let $m_\ell = cb_\ell(b_\ell - 1) + 1$. We choose a function $h_\ell \in H_{m_\ell}$ which maps B_ℓ injectively into $0..m_\ell - 1$. Half of the functions in H_{m_ℓ} have this property by Lemma 4.6 applied to B_ℓ. In other words, h_ℓ maps B_ℓ injectively into a table of size m_ℓ. We stack the various tables on top of each other to obtain one large table of size $\sum_\ell m_\ell$. In this large table, the subtable for B_ℓ starts at position $s_\ell = m_0 + m_1 + \dots + m_{\ell-1}$. Then

$$\ell := h(x); \quad \textbf{return } s_\ell + h_\ell(x)$$

computes an injective function on S. This function is bounded by

$$\sum_\ell m_\ell \leq \lceil \alpha n \rceil + c \cdot \sum_\ell b_\ell(b_\ell - 1)$$
$$\leq 1 + \alpha n + c \cdot C(h)$$
$$\leq 1 + \alpha n + c \cdot 2cn/\alpha$$
$$\leq 1 + (\alpha + 2c^2/\alpha)n,$$

and hence we have constructed a perfect hash function that maps S into a linearly sized range, namely $0..(\alpha + 2c^2/\alpha)n$. In the derivation above, the first inequality uses the definition of the m_ℓ's, the second inequality uses Lemma 4.7, and the third inequality uses $C(h) \leq 2cn/\alpha$. The choice $\alpha = \sqrt{2}c$ minimizes the size of the range. For $c = 1$, the size of the range is $2\sqrt{2}n$.

Theorem 4.8. *For any set of n keys, a perfect hash function with range $0..2\sqrt{2}n$ can be constructed in linear expected time.*

Constructions with smaller ranges are known. Also, it is possible to support insertions and deletions.

Exercise 4.18 (dynamization). We outline a scheme for "dynamization" here. Consider a fixed S, and choose $h \in H_{2\lceil \alpha n \rceil}$. For any ℓ, let $m_\ell = 2cb_\ell(b_\ell - 1) + 1$, i.e., all m's are chosen to be twice as large as in the static scheme. Construct a perfect hash function as above. Insertion of a new x is handled as follows. Assume that h maps x onto ℓ. If h_ℓ is no longer injective, choose a new h_ℓ. If b_ℓ becomes so large that $m_\ell = cb_\ell(b_\ell - 1) + 1$, choose a new h.

4.6 Implementation Notes

Although hashing is an algorithmically simple concept, a clean, efficient, robust implementation can be surprisingly nontrivial. Less surprisingly, the hash functions are the most important issue. Most applications seem to use simple, very fast hash functions based on exclusive-OR, shifting, and table lookup rather than universal hash functions; see, for example, www.burtleburtle.net/bob/hash/doobs.html or search for "hash table" on the Internet. Although these functions seem to work well in practice, we believe that the universal families of hash functions described in Sect. 4.2 are competitive. Unfortunately, there is no implementation study covering all of the fastest families. Thorup [191] implemented a fast family with additional properties. In particular, the family $H^{\oplus[]}$ considered in Exercise 4.15 should be suitable for integer keys, and Exercise 4.8 formulates a good function for strings. It might be possible to implement the latter function to run particularly fast using the SIMD instructions of modern processors that allow the parallel execution of several operations.

Hashing with chaining uses only very specialized operations on sequences, for which singly linked lists are ideally suited. Since these lists are extremely short, some deviations from the implementation scheme described in Sect. 3.1 are in order. In particular, it would be wasteful to store a dummy item with each list. Instead, one should use a single shared dummy item to mark the ends of all lists. This item can then be used as a sentinel element for *find* and *remove*, as in the function *findNext* in Sect. 3.1.1. This trick not only saves space, but also makes it likely that the dummy item will reside in the cache memory.

With respect to the first element of the lists, there are two alternatives. One can either use a table of pointers and store the first element outside the table, or store the first element of each list directly in the table. We refer to these alternatives as *slim tables* and *fat tables*, respectively. Fat tables are usually faster and more space-efficient. Slim tables are superior when the elements are very large. Observe that a slim table wastes the space occupied by m pointers and that a fat table wastes the space of the unoccupied table positions (see Exercise 4.6). Slim tables also have the advantage of referential integrity even when tables are reallocated. We have already observed this complication for unbounded arrays in Sect. 3.6.

Comparing the space consumption of hashing with chaining and hashing with linear probing is even more subtle than is outlined in Sect. 4.4. On the one hand, linked lists burden the memory management with many small pieces of allocated memory; see Sect. 3.1.1 for a discussion of memory management for linked lists.

On the other hand, implementations of unbounded hash tables based on chaining can avoid occupying two tables during reallocation by using the following method. First, concatenate all lists into a single list L. Deallocate the old table. Only then, allocate the new table. Finally, scan L, moving the elements to the new table.

Exercise 4.19. Implement hashing with chaining and hashing with linear probing on your own machine using your favorite programming language. Compare their performance experimentally. Also, compare your implementations with hash tables available in software libraries. Use elements of size eight bytes.

Exercise 4.20 (large elements). Repeat the above measurements with element sizes of 32 and 128. Also, add an implementation of *slim chaining*, where table entries only store pointers to the first list element.

Exercise 4.21 (large keys). Discuss the impact of large keys on the relative merits of chaining versus linear probing. Which variant will profit? Why?

Exercise 4.22. Implement a hash table data type for very large tables stored in a file. Should you use chaining or linear probing? Why?

4.6.1 C++

The C++ standard library does not (yet) define a hash table data type. However, the popular implementation by SGI (http://www.sgi.com/tech/stl/) offers several variants: *hash_set*, *hash_map*, *hash_multiset*, and *hash_multimap*.[7] Here "set" stands for the kind of interface used in this chapter, whereas a "map" is an associative array indexed by keys. The prefix "multi" indicates data types that allow multiple elements with the same key. Hash functions are implemented as *function objects*, i.e., the class *hash<T>* overloads the operator "( )" so that an object can be used like a function. The reason for this approach is that it allows the hash function to store internal state such as random coefficients.

LEDA [118] offers several hashing-based implementations of dictionaries. The class $h\_array\langle Key, T\rangle$ offers associative arrays for storing objects of type T. This class requires a user-defined hash function $int\ Hash(Key\&)$ that returns an integer value which is then mapped to a table index by LEDA. The implementation uses hashing with chaining and adapts the table size to the number of elements stored. The class *map* is similar but uses a built-in hash function.

Exercise 4.23 (associative arrays). Implement a C++ class for associative arrays. Support *operator* [ ] for any index type that supports a hash function. Make sure that H[x] = ... works as expected if x is the key of a new element.

4.6.2 Java

The class *java.util.HashMap* implements unbounded hash tables using the function *hashCode* defined in the class *Object* as a hash function.

---

[7] Future versions of the standard will have these data types using the word "*unordered*" instead of the word "*hash*".

4.7 Historical Notes and Further Findings

Hashing with chaining and hashing with linear probing were used as early as the 1950s [153]. The analysis of hashing began soon after. In the 1960s and 1970s, average-case analysis in the spirit of Theorem 4.1 and Exercise 4.7 prevailed. Various schemes for random sets of keys or random hash functions were analyzed. An early survey paper was written by Morris [143]. The book [112] contains a wealth of material. For example, it analyzes linear probing assuming random hash functions. Let n denote the number of elements stored, let m denote the size of the table and set $\alpha = n/m$. The expected number T_{fail} of table accesses for an unsuccessful search and the number T_{success} for a successful search are about

$$T_{\text{fail}} \approx \frac{1}{2}\left(1 + \left(\frac{1}{1-\alpha}\right)^2\right) \text{ and } T_{\text{success}} \approx \frac{1}{2}\left(1 + \frac{1}{1-\alpha}\right),$$

respectively. Note that these numbers become very large when n approaches m, i.e., it is not a good idea to fill a linear-probing table almost completely.

Universal hash functions were introduced by Carter and Wegman [34]. The original paper proved Theorem 4.3 and introduced the universal classes discussed in Exercise 4.11. More on universal hashing can be found in [10].

Perfect hashing was a black art until Fredman, Komlos, and Szemeredi [66] introduced the construction shown in Theorem 4.8. Dynamization is due to Dietzfelbinger et al. [54]. Cuckoo hashing [152] is an alternative approach to perfect hashing.

A *minimal perfect hash function* bijectively maps a set $S \subseteq 0..U - 1$ to the range $0..n - 1$, where $n = |S|$. The art is to do this in constant time and with very little space – $\Omega(n)$ bits is a lower bound. There are now practicable schemes that achieve this bound [29]. One variant assumes three truly random hash functions[8] $h_i : 0..U - 1 \to im/3..(i+1)m/3 - 1$ for $i \in 0..2$ and $m \approx 1.23n$. In a first *mapping step*, a key $k \in 0..U - 1$ is mapped to

$$p(k) = h_i(k), \text{ where } i = g(h_0(k)) \oplus g(h_1(k)) \oplus g(h_2(k)) \bmod 3,$$

and $g : 0..\alpha n \to \{0,1,2\}$ is a lookup table that is precomputed using some simple greedy algorithm. In a second *ranking step*, the set $0..\alpha n$ is mapped to $0..n - 1$, i.e., $h(k) = rank(p(k))$, where $rank(i) = |\{k \in S : p(k) \leq i\}|$. This ranking problem is a standard problem in the field of *succinct data structures* and can be supported in constant time using $O(n)$ bits of space.

Universal hashing bounds the probability of any two keys colliding. A more general notion is k-way independence, where k is a positive integer. A family H of hash functions is k-*way independent* if for some constant c, any k distinct keys x_1 to x_k, and any k hash values a_1 to a_k, $prob(h(x_1) = a_1 \wedge \cdots \wedge h(x_k) = a_k) \leq c/m^k$. The polynomials of degree $k - 1$ with random coefficients are a simple k-wise independent family of hash functions [34] (see Exercise 4.12).

---

[8] Actually implementing such hash functions would require $\Omega(n\log n)$ bits. However, this problem can be circumvented by first splitting S into many small *buckets*. We can then use the same set of fully random hash functions for all the buckets [55].

Cryptographic hash functions need stronger properties than what we need for hash tables. Roughly, for a value x, it should be difficult to come up with a value x' such that $h(x') = h(x)$.

5

Sorting and Selection

Telephone directories are sorted alphabetically by last name. Why? Because a sorted index can be searched quickly. Even in the telephone directory of a huge city, one can usually find a name in a few seconds. In an unsorted index, nobody would even try to find a name. To a first approximation, this chapter teaches you how to turn an unordered collection of elements into an ordered collection, i.e., how to sort the collection. However, sorting has many other uses as well. An early example of a massive data-processing task was the statistical evaluation of census data; 1500 people needed seven years to manually process data from the US census in 1880. The engineer Herman Hollerith,[1] who participated in this evaluation as a statistician, spent much of the ten years to the next census developing counting and sorting machines for mechanizing this gigantic endeavor. Although the 1890 census had to evaluate more people and more questions, the basic evaluation was finished in 1891. Hollerith's company continued to play an important role in the development of the information-processing industry; since 1924, it has been known as International Business Machines (IBM). Sorting is important for census statistics because one often wants to form subcollections, for example, all persons between age 20 and 30 and living on a farm. Two applications of sorting solve the problem. First, we sort all persons by age and form the subcollection of persons between 20 and 30 years of age. Then we sort the subcollection by home and extract the subcollection of persons living on a farm.

Although we probably all have an intuitive concept of what *sorting* is about, let us give a formal definition. The input is a sequence $s = \langle e_1, \ldots, e_n \rangle$ of n elements. Each element e_i has an associated *key* $k_i = key(e_i)$. The keys come from an ordered universe, i.e., there is a *linear order* $\leq$ defined on the keys.[2] For ease of notation, we extend the comparison relation to elements so that $e \leq e'$ if and only

---

[1] The photograph was taken by C. M. Bell (see US Library of Congress's Prints and Photographs Division, ID cph.3c15982).

[2] A linear order is a reflexive, transitive, and weakly antisymmetric relation. In contrast to a *total order*, it allows equivalent elements (see Appendix A for details).

if $key(e) \leq key(e')$. The task is to produce a sequence $s' = \langle e'_1, \ldots, e'_n \rangle$ such that s' is a permutation of s and such that $e'_1 \leq e'_2 \leq \cdots \leq e'_n$. Observe that the ordering of equivalent elements is arbitrary.

Although different comparison relations for the same data type may make sense, the most frequent relations are the obvious order for numbers and the *lexicographic order* (see Appendix A) for tuples, strings, and sequences. The lexicographic order for strings comes in different flavors. We may treat corresponding lower-case and upper-case characters as being equivalent, and different rules for treating accented characters are used in different contexts.

Exercise 5.1. Given linear orders $\leq_A$ for A and $\leq_B$ for B, define a linear order on $A \times B$.

Exercise 5.2. Define a total order for complex numbers with the property that $x \leq y$ implies $|x| \leq |y|$.

Sorting is a ubiquitous algorithmic tool; it is frequently used as a preprocessing step in more complex algorithms. We shall give some examples.

- *Preprocessing for fast search.* In Sect. 2.5 on binary search, we have already seen that a sorted directory is easier to search, both for humans and computers. Moreover, a sorted directory supports additional operations, such as finding all elements in a certain range. We shall discuss searching in more detail in Chap. 7. Hashing is a method for searching unordered sets.
- *Grouping.* Often, we want to bring equal elements together to count them, eliminate duplicates, or otherwise process them. Again, hashing is an alternative. But sorting has advantages, since we shall see rather fast, space-efficient, deterministic sorting algorithm that scale to huge data sets.
- *Processing in a sorted order.* Certain algorithms become very simple if the inputs are processed in sorted order. Exercise 5.3 gives an example. Other examples are Kruskal's algorithm in Sect. 11.3 and several of the algorithms for the knapsack problem in Chap. 12. You may also want to remember sorting when you solve Exercise 8.6 on interval graphs.

In Sect. 5.1, we shall introduce several simple sorting algorithms. They have quadratic complexity, but are still useful for small input sizes. Moreover, we shall learn some low-level optimizations. Section 5.2 introduces *mergesort*, a simple divide-and-conquer sorting algorithm that runs in time $O(n \log n)$. Section 5.3 establishes that this bound is optimal for all *comparison-based* algorithms, i.e., algorithms that treat elements as black boxes that can only be compared and moved around. The *quicksort* algorithm described in Sect. 5.4 is again based on the divide-and-conquer principle and is perhaps the most frequently used sorting algorithm. Quicksort is also a good example of a randomized algorithm. The idea behind quicksort leads to a simple algorithm for a problem related to sorting. Section 5.5 explains how the k-th smallest of n elements can be *selected* in time $O(n)$. Sorting can be made even faster than the lower bound obtained in Sect. 5.3 by looking at the bit patterns of the keys, as explained in Sect. 5.6. Finally, Section 5.7 generalizes quicksort and mergesort to very good algorithms for sorting inputs that do not fit into internal memory.

Exercise 5.3 (a simple scheduling problem). A hotel manager has to process n advance bookings of rooms for the next season. His hotel has k identical rooms. Bookings contain an arrival date and a departure date. He wants to find out whether there are enough rooms in the hotel to satisfy the demand. Design an algorithm that solves this problem in time $O(n\log n)$. Hint: consider the set of all arrivals and departures. Sort the set and process it in sorted order.

Exercise 5.4 (sorting with a small set of keys). Design an algorithm that sorts n elements in $O(k\log k + n)$ expected time if there are only k different keys appearing in the input. Hint: combine hashing and sorting.

Exercise 5.5 (checking). It is easy to check whether a sorting routine produces a sorted output. It is less easy to check whether the output is also a permutation of the input. But here is a fast and simple Monte Carlo algorithm for integers: (a) Show that $\langle e_1, \dots, e_n \rangle$ is a permutation of $\langle e_1', \dots, e_n' \rangle$ iff the polynomial

$$q(z) := \prod_{i=1}^{n} (z - e_i) - \prod_{i=1}^{n} (z - e_i')$$

is identically zero. Here, z is a variable. (b) For any $\varepsilon > 0$, let p be a prime with $p > \max\{n/\varepsilon, e_1, \dots, e_n, e_1', \dots, e_n'\}$. Now the idea is to evaluate the above polynomial mod p for a random value $z \in [0..p-1]$. Show that if $\langle e_1, \dots, e_n \rangle$ is *not* a permutation of $\langle e_1', \dots, e_n' \rangle$, then the result of the evaluation is zero with probability at most ε. Hint: a nonzero polynomial of degree n has at most n zeros.

5.1 Simple Sorters

We shall introduce two simple sorting techniques here: *selection sort* and *insertion sort*.

Selection sort repeatedly selects the smallest element from the input sequence, deletes it, and adds it to the end of the output sequence. The output sequence is initially empty. The process continues until the input sequence is exhausted. For example,

$$\langle\rangle, \langle 4,7,1,1 \rangle \rightsquigarrow \langle 1 \rangle, \langle 4,7,1 \rangle \rightsquigarrow \langle 1,1 \rangle, \langle 4,7 \rangle \rightsquigarrow \langle 1,1,4 \rangle, \langle 7 \rangle \rightsquigarrow \langle 1,1,4,7 \rangle, \langle\rangle \ .$$

The algorithm can be implemented such that it uses a single array of n elements and works *in-place*, i.e., it needs no additional storage beyond the input array and a constant amount of space for loop counters, etc. The running time is quadratic.

Exercise 5.6 (simple selection sort). Implement selection sort so that it sorts an array with n elements in time $O(n^2)$ by repeatedly scanning the input sequence. The algorithm should be in-place, i.e., the input sequence and the output sequence should share the same array. Hint: the implementation operates in n phases numbered 1 to n. At the beginning of the i-th phase, the first $i-1$ locations of the array contain the $i-1$ smallest elements in sorted order and the remaining $n-i+1$ locations contain the remaining elements in arbitrary order.

In Sect. 6.5, we shall learn about a more sophisticated implementation where the input sequence is maintained as a *priority queue*. Priority queues support efficient repeated selection of the minimum element. The resulting algorithm runs in time $O(n \log n)$ and is frequently used. It is efficient, it is deterministic, it works in-place, and the input sequence can be dynamically extended by elements that are larger than all previously selected elements. The last feature is important in discrete-event simulations, where events are to be processed in increasing order of time and processing an event may generate further events in the future.

Selection sort maintains the invariant that the output sequence is sorted by carefully choosing the element to be deleted from the input sequence. *Insertion sort* maintains the same invariant by choosing an arbitrary element of the input sequence but taking care to insert this element at the right place in the output sequence. For example,

$$\langle\rangle, \langle 4,7,1,1\rangle \rightsquigarrow \langle 4\rangle, \langle 7,1,1\rangle \rightsquigarrow \langle 4,7\rangle, \langle 1,1\rangle \rightsquigarrow \langle 1,4,7\rangle, \langle 1\rangle \rightsquigarrow \langle 1,1,4,7\rangle, \langle\rangle .$$

Figure 5.1 gives an in-place array implementation of insertion sort. The implementation is straightforward except for a small trick that allows the inner loop to use only a single comparison. When the element e to be inserted is smaller than all previously inserted elements, it can be inserted at the beginning without further tests. Otherwise, it suffices to scan the sorted part of a from right to left while e is smaller than the current element. This process has to stop, because $a[1] \leq e$.

In the worst case, insertion sort is quite slow. For example, if the input is sorted in decreasing order, each input element is moved all the way to $a[1]$, i.e., in iteration i of the outer loop, i elements have to be moved. Overall, we obtain

$$\sum_{i=2}^{n}(i-1) = -n + \sum_{i=1}^{n} i = \frac{n(n+1)}{2} - n = \frac{n(n-1)}{2} = \Omega(n^2)$$

movements of elements (see also (A.11)).

Nevertheless, insertion sort is useful. It is fast for small inputs (say, $n \leq 10$) and hence can be used as the base case in divide-and-conquer algorithms for sorting.

Procedure *insertionSort*(a : *Array* $[1..n]$ **of** *Element*)
  for $i := 2$ **to** n **do**
    invariant $a[1] \leq \cdots \leq a[i-1]$
    // move $a[i]$ to the right place
    $e := a[i]$
    if $e < a[1]$ **then**   // new minimum
        for $j := i$ **downto** 2 **do** $a[j] := a[j-1]$
        $a[1] := e$
    else   // use $a[1]$ as a sentinel
        for $j := i$ **downto** $-\infty$ **while** $a[j-1] > e$ **do** $a[j] := a[j-1]$
        $a[j] := e$

Fig. 5.1. Insertion sort

Furthermore, in some applications the input is already "almost" sorted, and in this situation insertion sort will be fast.

Exercise 5.7 (almost sorted inputs). Prove that insertion sort runs in time $O(n + D)$ where $D = \sum_i |r(e_i) - i|$ and $r(e_i)$ is the *rank* (position) of e_i in the sorted output.

Exercise 5.8 (average-case analysis). Assume that the input to an insertion sort is a permutation of the numbers 1 to n. Show that the average execution time over all possible permutations is $\Omega(n^2)$. Hint: argue formally that about one-third of the input elements in the right third of the array have to be moved to the left third of the array. Can you improve the argument to show that, on average, $n^2/4 - O(n)$ iterations of the inner loop are needed?

Exercise 5.9 (insertion sort with few comparisons). Modify the inner loops of the array-based insertion sort algorithm in Fig. 5.1 so that it needs only $O(n \log n)$ comparisons between elements. Hint: use binary search as discussed in Chap. 7. What is the running time of this modification of insertion sort?

Exercise 5.10 (efficient insertion sort?). Use the data structure for sorted sequences described in Chap. 7 to derive a variant of insertion sort that runs in time $O(n \log n)$.

*Exercise 5.11 (formal verification). Use your favorite verification formalism, for example Hoare calculus, to prove that insertion sort produces a permutation of the input (i.e., it produces a sorted permutation of the input).

5.2 Mergesort – an $O(n \log n)$ Sorting Algorithm

Mergesort is a straightforward application of the divide-and-conquer principle. The unsorted sequence is split into two parts of about equal size. The parts are sorted recursively, and the sorted parts are merged into a single sorted sequence. This approach is efficient because merging two sorted sequences a and b is quite simple. The globally smallest element is either the first element of a or the first element of b. So we move the smaller element to the output, find the second smallest element using the same approach, and iterate until all elements have been moved to the output. Figure 5.2 gives pseudocode, and Figure 5.3 illustrates a sample execution. If the sequences are represented as linked lists (see, Sect. 3.1), no allocation and deallocation of list items is needed. Each iteration of the inner loop of *merge* performs one element comparison and moves one element to the output. Each iteration takes constant time. Hence, merging runs in linear time.

Theorem 5.1. *The function merge, applied to sequences of total length n, executes in time $O(n)$ and performs at most $n - 1$ element comparisons.*

For the running time of mergesort, we obtain the following result.

Theorem 5.2. *Mergesort runs in time $O(n \log n)$ and performs no more than $\lceil n \log n \rceil$ element comparisons.*

Function $mergeSort(\langle e_1, \ldots, e_n \rangle)$: *Sequence* **of** *Element*
  if $n = 1$ **then return** $\langle e_1 \rangle$
  else return $merge($ $mergeSort(\langle e_1, \ldots, e_{\lfloor n/2 \rfloor} \rangle),$
                  $mergeSort(\langle e_{\lfloor n/2 \rfloor + 1}, \ldots, e_n \rangle))$

// merging two sequences represented as lists
Function $merge(a, b :$ *Sequence* **of** *Element*) : *Sequence* **of** *Element*
  $c := \langle \rangle$
  loop
    invariant a, b, and c are sorted and $\forall e \in c, e' \in a \cup b : e \leq e'$
    if $a.isEmpty$ **then** $c.concat(b);$ **return** c
    if $b.isEmpty$ **then** $c.concat(a);$ **return** c
    if $a.first \leq b.first$ **then** $c.moveToBack(a.first)$
    else $c.moveToBack(b.first)$

Fig. 5.2. Mergesort

a	b	c	operation
$\langle 1,2,7 \rangle$	$\langle 1,2,8,8 \rangle$	$\langle \rangle$	move a
$\langle 2,7 \rangle$	$\langle 1,2,8,8 \rangle$	$\langle 1 \rangle$	move b
$\langle 2,7 \rangle$	$\langle 2,8,8 \rangle$	$\langle 1,1 \rangle$	move a
$\langle 7 \rangle$	$\langle 2,8,8 \rangle$	$\langle 1,1,2 \rangle$	move b
$\langle 7 \rangle$	$\langle 8,8 \rangle$	$\langle 1,1,2,2 \rangle$	move a
$\langle \rangle$	$\langle 8,8 \rangle$	$\langle 1,1,2,2,7 \rangle$	concat b
$\langle \rangle$	$\langle \rangle$	$\langle 1,1,2,2,7,8,8 \rangle$	

Fig. 5.3. Execution of $mergeSort(\langle 2,7,1,8,2,8,1 \rangle)$. The *left* part illustrates the recursion in *mergeSort* and the *right* part illustrates the *merge* in the outermost call

Proof. Let $C(n)$ denote the worst-case number of element comparisons performed. We have $C(1) = 0$ and $C(n) \leq C(\lfloor n/2 \rfloor) + C(\lceil n/2 \rceil) + n - 1$, using Theorem 5.1. The master theorem for recurrence relations (2.5) suggests that $C(n) = O(n \log n)$. We shall give two proofs. The first proof shows that $C(n) \leq 2n \lceil \log n \rceil$, and the second proof shows that $C(n) \leq n \lceil \log n \rceil$.

For n a power of two, we define $D(1) = 0$ and $D(n) = 2D(n/2) + n$. Then $D(n) = n \log n$ for n a power of two, by the master theorem for recurrence relations. We claim that $C(n) \leq D(2^k)$, where k is such that $2^{k-1} < n \leq 2^k$. Then $C(n) \leq D(2^k) = 2^k k \leq 2n \lceil \log n \rceil$. It remains to argue the inequality $C(n) \leq D(2^k)$. We use induction on k. For $k = 0$, we have $n = 1$ and $C(1) = 0 = D(1)$, and the claim certainly holds. For $k > 1$, we observe that $\lfloor n/2 \rfloor \leq \lceil n/2 \rceil \leq 2^{k-1}$, and hence

$$C(n) \leq C(\lfloor n/2 \rfloor) + C(\lceil n/2 \rceil) + n - 1 \leq 2D(2^{k-1}) + 2^k - 1 \leq D(2^k) \, .$$

This completes the first proof. We turn now to the second, refined proof. We prove that

$$C(n) \leq n \lceil \log n \rceil - 2^{\lceil \log n \rceil} + 1 \leq n \log n$$

by induction over n. For $n = 1$, the claim is certainly true. So, assume $n > 1$. We distinguish two cases. Assume first that we have $2^{k-1} < \lfloor n/2 \rfloor \leq \lceil n/2 \rceil \leq 2^k$ for some integer k. Then $\lceil \log \lfloor n/2 \rfloor \rceil = \lceil \log \lceil n/2 \rceil \rceil = k$ and $\lceil \log n \rceil = k+1$, and hence

$$
\begin{aligned}
C(n) &\leq C(\lfloor n/2 \rfloor) + C(\lceil n/2 \rceil) + n - 1 \\
&\leq \left(\lfloor n/2 \rfloor k - 2^k + 1 \right) + \left(\lceil n/2 \rceil k - 2^k + 1 \right) + n - 1 \\
&= nk + n - 2^{k+1} + 1 = n(k+1) - 2^{k+1} + 1 = n \lceil \log n \rceil - 2^{\lceil \log n \rceil} + 1 .
\end{aligned}
$$

Otherwise, we have $\lfloor n/2 \rfloor = 2^{k-1}$ and $\lceil n/2 \rceil = 2^{k-1} + 1$ for some integer k, and therefore $\lceil \log \lfloor n/2 \rfloor \rceil = k - 1$, $\lceil \log \lceil n/2 \rceil \rceil = k$, and $\lceil \log n \rceil = k+1$. Thus

$$
\begin{aligned}
C(n) &\leq C(\lfloor n/2 \rfloor) + C(\lceil n/2 \rceil) + n - 1 \\
&\leq \left(2^{k-1}(k-1) - 2^{k-1} + 1 \right) + \left((2^{k-1} + 1)k - 2^k + 1 \right) + 2^k + 1 - 1 \\
&= (2^k + 1)k - 2^{k-1} - 2^{k-1} + 1 + 1 \\
&= (2^k + 1)(k+1) - 2^{k+1} + 1 = n \lceil \log n \rceil - 2^{\lceil \log n \rceil} + 1 .
\end{aligned}
$$

The bound for the execution time can be verified using a similar recurrence relation.

$\square$

Mergesort is the method of choice for sorting linked lists and is therefore frequently used in functional and logical programming languages that have lists as their primary data structure. In Sect. 5.3, we shall see that mergesort is basically optimal as far as the number of comparisons is concerned; so it is also a good choice if comparisons are expensive. When implemented using arrays, mergesort has the additional advantage that it streams through memory in a sequential way. This makes it efficient in memory hierarchies. Section 5.7 has more on that issue. Mergesort is still not the usual method of choice for an efficient array-based implementation, however, since *merge* does not work in-place. (But see Exercise 5.17 for a possible way out.)

Exercise 5.12. Explain how to insert k new elements into a sorted list of size n in time $O(k \log k + n)$.

Exercise 5.13. We discussed *merge* for lists but used abstract sequences for the description of *mergeSort*. Give the details of *mergeSort* for linked lists.

Exercise 5.14. Implement mergesort in a functional programming language.

Exercise 5.15. Give an efficient array-based implementation of mergesort in your favorite imperative programming language. Besides the input array, allocate one auxiliary array of size n at the beginning and then use these two arrays to store all intermediate results. Can you improve the running time by switching to insertion sort for small inputs? If so, what is the optimal switching point in your implementation?

Exercise 5.16. The way we describe *merge*, there are three comparisons for each loop iteration – one element comparison and two termination tests. Develop a variant using sentinels that needs only one termination test. Can you do this task without appending dummy elements to the sequences?

Exercise 5.17. Exercise 3.20 introduced a list-of-blocks representation for sequences. Implement merging and mergesort for this data structure. During merging, reuse emptied input blocks for the output sequence. Compare the space and time efficiency of mergesort for this data structure, for plain linked lists, and for arrays. Pay attention to constant factors.

5.3 A Lower Bound

Algorithms give upper bounds on the complexity of a problem. By the preceding discussion, we know that we can sort n items in time $O(n \log n)$. Can we do better, and maybe even achieve linear time? A "yes" answer requires a better algorithm and its analysis. But how could we potentially argue a "no" answer? We would have to argue that no algorithm, however ingenious, can run in time $o(n \log n)$. Such an argument is called a *lower bound*. So what is the answer? The answer is both no and yes. The answer is no, if we restrict ourselves to comparison-based algorithms, and the answer is yes if we go beyond comparison-based algorithms. We shall discuss non-comparison-based sorting in Sect. 5.6.

So what is a comparison-based sorting algorithm? The input is a set $\{e_1, \ldots, e_n\}$ of n elements, and the only way the algorithm can learn about its input is by comparing elements. In particular, it is not allowed to exploit the representation of keys, for example as bit strings. Deterministic comparison-based algorithms can be viewed as trees. They make an initial comparison; for instance, the algorithms asks "$e_i \leq e_j$?", with outcomes yes and no. On the basis of the outcome, the algorithm proceeds to the next comparison. The key point is that the comparison made next depends only on the outcome of all preceding comparisons and nothing else. Figure 5.4 shows a sorting tree for three elements.

When the algorithm terminates, it must have collected sufficient information so that it can commit to a permutation of the input. When can it commit? We perform the following thought experiment. We assume that the input keys are distinct, and consider any of the $n!$ permutations of the input, say π. The permutation π corresponds to the situation that $e_{\pi(1)} < e_{\pi(2)} < \cdots < e_{\pi(n)}$. We answer all questions posed by the algorithm so that they conform to the ordering defined by π. This will lead us to a leaf ℓ_π of the comparison tree.

Lemma 5.3. *Let π and σ be two distinct permutations of n elements. The leaves ℓ_π and ℓ_σ must then be distinct.*

Proof. Assume otherwise. In a leaf, the algorithm commits to some ordering of the input and so it cannot commit to both π and σ. Say it commits to π. Then, on an input ordered according to σ, the algorithm is incorrect, which is a contradiction.   □

The lemma above tells us that any comparison tree for sorting must have at least $n!$ leaves. Since a tree of depth T has at most 2^T leaves, we must have

$$2^T \geq n! \quad \text{or} \quad T \geq \log n! \, .$$

Via Stirling's approximation to the factorial (A.9), we obtain

$$T \geq \log n! \geq \log \left(\frac{n}{e}\right)^n = n \log n - n \log e \, .$$

Theorem 5.4. *Any comparison-based sorting algorithm needs $n \log n - O(n)$ comparisons in the worst case.*

We state without proof that this bound also applies to randomized sorting algorithms and to the average-case complexity of sorting, i.e., worst-case instances are not much more difficult than random instances. Furthermore, the bound applies even if we only want to solve the seemingly simpler problem of checking whether some element appears twice in a sequence.

Theorem 5.5. *Any comparison-based sorting algorithm needs $n \log n - O(n)$ comparisons on average, i.e.,*

$$\frac{\sum_\pi d_\pi}{n!} = n \log n - O(n) \, ,$$

where the sum extends over all $n!$ permutations of the n elements and d_π is the depth of the leaf ℓ_π.

Exercise 5.18. Show that any comparison-based algorithm for determining the smallest of n elements requires $n - 1$ comparisons. Show also that any comparison-based algorithm for determining the smallest and second smallest elements of n elements requires at least $n - 1 + \log n$ comparisons. Give an algorithm with this performance.

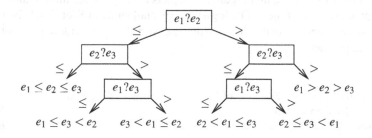

Fig. 5.4. A tree that sorts three elements. We first compare e_1 and e_2. If $e_1 \leq e_2$, we compare e_2 with e_3. If $e_2 \leq e_3$, we have $e_1 \leq e_2 \leq e_3$ and are finished. Otherwise, we compare e_1 with e_3. For either outcome, we are finished. If $e_1 > e_2$, we compare e_2 with e_3. If $e_2 > e_3$, we have $e_1 > e_2 > e_3$ and are finished. Otherwise, we compare e_1 with e_3. For either outcome, we are finished. The worst-case number of comparisons is three. The average number is $(2 + 3 + 3 + 2 + 3 + 3)/6 = 8/3$

Exercise 5.19. The *element uniqueness problem* is the task of deciding whether in a set of n elements, all elements are pairwise distinct. Argue that comparison-based algorithms require $\Omega(n\log n)$ comparisons. Why does this not contradict the fact that we can solve the problem in linear expected time using hashing?

Exercise 5.20 (lower bound for average case). With the notation above, let d_π be the depth of the leaf ℓ_π. Argue that $A = (1/n!)\sum_\pi d_\pi$ is the average-case complexity of a comparison-based sorting algorithm. Try to show that $A \geq \log n!$. Hint: prove first that $\sum_\pi 2^{-d_\pi} \leq 1$. Then consider the minimization problem "minimize $\sum_\pi d_\pi$ subject to $\sum_\pi 2^{-d_\pi} \leq 1$". Argue that the minimum is attained when all d_i's are equal.

Exercise 5.21 (sorting small inputs optimally). Give an algorithm for sorting k elements using at most $\lceil \log k! \rceil$ element comparisons. (a) For $k \in \{2,3,4\}$, use merge-sort. (b) For $k = 5$, you are allowed to use seven comparisons. This is difficult. Merge-sort does not do the job, as it uses up to eight comparisons. (c) For $k \in \{6,7,8\}$, use the case $k = 5$ as a subroutine.

5.4 Quicksort

Quicksort is a divide-and-conquer algorithm that is complementary to the mergesort algorithm of Sect. 5.2. Quicksort does all the difficult work *before* the recursive calls. The idea is to distribute the input elements into two or more sequences that represent nonoverlapping ranges of key values. Then, it suffices to sort the shorter sequences recursively and concatenate the results. To make the duality to mergesort complete, we would like to split the input into two sequences of equal size. Unfortunately, this is a nontrivial task. However, we can come close by picking a random splitter element. The splitter element is usually called the *pivot*. Let p denote the pivot element chosen. Elements are classified into three sequences a, b, and c of elements that are smaller than, equal to, or larger than p, respectively. Figure 5.5 gives a high-level realization of this idea, and Figure 5.6 depicts a sample execution. Quicksort has an expected execution time of $O(n\log n)$, as we shall show in Sect. 5.4.1. In Sect. 5.4.2, we discuss refinements that have made quicksort the most widely used sorting algorithm in practice.

Function *quickSort*(s : *Sequence* **of** *Element*) : *Sequence* **of** *Element*
    if $|s| \leq 1$ **then return** s // base case
    pick $p \in s$ uniformly at random   // pivot key
    $a := \langle e \in s : e < p \rangle$
    $b := \langle e \in s : e = p \rangle$
    $c := \langle e \in s : e > p \rangle$
    return *concatenation of quickSort*(a), b, *and quickSort*(c)

Fig. 5.5. High-level formulation of quicksort for lists

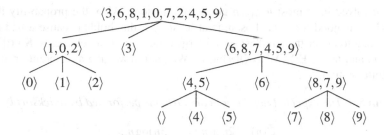

Fig. 5.6. Execution of *quickSort* (Fig. 5.5) on $\langle 3,6,8,1,0,7,2,4,5,9 \rangle$ using the first element of a subsequence as the pivot. The first call of quicksort uses 3 as the pivot and generates the subproblems $\langle 1,0,2 \rangle$, $\langle 3 \rangle$, and $\langle 6,8,7,4,5,9 \rangle$. The recursive call for the third subproblem uses 6 as a pivot and generates the subproblems $\langle 4,5 \rangle$, $\langle 6 \rangle$, and $\langle 8,7,9 \rangle$

5.4.1 Analysis

To analyze the running time of quicksort for an input sequence $s = \langle e_1, \ldots, e_n \rangle$, we focus on the number of element comparisons performed. We allow *three-way* comparisons here, with possible outcomes "smaller", "equal", and "larger". Other operations contribute only constant factors and small additive terms to the execution time.

Let $C(n)$ denote the worst-case number of comparisons needed for any input sequence of size n and any choice of pivots. The worst-case performance is easily determined. The subsequences a, b, and c in Fig. 5.5 are formed by comparing the pivot with all other elements. This makes $n-1$ comparisons. Assume there are k elements smaller than the pivot and k' elements larger than the pivot. We obtain $C(0) = C(1) = 0$ and

$$C(n) \le n - 1 + \max \left\{ C(k) + C(k') : 0 \le k \le n-1, 0 \le k' < n-k \right\} .$$

It is easy to verify by induction that

$$C(n) \le \frac{n(n-1)}{2} = \Theta(n^2) .$$

The worst case occurs if all elements are different and we always pick the largest or smallest element as the pivot. Thus $C(n) = n(n-1)/2$.

The expected performance is much better. We first argue for an $\mathrm{O}(n \log n)$ bound and then show a bound of $2n \ln n$. We concentrate on the case where all elements are different. Other cases are easier because a pivot that occurs several times results in a larger middle sequence b that need not be processed any further. Consider a fixed element e_i, and let X_i denote the total number of times e_i is compared with a pivot element. Then $\sum_i X_i$ is the total number of comparisons. Whenever e_i is compared with a pivot element, it ends up in a smaller subproblem. Therefore, $X_i \le n-1$, and we have another proof for the quadratic upper bound. Let us call a comparison "good" for e_i if e_i moves to a subproblem of at most three-quarters the size. Any e_i

can be involved in at most $\log_{4/3} n$ good comparisons. Also, the probability that a pivot which is good for e_i is chosen, is at least $1/2$; this holds because a bad pivot must belong to either the smallest or the largest quarter of the elements. So $E[X_i] \leq 2\log_{4/3} n$, and hence $E[\sum_i X_i] = O(n \log n)$. We shall now give a different argument and a better bound.

Theorem 5.6. *The expected number of comparisons performed by quicksort is*

$$\bar{C}(n) \leq 2n \ln n \leq 1.45 n \log n .$$

Proof. Let $s' = \langle e'_1, \ldots, e'_n \rangle$ denote the elements of the input sequence in sorted order. Elements e'_i and e'_j are compared at most once, and only if one of them is picked as a pivot. Hence, we can count comparisons by looking at the indicator random variables X_{ij}, $i < j$, where $X_{ij} = 1$ if e'_i and e'_j are compared and $X_{ij} = 0$ otherwise. We obtain

$$\bar{C}(n) = E\left[\sum_{i=1}^n \sum_{j=i+1}^n X_{ij} \right] = \sum_{i=1}^n \sum_{j=i+1}^n E[X_{ij}] = \sum_{i=1}^n \sum_{j=i+1}^n \text{prob}(X_{ij} = 1) .$$

The middle transformation follows from the linearity of expectations (A.2). The last equation uses the definition of the expectation of an indicator random variable $E[X_{ij}] = \text{prob}(X_{ij} = 1)$. Before we can further simplify the expression for $\bar{C}(n)$, we need to determine the probability of X_{ij} being 1.

Lemma 5.7. *For any $i < j$, $\text{prob}(X_{ij} = 1) = \dfrac{2}{j-i+1}$.*

Proof. Consider the $j-i+1$-element set $M = \{e'_i, \ldots, e'_j\}$. As long as no pivot from M is selected, e'_i and e'_j are not compared, but all elements from M are passed to the same recursive calls. Eventually, a pivot p from M is selected. Each element in M has the same chance $1/|M|$ of being selected. If $p = e'_i$ or $p = e'_j$ we have $X_{ij} = 1$. The probability for this event is $2/|M| = 2/(j-i+1)$. Otherwise, e'_i and e'_j are passed to different recursive calls, so that they will never be compared.   □

Now we can finish proving Theorem 5.6 using relatively simple calculations:

$$\bar{C}(n) = \sum_{i=1}^n \sum_{j=i+1}^n \text{prob}(X_{ij} = 1) = \sum_{i=1}^n \sum_{j=i+1}^n \frac{2}{j-i+1} = \sum_{i=1}^n \sum_{k=2}^{n-i+1} \frac{2}{k}$$

$$\leq \sum_{i=1}^n \sum_{k=2}^n \frac{2}{k} = 2n \sum_{k=2}^n \frac{1}{k} = 2n(H_n - 1) \leq 2n(1 + \ln n - 1) = 2n \ln n .$$

For the last three steps, recall the properties of the n-th harmonic number $H_n := \sum_{k=1}^n 1/k \leq 1 + \ln n$ (A.12).   □

Note that the calculations in Sect. 2.8 for left-to-right maxima were very similar, although we had quite a different problem at hand.

5.4.2 *Refinements

We shall now discuss refinements of the basic quicksort algorithm. The resulting algorithm, called *qsort*, works in-place, and is fast and space-efficient. Figure 5.7 shows the pseudocode, and Figure 5.8 shows a sample execution. The refinements are nontrivial and we need to discuss them carefully.

Procedure $qSort(a : Array$ **of** $Element$; $\ell, r : \mathbb{N})$	// Sort the subarray $a[\ell..r]$
while $r - \ell + 1 > n_0$ **do**	// Use divide-and-conquer.
$j := pickPivotPos(a, \ell, r)$	// Pick a pivot element and
$swap(a[\ell], a[j])$	// bring it to the first position.
$p := a[\ell]$	// p is the pivot now.
$i := \ell$; $j := r$	
repeat	// a: $\boxed{\ell \quad\quad i\rightarrow\ \leftarrow j \quad\quad r}$
while $a[i] < p$ **do** $i{+}{+}$	// Skip over elements
while $a[j] > p$ **do** $j{-}{-}$	// already in the correct subarray.
if $i \le j$ **then**	// If partitioning is not yet complete,
$swap(a[i], a[j])$; $i{+}{+}$; $j{-}{-}$	// (*) swap misplaced elements and go on.
until $i > j$	// Partitioning is complete.
if $i < (\ell + r)/2$ **then** $qSort(a, \ell, j)$; $\ell := i$	// Recurse on
else $qSort(a, i, r)$; $r := j$	// smaller subproblem.
endwhile	
$insertionSort(a[\ell..r])$	// faster for small $r - \ell$

Fig. 5.7. Refined quicksort for arrays

The function *qsort* operates on an array a. The arguments ℓ and r specify the subarray to be sorted. The outermost call is $qsort(a, 1, n)$. If the size of the subproblem is smaller than some constant n_0, we resort to a simple algorithm[3] such as the insertion sort shown in Fig. 5.1. The best choice for n_0 depends on many details of the machine and compiler and needs to be determined experimentally; a value somewhere between 10 and 40 should work fine under a variety of conditions.

The pivot element is chosen by a function *pickPivotPos* that we shall not specify further. The correctness does not depend on the choice of the pivot, but the efficiency does. Possible choices are the first element; a random element; the median ("middle") element of the first, middle, and last elements; and the median of a random sample consisting of k elements, where k is either a small constant, say three, or a number depending on the problem size, say $\lceil \sqrt{r - \ell + 1} \rceil$. The first choice requires the least amount of work, but gives little control over the size of the subproblems; the last choice requires a nontrivial but still sublinear amount of work, but yields balanced

---

[3] Some authors propose leaving small pieces unsorted and cleaning up at the end using a single insertion sort that will be fast, according to Exercise 5.7. Although this nice trick reduces the number of instructions executed, the solution shown is faster on modern machines because the subarray to be sorted will already be in cache.

```
i →              ← j          3 6 8 1 0 7 2 4 5 9
3 6 8 1 0 7 2 4 5 9           2 0 1│8 6 7 3 4 5 9
2 6 8 1 0 7 3 4 5 9           1 0│2│5 6 7 3 4│8 9
2 0 8 1 6 7 3 4 5 9           0 1│ │4 3│7 6 5│8 9
2 0 1 8 6 7 3 4 5 9               │3 4│5 6│7│
      j i                        │   │5 6│ │
```

Fig. 5.8. Execution of *qSort* (Fig. 5.7) on $\langle 3,6,8,1,0,7,2,4,5,9 \rangle$ using the first element as the pivot and $n_0 = 1$. The *left-hand side* illustrates the first partitioning step, showing elements in **bold** that have just been swapped. The *right-hand side* shows the result of the recursive partitioning operations

subproblems with high probability. After selecting the pivot p, we swap it into the first position of the subarray (= position ℓ of the full array).

The repeat–until loop partitions the subarray into two proper (smaller) subarrays. It maintains two indices i and j. Initially, i is at the left end of the subarray and j is at the right end; i scans to the right, and j scans to the left. After termination of the loop, we have $i = j+1$ or $i = j+2$, all elements in the subarray $a[\ell..j]$ are no larger than p, all elements in the subarray $a[i..r]$ are no smaller than p, each subarray is a proper subarray, and, if $i = j+2$, $a[i+1]$ is equal to p. So, recursive calls $qSort(a,\ell,j)$ and $qsort(a,i,r)$ will complete the sort. We make these recursive calls in a nonstandard fashion; this is discussed below.

Let us see in more detail how the partitioning loops work. In the first iteration of the repeat loop, i does not advance at all but remains at ℓ, and j moves left to the rightmost element no larger than p. So j ends at ℓ or at a larger value; generally, the latter is the case. In either case, we have $i \leq j$. We swap $a[i]$ and $a[j]$, increment i, and decrement j. In order to describe the total effect more generally, we distinguish cases.

If p is the unique smallest element of the subarray, j moves all the way to ℓ, the swap has no effect, and $j = \ell - 1$ and $i = \ell + 1$ after the increment and decrement. We have an empty subproblem $\ell..\ell - 1$ and a subproblem $\ell + 1..r$. Partitioning is complete, and both subproblems are proper subproblems.

If j moves down to $i+1$, we swap, increment i to $\ell + 1$, and decrement j to ℓ. Partitioning is complete, and we have the subproblems $\ell..\ell$ and $\ell + 1..r$. Both subarrays are proper subarrays.

If j stops at an index larger than $i+1$, we have $\ell < i \leq j < r$ after executing the line in Fig. 5.7 marked (*). Also, all elements left of i are at most p (and there is at least one such element), and all elements right of j are at least p (and there is at least one such element). Since the scan loop for i skips only over elements smaller than p and the scan loop for j skips only over elements larger than p, further iterations of the repeat loop maintain this invariant. Also, all further scan loops are guaranteed to terminate by the claims in parentheses and so there is no need for an index-out-of-bounds check in the scan loops. In other words, the scan loops are as concise as possible; they consist of a test and an increment or decrement.

Let us next study how the repeat loop terminates. If we have $i \leq j+2$ after the scan loops, we have $i \leq j$ in the termination test. Hence, we continue the loop. If we have $i = j-1$ after the scan loops, we swap, increment i, and decrement j. So $i = j+1$, and the repeat loop terminates with the proper subproblems $\ell..j$ and $i..r$. The case $i = j$ after the scan loops can occur only if $a[i] = p$. In this case, the swap has no effect. After incrementing i and decrementing j, we have $i = j+2$, resulting in the proper subproblems $\ell..j$ and $j+2..r$, separated by one occurrence of p. Finally, when $i > j$ after the scan loops, then either i goes beyond j in the first scan loop, or j goes below i in the second scan loop. By our invariant, i must stop at $j+1$ in the first case, and then j does not move in its scan loop or j must stop at $i-1$ in the second case. In either case, we have $i = j+1$ after the scan loops. The line marked (*) is not executed, so that we have subproblems $\ell..j$ and $i..r$, and both subproblems are proper.

We have now shown that the partitioning step is correct, terminates, and generates proper subproblems.

Exercise 5.22. Is it safe to make the scan loops skip over elements equal to p? Is this safe if it is known that the elements of the array are pairwise distinct?

The refined quicksort handles recursion in a seemingly strange way. Recall that we need to make the recursive calls $qSort(a, \ell, j)$ and $qSort(a, i, r)$. We may make these calls in either order. We exploit this flexibility by making the call for the smaller subproblem first. The call for the larger subproblem would then be the last thing done in $qSort$. This situation is known as *tail recursion* in the programming-language literature. Tail recursion can be eliminated by setting the parameters (ℓ and r) to the right values and jumping to the first line of the procedure. This is precisely what the while loop does. Why is this manipulation useful? Because it guarantees that the recursion stack stays logarithmically bounded; the precise bound is $\lceil \log(n/n_0) \rceil$. This follows from the fact that we make a single recursive call for a subproblem which is at most half the size.

Exercise 5.23. What is the maximal depth of the recursion stack without the "smaller subproblem first" strategy? Give a worst-case example.

*Exercise 5.24 (sorting strings using multikey quicksort [22]). Let s be a sequence of n strings. We assume that each string ends in a special character that is different from all "normal" characters. Show that the function $mkqSort(s, 1)$ below sorts a sequence s consisting of *different* strings. What goes wrong if s contains equal strings? Solve this problem. Show that the expected execution time of $mkqSort$ is $O(N + n \log n)$ if $N = \sum_{e \in s} |e|$.

Function $mkqSort(s : Sequence \text{ of } String, i : \mathbb{N}) : Sequence \text{ of } String$
    assert $\forall e, e' \in s : e[1..i-1] = e'[1..i-1]$
    if $|s| \leq 1$ **then return** s // base case
    pick $p \in s$ uniformly at random   // pivot character
    return concatenation of $mkqSort(\langle e \in s : e[i] < p[i] \rangle, i)$,
                              $mkqSort(\langle e \in s : e[i] = p[i] \rangle, i+1)$, *and*
                              $mkqSort(\langle e \in s : e[i] > p[i] \rangle, i)$

Exercise 5.25. Implement several different versions of *qSort* in your favorite programming language. Use and do not use the refinements discussed in this section, and study the effect on running time and space consumption.

5.5 Selection

Selection refers to a class of problems that are easily reduced to sorting but do not require the full power of sorting. Let $s = \langle e_1, \dots, e_n \rangle$ be a sequence and call its sorted version $s' = \langle e'_1, \dots, e'_n \rangle$. Selection of the smallest element requires determining e'_1, selection of the largest requires determining e'_n, and selection of the k-th smallest requires determining e'_k. Selection of the median refers to selecting $e_{\lfloor n/2 \rfloor}$. Selection of the median and also of quartiles is a basic problem in statistics. It is easy to determine the smallest element or the smallest and the largest element by a single scan of a sequence in linear time. We now show that the k-th smallest element can also be determined in linear time. The simple recursive procedure shown in Fig. 5.9 solves the problem.

This procedure is akin to quicksort and is therefore called *quickselect*. The key insight is that it suffices to follow one of the recursive calls. As before, a pivot is chosen, and the input sequence s is partitioned into subsequences a, b, and c containing the elements smaller than the pivot, equal to the pivot, and larger than the pivot, respectively. If $|a| \geq k$, we recurse on a, and if $k > |a| + |b|$, we recurse on c with a suitably adjusted k. If $|a| < k \leq |a| + |b|$, the task is solved: the pivot has rank k and we return it. Observe that the latter case also covers the situation $|s| = k = 1$, and hence no special base case is needed. Figure 5.10 illustrates the execution of quickselect.

```
// Find an element with rank k
Function select(s : Sequence of Element; k : ℕ) : Element
    assert |s| ≥ k
    pick p ∈ s uniformly at random                                    // pivot key
    a := ⟨e ∈ s : e < p⟩
    if |a| ≥ k then return select(a, k)                               //  [  a  ]ᵏ
    b := ⟨e ∈ s : e = p⟩
    if |a| + |b| ≥ k then return p                                    //  [ a | b = ⟨p,...,p⟩ ]ᵏ
    c := ⟨e ∈ s : e > p⟩
    return select(c, k − |a| − |b|)                                   //  [ a | b | c ]ᵏ
```

Fig. 5.9. Quickselect

s	k	p	a	b	c
$\langle 3,1,4,5,9,2,6,5,3,5,8 \rangle$	6	2	$\langle 1 \rangle$	$\langle 2 \rangle$	$\langle 3,4,5,9,6,5,3,5,8 \rangle$
$\langle 3,4,5,9,\mathbf{6},5,3,5,8 \rangle$	4	6	$\langle 3,4,5,5,3,4 \rangle$	$\langle 6 \rangle$	$\langle 9,8 \rangle$
$\langle 3,4,\mathbf{5},5,3,5 \rangle$	4	5	$\langle 3,4,3 \rangle$	$\langle 5,5,5 \rangle$	$\langle \rangle$

Fig. 5.10. The execution of $select(\langle 3,1,4,5,9,2,6,5,3,5,8,6 \rangle, 6)$. The middle element (**bold**) of the current s is used as the pivot p

As for quicksort, the worst-case execution time of quickselect is quadratic. But the expected execution time is linear and hence is a logarithmic factor faster than quicksort.

Theorem 5.8. *The quickselect algorithm runs in expected time* $O(n)$ *on an input of size* n.

Proof. We shall give an analysis that is simple and shows a linear expected execution time. It does not give the smallest constant possible. Let $T(n)$ denote the expected execution time of quickselect. We call a pivot *good* if neither $|a|$ nor $|c|$ is larger than $2n/3$. Let γ denote the probability that a pivot is good; then $\gamma \geq 1/3$. We now make the conservative assumption that the problem size in the recursive call is reduced only for good pivots and that, even then, it is reduced only by a factor of $2/3$. Since the work outside the recursive call is linear in n, there is an appropriate constant c such that

$$T(n) \leq cn + \gamma T\left(\frac{2n}{3}\right) + (1-\gamma)T(n).$$

Solving for $T(n)$ yields

$$T(n) \leq \frac{cn}{\gamma} + T\left(\frac{2n}{3}\right) \leq 3cn + T\left(\frac{2n}{3}\right) \leq 3c\left(n + \frac{2n}{3} + \frac{4n}{9} + \ldots\right)$$

$$\leq 3cn \sum_{i \geq 0} \left(\frac{2}{3}\right)^i \leq 3cn \frac{1}{1 - 2/3} = 9cn.$$

$\square$

Exercise 5.26. Modify quickselect so that it returns the k smallest elements.

Exercise 5.27. Give a selection algorithm that permutes an array in such a way that the k smallest elements are in entries $a[1], \ldots, a[k]$. No further ordering is required except that $a[k]$ should have rank k. Adapt the implementation tricks used in the array-based quicksort to obtain a nonrecursive algorithm with fast inner loops.

Exercise 5.28 (streaming selection).

(a) Develop an algorithm that finds the k-th smallest element of a sequence that is presented to you one element at a time in an order you cannot control. You have only space $O(k)$ available. This models a situation where voluminous data arrives over a network or at a sensor.
(b) Refine your algorithm so that it achieves a running time $O(n \log k)$. You may want to read some of Chap. 6 first.
*(c) Refine the algorithm and its analysis further so that your algorithm runs in average-case time $O(n)$ if $k = O(n/\log n)$. Here, "average" means that all orders of the elements in the input sequence are equally likely.

5.6 Breaking the Lower Bound

The title of this section is, of course, nonsense. A lower bound is an absolute statement. It states that, in a certain model of computation, a certain task cannot be carried out faster than the bound. So a lower bound cannot be broken. But be careful. It cannot be broken within the model of computation used. The lower bound does not exclude the possibility that a faster solution exists in a richer model of computation. In fact, we may even interpret the lower bound as a guideline for getting faster. It tells us that we must enlarge our repertoire of basic operations in order to get faster.

What does this mean in the case of sorting? So far, we have restricted ourselves to comparison-based sorting. The only way to learn about the order of items was by comparing two of them. For structured keys, there are more effective ways to gain information, and this will allow us to break the $\Omega(n \log n)$ lower bound valid for comparison-based sorting. For example, numbers and strings have structure; they are sequences of digits and characters, respectively.

Let us start with a very simple algorithm *Ksort* that is fast if the keys are small integers, say in the range $0..K-1$. The algorithm runs in time $O(n+K)$. We use an array $b[0..K-1]$ of *buckets* that are initially empty. We then scan the input and insert an element with key k into bucket $b[k]$. This can be done in constant time per element, for example by using linked lists for the buckets. Finally, we concatenate all the nonempty buckets to obtain a sorted output. Figure 5.11 gives the pseudocode. For example, if the elements are pairs whose first element is a key in the range $0..3$ and

$$s = \langle (3,a), (1,b), (2,c), (3,d), (0,e), (0,f), (3,g), (2,h), (1,i) \rangle ,$$

we obtain $b = [\langle (0,e), (0,f) \rangle, \ \langle (1,b), (1,i) \rangle, \ \langle (2,c), (2,h) \rangle, \ \langle (3,a), (3,d), (3,g) \rangle]$ and output $\langle (0,e), (0,f), (1,b), (1,i), (2,c), (2,h), (3,a), (3,d), (3,g) \rangle$. This example illustrates an important property of *Ksort*. It is *stable*, i.e., elements with the same key inherit their relative order from the input sequence. Here, it is crucial that elements are *appended* to their respective bucket.

KSort can be used as a building block for sorting larger keys. The idea behind *radix sort* is to view integer keys as numbers represented by digits in the range $0..K-1$. Then *KSort* is applied once for each digit. Figure 5.12 gives a radix-sorting algorithm for keys in the range $0..K^d-1$ that runs in time $O(d(n+K))$. The elements are first sorted by their least significant digit (*LSD radix sort*), then by the second least significant digit, and so on until the most significant digit is used for sorting. It is not obvious why this works. The correctness rests on the stability of

Procedure *KSort(s : Sequence of Element)*
$b = \langle \langle \rangle, \ldots, \langle \rangle \rangle$: *Array* $[0..K-1]$ **of** *Sequence* **of** *Element*
foreach $e \in s$ **do** $b[key(e)].pushBack(e)$ //
$s := concatenation\ of\ b[0], \ldots, b[K-1]$

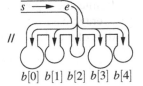

b[0] b[1] b[2] b[3] b[4]

Fig. 5.11. Sorting with keys in the range $0..K-1$

Procedure *LSDRadixSort*(*s* : *Sequence* **of** *Element*)
 for $i := 0$ **to** $d - 1$ **do**   digits
  redefine *key*(*x*) as $(x \ \text{div} \ K^i) \ \text{mod} \ K$ // $x \ \boxed{d-1} \ \cdots \ \boxed{i} \ \cdots \ \boxed{} \ \boxed{0}$
  KSort(*s*)   *key*(*x*)
  invariant *s* is sorted with respect to digits *i*..0

Fig. 5.12. Sorting with keys in $0..K^d - 1$ using least significant digit (LSD) radix sort

Procedure *uniformSort*(*s* : *Sequence* **of** *Element*)
 $n := |s|$
 $b = \langle\langle\rangle, \ldots, \langle\rangle\rangle$: *Array* $[0..n - 1]$ **of** *Sequence* **of** *Element*
 foreach $e \in s$ **do** $b[\lfloor key(e) \cdot n \rfloor].pushBack(e)$
 for $i := 0$ **to** $n - 1$ **do** sort $b[i]$ in time $O(|b[i]| \log |b[i]|)$
 $s :=$ *concatenation of* $b[0], \ldots, b[n - 1]$

Fig. 5.13. Sorting random keys in the range $[0, 1)$

Ksort. Since *KSort* is stable, the elements with the same *i*-th digit remain sorted with respect to digits $i - 1..0$ during the sorting process with respect to digit *i*. For example, if $K = 10$, $d = 3$, and

$$s = \langle 017, 042, 666, 007, 111, 911, 999 \rangle, \text{ we successively obtain}$$
$$s = \langle \mathbf{1}11, \mathbf{9}11, 0\mathbf{4}2, 6\mathbf{6}6, 0\mathbf{1}7, 0\mathbf{0}7, 9\mathbf{9}9 \rangle,$$
$$s = \langle 0\mathbf{0}7, \mathbf{1}11, \mathbf{9}11, 0\mathbf{1}7, 0\mathbf{4}2, 6\mathbf{6}6, 9\mathbf{9}9 \rangle, \text{ and}$$
$$s = \langle \mathbf{0}07, \mathbf{0}17, \mathbf{0}42, \mathbf{1}11, \mathbf{6}66, \mathbf{9}11, \mathbf{9}99 \rangle.$$

Radix sort starting with the most significant digit (*MSD radix sort*) is also possible. We apply *KSort* to the most significant digit and then sort each bucket recursively. The only problem is that the buckets might be much smaller than *K*, so that it would be expensive to apply *KSort* to small buckets. We then have to switch to another algorithm. This works particularly well if we can assume that the keys are uniformly distributed. More specifically, let us now assume that the keys are real numbers with $0 \leq key(e) < 1$. The algorithm *uniformSort* in Fig. 5.13 scales these keys to integers between 0 and $n - 1 = |s| - 1$, and groups them into *n* buckets, where bucket $b[i]$ is responsible for keys in the range $[i/n, (i + 1)/n)$. For example, if $s = \langle 0.8, 0.4, 0.7, 0.6, 0.3 \rangle$, we obtain five buckets responsible for intervals of size 0.2, and

$$b = [\langle\rangle, \ \langle 0.3 \rangle, \ \langle 0.4 \rangle, \ \langle 0.7, 0.6 \rangle, \ \langle 0.8 \rangle] ;$$

only $b[3] = \langle 0.7, 0.6 \rangle$ is a nontrivial subproblem. *uniformSort* is very efficient for *random* keys.

Theorem 5.9. *If the keys are independent uniformly distributed random values in* $[0, 1)$*, uniformSort sorts n keys in expected time* $O(n)$ *and worst-case time* $O(n \log n)$*.*

Proof. We leave the worst-case bound as an exercise and concentrate on the average case. The total execution time T is $O(n)$ for setting up the buckets and concatenating the sorted buckets, plus the time for sorting the buckets. Let T_i denote the time for sorting the i-th bucket. We obtain

$$\mathrm{E}[T] = O(n) + \mathrm{E}\left[\sum_{i<n} T_i\right] = O(n) + \sum_{i<n} \mathrm{E}[T_i] = O(n) + n\mathrm{E}[T_0] \ .$$

The second equality follows from the linearity of expectations (A.2), and the third equality uses the fact that all bucket sizes have the same distribution for uniformly distributed inputs. Hence, it remains to show that $\mathrm{E}[T_0] = O(1)$. We shall prove the stronger claim that $\mathrm{E}[T_0] = O(1)$ even if a quadratic-time algorithm such as insertion sort is used for sorting the buckets. The analysis is similar to the arguments used to analyze the behavior of hashing in Chap. 4.

Let $B_0 = |b[0]|$. We have $\mathrm{E}[T_0] = O\big(\mathrm{E}[B_0^2]\big)$. The random variable B_0 obeys a binomial distribution (A.7) with n trials and success probability $1/n$, and hence

$$\mathrm{prob}(B_0 = i) = \binom{n}{i}\left(\frac{1}{n}\right)^i\left(1 - \frac{1}{n}\right)^{n-i} \le \frac{n^i}{i!}\frac{1}{n^i} = \frac{1}{i!} \le \left(\frac{e}{i}\right)^i \ ,$$

where the last inequality follows from Stirling's approximation to the factorial (A.9). We obtain

$$\mathrm{E}[B_0^2] = \sum_{i\le n} i^2 \mathrm{prob}(B_0 = i) \le \sum_{i\le n} i^2 \left(\frac{e}{i}\right)^i$$

$$\le \sum_{i\le 5} i^2 \left(\frac{e}{i}\right)^i + e^2 \sum_{i\ge 6} \left(\frac{e}{i}\right)^{i-2}$$

$$\le O(1) + e^2 \sum_{i\ge 6} \left(\frac{1}{2}\right)^{i-2} = O(1) \ ,$$

and hence $\mathrm{E}[T] = O(n)$ (note that the split at $i = 6$ allows us to conclude that $e/i \le 1/2$). □

*Exercise 5.29. Implement an efficient sorting algorithm for elements with keys in the range $0..K - 1$ that uses the data structure of Exercise 3.20 for the input and output. The space consumption should be $n + O(n/B + KB)$ for n elements, and blocks of size B.

5.7 *External Sorting

Sometimes the input is so huge that it does not fit into internal memory. In this section, we shall learn how to sort such data sets in the external-memory model introduced in Sect. 2.2. This model distinguishes between a fast internal memory of size M and a large external memory. Data is moved in the memory hierarchy in

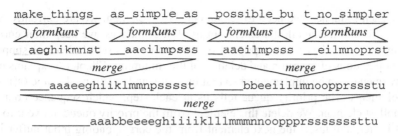

Fig. 5.14. An example of two-way mergesort with initial runs of length 12

blocks of size B. Scanning data is fast in external memory and mergesort is based on scanning. We therefore take mergesort as the starting point for external-memory sorting.

Assume that the input is given as an array in external memory. We shall describe a nonrecursive implementation for the case where the number of elements n is divisible by B. We load subarrays of size M into internal memory, sort them using our favorite algorithm, for example $qSort$, and write the sorted subarrays back to external memory. We refer to the sorted subarrays as *runs*. The *run formation phase* takes n/B block reads and n/B block writes, i.e., a total of $2n/B$ I/Os. We then merge pairs of runs into larger runs in $\lceil \log(n/M) \rceil$ *merge phases*, ending up with a single sorted run. Figure 5.14 gives an example for $n = 48$ and runs of length 12.

How do we merge two runs? We keep one block from each of the two input runs and from the output run in internal memory. We call these blocks *buffers*. Initially, the input buffers are filled with the first B elements of the input runs, and the output buffer is empty. We compare the leading elements of the input buffers and move the smaller element to the output buffer. If an input buffer becomes empty, we fetch the next block of the corresponding input run; if the output buffer becomes full, we write it to external memory.

Each merge phase reads all current runs and writes new runs of twice the length. Therefore, each phase needs n/B block reads and n/B block writes. Summing over all phases, we obtain $(2n/B)(1 + \lceil \log n/M \rceil)$ I/Os. This technique works provided that $M \geq 3B$.

5.7.1 Multiway Mergesort

In general, internal memory can hold many blocks and not just three. We shall describe how to make full use of the available internal memory during merging. The idea is to merge more than just two runs; this will reduce the number of phases. In *k-way merging*, we merge k sorted sequences into a single output sequence. In each step we find the input sequence with the smallest first element. This element is removed and appended to the output sequence. External-memory implementation is easy as long as we have enough internal memory for k input buffer blocks, one output buffer block, and a small amount of additional storage.

For each sequence, we need to remember which element we are currently considering. To find the smallest element out of all k sequences, we keep their current elements in a *priority queue*. A priority queue maintains a set of elements supporting the operations of insertion and deletion of the minimum. Chapter 6 explains how priority queues can be implemented so that insertion and deletion take time $O(\log k)$ for k elements. The priority queue tells us at each step, which sequence contains the smallest element. We delete this element from the priority queue, move it to the output buffer, and insert the next element from the corresponding input buffer into the priority queue. If an input buffer runs dry, we fetch the next block of the corresponding sequence, and if the output buffer becomes full, we write it to the external memory.

How large can we choose k? We need to keep $k+1$ blocks in internal memory and we need a priority queue for k keys. So we need $(k+1)B + O(k) \leq M$ or $k = O(M/B)$. The number of merging phases is reduced to $\lceil \log_k(n/M) \rceil$, and hence the total number of I/Os becomes

$$2\frac{n}{B}\left(1 + \left\lceil \log_{M/B} \frac{n}{M} \right\rceil\right) .\tag{5.1}$$

The difference from binary merging is the much larger base of the logarithm. Interestingly, the above upper bound for the I/O complexity of sorting is also a lower bound [5], i.e., under fairly general assumptions, no external sorting algorithm with fewer I/O operations is possible.

In practice, the number of merge phases will be very small. Observe that a single merge phase suffices as long as $n \leq M^2/B$. We first form M/B runs of length M each and then merge these runs into a single sorted sequence. If internal memory stands for DRAM and "external memory" stands for hard disks, this bound on n is no real restriction, for all practical system configurations.

Exercise 5.30. Show that a multiway mergesort needs only $O(n\log n)$ element comparisons.

Exercise 5.31 (balanced systems). Study the current market prices of computers, internal memory, and mass storage (currently hard disks). Also, estimate the block size needed to achieve good bandwidth for I/O. Can you find any configuration where multiway mergesort would require more than one merging phase for sorting an input that fills all the disks in the system? If so, what fraction of the cost of that system would you have to spend on additional internal memory to go back to a single merging phase?

5.7.2 Sample Sort

The most popular internal-memory sorting algorithm is not mergesort but quicksort. So it is natural to look for an external-memory sorting algorithm based on quicksort. We shall sketch *sample sort*. In expectation, it has the same performance guarantees as multiway mergesort (5.1). Sample sort is easier to adapt to parallel disks and parallel processors than merging-based algorithms. Furthermore, similar algorithms can be used for fast external sorting of integer keys along the lines of Sect. 5.6.

Instead of the single pivot element of quicksort, we now use $k-1$ *splitter elements* $s_1, \ldots, s_{k-1}$ to split an input sequence into k output sequences, or *buckets*. Bucket i gets the elements e for which $s_{i-1} \leq e < s_i$. To simplify matters, we define the artificial splitters $s_0 = -\infty$ and $s_k = \infty$ and assume that all elements have different keys. The splitters should be chosen in such a way that the buckets have a size of roughly n/k. The buckets are then sorted recursively. In particular, buckets that fit into the internal memory can subsequently be sorted internally. Note the similarity to MSD-radix sort described in Sect. 5.6.

The main challenge is to find good splitters quickly. Sample sort uses a fast, simple randomized strategy. For some integer a, we randomly choose $(a+1)k-1$ *sample* elements from the input. The sample S is then sorted internally, and we define the splitters as $s_i = S[(a+1)i]$ for $1 \leq i \leq k-1$, i.e., consecutive splitters are separated by a samples, the first splitter is preceded by a samples, and the last splitter is followed by a samples. Taking $a = 0$ results in a small sample set, but the splitting will not be very good. Moving all elements to the sample will result in perfect splitters, but the sample will be too big. The following analysis shows that setting $a = O(\log k)$ achieves roughly equal bucket sizes at low cost for sampling and sorting the sample.

The most I/O-intensive part of sample sort is the k-way distribution of the input sequence to the buckets. We keep one buffer block for the input sequence and one buffer block for each bucket. These buffers are handled analogously to the buffer blocks in k-way merging. If the splitters are kept in a sorted array, we can find the right bucket for an input element e in time $O(\log k)$ using binary search.

Theorem 5.10. *Sample sort uses*

$$O\left(\frac{n}{B}\left(1 + \left\lceil \log_{M/B} \frac{n}{M} \right\rceil\right)\right)$$

expected I/O steps for sorting n elements. The internal work is $O(n \log n)$.

We leave the detailed proof to the reader and describe only the key ingredient of the analysis here. We use $k = \Theta(\min(n/M, M/B))$ buckets and a sample of size $O(k \log k)$. The following lemma shows that with this sample size, it is unlikely that any bucket has a size much larger than the average. We hide the constant factors behind $O(\cdot)$ notation because our analysis is not very tight in this respect.

Lemma 5.11. *Let $k \geq 2$ and $a+1 = 12 \ln k$. A sample of size $(a+1)k-1$ suffices to ensure that no bucket receives more than $4n/k$ elements with probability at least $1/2$.*

Proof. As in our analysis of quicksort (Theorem 5.6), it is useful to study the sorted version $s' = \langle e'_1, \ldots, e'_n \rangle$ of the input. Assume that there is a bucket with at least $4n/k$ elements assigned to it. We estimate the probability of this event.

We split s' into $k/2$ segments of length $2n/k$. The j-th segment t_j contains elements $e'_{2jn/k+1}$ to $e'_{2(j+1)n/k}$. If $4n/k$ elements end up in some bucket, there must be some segment t_j such that all its elements end up in the same bucket. This can only happen if fewer than $a+1$ samples are taken from t_j, because otherwise at least one splitter would be chosen from t_j and its elements would not end up in a single bucket. Let us concentrate on a fixed j.

We use a random variable X to denote the number of samples taken from t_j. Recall that we take $(a+1)k-1$ samples. For each sample i, $1 \le i \le (a+1)k-1$, we define an indicator variable X_i with $X_i = 1$ if the i-th sample is taken from t_j and $X_i = 0$ otherwise. Then $X = \sum_{1 \le i \le (a+1)k-1} X_i$. Also, the X_i's are independent, and $\mathrm{prob}(X_i = 1) = 2/k$. Independence allows us to use the Chernoff bound (A.5) to estimate the probability that $X < a+1$. We have

$$\mathrm{E}[X] = ((a+1)k-1) \cdot \frac{2}{k} = 2(a+1) - \frac{2}{k} \ge \frac{3(a+1)}{2} .$$

Hence $X < a+1$ implies $X < (1-1/3)\mathrm{E}[X]$, and so we can use (A.5) with $\varepsilon = 1/3$. Thus

$$\mathrm{prob}(X < a+1) \le e^{-(1/9)\mathrm{E}[X]/2} \le e^{-(a+1)/12} = e^{-\ln k} = \frac{1}{k} .$$

The probability that an insufficient number of samples is chosen from a fixed t_j is thus at most $1/k$, and hence the probability that an insufficient number is chosen from some t_j is at most $(k/2) \cdot (1/k) = 1/2$. Thus, with probability at least $1/2$, each bucket receives fewer than $4n/k$ elements.   ☐

Exercise 5.32. Work out the details of an external-memory implementation of sample sort. In particular, explain how to implement multiway distribution using $2n/B + k+1$ I/O steps if the internal memory is large enough to store $k+1$ blocks of data and $\mathrm{O}(k)$ additional elements.

Exercise 5.33 (many equal keys). Explain how to generalize multiway distribution so that it still works if some keys occur very often. Hint: there are at least two different solutions. One uses the sample to find out which elements are frequent. Another solution makes all elements unique by interpreting an element e at an input position i as the pair (e, i).

*Exercise 5.34 (more accurate distribution). A larger sample size improves the quality of the distribution. Prove that a sample of size $\mathrm{O}\big((k/\varepsilon^2)\log(k/\varepsilon m)\big)$ guarantees, with probability (at least $1 - 1/m$), that no bucket has more than $(1+\varepsilon)n/k$ elements. Can you get rid of the ε in the logarithmic factor?

5.8 Implementation Notes

Comparison-based sorting algorithms are usually available in standard libraries, and so you may not have to implement one yourself. Many libraries use tuned implementations of quicksort.

Canned non-comparison-based sorting routines are less readily available. Figure 5.15 shows a careful array-based implementation of *Ksort*. It works well for

Procedure *KSortArray(a,b : Array* [1..n] **of** *Element)*
   $c = \langle 0,\ldots,0\rangle$: *Array* [0..K − 1] **of** ℕ   // counters for each bucket
   for $i := 1$ **to** n **do** $c[key(a[i])]$++   // Count bucket sizes

   $C := 0$
   for $k := 0$ **to** $K − 1$ **do** $(C, c[k]) := (C + c[k], C)$ // Store $\sum_{i<k} c[k]$ in $c[k]$.

   for $i := 1$ **to** n **do**   // Distribute $a[i]$
      $b[c[key(a[i])]] := a[i]$
      $c[key(a[i])]$++

Fig. 5.15. Array-based sorting with keys in the range $0..K − 1$. The input is an unsorted array
a. The output is b, containing the elements of a in sorted order. We first count the number of
inputs for each key. Then we form the partial sums of the counts. Finally, we write each input
element to the correct position in the output array

small to medium-sized problems. For large K and n, it suffers from the problem that
the distribution of elements to the buckets may cause a cache fault for every element.

To fix this problem, one can use multiphase algorithms similar to MSD radix sort.
The number K of output sequences should be chosen in such a way that one block
from each bucket is kept in the cache (see also [134]). The distribution degree K can
be larger when the subarray to be sorted fits into the cache. We can then switch to a
variant of *uniformSort* (see Fig. 5.13).

Another important practical aspect concerns the type of elements to be sorted.
Sometimes we have rather large elements that are sorted with respect to small keys.
For example, you may want to sort an employee database by last name. In this situation, it makes sense to first extract the keys and store them in an array together
with pointers to the original elements. Then, only the key–pointer pairs are sorted.
If the original elements need to be brought into sorted order, they can be permuted
accordingly in linear time using the sorted key–pointer pairs.

Multiway merging of a small number of sequences (perhaps up to eight) deserves
special mention. In this case, the priority queue can be kept in the processor registers
[160, 206].

5.8.1 C/C++

Sorting is one of the few algorithms that is part of the C standard library. However,
the C sorting routine *qsort* is slower and harder to use than the C++ function *sort*.
The main reason is that the comparison function is passed as a function pointer and is
called for every element comparison. In contrast, *sort* uses the template mechanism
of C++ to figure out at compile time how comparisons are performed so that the
code generated for comparisons is often a single machine instruction. The parameters passed to *sort* are an iterator pointing to the start of the sequence to be sorted,
and an iterator pointing after the end of the sequence. In our experiments using an
Intel Pentium III and GCC 2.95, *sort* on arrays ran faster than our manual implementation of quicksort. One possible reason is that compiler designers may tune their

code optimizers until they find that good code for the library version of quicksort is generated. There is an efficient parallel-disk external-memory sorter in STXXL [48], an external-memory implementation of the STL. Efficient parallel sorters (parallel quicksort and parallel multiway mergesort) for multicore machines are available with the Multi-Core Standard Template Library [180, 125].

Exercise 5.35. Give a C or C++ implementation of the procedure *qSort* in Fig. 5.7. Use only two parameters: a pointer to the (sub)array to be sorted, and its size.

5.8.2 Java

The Java 6 platform provides a method *sort* which implements a stable binary merge-sort for *Arrays* and *Collections*. One can use a customizable *Comparator*, but there is also a default implementation for all classes supporting the interface *Comparable*.

5.9 Historical Notes and Further Findings

In later chapters, we shall discuss several generalizations of sorting. Chapter 6 discusses priority queues, a data structure that supports insertions of elements and removal of the smallest element. In particular, inserting n elements followed by repeated deletion of the minimum amounts to sorting. Fast priority queues result in quite good sorting algorithms. A further generalization is the *search trees* introduced in Chap. 7, a data structure for maintaining a sorted list that allows searching, inserting, and removing elements in logarithmic time.

We have seen several simple, elegant, and efficient randomized algorithms in this chapter. An interesting question is whether these algorithms can be replaced by deterministic ones. Blum et al. [25] described a deterministic median selection algorithm that is similar to the randomized algorithm discussed in Sect. 5.5. This deterministic algorithm makes pivot selection more reliable using recursion: it splits the input set into subsets of five elements, determines the median of each subset by sorting the five-element subset, then determines the median of the $n/5$ medians by calling the algorithm recursively, and finally uses the median of the medians as the splitter. The resulting algorithm has linear worst-case execution time, but the large constant factor makes the algorithm impractical. (We invite the reader to set up a recurrence for the running time and to show that it has a linear solution.)

There are quite practical ways to reduce the expected number of comparisons required by quicksort. Using the median of three random elements yields an algorithm with about $1.188n \log n$ comparisons. The median of three medians of three-element subsets brings this down to $\approx 1.094n \log n$ [20]. The number of comparisons can be reduced further by making the number of elements considered for pivot selection dependent on the size of the subproblem. Martinez and Roura [123] showed that for a subproblem of size m, the median of $\Theta(\sqrt{m})$ elements is a good choice for the pivot. With this approach, the total number of comparisons becomes $(1 + o(1))n \log n$, i.e., it matches the lower bound of $n \log n - O(n)$ up to lower-order terms. Interestingly, the above optimizations can be counterproductive. Although fewer instructions are executed, it becomes impossible to predict when the inner while loops of quicksort will be aborted. Since modern, deeply pipelined processors only work efficiently when they can predict the directions of branches taken, the net effect on performance can even be negative [102]. Therefore, in [167] , a comparison-based sorting algorithm that avoids conditional branch instructions was developed. An interesting deterministic variant of quicksort is proportion-extend sort [38].

A classical sorting algorithm of some historical interest is *Shell sort* [174, 100], a generalization of insertion sort, that gains efficiency by also comparing nonadjacent elements. It is still open whether some variant of Shell sort achieves $O(n \log n)$ average running time [100, 124].

There are some interesting techniques for improving external multiway mergesort. The *snow plow* heuristic [112, Sect. 5.4.1] forms runs of expected size $2M$ using a fast memory of size M: whenever an element is selected from the internal priority queue and written to the output buffer and the next element in the input buffer can extend the current run, we add it to the priority queue. Also, the use of *tournament trees* instead of general priority queues leads to a further improvement of multiway merging [112].

Parallelism can be used to improve the sorting of very large data sets, either in the form of a uniprocessor using parallel disks or in the form of a multiprocessor. Multiway mergesort and distribution sort can be adapted to D parallel disks by *striping*, i.e., any D consecutive blocks in a run or bucket are evenly distributed over the disks. Using randomization, this idea can be developed into almost optimal algorithms that also overlap I/O and computation [49]. The sample sort algorithm of Sect. 5.7.2 can be adapted to parallel machines [24] and results in an efficient parallel sorter.

We have seen linear-time algorithms for highly structured inputs. A quite general model, for which the $n \log n$ lower bound does not hold, is the *word model*. In this model, keys are integers that fit into a single memory cell, say 32- or 64-bit keys, and the standard operations on words (bitwise-AND, bitwise-OR, addition, . . .) are available in constant time. In this model, sorting is possible in deterministic time $O(n \log \log n)$ [11]. With randomization, even $O(n\sqrt{\log \log n})$ is possible [85]. *Flash sort* [149] is a distribution-based algorithm that works almost in-place.

Exercise 5.36 (Unix spellchecking). Assume you have a dictionary consisting of a sorted sequence of correctly spelled words. To check a text, you convert it to a sequence of words, sort it, scan the text and dictionary simultaneously, and output the words in the text that do not appear in the dictionary. Implement this spellchecker using Unix tools in a small number of lines of code. Can you do this in one line?

6

Priority Queues

The company TMG markets tailor-made first-rate garments. It organizes marketing, measurements, etc., but outsources the actual fabrication to independent tailors. The company keeps 20% of the revenue. When the company was founded in the 19th century, there were five subcontractors. Now it controls 15% of the world market and there are thousands of subcontractors worldwide.

Your task is to assign orders to the subcontractors. The rule is that an order is assigned to the tailor who has so far (in the current year) been assigned the smallest total value of orders. Your ancestors used a blackboard to keep track of the current total value of orders for each tailor; in computer science terms, they kept a list of values and spent linear time to find the correct tailor. The business has outgrown this solution. Can you come up with a more scalable solution where you have to look only at a small number of values to decide who will be assigned the next order?

In the following year the rules are changed. In order to encourage timely delivery, the orders are now assigned to the tailor with the smallest value of unfinished *orders, i.e., whenever a finished order arrives, you have to deduct the value of the order from the backlog of the tailor who executed it. Is your strategy for assigning orders flexible enough to handle this efficiently?*

Priority queues are the data structure required for the problem above and for many other applications. We start our discussion with the precise specification. Priority queues maintain a set M of *Element*s with *Key*s under the following operations:

- $M.build(\{e_1,\ldots,e_n\})$: $M := \{e_1,\ldots,e_n\}$.
- $M.insert(e)$: $M := M \cup \{e\}$.
- $M.\min$: **return** $\min M$.
- $M.deleteMin$: $e := \min M$; $M := M \setminus \{e\}$; **return** e.

This is enough for the first part of our example. Each year, we build a new priority queue containing an *Element* with a *Key* of zero for each contract tailor. To assign an order, we delete the smallest *Element*, add the order value to its *Key*, and reinsert it. Section 6.1 presents a simple, efficient implementation of this basic functionality.

---

[0] The photograph shows a queue at the Mao Mausoleum (V. Berger, see http://commons.wikimedia.org/wiki/Image:Zhengyangmen01.jpg).

Addressable priority queues additionally support operations on arbitrary elements addressed by an element handle h:

- *insert*:   as before, but return a handle to the element inserted.
- *remove*(h):   remove the element specified by the handle h.
- *decreaseKey*(h,k): decrease the key of the element specified by the handle h to k.
- $M.merge(Q)$: $M := M \cup Q$; $Q := \emptyset$.

In our example, the operation *remove* might be helpful when a contractor is fired because he/she delivers poor quality. Using this operation together with *insert*, we can also implement the "new contract rules": when an order is delivered, we remove the *Element* for the contractor who executed the order, subtract the value of the order from its *Key* value, and reinsert the *Element*. *DecreaseKey* streamlines this process to a single operation. In Sect. 6.2, we shall see that this is not just convenient but that decreasing keys can be implemented more efficiently than arbitrary element updates.

Priority queues have many applications. For example, in Sect. 12.2, we shall see that our introductory example can also be viewed as a greedy algorithm for a machine-scheduling problem. Also, the rather naive selection-sort algorithm of Sect. 5.1 can be implemented efficiently now: first, insert all elements into a priority queue, and then repeatedly delete the smallest element and output it. A tuned version of this idea is described in Sect. 6.1. The resulting *heapsort* algorithm is popular because it needs no additional space and is worst-case efficient.

In a *discrete-event simulation*, one has to maintain a set of pending events. Each event happens at some scheduled point in time and creates zero or more new events in the future. Pending events are kept in a priority queue. The main loop of the simulation deletes the next event from the queue, executes it, and inserts newly generated events into the priority queue. Note that the priorities (times) of the deleted elements (simulated events) increase monotonically during the simulation. It turns out that many applications of priority queues have this monotonicity property. Section 10.5 explains how to exploit monotonicity for integer keys.

Another application of monotone priority queues is the *best-first branch-and-bound* approach to optimization described in Sect. 12.4. Here, the elements are partial solutions of an optimization problem and the keys are optimistic estimates of the obtainable solution quality. The algorithm repeatedly removes the best-looking partial solution, refines it, and inserts zero or more new partial solutions.

We shall see two applications of addressable priority queues in the chapters on graph algorithms. In both applications, the priority queue stores nodes of a graph. Dijkstra's algorithm for computing shortest paths (Sect. 10.3) uses a monotone priority queue where the keys are path lengths. The Jarník–Prim algorithm for computing minimum spanning trees (Sect. 11.2) uses a (nonmonotone) priority queue where the keys are the weights of edges connecting a node to a partial spanning tree. In both algorithms, there can be a *decreaseKey* operation for each edge, whereas there is at most one *insert* and *deleteMin* for each node. Observe that the number of edges may be much larger than the number of nodes, and hence the implementation of *decreaseKey* deserves special attention.

Exercise 6.1. Show how to implement bounded nonaddressable priority queues using arrays. The maximal size of the queue is w and when the queue has a size n, the first n entries of the array are used. Compare the complexity of the queue operations for two implementations: one by unsorted arrays and one by sorted arrays.

Exercise 6.2. Show how to implement addressable priority queues using doubly linked lists. Each list item represents an element in the queue, and a handle is a handle of a list item. Compare the complexity of the queue operations for two implementations: one by sorted lists and one by unsorted lists.

6.1 Binary Heaps

Heaps are a simple and efficient implementation of nonaddressable bounded priority queues [208]. They can be made unbounded in the same way as bounded arrays can be made unbounded (see Sect. 3.2). Heaps can also be made addressable, but we shall see better addressable queues in later sections.

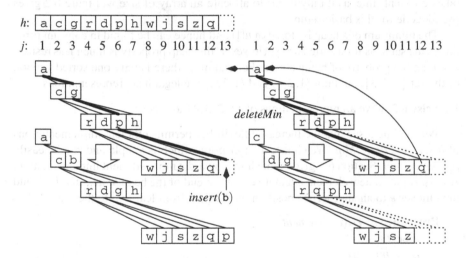

Fig. 6.1. The *top part* shows a heap with $n = 12$ elements stored in an array h with $w = 13$ entries. The root corresponds to index 1. The children of the root correspond to indices 2 and 3. The children of node i have indices $2i$ and $2i + 1$ (if they exist). The parent of a node i, $i \geq 2$, has index $\lfloor i/2 \rfloor$. The elements stored in this implicitly defined tree fulfill the invariant that parents are no larger than their children, i.e., the tree is heap-ordered. The *left part* shows the effect of inserting b. The thick edges mark a path from the rightmost leaf to the root. The new element b is moved up this path until its parent is smaller. The remaining elements on the path are moved down to make room for b. The *right part* shows the effect of deleting the minimum. The thick edges mark the path p that starts at the root and always proceeds to the child with the smaller *Key*. The element q is provisionally moved to the root and then moves down p until its successors are larger. The remaining elements move up to make room for q

Class *BinaryHeapPQ*(w : $\mathbb{N}$) **of** *Element*
  h : *Array* $[1..w]$ **of** *Element*   // The *heap* h is
  $n = 0$: $\mathbb{N}$ // initially *empty* and has the
  invariant $\forall j \in 2..n : h[\lfloor j/2 \rfloor] \leq h[j]$ // *heap property* which implies that
  Function min **assert** $n > 0$; **return** $h[1]$ // the *root* is the *min*imum.

Fig. 6.2. A class for a priority queue based on binary heaps whose size is bounded by w

We use an array $h[1..w]$ that stores the elements of the queue. The first n entries of the array are used. The array is *heap-ordered*, i.e.,

$$\text{for } j \text{ with } 2 < j \leq n: \quad h[\lfloor j/2 \rfloor] \leq h[j].$$

What does "heap-ordered" mean? The key to understanding this definition is a bijection between positive integers and the nodes of a complete binary tree, as illustrated in Fig. 6.1. In a heap the minimum element is stored in the root (= array position 1). Thus min takes time $O(1)$. Creating an empty heap with space for w elements also takes constant time, as it only needs to allocate an array of size w. Figure 6.2 gives pseudocode for this basic setup.

The minimum of a heap is stored in $h[1]$ and hence can be found in constant time; this is the same as for a sorted array. However, the heap property is much less restrictive than the property of being sorted. For example, there is only one sorted version of the set $\{1,2,3\}$, but both $\langle 1,2,3 \rangle$ and $\langle 1,3,2 \rangle$ are legal heap representations.

Exercise 6.3. Give all representations of $\{1,2,3,4\}$ as a heap.

We shall next see that the increased flexibility permits efficient implementations of *insert* and *deleteMin*. We choose a description which is simple and can be easily proven correct. Section 6.4 gives some hints toward a more efficient implementation. An *insert* puts a new element e tentatively at the end of the heap h, i.e., into $h[n]$, and then moves e to an appropriate position on the path from leaf $h[n]$ to the root:

Procedure *insert*(e : *Element*)
  assert $n < w$
  n++; $h[n] := e$
  siftUp(n)

Here *siftUp*(s) moves the contents of node s toward the root until the heap property holds (see. Fig. 6.1).

Procedure *siftUp*(i : $\mathbb{N}$)
  assert the heap property holds except maybe at position i
  if $i = 1 \vee h[\lfloor i/2 \rfloor] \leq h[i]$ **then return**
  assert the heap property holds except for position i
  swap($h[i], h[\lfloor i/2 \rfloor]$)
  assert the heap property holds except maybe for position $\lfloor i/2 \rfloor$
  siftUp($\lfloor i/2 \rfloor$)

Correctness follows from the invariants stated.

Exercise 6.4. Show that the running time of *siftUp*(n) is $O(\log n)$ and hence an *insert* takes time $O(\log n)$.

A *deleteMin* returns the contents of the root and replaces them by the contents of node n. Since $h[n]$ might be larger than $h[2]$ or $h[3]$, this manipulation may violate the heap property at position 2 or 3. This possible violation is repaired using *siftDown*:

> **Function** *deleteMin* : *Element*
>   **assert** $n > 0$
>   *result* = $h[1]$: *Element*
> $h[1] := h[n]$; $n--$
>   *siftDown*(1)
>   **return** *result*

The procedure *siftDown*(1) moves the new contents of the root down the tree until the heap property holds. More precisely, consider the path p that starts at the root and always proceeds to the child with the smaller key (see Fig. 6.1); in the case of equal keys, the choice is arbitrary. We extend the path until all children (there may be zero, one, or two) have a key no larger than $h[1]$. We put $h[1]$ into this position and move all elements on path p up by one position. In this way, the heap property is restored. This strategy is most easily formulated as a recursive procedure. A call of the following procedure *siftDown*(i) repairs the heap property in the subtree rooted at i, assuming that it holds already for the subtrees rooted at $2i$ and $2i + 1$; the heap property holds in the subtree rooted at i if we have $h[\lfloor j/2 \rfloor] \leq h[j]$ for all proper descendants j of i:

> **Procedure** *siftDown*$(i : \mathbb{N})$
>   **assert** the heap property holds for the trees rooted at $j = 2i$ and $j = 2i + 1$
>   **if** $2i \leq n$ **then**   // i is not a leaf
>   **if** $2i + 1 > n \vee h[2i] \leq h[2i + 1]$ **then** $m := 2i$ **else** $m := 2i + 1$
>   **assert** the sibling of m does not exist or it has a larger key than m
>   **if** $h[i] > h[m]$ **then**   // the heap property is violated
>   *swap*$(h[i], h[m])$
>   *siftDown*(m)
>   **assert** the heap property holds for the tree rooted at i

Exercise 6.5. Our current implementation of *siftDown* needs about $2 \log n$ element comparisons. Show how to reduce this to $\log n + O(\log \log n)$. Hint: determine the path p first and then perform a binary search on this path to find the proper position for $h[1]$. Section 6.5 has more on variants of *siftDown*.

We can obviously build a heap from n elements by inserting them one after the other in $O(n \log n)$ total time. Interestingly, we can do better by establishing the heap property in a bottom-up fashion: *siftDown* allows us to establish the heap property for a subtree of height $k + 1$ provided the heap property holds for its subtrees of height k. The following exercise asks you to work out the details of this idea.

Exercise 6.6 (*buildHeap*). Assume that you are given an arbitrary array $h[1..n]$ and want to establish the heap property on it by permuting its entries. Consider two procedures for achieving this:

Procedure *buildHeapBackwards*
    for $i := \lfloor n/2 \rfloor$ **downto** 1 **do** *siftDown(i)*

Procedure *buildHeapRecursive*$(i : \mathbb{N})$
    if $4i \leq n$ **then**
        buildHeapRecursive(2i)
        buildHeapRecursive(2i + 1)
    siftDown(i)

(a) Show that both *buildHeapBackwards* and *buildHeapRecursive*(1) establish the heap property everywhere.
(b) Implement both algorithms efficiently and compare their running times for random integers and $n \in \{10^i : 2 \leq i \leq 8\}$. It will be important how efficiently you implement *buildHeapRecursive*. In particular, it might make sense to unravel the recursion for small subtrees.
*(c) For large n, the main difference between the two algorithms is in memory hierarchy effects. Analyze the number of I/O operations required by the two algorithms in the external-memory model described at the end of Sect. 2.2. In particular, show that if the block size is B and the fast memory has size $M = \Omega(B \log B)$, then *buildHeapRecursive* needs only $O(n/B)$ I/O operations.

The following theorem summarizes our results on binary heaps.

Theorem 6.1. *The heap implementation of nonaddressable priority queues realizes creating an empty heap and finding the minimum element in constant time, deleteMin and insert in logarithmic time* $O(\log n)$, *and build in linear time.*

Proof. The binary tree represented by a heap of n elements has a height of $k = \lfloor \log n \rfloor$. *insert* and *deleteMin* explore one root-to-leaf path and hence have logarithmic running time; min returns the contents of the root and hence takes constant time. Creating an empty heap amounts to allocating an array and therefore takes constant time. *build* calls *siftDown* for at most 2^ℓ nodes of depth ℓ. Such a call takes time $O(k - \ell)$. Thus total the time is

$$O\left(\sum_{0 \leq \ell < k} 2^\ell (k - \ell)\right) = O\left(2^k \sum_{0 \leq \ell < k} \frac{k - \ell}{2^{k-\ell}}\right) = O\left(2^k \sum_{j \geq 1} \frac{j}{2^j}\right) = O(n) \ .$$

The last equality uses (A.14). $\qquad\qquad\qquad\qquad\qquad\qquad\qquad\qquad\qquad\qquad\qquad$ □

Heaps are the basis of *heapsort*. We first *build* a heap from the elements and then repeatedly perform *deleteMin*. Before the i-th *deleteMin* operation, the i-th smallest element is stored at the root $h[1]$. We swap $h[1]$ and $h[n - i + 1]$ and sift the new root down to its appropriate position. At the end, h stores the elements sorted in decreasing order. Of course, we can also sort in increasing order by using a *max-priority queue*, i.e., a data structure supporting the operations of *insert* and of deleting the maximum.

Heaps do not immediately implement the data type addressable priority queue, since elements are moved around in the array h during insertion and deletion. Thus the array indices cannot be used as handles.

Exercise 6.7 (addressable binary heaps). Extend heaps to an implementation of addressable priority queues. How many additional pointers per element do you need? There is a solution with two additional pointers per element.

*Exercise 6.8 (bulk insertion). Design an algorithm for inserting k new elements into an n-element heap. Give an algorithm that runs in time $O(k + \log n)$. Hint: use a bottom-up approach similar to that for heap construction.

6.2 Addressable Priority Queues

Binary heaps have a rather rigid structure. All n elements are arranged into a single binary tree of height $\lfloor \log n \rfloor$. In order to obtain faster implementations of the operations *insert*, *decreaseKey*, *remove*, and *merge*, we now look at structures which are more flexible. The single, complete binary tree is replaced by a collection of trees (i.e., a forest) with arbitrary shape. Each tree is still *heap-ordered*, i.e., no child is smaller than its parent. In other words, the sequence of keys along any root-to-leaf path is nondecreasing. Figure 6.4 shows a heap-ordered forest. Furthermore, the elements of the queue are now stored in *heap items* that have a persistent location in memory. Hence, pointers to heap items can serve as *handles* to priority queue elements. The tree structure is explicitly defined using pointers between items.

We shall discuss several variants of addressable priority queues. We start with the common principles underlying all of them. Figure 6.3 summarizes the commonalities.

In order to keep track of the current minimum, we maintain the handle to the root containing it. We use *minPtr* to denote this handle. The forest is manipulated using three simple operations: adding a new tree (and keeping *minPtr* up to date), combining two trees into a single one, and cutting out a subtree, making it a tree of its own.

An *insert* adds a new single-node tree to the forest. So a sequence of n inserts into an initially empty heap will simply create n single-node trees. The cost of an insert is clearly $O(1)$.

A *deleteMin* operation removes the node indicated by *minPtr*. This turns all children of the removed node into roots. We then scan the set of roots (old and new) to find the new minimum, a potentially very costly process. We also perform some rebalancing, i.e., we combine trees into larger ones. The details of this process distinguish different kinds of addressable priority queue and are the key to efficiency.

We turn now to *decreaseKey*(h, k) which decreases the key value at a handle h to k. Of course, k must not be larger than the old key stored with h. Decreasing the

Class *Handle* = **Pointer to** *PQItem*

Class *AddressablePQ*

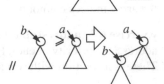

    minPtr : *Handle*   // root that stores the minimum

    roots : **Set of** *Handle*   // pointers to tree roots

    Function min **return** element stored at *minPtr*

    Procedure *link*(*a,b* : *Handle*)

        assert $a \leq b$

        remove *b* from *roots*

        make *a* the parent of *b*   //

    Procedure *combine*(*a,b* : *Handle*)

        assert *a* and *b* are tree roots

        if $a \leq b$ **then** *link*(*a,b*) **else** *link*(*b,a*)

    Procedure *newTree*(*h* : *Handle*)

        roots := *roots* $\cup$ {*h*}

        if $*h <$ min **then** *minPtr* := *h*

    Procedure *cut*(*h* : *Handle*)

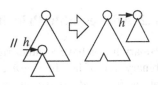

        remove the subtree rooted at *h* from its tree   // *h*

        newTree(*h*)

    Function *insert*(*e* : *Element*) : *Handle*

        i:=a *Handle* for a new *PQItem* storing *e*

        newTree(*i*)

        return *i*

    Function *deleteMin* : *Element*

        e:= the *Element* stored in *minPtr*

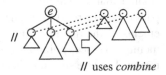

        foreach child *h* of the root at *minPtr* **do** *cut*(*h*)   //

        dispose *minPtr*

        perform some rebalancing and update *minPtr*   // uses *combine*

        return *e*

    Procedure *decreaseKey*(*h* : *Handle*, *k* : *Key*)

        change the key of *h* to *k*

        if *h* is not a root **then**

            cut(*h*);   possibly perform some rebalancing

    Procedure *remove*(*h* : *Handle*)   *decreaseKey*(*h*, $-\infty$); *deleteMin*

    Procedure *merge*(*o* : *AddressablePQ*)

        if $*minPtr > *(o.minPtr)$ **then** *minPtr* := *o.minPtr*

        roots := *roots* $\cup$ *o.roots*

        o.roots := $\emptyset$;   possibly perform some rebalancing

Fig. 6.3. Addressable priority queues

Fig. 6.4. A heap-ordered forest representing the set $\{0, 1, 3, 4, 5, 7, 8\}$

key associated with h may destroy the heap property because h may now be smaller than its parent. In order to maintain the heap property, we cut the subtree rooted at h and turn h into a root. This sounds simple enough, but may create highly skewed trees. Therefore, some variants of addressable priority queues perform additional operations to keep the trees in shape.

The remaining operations are easy. We can *remove* an item from the queue by first decreasing its key so that it becomes the minimum item in the queue, and then perform a *deleteMin*. To merge a queue o into another queue we compute the union of *roots* and *o.roots*. To update *minPtr*, it suffices to compare the minima of the merged queues. If the root sets are represented by linked lists, and no additional balancing is done, a merge needs only constant time.

In the remainder of this section we shall discuss particular implementations of addressable priority queues.

6.2.1 Pairing Heaps

Pairing heaps [67] use a very simple technique for rebalancing. Pairing heaps are efficient in practice; however a full theoretical analysis is missing. They rebalance only in *deleteMin*. If $\langle r_1, \ldots, r_k \rangle$ is the sequence of root nodes stored in *roots*, then *deleteMin* combines r_1 with r_2, r_3 with r_4, etc., i.e., the *roots* are *paired*. Figure 6.5 gives an example.

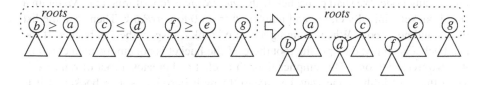

Fig. 6.5. The *deleteMin* operation for pairing heaps combines pairs of root nodes

Exercise 6.9 (three-pointer items). Explain how to implement pairing heaps using three pointers per heap item i: one to the oldest child (i.e., the child linked first to i), one to the next younger sibling (if any), and one to the next older sibling. If there is no older sibling, the third pointer goes to the parent. Figure 6.8 gives an example.

*Exercise 6.10 (two-pointer items). Explain how to implement pairing heaps using two pointers per heap item: one to the oldest child and one to next younger sibling. If there is no younger sibling, the second pointer goes to the parent. Figure 6.8 gives an example.

6.2.2 *Fibonacci Heaps

Fibonacci heaps [68] use more intensive balancing operations than do pairing heaps. This paves the way to a theoretical analysis. In particular, we obtain logarithmic

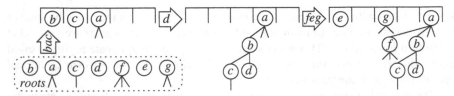

Fig. 6.6. An example of the development of the bucket array during execution of *deleteMin* for a Fibonacci heap. The arrows indicate the roots scanned. Note that scanning *d* leads to a cascade of three combine operations

amortized time for *remove* and *deleteMin* and worst-case constant time for all other operations.

Each item of a Fibonacci heap stores four pointers that identify its parent, one child, and two siblings (see Fig. 6.8). The children of each node form a doubly linked circular list using the sibling pointers. The sibling pointers of the root nodes can be used to represent *roots* in a similar way. Parent pointers of roots and child pointers of leaf nodes have a special value, for example, a null pointer.

In addition, every heap item contains a field *rank*. The *rank* of an item is the number of its children. In Fibonacci heaps, *deleteMin* links roots of equal rank r. The surviving root will then obtain a rank of $r + 1$. An efficient method to combine trees of equal rank is as follows. Let *maxRank* be an upper bound on the maximal rank of any node. We shall prove below that *maxRank* is logarithmic in n. Maintain a set of buckets, initially empty and numbered from 0 to *maxRank*. Then scan the list of old and new roots. When scanning a root of rank i, inspect the i-th bucket. If the i-th bucket is empty, then put the root there. If the bucket is nonempty, then combine the two trees into one. This empties the i-th bucket and creates a root of rank $i + 1$. Treat this root in the same way, i.e., try to throw it into the $i + 1$-th bucket. If it is occupied, combine .... When all roots have been processed in this way, we have a collection of trees whose roots have pairwise distinct ranks (see Figure 6.6).

A *deleteMin* can be very expensive if there are many roots. For example, a *deleteMin* following n insertions has a cost $\Omega(n)$. However, in an amortized sense, the cost of *deletemin* is O(*maxRank*). The reader must be familiar with the technique of amortized analysis (see Sect. 3.3) before proceeding further. For the amortized analysis, we postulate that each root holds one token. Tokens pay for a constant amount of computing time.

Lemma 6.2. *The amortized complexity of deleteMin is* O(*maxRank*).

Proof. A *deleteMin* first calls *newTree* at most *maxRank* times (since the degree of the old minimum is bounded by *maxRank*) and then initializes an array of size *maxRank*. Thus its running time is O(*maxRank*) and it needs to create *maxRank* new tokens. The remaining time is proportional to the number of *combine* operations performed. Each *combine* turns a root into a nonroot and is paid for by the token associated with the node turning into a nonroot.   □

How can we guarantee that *maxRank* stays small? Let us consider a simple situation first. Suppose that we perform a sequence of insertions followed by a one *deleteMin*. In this situation, we start with a certain number of single-node trees and all trees formed by combining are *binomial trees*, as shown in Fig. 6.7. The binomial tree B_0 consists of a single node, and the binomial tree B_{i+1} is obtained by combining two copies of B_i. This implies that the root of B_i has rank i and that B_i contains exactly 2^i nodes. Thus the rank of a binomial tree is logarithmic in the size of the tree.

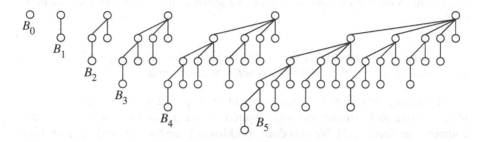

Fig. 6.7. The binomial trees of ranks zero to five

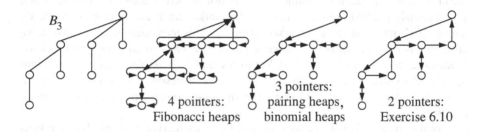

Fig. 6.8. Three ways to represent trees of nonuniform degree. The binomial tree of rank three, B_3, is used as an example

Unfortunately, *decreaseKey* may destroy the nice structure of binomial trees. Suppose an item v is cut out. We now have to decrease the rank of its parent w. The problem is that the size of the subtrees rooted at the ancestors of w has decreased but their rank has not changed, and hence we can no longer claim that the size of a tree stays exponential in the rank of its root. Therefore, we have to perform some rebalancing to keep the trees in shape. An old solution [202] is to keep all trees in the heap binomial. However, this causes logarithmic cost for a *decreaseKey*.

*Exercise 6.11 (binomial heaps). Work out the details of this idea. Hint: cut the following links. For each ancestor of v and for v itself, cut the link to its parent. For

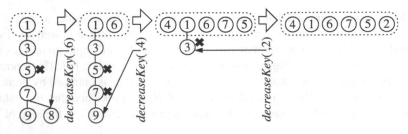

Fig. 6.9. An example of cascading cuts. Marks are drawn as crosses. Note that roots are never marked

each sibling of v of rank higher than v, cut the link to its parent. Argue that the trees stay binomial and that the cost of *decreaseKey* is logarithmic.

Fibonacci heaps allow the trees to go out of shape but in a controlled way. The idea is surprisingly simple and was inspired by the amortized analysis of binary counters (see Sect. 3.2.3). We introduce an additional flag for each node. A node may be marked or not. Roots are never marked. In particular, when *newTree(h)* is called in *deleteMin*, it removes the mark from h (if any). Thus when *combine* combines two trees into one, neither node is marked.

When a nonroot item x loses a child because *decreaseKey* has been applied to the child, x is marked; this assumes that x is not already marked. Otherwise, when x was already marked, we cut x, remove the mark from x, and attempt to mark x's parent. If x's parent is already marked, then .... This technique is called *cascading cuts*. In other words, suppose that we apply *decreaseKey* to an item v and that the k nearest ancestors of v are marked. We turn v and the k nearest ancestors of v into roots, unmark them, and mark the $k+1$-th nearest ancestor of v (if it is not a root). Figure 6.9 gives an example. Observe the similarity to carry propagation in binary addition.

For the amortized analysis, we postulate that each marked node holds two tokens and each root holds one token. Please check that this assumption does not invalidate the proof of Lemma 6.2.

Lemma 6.3. *The amortized complexity of decreaseKey is constant.*

Proof. Assume that we decrease the key of item v and that the k nearest ancestors of v are marked. Here, $k \geq 0$. The running time of the operation is $O(1+k)$. Each of the k marked ancestors carries two tokens, i.e., we have a total of $2k$ tokens available. We create $k+1$ new roots and need one token for each of them. Also, we mark one unmarked node and need two tokens for it. Thus we need a total of $k+3$ tokens. In other words, $k-3$ tokens are freed. They pay for all but $O(1)$ of the cost of *decreaseKey*. Thus the amortized cost of *decreaseKey* is constant.   □

How do cascading cuts affect the size of trees? We shall show that it stays exponential in the rank of the root. In order to do so, we need some notation. Recall the sequence 0, 1, 1, 2, 3, 5, 8, ... of Fibonacci numbers. These are defined by the recurrence $F_0 = 0$, $F_1 = 1$, and $F_i = F_{i-1} + F_{i-2}$ for $i \geq 2$. It is well known that $F_{i+1} \geq ((1 + \sqrt{5})/2)^i \geq 1.618^i$ for all $i \geq 0$.

Exercise 6.12. Prove that $F_{i+2} \geq ((1 + \sqrt{5})/2)^i \geq 1.618^i$ for all $i \geq 0$ by induction.

Lemma 6.4. *Let v be any item in a Fibonacci heap and let i be the rank of v. The subtree rooted at v then contains at least F_{i+2} nodes. In a Fibonacci heap with n items, all ranks are bounded by $1.4404 \log n$.*

Proof. Consider an arbitrary item v of rank i. Order the children of v by the time at which they were made children of v. Let w_j be the j-th child, $1 \leq j \leq i$. When w_j was made a child of v, both nodes had the same rank. Also, since at least the nodes $w_1, \ldots, w_{j-1}$ were children of v at that time, the rank of v was at least $j - 1$ then. The rank of w_j has decreased by at most 1 since then, because otherwise w_j would no longer be a child of v. Thus the current rank of w_j is at least $j - 2$.

We can now set up a recurrence for the minimal number S_i of nodes in a tree whose root has rank i. Clearly, $S_0 = 1$, $S_1 = 2$, and $S_i \geq 2 + S_0 + S_1 + \cdots + S_{i-2}$. The latter inequality follows from the fact that for $j \geq 2$, the number of nodes in the subtree with root w_j is at least S_{j-2}, and that we can also count the nodes v and w_1. The recurrence above (with = instead of $\geq$) generates the sequence 1, 2, 3, 5, 8, ... which is identical to the Fibonacci sequence (minus its first two elements).

Let us verify this by induction. Let $T_0 = 1$, $T_1 = 2$, and $T_i = 2 + T_0 + \cdots + T_{i-2}$ for $i \geq 2$. Then, for $i \geq 2$, $T_{i+1} - T_i = 2 + T_0 + \cdots + T_{i-1} - 2 - T_0 - \cdots - T_{i-2} = T_{i-1}$, i.e., $T_{i+1} = T_i + T_{i-1}$. This proves $T_i = F_{i+2}$.

For the second claim, we observe that $F_{i+2} \leq n$ implies $i \cdot \log((1 + \sqrt{5})/2) \leq \log n$, which in turn implies $i \leq 1.4404 \log n$. $\qquad \square$

This concludes our treatment of Fibonacci heaps. We have shown the following result.

Theorem 6.5. *The following time bounds hold for Fibonacci heaps: min, insert, and merge take worst-case constant time; decreaseKey takes amortized constant time, and remove and deleteMin take an amortized time logarithmic in the size of the queue.*

Exercise 6.13. Describe a variant of Fibonacci heaps where all roots have distinct ranks.

6.3 *External Memory

We now go back to nonaddressable priority queues and consider their cache efficiency and I/O efficiency. A weakness of binary heaps is that the *siftDown* operation goes down the tree in an unpredictable fashion. This leads to many cache faults and makes binary heaps prohibitively slow when they do not fit into the main memory.

We now outline a data structure for (nonadressable) priority queues with more regular memory accesses. It is also a good example of a generally useful design principle: construction of a data structure out of simpler, known components and algorithms.

In this case, the components are internal-memory priority queues, sorting, and multiway merging (see also Sect. 5.7.1). Figure 6.10 depicts the basic design. The data structure consists of two priority queues Q and Q' (e.g., binary heaps) and k sorted sequences $S_1, \ldots, S_k$. Each element of the priority queue is stored either in the *insertion queue* Q, in the *deletion queue* Q', or in one of the sorted sequences. The size of Q is limited to a parameter m. The *deletion queue* Q' stores the smallest element of each sequence, together with the index of the sequence holding the element.

New elements are inserted into the insertion queue. If the insertion queue is full, it is first emptied. In this case, its elements form a new sorted sequence:

Procedure *insert*(e : *Element*)
    if $|Q| = m$ **then**
        k++; $S_k := sort(Q)$; $Q := \emptyset$; $Q'.insert((S_k.popFront, k))$
    $Q.insert(e)$

The minimum is stored either in Q or in Q'. If the minimum is in Q' and comes from sequence S_i, the next largest element of S_i is inserted into Q':

Function *deleteMin*
    if $\min Q \leq \min Q'$ **then** $e := Q.deleteMin$ // assume $\min \emptyset = \infty$
    else $(e, i) := Q'.deleteMin$
          if $S_i \neq \langle \rangle$ **then** $Q'.insert((S_i.popFront, i))$
    return e

It remains to explain how the ingredients of our data structure are mapped to the memory hierarchy. The queues Q and Q' are stored in internal memory. The size bound m for Q should be a constant fraction of the internal-memory size M and a multiple of the block size B. The sequences S_i are largely kept externally. Initially, only the B smallest elements of S_i are kept in an internal-memory buffer b_i. When the last element of b_i is removed, the next B elements of S_i are loaded. Note that we are effectively merging the sequences S_i. This is similar to our multiway merging

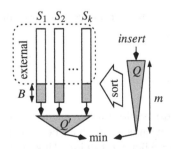

Fig. 6.10. Schematic view of an external-memory priority queue

algorithm described in Sect. 5.7.1. Each inserted element is written to disk at most once and fetched back to internal memory at most once. Since all disk accesses are in units of at least a full block, the I/O requirement of our algorithm is at most n/B for n queue operations.

Our total requirement for internal memory is at most $m + kB + 2k$. This is below the total fast-memory size M if $m = M/2$ and $k \leq \lfloor (M/2 - 2k)/B \rfloor \approx M/(2B)$. If there are many insertions, the internal memory may eventually overflow. However, the earliest this can happen is after $m(1 + \lfloor (M/2 - 2k)/B \rfloor) \approx M^2/(4B)$ insertions. For example, if we have 1 Gbyte of main memory, 8-byte elements, and 512 Kbyte disk blocks, we have $M = 2^{27}$ and $B = 2^{16}$ (measured in elements). We can then perform about 2^{36} insertions – enough for 128 Gbyte of data. Similarly to external mergesort, we can handle larger amounts of data by performing multiple phases of multiway merging (see, [31, 164]). The data structure becomes considerably more complicated, but it turns out that the I/O requirement for n insertions and deletions is about the same as for sorting n elements. An implementation of this idea is two to three times faster than binary heaps for the hierarchy between cache and main memory [164]. There are also implementations for external memory [48].

6.4 Implementation Notes

There are various places where *sentinels* (see Chap. 3) can be used to simplify or (slightly) accelerate the implementation of priority queues. Since sentinels may require additional knowledge about key values, this could make a reusable implementation more difficult, however.

- If $h[0]$ stores a *Key* no larger than any *Key* ever inserted into a binary heap, then *siftUp* need not treat the case $i = 1$ in a special way.
- If $h[n + 1]$ stores a *Key* no smaller than any *Key* ever inserted into a binary heap, then *siftDown* need not treat the case $2i + 1 > n$ in a special way. If such large keys are stored in $h[n + 1..2n + 1]$, then the case $2i > n$ can also be eliminated.
- Addressable priority queues can use a special dummy item rather than a null pointer.

For simplicity we have formulated the operations *siftDown* and *siftUp* for binary heaps using recursion. It might be a little faster to implement them iteratively instead. Similarly, the *swap* operations could be replaced by unidirectional move operations thus halving the number of memory accesses.

Exercise 6.14. Give iterative versions of *siftDown* and *siftUp*. Also replace the *swap* operations.

Some compilers do the recursion elimination for you.

As for sequences, memory management for items of addressable priority queues can be critical for performance. Often, a particular application may be able to do this more efficiently than a general-purpose library. For example, many graph algorithms use a priority queue of nodes. In this case, items can be incorporated into nodes.

There are priority queues that work efficiently for integer keys. It should be noted that these queues can also be used for floating-point numbers. Indeed, the IEEE floating-point standard has the interesting property that for any valid floating-point numbers a and b, $a \leq b$ if and only if $bits(a) \leq bits(b)$, where $bits(x)$ denotes the reinterpretation of x as an unsigned integer.

6.4.1 C++

The STL class *priority_queue* offers nonaddressable priority queues implemented using binary heaps. The external-memory library STXXL [48] offers an external-memory priority queue. LEDA [118] implements a wide variety of addressable priority queues, including pairing heaps and Fibonacci heaps.

6.4.2 Java

The class *java.util.PriorityQueue* supports addressable priority queues to the extent that *remove* is implemented. However, *decreaseKey* and *merge* are not supported. Also, it seems that the current implementation of *remove* needs time $\Theta(n)$! JDSL [78] offers an addressable priority queue *jdsl.core.api.PriorityQueue*, which is currently implemented as a binary heap.

6.5 Historical Notes and Further Findings

There is an interesting Internet survey[1] of priority queues. It lists the following applications: (shortest-) path planning (see Chap. 10), discrete-event simulation, coding and compression, scheduling in operating systems, computing maximum flows, and branch-and-bound (see Sect. 12.4).

In Sect. 6.1 we saw an implementation of *deleteMin* by top-down search that needs about $2\log n$ element comparisons, and a variant using binary search that needs only $\log n + O(\log\log n)$ element comparisons. The latter is mostly of theoretical interest. Interestingly, a very simple "bottom-up" algorithm can be even better: The old minimum is removed and the resulting hole is sifted down all the way to the bottom of the heap. Only then, the rightmost element fills the hole and is subsequently sifted up. When used for sorting, the resulting *Bottom-up heapsort* requires $\frac{3}{2}n\log n + O(n)$ comparisons in the worst case and $n\log n + O(1)$ in the average case [204, 61, 169]. While bottom-up heapsort is simple and practical, our own experiments indicate that it is not faster than the usual top-down variant (for integer keys). This surprised us. The explanation might be that the outcomes of the comparisons saved by the bottom-up variant are easy to predict. Modern hardware executes such predictable comparisons very efficiently (see [167] for more discussion).

The recursive *buildHeap* routine in Exercise 6.6 is an example of a *cache-oblivious algorithm* [69]. This algorithm is efficient in the external-memory model even though it does not explicitly use the block size or cache size.

---

[1] http://www.leekillough.com/heaps/survey_results.html

Pairing heaps [67] have constant amortized complexity for *insert* and *merge* [96] and logarithmic amortized complexity for *deleteMin*. The best analysis is that due to Pettie [154]. Fredman [65] has given operation sequences consisting of $O(n)$ insertions and *deleteMins* and $O(n\log n)$ *decreaseKeys* that require time $\Omega(n\log n\log\log n)$ for a family of addressable priority queues that includes all previously proposed variants of pairing heaps.

The family of addressable priority queues is large. Vuillemin [202] introduced binomial heaps, and Fredman and Tarjan [68] invented Fibonacci heaps. Høyer [94] described additional balancing operations that are akin to the operations used for search trees. One such operation yields *thin heaps* [103], which have performance guarantees similar to Fibonacci heaps and do without parent pointers and mark bits. It is likely that thin heaps are faster in practice than Fibonacci heaps. There are also priority queues with worst-case bounds asymptotically as good as the amortized bounds that we have seen for Fibonacci heaps [30]. The basic idea is to tolerate violations of the heap property and to continuously invest some work in reducing these violations. Another interesting variant is *fat heaps* [103].

Many applications need priority queues for integer keys only. For this special case, there are more efficient priority queues. The best theoretical bounds so far are constant time for *decreaseKey* and *insert* and $O(\log\log n)$ time for *deleteMin* [193, 136]. Using randomization, the time bound can even be reduced to $O(\sqrt{\log\log n})$ [85]. The algorithms are fairly complex. However, integer priority queues that also have the *monotonicity property* can be simple and practical. Section 10.3 gives examples. *Calendar queues* [33] are popular in the discrete-event simulation community. These are a variant of the *bucket queues* described in Sect. 10.5.1.

7

Sorted Sequences

All of us spend a significant part of our time on searching, and so do computers: they look up telephone numbers, balances of bank accounts, flight reservations, bills and payments, ... In many applications, we want to search dynamic collections of data. New bookings are entered into reservation systems, reservations are changed or cancelled, and bookings turn into actual flights. We have already seen one solution to the problem, namely hashing. It is often desirable to keep a dynamic collection sorted. The "manual data structure" used for this purpose is a filing-card box. We can insert new cards at any position, we can remove cards, we can go through the cards in sorted order, and we can use some kind of binary search to find a particular card. Large libraries used to have filing-card boxes with hundreds of thousands of cards.[1]

Formally, we want to maintain a *sorted sequence*, i.e. a sequence of *Element*s sorted by their *Key* value, under the following operations:

- $M.locate(k : Key)$:   **return** $\min\{e \in M : e \geq k\}$.
- $M.insert(e : Element)$: $M := M \cup \{e\}$.
- $M.remove(k : Key)$: $M := M \setminus \{e \in M : key(e) = k\}$.

Here, M is the set of elements stored in the sequence. For simplicity, we assume that the elements have pairwise distinct keys. We shall reconsider this assumption in Exercise 7.10. We shall show that these operations can be implemented to run in time $O(\log n)$, where n denotes the size of the sequence. How do sorted sequences compare with the data structures known to us from previous chapters? They are more flexible than sorted arrays, because they efficiently support *insert* and *remove*. They are slower but also more powerful than hash tables, since *locate* also works when there is no element with key k in M. Priority queues are a special case of sorted sequences; they can only locate and remove the smallest element.

Our basic realization of a sorted sequence consists of a sorted doubly linked list with an additional navigation data structure supporting *locate*. Figure 7.1 illustrates this approach. Recall that a doubly linked list for n elements consists of $n + 1$ items,

---

[1] The above photograph is from the catalogue of the University of Graz (Dr. M. Gossler).

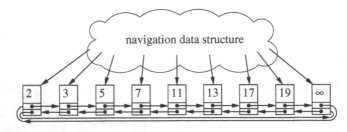

Fig. 7.1. A sorted sequence as a doubly linked list plus a navigation data structure

one for each element and one additional "dummy item". We use the dummy item to store a special key value $+\infty$ which is larger than all conceivable keys. We can then define the result of *locate*(k) as the handle to the smallest list item $e \geq k$. If k is larger than all keys in M, *locate* will return a handle to the dummy item. In Sect. 3.1.1, we learned that doubly linked lists support a large set of operations; most of them can also be implemented efficiently for sorted sequences. For example, we "inherit" constant-time implementations for *first*, *last*, *succ*, and *pred*. We shall see constant-amortized-time implementations for *remove*(h : *Handle*), *insertBefore*, and *insertAfter*, and logarithmic-time algorithms for concatenating and splitting sorted sequences. The indexing operator [·] and finding the position of an element in the sequence also take logarithmic time. Before we delve into a description of the navigation data structure, let us look at some concrete applications of sorted sequences.

Best-first heuristics. Assume that we want to pack some items into a set of bins. The items arrive one at a time and have to be put into a bin immediately. Each item i has a weight $w(i)$, and each bin has a maximum capacity. The goal is to minimize the number of bins used. One successful heuristic solution to this problem is to put item i into the bin that fits best, i.e., the bin whose remaining capacity is the smallest among all bins that have a residual capacity at least as large as $w(i)$ [41]. To implement this algorithm, we can keep the bins in a sequence q sorted by their residual capacity. To place an item, we call $q.locate(w(i))$, remove the bin that we have found, reduce its residual capacity by $w(i)$, and reinsert it into q. See also Exercise 12.8.

Sweep-line algorithms. Assume that you have a set of horizontal and vertical line segments in the plane and want to find all points where two segments intersect. A sweep-line algorithm moves a vertical line over the plane from left to right and maintains the set of horizontal lines that intersect the sweep line in a sorted sequence q. When the left endpoint of a horizontal segment is reached, it is inserted into q, and when its right endpoint is reached, it is removed from q. When a vertical line segment is reached at a position x that spans the vertical range $[y, y']$, we call $s.locate(y)$ and scan q until we reach the key y'.[2] All horizontal line segments discovered during this scan define an intersection. The sweeping algorithm can be generalized to arbitrary line segments [21], curved objects, and many other geometric problems [46].

---

[2] This *range query* operation is also discussed in Sect. 7.3.

Database indexes. A key problem in databases is to make large collections of data efficiently searchable. A variant of the (a, b)-tree data structure described in Sect. 7.2 is one of the most important data structures used for databases.

The most popular navigation data structure is that of *search trees*. We shall frequently use the name of the navigation data structure to refer to the entire sorted sequence data structure.[3] We shall introduce search tree algorithms in three steps. As a warm-up, Sect. 7.1 introduces (unbalanced) *binary search trees* that support *locate* in $O(\log n)$ time under certain favorable circumstances. Since binary search trees are somewhat difficult to maintain under insertions and removals, we then switch to a generalization, (a, b)-trees that allows search tree nodes of larger degree. Section 7.2 explains how (a, b)-trees can be used to implement all three basic operations in logarithmic worst-case time. In Sects. 7.3 and 7.5, we shall augment search trees with additional mechanisms that support further operations. Section 7.4 takes a closer look at the (amortized) cost of update operations.

7.1 Binary Search Trees

Navigating a search tree is a bit like asking your way around in a foreign city. You ask a question, follow the advice given, ask again, follow the advice again, ..., until you reach your destination.

A *binary search tree* is a tree whose leaves store the elements of a sorted sequence in sorted order from left to right. In order to locate a key k, we start at the root of the tree and follow the unique path to the appropriate leaf. How do we identify the correct path? To this end, the interior nodes of a search tree store keys that guide the search; we call these keys *splitter* keys. Every nonleaf node in a binary search tree with $n \geq 2$ leaves has exactly two children, a *left* child and a *right* child. The splitter key s associated with a node has the property that all keys k stored in the left subtree satisfy $k \leq s$ and all keys k stored in the right subtree satisfy $k > s$.

With these definitions in place, it is clear how to identify the correct path when locating k. Let s be the splitter key of the current node. If $k \leq s$, go left. Otherwise, go right. Figure 7.2 gives an example. Recall that the height of a tree is the length of its longest root–leaf path. The height therefore tells us the maximum number of search steps needed to *locate* a leaf.

Exercise 7.1. Prove that a binary search tree with $n \geq 2$ leaves can be arranged such that it has height $\lceil \log n \rceil$.

A search tree with height $\lceil \log n \rceil$ is called *perfectly balanced*. The resulting logarithmic search time is a dramatic improvement compared with the $\Omega(n)$ time needed for scanning a list. The bad news is that it is expensive to keep perfect balance when elements are inserted and removed. To understand this better, let us consider the "naive" insertion routine depicted in Fig. 7.3. We locate the key k of the new element e before its successor e', insert e into the list, and then introduce a new node v with

---

[3] There is also a variant of search trees where the elements are stored in all nodes of the tree.

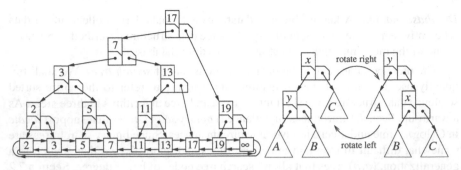

Fig. 7.2. *Left*: the sequence $\langle 2,3,5,7,11,13,17,19 \rangle$ represented by a binary search tree. In each node, we show the splitter key at the top and the pointers to the children at the bottom. *Right*: rotation of a binary search tree. The triangles indicate subtrees. Observe that the ancestor relationship between nodes x and y is interchanged

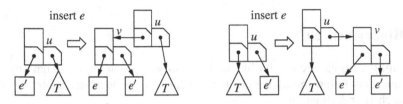

Fig. 7.3. Naive insertion into a binary search tree. A triangle indicates an entire subtree

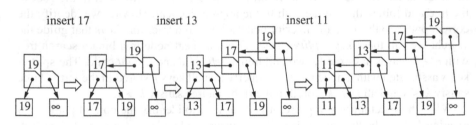

Fig. 7.4. Naively inserting sorted elements leads to a degenerate tree

left child e and right child e'. The old parent u of e' now points to v. In the worst case, every insertion operation will locate a leaf at the maximum depth so that the height of the tree increases every time. Figure 7.4 gives an example: the tree may degenerate to a list; we are back to scanning.

An easy solution to this problem is a healthy portion of optimism; perhaps it will not come to the worst. Indeed, if we insert n elements in *random* order, the expected height of the search tree is $\approx 2.99 \log n$ [51]. We shall not prove this here, but outline a connection to quicksort to make the result plausible. For example, consider how the tree in Fig. 7.2 can be built using naive insertion. We first insert 17; this splits the set into subsets $\{2,3,5,7,11,13\}$ and $\{19\}$. From the elements in the left subset, we first insert 7; this splits the left subset into $\{2,3,5\}$ and $\{11,13\}$. In quicksort terminology, we would say that 17 is chosen as the splitter in the top-level call and that 7 is chosen as the splitter in the left recursive call. So building a binary search tree and quicksort are completely analogous processes; the same comparisons are made, but at different times. Every element of the set is compared with 17. In quicksort, these comparisons take place when the set is split in the top-level call. In building a binary search tree, these comparisons take place when the elements of the set are inserted. So the comparison between 17 and 11 takes place either in the top-level call of quicksort or when 11 is inserted into the tree. We have seen (Theorem 5.6) that the expected number of comparisons in a randomized quicksort of n elements is $O(n\log n)$. By the above correspondence, the expected number of comparisons in building a binary tree by random insertions is also $O(n\log n)$. Thus any insertion requires $O(\log n)$ comparisons on average. Even more is true; with high probability each single insertion requires $O(\log n)$ comparisons, and the expected height is $\approx 2.99\log n$.

Can we guarantee that the height stays logarithmic in the worst case? Yes and there are many different ways to achieve logarithmic height. We shall survey these techniques in Sect. 7.7 and discuss two solutions in detail in Sect. 7.2. We shall first discuss a solution which allows nodes of varying degree, and then show how to balance binary trees using rotations.

Exercise 7.2. Figure 7.2 indicates how the shape of a binary tree can be changed by a transformation called *rotation*. Apply rotations to the tree in Fig. 7.2 so that the node labelled 11 becomes the root of the tree.

Exercise 7.3. Explain how to implement an *implicit* binary search tree, i.e., the tree is stored in an array using the same mapping of the tree structure to array positions as in the binary heaps discussed in Sect. 6.1. What are the advantages and disadvantages compared with a pointer-based implementation? Compare searching in an implicit binary tree with binary searching in a sorted array.

7.2 (a,b)-Trees and Red–Black Trees

An (a,b)-tree is a search tree where all interior nodes, except for the root, have an outdegree between a and b. Here, a and b are constants. The root has degree one for a trivial tree with a single leaf. Otherwise, the root has a degree between 2 and b. For $a \geq 2$ and $b \geq 2a - 1$, the flexibility in node degrees allows us to efficiently maintain the invariant that *all leaves have the same depth*, as we shall see in a short while. Consider a node with outdegree d. With such a node, we associate an array $c[1..d]$ of pointers to children and a sorted array $s[1..d-1]$ of $d - 1$ splitter keys. The splitters guide the search. To simplify the notation, we additionally define $s[0] = -\infty$ and $s[d] = \infty$. The keys of the elements e contained in the i-th child $c[i]$, $1 \leq i \leq d$, lie between the $i - 1$-th splitter (exclusive) and the i-th splitter (inclusive), i.e., $s[i-1] < key(e) \leq s[i]$. Figure 7.5 shows a $(2,4)$-tree storing the sequence $\langle 2,3,5,7,11,13,17,19 \rangle$.

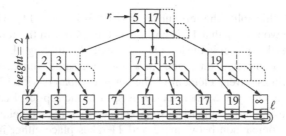

Fig. 7.5. Representation of $\langle 2,3,5,7,11,13,17,19\rangle$ by a $(2,4)$-tree. The tree has height 2

Class *ABHandle* : **Pointer** *to ABItem or Item*
// an ABItem (Item) is an item in the navigation data structure (doubly linked list)

Class *ABItem*(*splitters* : *Sequence* **of** *Key, children* : *Sequence* **of** *ABHandle*)
    $d = |children|$: $1..b$ // outdegree
    $s = splitters$: *Array* $[1..b-1]$ **of** *Key*
    $c = children$: *Array* $[1..b]$ **of** *Handle*

    Function *locateLocally*(k : *Key*) : $\mathbb{N}$
      return $\min\{i \in 1..d : k \leq s[i]\}$

    Function *locateRec*(k : *Key, h* : $\mathbb{N}$) : *Handle*
      i:=*locateLocally*(k)
      if $h = 1$ **then return** $c[i]$
      else return $c[i] \rightarrow$*locateRec*(k, $h-1$)   //

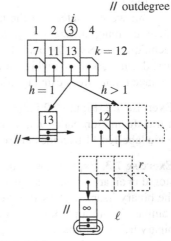

Class *ABTree*($a \geq 2$: $\mathbb{N}$, $b \geq 2a-1$: $\mathbb{N}$) **of** *Element*
    $\ell = \langle\rangle$: *List* **of** *Element*
    r : *ABItem*($\langle\rangle, \langle\ell.head\rangle$)
    height = 1 : $\mathbb{N}$ //

    // Locate the smallest Item with key $k' \geq k$
    Function *locate*(k : *Key*) : *Handle* **return** r.*locateRec*(k, *height*)

Fig. 7.6. (a,b)-trees. An *ABItem* is constructed from a sequence of keys and a sequence of handles to the children. The outdegree is the number of children. We allocate space for the maximum possible outdegree b. There are two functions local to *ABItem*: *locateLocally*(k) locates k among the splitters and *locateRec*(k,h) assumes that the *ABItem* has height h and descends h levels down the tree. The constructor for *ABTree* creates a tree for the empty sequence. The tree has a single leaf, the dummy element, and the root has degree one. Locating a key k in an (a,b)-tree is solved by calling r.*locateRec*(k,h), where r is the root and h is the height of the tree

Lemma 7.1. *An (a,b)-tree for n elements has a height at most*

$$1 + \left\lfloor \log_a \frac{n+1}{2} \right\rfloor .$$

Proof. The tree has $n+1$ leaves, where the "$+1$" accounts for the dummy leaf $+\infty$. If $n=0$, the root has degree one and there is a single leaf. So, assume $n \geq 1$. Let h be the height of the tree. Since the root has degree at least two and every other node has degree at least a, the number of leaves is at least $2a^{h-1}$. So $n+1 \geq 2a^{h-1}$, or $h \leq 1+\log_a(n+1)/2$. Since the height is an integer, the bound follows.   □

Exercise 7.4. Prove that the height of an (a,b)-tree for n elements is at least $\lceil \log_b(n+1) \rceil$. Prove that this bound and the bound given in Lemma 7.1 are tight.

Searching in an (a,b)-tree is only slightly more complicated than searching in a binary tree. Instead of performing a single comparison at a nonleaf node, we have to find the correct child among up to b choices. Using binary search, we need at most $\lceil \log b \rceil$ comparisons for each node on the search path. Figure 7.6 gives pseudocode for (a,b)-trees and the *locate* operation. Recall that we use the search tree as a way to locate items of a doubly linked list and that the dummy list item is considered to have key value ∞. This dummy item is the rightmost leaf in the search tree. Hence, there is no need to treat the special case of root degree 0, and the handle of the dummy item can serve as a return value when one is locating a key larger than all values in the sequence.

Exercise 7.5. Prove that the total number of comparisons in a search is bounded by $\lceil \log b \rceil (1+\log_a(n+1)/2)$. Assume $b \leq 2a$. Show that this number is $O(\log b) + O(\log n)$. What is the constant in front of the $\log n$ term?

To *insert* an element e, we first descend the tree recursively to find the smallest sequence element $e' \geq e$. If e and e' have equal keys, e' is replaced by e.

Otherwise, e is inserted into the sorted list ℓ before e'. If e' was the i-th child $c[i]$ of its parent node v, then e will become the new $c[i]$ and $key(e)$ becomes the corresponding splitter element $s[i]$. The old children $c[i..d]$ and their corresponding splitters $s[i..d-1]$ are shifted one position to the right. If d was less than b, d can be incremented and we are finished.

The difficult part is when a node v already has a degree $d=b$ and now would get a degree $b+1$. Let s' denote the splitters of this illegal node, c' its children, and

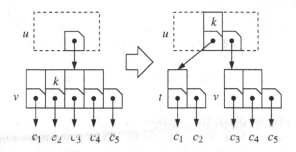

Fig. 7.7. Node splitting: the node v of degree $b+1$ (here 5) is split into a node of degree $\lfloor (b+1)/2 \rfloor$ and a node of degree $\lceil (b+1)/2 \rceil$. The degree of the parent increases by one. The splitter key separating the two "parts" of v is moved to the parent

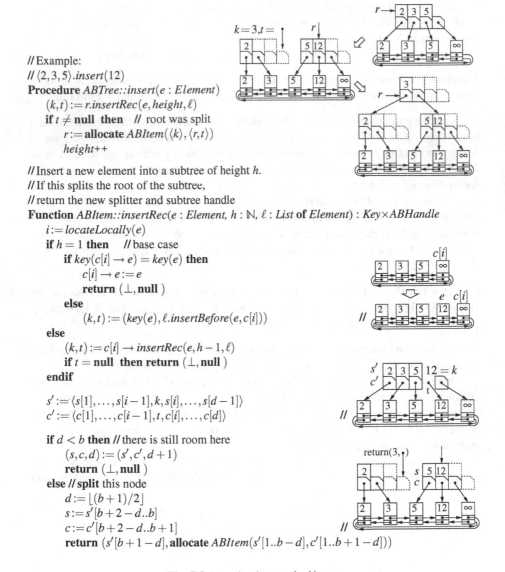

// Example:
// $\langle 2,3,5 \rangle .insert(12)$

Procedure *ABTree::insert(e : Element)*
   $(k,t) := r.insertRec(e, height, \ell)$
   if $t \neq$ **null then**   // root was split
      $r :=$ **allocate** $ABItem(\langle k \rangle, \langle r,t \rangle)$
      height++

// Insert a new element into a subtree of height h.
// If this splits the root of the subtree,
// return the new splitter and subtree handle

Function *ABItem::insertRec(e : Element, h : ℕ, ℓ : List of Element) : Key×ABHandle*
   $i := locateLocally(e)$
   if $h = 1$ **then**   // base case
      if $key(c[i] \rightarrow e) = key(e)$ **then**
         $c[i] \rightarrow e := e$
         return $(\perp, \textbf{null})$
      else
         $(k,t) := (key(e), \ell.insertBefore(e, c[i]))$
   else
      $(k,t) := c[i] \rightarrow insertRec(e, h-1, \ell)$
      if $t =$ **null then return** $(\perp, \textbf{null})$
   endif

$s' := \langle s[1], \ldots, s[i-1], k, s[i], \ldots, s[d-1] \rangle$
$c' := \langle c[1], \ldots, c[i-1], t, c[i], \ldots, c[d] \rangle$

if $d < b$ **then** // there is still room here
   $(s,c,d) := (s',c',d+1)$
   return $(\perp, \textbf{null})$
else // **split** this node
   $d := \lfloor (b+1)/2 \rfloor$
   $s := s'[b+2-d..b]$
   $c := c'[b+2-d..b+1]$
   return $(s'[b+1-d], \textbf{allocate } ABItem(s'[1..b-d], c'[1..b+1-d]))$

Fig. 7.8. Insertion into an (a,b)-tree

u the parent of v (if it exists). The solution is to *split* v in the middle (see Fig. 7.7). More precisely, we create a new node t to the left of v and reduce the degree of v to $d = \lceil (b+1)/2 \rceil$ by moving the $b+1-d$ leftmost child pointers $c'[1..b+1-d]$ and the corresponding keys $s'[1..b-d]$. The old node v keeps the d rightmost child pointers $c'[b+2-d..b+1]$ and the corresponding splitters $s'[b+2-d..b]$.

The "leftover" middle key $k = s'[b + 1 - d]$ is an upper bound for the keys reachable from t. It and the pointer to t are needed in the predecessor u of v. The situation for u is analogous to the situation for v before the insertion: if v was the i-th child of u, t displaces it to the right. Now t becomes the i-th child, and k is inserted as the i-th splitter. The addition of t as an additional child of u increases the degree of u. If the degree of u becomes $b + 1$, we split u. The process continues until either some ancestor of v has room to accommodate the new child or the root is split.

In the latter case, we allocate a new root node pointing to the two fragments of the old root. This is the only situation where the height of the tree can increase. In this case, the depth of all leaves increases by one, i.e., we maintain the invariant that all leaves have the same depth. Since the height of the tree is $O(\log n)$ (see Lemma 7.1), we obtain a worst-case execution time of $O(\log n)$ for *insert*. Pseudocode is shown in Fig. 7.8.[4]

We still need to argue that *insert* leaves us with a correct (a, b)-tree. When we split a node of degree $b + 1$, we create nodes of degree $d = \lceil (b + 1)/2 \rceil$ and $b + 1 - d$. Both degrees are clearly at most b. Also, $b + 1 - \lceil (b + 1)/2 \rceil \geq a$ if $b \geq 2a - 1$. Convince yourself that $b = 2a - 2$ will not work.

Exercise 7.6. It is tempting to streamline *insert* by calling *locate* to replace the initial descent of the tree. Why does this not work? Would it work if every node had a pointer to its parent?

We now turn to the operation *remove*. The approach is similar to what we already know from our study of *insert*. We locate the element to be removed, remove it from the sorted list, and repair possible violations of invariants on the way back up. Figure 7.9 shows pseudocode. When a parent u notices that the degree of its child $c[i]$ has dropped to $a - 1$, it combines this child with one of its neighbors $c[i - 1]$ or $c[i + 1]$ to repair the invariant. There are two cases illustrated in Fig. 7.10. If the neighbor has degree larger than a, we can *balance* the degrees by transferring some nodes from the neighbor. If the neighbor has degree a, balancing cannot help since both nodes together have only $2a - 1$ children, so that we cannot give a children to both of them. However, in this case we can *fuse* them into a single node, since the requirement $b \geq 2a - 1$ ensures that the fused node has degree b at most.

To fuse a node $c[i]$ with its right neighbor $c[i + 1]$, we concatenate their child arrays. To obtain the corresponding splitters, we need to place the splitter $s[i]$ of the parent between the splitter arrays. The fused node replaces $c[i + 1]$, $c[i]$ is deallocated, and $c[i]$, together with the splitter $s[i]$, is removed from the parent node.

Exercise 7.7. Suppose a node v has been produced by fusing two nodes as described above. Prove that the ordering invariant is maintained: an element e reachable through child $v.c[i]$ has key $v.s[i - 1] < key(e) \leq v.s[i]$ for $1 \leq i \leq v.d$.

Balancing two neighbors is equivalent to first fusing them and then splitting the result, as in the operation *insert*. Since fusing two nodes decreases the degree of their

---

[4] We borrow the notation $C :: m$ from C++ to define a method m for class C.

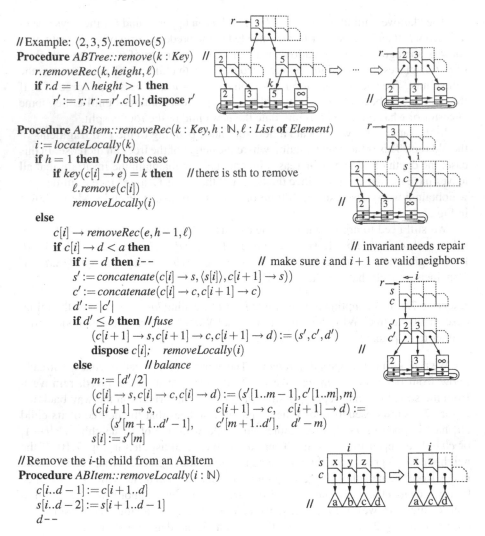

// Example: ⟨2, 3, 5⟩.remove(5)
Procedure *ABTree::remove(k : Key)* //
  r.removeRec(k, height, ℓ)
  if *r.d = 1 ∧ height > 1* **then**
    r′ := r; r := r′.c[1]; **dispose** *r′*

Procedure *ABItem::removeRec(k : Key, h : ℕ, ℓ : List of Element)*
  i := locateLocally(k)
  if *h = 1* **then**   // base case
    if *key(c[i] → e) = k* **then**   // there is sth to remove
      ℓ.remove(c[i])
      removeLocally(i)
  else
    c[i] → removeRec(e, h − 1, ℓ)
    if *c[i] → d < a* **then**   // invariant needs repair
      if *i = d* **then** *i−−*   // make sure *i* and *i + 1* are valid neighbors
      s′ := concatenate(c[i] → s, ⟨s[i]⟩, c[i + 1] → s))
      c′ := concatenate(c[i] → c, c[i + 1] → c)
      d′ := |c′|
      if *d′ ≤ b* **then** //fuse
        (c[i + 1] → s, c[i + 1] → c, c[i + 1] → d) := (s′, c′, d′)
        dispose *c[i];*   *removeLocally(i)*
      else   // balance
        m := ⌈d′/2⌉
        (c[i] → s, c[i] → c, c[i] → d) := (s′[1..m − 1], c′[1..m], m)
        (c[i + 1] → s,   c[i + 1] → c,   c[i + 1] → d) :=
          (s′[m + 1..d′ − 1],   c′[m + 1..d′],   d′ − m)
        s[i] := s′[m]

// Remove the *i*-th child from an ABItem
Procedure *ABItem::removeLocally(i : ℕ)*
  c[i..d − 1] := c[i + 1..d]
  s[i..d − 2] := s[i + 1..d − 1]
  d−−

Fig. 7.9. Removal from an (a, b)-tree

parent, the need to fuse or balance might propagate up the tree. If the degree of the root drops to one, we do one of two things. If the tree has height one and hence contains only a single element, there is nothing to do and we are finished. Otherwise, we deallocate the root and replace it by its sole child. The height of the tree decreases by one.

The execution time of *remove* is also proportional to the height of the tree and hence logarithmic in the size of the sorted sequence. We summarize the performance of (a, b)-trees in the following theorem.

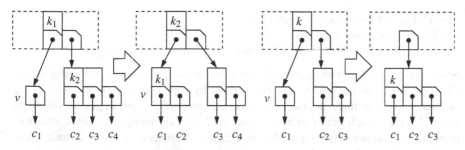

Fig. 7.10. Node balancing and fusing in (2,4)-trees: node v has degree $a-1$ (here 1). In the situation on the *left*, it has a sibling of degree $a+1$ or more (here 3), and we *balance* the degrees. In the situation on the *right*, the sibling has degree a and we *fuse* v and its sibling. Observe how keys are moved. When two nodes are fused, the degree of the parent decreases

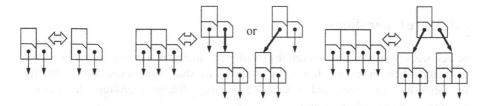

Fig. 7.11. The correspondence between (2,4)-trees and red–black trees. Nodes of degree 2, 3, and 4 as shown on the *left* correspond to the configurations on the *right*. Red edges are shown in **bold**

Theorem 7.2. *For any integers a and b with $a \geq 2$ and $b \geq 2a - 1$, (a,b)-trees support the operations insert, remove, and locate on sorted sequences of size n in time* $O(\log n)$.

Exercise 7.8. Give a more detailed implementation of *locateLocally* based on binary search that needs at most $\lceil \log b \rceil$ comparisons. Your code should avoid both explicit use of infinite key values and special case treatments for extreme cases.

Exercise 7.9. Suppose $a = 2^k$ and $b = 2a$. Show that $(1 + \frac{1}{k}) \log n + 1$ element comparisons suffice to execute a *locate* operation in an (a,b)-tree. Hint: it is *not* quite sufficient to combine Exercise 7.4 with Exercise 7.8 since this would give you an additional term $+k$.

Exercise 7.10. Extend (a,b)-trees so that they can handle multiple occurrences of the same key. Elements with identical keys should be treated last-in first-out, i.e., $remove(k)$ should remove the least recently inserted element with key k.

*Exercise 7.11 (red–black trees). A *red–black tree* is a binary search tree where the edges are colored either red or black. The *black depth* of a node v is the number of black edges on the path from the root to v. The following invariants have to hold:

(a) All leaves have the same black depth.
(b) Edges into leaves are black.
(c) No path from the root to a leaf contains two consecutive red edges.

Show that red–black trees and $(2,4)$-trees are isomorphic in the following sense: $(2,4)$-trees can be mapped to red–black trees by replacing nodes of degree three or four by two or three nodes, respectively, connected by red edges as shown in Fig. 7.11. Red–black trees can be mapped to $(2,4)$-trees using the inverse transformation, i.e., components induced by red edges are replaced by a single node. Now explain how to implement $(2,4)$-trees using a representation as a red–black tree.[5] Explain how the operations of expanding, shrinking, splitting, merging, and balancing nodes of the $(2,4)$-tree can be translated into recoloring and rotation operations in the red–black tree. Colors are stored at the target nodes of the corresponding edges.

7.3 More Operations

Search trees support many operations in addition to *insert*, *remove*, and *locate*. We shall study them in two batches. In this section, we shall discuss operations directly supported by (a,b)-trees, and in Sect. 7.5 we shall discuss operations that require augmentation of the data structure.

- *min/max.* The constant-time operations *first* and *last* on a sorted list give us the smallest and the largest element in the sequence in constant time. In particular, search trees implement *double-ended priority queues*, i.e., sets that allow locating and removing both the smallest and the largest element in logarithmic time. For example, in Fig. 7.5, the dummy element of list ℓ gives us access to the smallest element, 2, and to the largest element, 19, via its *next* and *prev* pointers, respectively.
- *Range queries.* To retrieve all elements with keys in the range $[x,y]$, we first locate x and then traverse the sorted list until we see an element with a key larger than y. This takes time $O(\log n + \text{output size})$. For example, the range query $[4,14]$ applied to the search tree in Fig. 7.5 will find the 5, it subsequently outputs 7, 11, 13, and it stops when it sees the 17.
- *Build/rebuild.* Exercise 7.12 asks you to give an algorithm that converts a sorted list or array into an (a,b)-tree in linear time. Even if we first have to sort the elements, this operation is much faster than inserting the elements one by one. We also obtain a more compact data structure this way.

Exercise 7.12. Explain how to construct an (a,b)-tree from a sorted list in linear time. Which $(2,4)$-tree does your routine construct for the sequence $\langle 1..17 \rangle$? Next, remove the elements 4, 9, and 16.

---

[5] This may be more space-efficient than a direct representation, if the keys are large.

7.3.1 *Concatenation

Two sorted sequences can be concatenated if the largest element of the first sequence is smaller than the smallest element of the second sequence. If sequences are represented as (a,b)-trees, two sequences q_1 and q_2 can be concatenated in time $O(\log\max(|q_1|,|q_2|))$. First, we remove the dummy item from q_1 and concatenate the underlying lists. Next, we fuse the root of one tree with an appropriate node of the other tree in such a way that the resulting tree remains sorted and balanced. More precisely, if $q_1.height \geq q_2.height$, we descend $q_1.height - q_2.height$ levels from the root of q_1 by following pointers to the rightmost children. The node v, that we reach is then fused with the root of q_2. The new splitter key required is the largest key in q_1. If the degree of v now exceeds b, v is split. From that point, the concatenation proceeds like an *insert* operation, propagating splits up the tree until the invariant is fulfilled or a new root node is created. The case $q_1.height < q_2.height$ is a mirror image. We descend $q_2.height - q_1.height$ levels from the root of q_2 by following pointers to the leftmost children, and fuse .... If we explicitly store the heights of the trees, the operation runs in time $O(1 + |q_1.height - q_2.height|) = O(\log(|q_1| + |q_2|))$. Figure 7.12 gives an example.

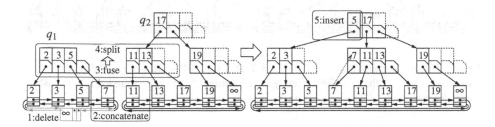

Fig. 7.12. Concatenating $(2,4)$-trees for $\langle 2,3,5,7 \rangle$ and $\langle 11,13,17,19 \rangle$

7.3.2 *Splitting

We now show how to split a sorted sequence at a given element in logarithmic time. Consider a sequence $q = \langle w,\ldots,x,y,\ldots,z \rangle$. Splitting q at y results in the sequences $q_1 = \langle w,\ldots,x \rangle$ and $q_2 = \langle y,\ldots,z \rangle$. We implement splitting as follows. Consider the path from the root to leaf y. We split each node v on this path into two nodes, v_ℓ and v_r. Node v_ℓ gets the children of v that are to the left of the path and v_r gets the children, that are to the right of the path. Some of these nodes may get no children. Each of the nodes with children can be viewed as the root of an (a,b)-tree. Concatenating the left trees and a new dummy sequence element yields the elements up to x. Concatenating $\langle y \rangle$ and the right trees produces the sequence of elements starting from y. We can do these $O(\log n)$ concatenations in total time $O(\log n)$ by exploiting the fact that the left trees have a strictly decreasing height and the right trees have a strictly increasing height. Let us look at the trees on the left in more detail. Let

r_1, r_2 to r_k be the roots of the trees on the left and let h_1, h_2 to h_h be their heights. Then $h_1 \geq h_2 \geq \ldots \geq h_k$. We first concatenate r_{k-1} and r_k in time $O(1 + h_{k-1} - h_k)$, then concatenate r_{k-2} with the result in time $O(1 + h_{k-2} - h_{k-1})$, then concatenate r_{k-3} with the result in time $O(1 + h_{k-2} - h_{k-1})$, and so on. The total time needed for all concatenations is $O(\sum_{1 \leq i < k}(1 + h_i - h_{i+1})) = O(k + h_1 - h_k) = O(\log n)$. Figure 7.13 gives an example.

Exercise 7.13. We glossed over one issue in the argument above. What is the height of the tree resulting from concatenating the trees with roots r_k to r_i? Show that the height is $h_i + O(1)$.

Exercise 7.14. Explain how to remove a subsequence $\langle e \in q : \alpha \leq e \leq \beta \rangle$ from an (a,b)-tree q in time $O(\log n)$.

split $< 2, 3, 5, 7, 11, 13, 17, 19 >$ at 11

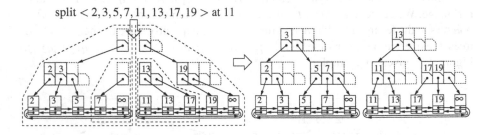

Fig. 7.13. Splitting the $(2,4)$-tree for $\langle 2, 3, 5, 7, 11, 13, 17, 19 \rangle$ shown in Fig. 7.5 produces the subtrees shown on the *left*. Subsequently concatenating the trees surrounded by the dashed lines leads to the $(2,4)$-trees shown on the *right*

7.4 Amortized Analysis of Update Operations

The best-case time for an insertion or removal is considerably smaller than the worst-case time. In the best case, we basically pay for locating the affected element, for updating the sequence, and for updating the bottommost internal node. The worst case is much slower. *Split* or *fuse* operations may propagate all the way up the tree.

Exercise 7.15. Give a sequence of n operations on $(2,3)$-trees that requires $\Omega(n \log n)$ *split* and *fuse* operations.

We now show that the *amortized* complexity is essentially equal to that of the best case if b is not at its minimum possible value but is at least $2a$. In Sect. 7.5.1, we shall see variants of *insert* and *remove* that turn out to have constant amortized complexity in the light of the analysis below.

Theorem 7.3. *Consider an (a,b)-tree with $b \geq 2a$ that is initially empty. For any sequence of n insert or remove operations, the total number of split or fuse operations is $O(n)$.*

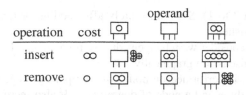

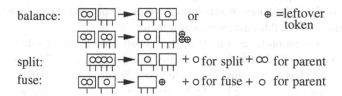

Fig. 7.14. The effect of (a, b)-tree operations on the token invariant. The *upper part* of the figure illustrates the addition or removal of a leaf. The two tokens charged for an insert are used as follows. When the leaf is added to a node of degree three or four, the two tokens are put on the node. When the leaf is added to a node of degree two, the two tokens are not needed, and the token from the node is also freed. The *lower part* illustrates the use of the tokens in *balance*, *split*, and *fuse* operations

Proof. We give the proof for $(2, 4)$-trees and leave the generalization to Exercise 7.16. We use the bank account method introduced in Sect. 3.3. *Split* and *fuse* operations are paid for by tokens. These operations cost one token each. We charge two tokens for each *insert* and one token for each *remove*. and claim that this suffices to pay for all *split* and *fuse* operations. Note that there is at most one *balance* operation for each *remove*, so that we can account for the cost of *balance* directly without an accounting detour. In order to do the accounting, we associate the tokens with the nodes of the tree and show that the nodes can hold tokens according to the following table (*the token invariant*):

degree	1	2	3	4	5
tokens	oo	o		oo	oooo

Note that we have included the cases of degree 1 and 5 that occur during rebalancing. The purpose of splitting and fusing is to remove these exceptional degrees.

Creating an empty sequence makes a list with one dummy item and a root of degree one. We charge two tokens for the *create* and put them on the root. Let us look next at insertions and removals. These operations add or remove a leaf and hence increase or decrease the degree of a node immediately above the leaf level. Increasing the degree of a node requires up to two additional tokens on the node (if the degree increases from 3 to 4 or from 4 to 5), and this is exactly what we charge for an insertion. If the degree grows from 2 to 3, we do not need additional tokens and we are overcharging for the insertion; there is no harm in this. Similarly, reducing the degree by one may require one additional token on the node (if the degree decreases from 3 to 2 or from 2 to 1). So, immediately after adding or removing a leaf, the token invariant is satisfied.

We need next to consider what happens during rebalancing. Figure 7.14 summarizes the following discussion graphically.

A *split* operation is performed on nodes of (temporary) degree five and results in a node of degree three and a node of degree two. It also increases the degree of the parent. The four tokens stored on the degree-five node are spent as follows: one token pays for the *split*, one token is put on the new node of degree two, and two tokens are used for the parent node. Again, we may not need the additional tokens for the parent node; in this case, we discard them.

A *balance* operation takes a node of degree one and a node of degree three or four and moves one child from the high-degree node to the node of degree one. If the high-degree node has degree three, we have two tokens available to us and need two tokens; if the high-degree node has degree four, we have four tokens available to us and need one token. In either case, the tokens available are sufficient to maintain the token invariant.

A *fuse* operation fuses a degree-one node with a degree-two node into a degree-three node and decreases the degree of the parent. We have three tokens available. We use one to pay for the operation and one to pay for the decrease of the degree of the parent. The third token is no longer needed, and we discard it.

Let us summarize. We charge two tokens for sequence creation, two tokens for each *insert*, and one token for each *remove*. These tokens suffice to pay one token each for every *split* or *fuse* operation. There is at most a constant amount of work for everything else done during an *insert* or *remove* operation. Hence, the total cost for n update operations is $O(n)$, and there are at most $2(n+1)$ *split* or *fuse* operations. $\Box$

*Exercise 7.16. Generalize the above proof to arbitrary a and b with $b \geq 2a$. Show that n *insert* or *remove* operations cause only $O(n/(b-2a+1))$ *fuse* or *split* operations.

*Exercise 7.17 (weight-balanced trees [150]). Consider the following variant of (a,b)-trees: the node-by-node invariant $d \geq a$ is relaxed to the global invariant that the tree has at least $2a^{height-1}$ leaves. A *remove* does not perform any *fuse* or *balance* operations. Instead, the whole tree is rebuilt using the routine described in Exercise 7.12 when the invariant is violated. Show that *remove* operations execute in $O(\log n)$ amortized time.

7.5 Augmented Search Trees

We show here that (a,b)-trees can support additional operations on sequences if we augment the data structure with additional information. However, augmentations come at a cost. They consume space and require time for keeping them up to date. Augmentations may also stand in each other's way.

Exercise 7.18 (reduction). Some operations on search trees can be carried out with the use of the navigation data structure alone and without the doubly linked list. Go through the operations discussed so far and discuss whether they require the *next* and *prev* pointers of linear lists. Range queries are a particular challenge.

7.5.1 Parent Pointers

Suppose we want to remove an element specified by the handle of a list item. In the basic implementation described in Sect. 7.2, the only thing we can do is to read the key k of the element and call *remove*(k). This would take logarithmic time for the search, although we know from Sect. 7.4 that the amortized number of *fuse* operations required to rebalance the tree is constant. This detour is not necessary if each node v of the tree stores a handle indicating its *parent* in the tree (and perhaps an index i such that $v.parent.c[i] = v$).

Exercise 7.19. Show that in (a, b)-trees with parent pointers, *remove*$(h : Item)$ and *insertAfter*$(h : Item)$ can be implemented to run in constant amortized time.

*Exercise 7.20 (avoiding augmentation). Outline a class *ABTreeIterator* that allows one to represent a position in an (a, b)-tree that has no parent pointers. Creating an iterator I is an extension of *search* and takes logarithmic time. The class should support the operations *remove* and *insertAfter* in constant amortized time. Hint: store the path to the current position.

*Exercise 7.21 (finger search). Augment search trees such that searching can profit from a "hint" given in the form of the handle of a *finger element* e'. If the sought element has rank r and the finger element e' has rank r', the search time should be $O(\log |r - r'|)$. Hint: one solution links all nodes at each level of the search tree into a doubly linked list.

*Exercise 7.22 (optimal merging). Explain how to use finger search to implement merging of two sorted sequences in time $O(n \log(m/n))$, where n is the size of the shorter sequence and m is the size of the longer sequence.

7.5.2 Subtree Sizes

Suppose that every nonleaf node t of a search tree stores its *size*, i.e., $t.size$ is the number of leaves in the subtree rooted at t. The k-th smallest element of the sorted sequence can then be selected in a time proportional to the height of the tree. For simplicity, we shall describe this for binary search trees. Let t denote the current search tree node, which is initialized to the root. The idea is to descend the tree while maintaining the invariant that the k-th element is contained in the subtree rooted at t. We also maintain the number i of elements that are to the *left* of t. Initially, $i = 0$. Let i' denote the size of the left subtree of t. If $i + i' \geq k$, then we set t to its left successor. Otherwise, t is set to its right successor and i is increased by i'. When a leaf is reached, the invariant ensures that the k-th element is reached. Figure 7.15 gives an example.

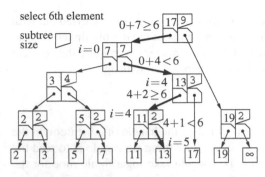

Fig. 7.15. Selecting the 6th smallest element from $\langle 2,3,5,7,11,13,17,19\rangle$ represented by a binary search tree. The **thick** arrows indicate the search path

Exercise 7.23. Generalize the above selection algorithm to (a,b)-trees. Develop two variants: one that needs time $O(b\log_a n)$ and stores only the subtree size and another variant that needs only time $O(\log n)$ and stores $d-1$ sums of subtree sizes in a node of degree d.

Exercise 7.24. Explain how to determine the rank of a sequence element with key k in logarithmic time.

Exercise 7.25. A colleague suggests supporting both logarithmic selection time and constant amortized update time by combining the augmentations described in Sects. 7.5.1 and 7.5.2. What will go wrong?

7.6 Implementation Notes

Our pseudocode for (a,b)-trees is close to an actual implementation in a language such as C++ except for a few oversimplifications. The temporary arrays s' and c' in the procedures *insertRec* and *removeRec* can be avoided by appropriate case distinctions. In particular, a *balance* operation will not require calling the memory manager. A *split* operation of a node v might be slightly faster if v keeps the left half rather than the right half. We did not formulate the operation this way because then the cases of inserting a new sequence element and splitting a node would no longer be the same from the point of view of their parent.

For large b, *locateLocally* should use binary search. For small b, a linear search might be better. Furthermore, we might want to have a specialized implementation for small, fixed values of a and b that *unrolls*[6] all the inner loops. Choosing b to be a power of two might simplify this task.

Of course, the values of a and b are important. Let us start with the cost of *locate*. There are two kinds of operation that dominate the execution time of *locate*: besides their inherent cost, element comparisons may cause branch mispredictions (see also Sect. 5.9); pointer dereferences may cause cache faults. Exercise 7.9 indicates that

---

[6] *Unrolling* a loop "**for** $i:=1$ **to** K **do** $body_i$" means replacing it by the *straight-line program* "$body_1; \ldots; body_K$". This saves the overhead required for loop control and may give other opportunities for simplifications.

element comparisons can be minimized by choosing a as a large power of two and $b = 2a$. Since the number of pointer dereferences is proportional to the height of the tree (see Exercise 7.4), large values of a are also good for this measure. Taking this reasoning to the extreme, we would obtain the best performance for $a \geq n$, i.e., a single sorted array. This is not astonishing. We have concentrated on searches, and static data structures are best if updates are neglected.

Insertions and deletions have an amortized cost of one *locate* plus a constant number of node reorganizations (*split*, *balance*, or *fuse*) with cost $O(b)$ each. We obtain a logarithmic amortized cost for update operations if $b = O(\log n)$. A more detailed analysis (see Exercise 7.16) would reveal that increasing b beyond $2a$ makes *split* and *fuse* operations less frequent and thus saves expensive calls to the memory manager associated with them. However, this measure has a slightly negative effect on the performance of *locate* and it clearly increases *space consumption*. Hence, b should remain close to $2a$.

Finally, let us take a closer look at the role of cache faults. A cache of size M can hold $\Theta(M/b)$ nodes. These are most likely to be the frequently accessed nodes close to the root. To a first approximation, the top $\log_a(M/b)$ levels of the tree are stored in the cache. Below this level, every pointer dereference is associated with a cache fault, i.e., we will have about $\log_a(bn/\Theta(M))$ cache faults in each *locate* operation. Since the cache blocks of processor caches start at addresses that are a multiple of the block size, it makes sense to *align* the starting addresses of search tree nodes with a cache block, i.e., to make sure that they also start at an address that is a multiple of the block size. Note that (a,b)-trees might well be more efficient than binary search for large data sets because we may save a factor of $\log a$ in cache faults.

Very large search trees are stored on disks. Under the name *B-trees* [16], (a,b)-trees are the workhorse of the indexing data structures in databases. In that case, internal nodes have a size of several kilobytes. Furthermore, the items of the linked list are also replaced by entire data blocks that store between a' and b' elements, for appropriate values of a' and b' (see also Exercise 3.20). These leaf blocks will then also be subject to splitting, balancing, and fusing operations. For example, assume that we have $a = 2^{10}$, the internal memory is large enough (a few megabytes) to cache the root and its children, and the data blocks store between 16 and 32 Kbyte of data. Then two disk accesses are sufficient to *locate* any element in a sorted sequence that takes 16 Gbyte of storage. Since putting elements into leaf blocks dramatically decreases the total space needed for the internal nodes and makes it possible to perform very fast range queries, this measure can also be useful for a cache-efficient internal-memory implementation. However, note that update operations may now move an element in memory and thus will invalidate element handles stored outside the data structure. There are many more tricks for implementing (external-memory) (a,b)-trees. We refer the reader to [79] and [141, Chaps. 2 and 14] for overviews. A good free implementation of B-trees is available in STXXL [48].

From the augmentations discussed in Sect. 7.5 and the implementation trade-offs discussed here, it becomes evident that *the* optimal implementation of sorted sequences does not exist but depends on the hardware and the operation mix relevant to the actual application. We believe that (a,b)-trees with $b = 2^k = 2a = O(\log n)$, augmented with parent pointers and a doubly linked list of leaves, are a sorted-sequence data structure that supports a wide range of operations efficiently.

Exercise 7.26. What choice of a and b for an (a,b)-tree guarantees that the number of I/O operations required for *insert*, *remove*, or *locate* is $O(\log_B(n/M))$? How many I/O operations are needed to *build* an n-element (a,b)-tree using the external sorting algorithm described in Sect. 5.7 as a subroutine? Compare this with the number of I/Os needed for building the tree naively using insertions. For example, try $M = 2^{29}$ bytes, $B = 2^{18}$ bytes[7], $n = 2^{32}$, and elements that have 8-byte keys and 8 bytes of associated information.

7.6.1 C++

The STL has four container classes *set*, *map*, *multiset*, and *multimap* for sorted sequences. The prefix *multi* means that there may be several elements with the same key. *Map*s offer the interface of an associative array (see also Chap. 4). For example, *someMap*[k] := x inserts or updates the element with key k and sets the associated information to x.

The most widespread implementation of sorted sequences in STL uses a variant of red–black trees with parent pointers, where elements are stored in all nodes rather than only in the leaves. None of the STL data types supports efficient splitting or concatenation of sorted sequences.

LEDA [118] offers a powerful interface *sortseq* that supports all important operations on sorted sequences, including finger search, concatenation, and splitting. Using an implementation parameter, there is a choice between (a,b)-trees, red–black trees, randomized search trees, weight-balanced trees, and skip lists.

7.6.2 Java

The Java library *java.util* offers the interface classes *SortedMap* and *SortedSet*, which correspond to the STL classes *set* and *map*, respectively. The corresponding implementation classes *TreeMap* and *TreeSet* are based on red–black trees.

7.7 Historical Notes and Further Findings

There is an entire zoo of sorted sequence data structures. Just about any of them will do if you just want to support *insert*, *remove*, and *locate* in logarithmic time. Performance differences for the basic operations are often more dependent on implementation details than on the fundamental properties of the underlying data structures. The differences show up in the additional operations.

---

[7] We are making a slight oversimplification here, since in practice one will use much smaller block sizes for organizing the tree than for sorting.

The first sorted-sequence data structure to support *insert*, *remove*, and *locate* in logarithmic time was AVL trees [4]. AVL trees are binary search trees which maintain the invariant that the heights of the subtrees of a node differ by one at the most. Since this is a strong balancing condition, *locate* is probably a little faster than in most competitors. On the other hand, AVL trees do *not* have constant amortized update costs. Another small disadvantage is that storing the heights of subtrees costs additional space. In comparison, red–black trees have slightly higher costs for *locate*, but they have faster updates and the single color bit can often be squeezed in somewhere. For example, pointers to items will always store even addresses, so that their least significant bit could be diverted to storing color information.

(2,3)-trees were introduced in [6]. The generalization to (a,b)-trees and the amortized analysis of Sect. 3.3 come from [95]. There, it was also shown that the total number of splitting and fusing operations at the nodes of any given height decreases exponentially with the height.

Splay trees [183] and some variants of randomized search trees [176] work even without any additional information besides one key and two successor pointers. A more interesting advantage of these data structures is their *adaptability* to nonuniform access frequencies. If an element e is accessed with probability p, these search trees will be reshaped over time to allow an access to e in a time $O(\log(1/p))$. This can be shown to be asymptotically optimal for any comparison-based data structure. However, this property leads to improved running time only for quite skewed access patterns because of the large constants.

Weight-balanced trees [150] balance the size of the subtrees instead of the height. They have the advantage that a node of weight w (= number of leaves of its subtree) is only rebalanced after $\Omega(w)$ insertions or deletions have passed through it [26].

There are so many *search tree* data structures for *sorted sequences* that these two terms are sometimes used as synonyms. However, there are also some equally interesting data structures for sorted sequences that are *not* based on search trees. Sorted arrays are a simple *static* data structure. Sparse tables [97] are an elegant way to make sorted arrays dynamic. The idea is to accept some empty cells to make insertion easier. Reference [19] extended sparse tables to a data structure which is asymptotically optimal in an amortized sense. Moreover, this data structure is a crucial ingredient for a sorted-sequence data structure [19] that is *cache-oblivious* [69], i.e., it is cache-efficient on any two levels of a memory hierarchy without even knowing the size of caches and cache blocks. The other ingredient is oblivious *static* search trees [69]; these are perfectly balanced binary search trees stored in an array such that any search path will exhibit good locality in any cache. We describe here the *van Emde Boas layout* used for this purpose, for the case where there are $n = 2^{2^k}$ leaves for some integer k. We store the top 2^{k-1} levels of the tree at the beginning of the array. After that, we store the 2^{k-1} subtrees of depth 2^{k-1}, allocating consecutive blocks of memory for them. We recursively allocate the resulting $1 + 2^{k-1}$ subtrees of depth 2^{k-1}. Static cache-oblivious search trees are practical in the sense that they can outperform binary search in a sorted array.

Skip lists [159] are based on another very simple idea. The starting point is a sorted linked list ℓ. The tedious task of scanning ℓ during *locate* can be accelerated by producing a shorter list ℓ' that contains only some of the elements in ℓ. If corresponding elements of ℓ and ℓ' are linked, it suffices to scan ℓ' and only descend to ℓ when approaching the searched element. This idea can be iterated by building shorter and shorter lists until only a single element remains in the highest-level list. This data structure supports all important operations efficiently in an expected sense. Randomness comes in because the decision about which elements to lift to a higher-level list is made randomly. Skip lists are particularly well suited for supporting finger search.

Yet another family of sorted-sequence data structures comes into play when we no longer consider keys as atomic objects. If keys are numbers given in binary representation, we can obtain faster data structures using ideas similar to the fast integer-sorting algorithms described in Sect. 5.6. For example, we can obtain sorted sequences with w-bit integer keys that support all operations in time $O(\log w)$ [198, 129]. At least for 32 bit keys, these ideas bring a considerable speedup in practice [47]. Not astonishingly, string keys are also important. For example, suppose we want to adapt (a, b)-trees to use variable-length strings as keys. If we want to keep a fixed size for node objects, we have to relax the condition on the minimal degree of a node. Two ideas can be used to avoid storing long string keys in many nodes. *Common prefixes* of keys need to be stored only once, often in the parent nodes. Furthermore, it suffices to store the *distinguishing prefixes* of keys in inner nodes, i.e., just enough characters to be able to distinguish different keys in the current node [83]. Taking these ideas to the extreme results in *tries* [64], a search tree data structure specifically designed for string keys: tries are trees whose edges are labeled by characters or strings. The characters along a root–leaf path represent a key. Using appropriate data structures for the inner nodes, a trie can be searched in time $O(s)$ for a string of size s.

We shall close with three interesting generalizations of sorted sequences. The first generalization is *multidimensional objects*, such as intervals or points in d-dimensional space. We refer to textbooks on geometry for this wide subject [46]. The second generalization is *persistence*. A data structure is persistent if it supports nondestructive updates. For example, after the insertion of an element, there may be two versions of the data structure, the one before the insertion and the one after the insertion – both can be searched [59]. The third generalization is *searching many sequences* [36, 37, 130]. In this setting, there are many sequences, and searches need to locate a key in all of them or a subset of them.

8

Graph Representation

Scientific results are mostly available in the form of articles in journals and conference proceedings, and on various Web[1] resources. These articles are not self-contained, but cite previous articles with related content. However, when you read an article from 1975 with an interesting partial result, you may often ask yourself what the current state of the art is. In particular, you would like to know which newer articles cite the old article. Projects such as Google Scholar provide this functionality by analyzing the reference sections of articles and building a database of articles that efficiently supports looking up articles that cite a given article.

We can easily model this situation by a directed graph. The graph has a node for each article and an edge for each citation. An edge (u,v) from article u to article v means that u cites v. In this terminology, every node (= article) stores all its outgoing edges (= the articles cited by it) but not the incoming edges (the articles citing it). If every node were also to store the incoming edges, it would be easy to find the citing articles. One of the main tasks of Google Scholar is to construct the reversed edges. This example shows that the cost of even a very basic elementary operation on a graph, namely finding all edges entering a particular node, depends heavily on the representation of the graph. If the incoming edges are stored explicitly, the operation is easy; if the incoming edges are not stored, the operation is nontrivial.

In this chapter, we shall give an introduction to the various possibilities for representing graphs in a computer. We focus mostly on directed graphs and assume that an undirected graph $G = (V, E)$ is represented as the corresponding (bi)directed graph $G' = (V, \bigcup_{\{u,v\} \in E} \{(u,v), (v,u)\})$. Figure 8.1 illustrates the concept of a bidirected graph. Most of the data structures presented also allow us to represent multiple parallel edges and self-loops. We start with a survey of the operations that we may want to support.

- *Accessing associated information.* Given a node or an edge, we frequently want to access information associated with it, for example the weight of an edge or the distance to a node. In many representations, nodes and edges are objects, and we can store this information directly as a member of these objects. If not otherwise mentioned, we assume that $V = 1..n$ so that information associated

---

[1] The picture above shows a spider web (USFWS, see http://commons.wikimedia.org/wiki/Image:Water_drops_on_spider_web.jpg).

with nodes can be stored in arrays. When all else fails, we can always store node or edge information in a hash table. Hence, accesses can be implemented to run in constant time. In the remainder of this book we abstract from the various options for realizing access by using the data types *NodeArray* and *EdgeArray* to indicate array-like data structures that can be indexed by nodes and by edges, respectively.

- *Navigation.* Given a node, we may want to access its outgoing edges. It turns out that this operation is at the heart of most graph algorithms. As we have seen in the example above, we sometimes also want to know the incoming edges.

- *Edge queries.* Given a pair of nodes (u, v), we may want to know whether this edge is in the graph. This can always be implemented using a hash table, but we may want to have something even faster. A more specialized but important query is to find the *reverse edge* (v, u) of a directed edge $(u, v) \in E$ if it exists. This operation can be implemented by storing additional pointers connecting edges with their reversals.

- *Construction, conversion and output.* The representation most suitable for the algorithmic problem at hand is not always the representation given initially. This is not a big problem, since most graph representations can be translated into each other in linear time.

- *Update.* Sometimes we want to add or remove nodes or edges. For example, the description of some algorithms is simplified if a node is added from which all other nodes can be reached (e.g. Fig. 10.10).

8.1 Unordered Edge Sequences

Perhaps the simplest representation of a graph is as an unordered sequence of edges. Each edge contains a pair of node indices and, possibly, associated information such as an edge weight. Whether these node pairs represent directed or undirected edges is merely a matter of interpretation. Sequence representation is often used for input and output. It is easy to add edges or nodes in constant time. However, many other operations, in particular navigation, take time $\Theta(m)$, which is forbiddingly slow. Only a few graph algorithms work well with the edge sequence representation; most algorithms require easy access to the edges incident on any given node. In this case the ordered representations discussed in the following sections are appropriate. In Chap. 11, we shall see two minimum-spanning-tree algorithms: one works well with an edge sequence representation and the other needs a more sophisticated data structure.

8.2 Adjacency Arrays – Static Graphs

To support easy access to the edges leaving any particular node, we can store the edges leaving any node in an array. If no additional information is stored with the edges, this array will just contain the indices of the target nodes. If the graph is *static*, i.e., does not change over time, we can concatenate all these little arrays into a single

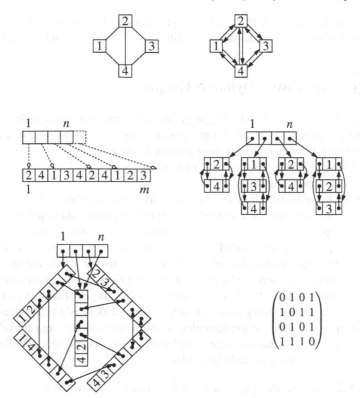

Fig. 8.1. The *first row* shows an undirected graph and the corresponding bidirected graph. The *second row* shows the adjacency array and adjacency list representations of this bidirected graph. The *third row* shows the linked-edge-objects representation and the adjacency matrix

edge array E. An additional array V stores the starting positions of the subarrays, i.e., for any node v, $V[v]$ is the index in E of the first edge out of V. It is convenient to add a dummy entry $V[n+1]$ with $V[n+1] = m+1$. The edges out of any node v are then easily accessible as $E[V[v]], \ldots, E[V[v+1]-1]$; the dummy entry ensures that this also holds true for node n. Figure 8.1 shows an example.

The memory consumption for storing a directed graph using adjacency arrays is $n + m + \Theta(1)$ words. This is even more compact than the $2m$ words needed for an edge sequence representation.

Adjacency array representations can be generalized to store additional information: we may store information associated with edges in separate arrays or within the edge array. If we also need incoming edges, we may use additional arrays V' and E' to store the reversed graph.

Exercise 8.1. Design a linear-time algorithm for converting an edge sequence representation of a directed graph into an adjacency array representation. You should use only $O(1)$ auxiliary space. Hint: view the problem as the task of sorting edges by their source node and adapt the integer-sorting algorithm shown in Fig. 5.15.

8.3 Adjacency Lists – Dynamic Graphs

Edge arrays are a compact and efficient graph representation. Their main disadvantage is that it is expensive to add or remove edges. For example, assume that we want to insert a new edge (u, v). Even if there is room in the edge array E to accommodate it, we still have to move the edges associated with nodes $u + 1$ to n one position to the right, which takes time $O(m)$.

In Chap. 3, we learned how to implement dynamic sequences. We can use any of the solutions presented there to produce a dynamic graph data structure. For each node v, we represent the sequence E_v of outgoing (or incoming, or outgoing and incoming) edges by an unbounded array or by a (singly or doubly) linked list. We inherit the advantages and disadvantages of the respective sequence representations. Unbounded arrays are more cache-efficient. Linked lists allow constant-time insertion and deletion of edges at arbitrary positions. Most graphs arising in practice are sparse in the sense that every node has only a few incident edges. Adjacency lists for sparse graphs should be implemented without the dummy item introduced in Sect. 3.1, because an additional item would waste considerable space. In the example in Fig. 8.1, we show circularly linked lists.

Exercise 8.2. Suppose the edges adjacent to a node u are stored in an unbounded array E_u, and an edge $e = (u, v)$ is specified by giving its position in E_u. Explain how to remove $e = (u, v)$ in constant amortized time. Hint: you do *not* have to maintain the relative order of the other edges.

Exercise 8.3. Explain how to implement the algorithm for testing whether a graph is acyclic discussed in Chap. 2.9 so that it runs in linear time, i.e., design an appropriate graph representation and an algorithm using it efficiently. Hint: maintain a queue of nodes with outdegree zero.

Bidirected graphs arise frequently. Undirected graphs are naturally presented as bidirected graphs, and some algorithms that operate on directed graphs need access not only to outgoing edges but also to incoming edges. In these situations, we frequently want to store the information associated with an undirected edge or a directed edge and its reversal only once. Also, we may want to have easy access from an edge to its reversal.

We shall describe two solutions. The first solution simply associates two additional pointers with every directed edge. One points to the reversal, and the other points to the information associated with the edge.

The second solution has only one item for each undirected edge (or pair of directed edges) and makes this item a member of two adjacency lists. So, the item for an undirected edge $\{u, v\}$ would be a member of lists E_u and E_v. If we want doubly linked adjacency information, the edge object for any edge $\{u, v\}$ stores four pointers: two are used for the doubly linked list representing E_u, and two are used for the doubly linked list representing E_v. Any node stores a pointer to some edge incident on it. Starting from it, all edges incident on the node can be traversed. The bottom part of Fig. 8.1 gives an example. A small complication lies in the fact that finding the other end of an edge now requires some work. Note that the edge object for an edge $\{u, v\}$ stores the endpoints in no particular order. Hence, when we explore the edges out of a node u, we must inspect both endpoints and then choose the one which is different from u. An elegant alternative is to store $u \oplus v$ in the edge object [145]. An exclusive OR with either endpoint then yields the other endpoint. Also, this representation saves space.

8.4 The Adjacency Matrix Representation

An n-node graph can be represented by an $n \times n$ *adjacency matrix* A. A_{ij} is 1 if $(i, j) \in E$ and 0 otherwise. Edge insertion or removal and edge queries work in constant time. It takes time $O(n)$ to obtain the edges entering or leaving a node. This is only efficient for very dense graphs with $m = \Omega(n^2)$. The storage requirement is n^2 bits. For very dense graphs, this may be better than the $n + m + O(1)$ words required for adjacency arrays. However, even for dense graphs, the advantage is small if additional edge information is needed.

Exercise 8.4. Explain how to represent an undirected graph with n nodes and without self-loops using $n(n-1)/2$ bits.

Perhaps more important than actually storing the adjacency matrix is the conceptual link between graphs and linear algebra introduced by the adjacency matrix. On the one hand, graph-theoretic problems can be solved using methods from linear algebra. For example, if $C = A^k$, then C_{ij} counts the number of paths from i to j with exactly k edges.

Exercise 8.5. Explain how to store an $n \times n$ matrix A with m nonzero entries using storage $O(m + n)$ such that a matrix–vector multiplication Ax can be performed in time $O(m + n)$. Describe the multiplication algorithm. Expand your representation so that products of the form $x^T A$ can also be computed in time $O(m + n)$.

On the other hand, graph-theoretic concepts can be useful for solving problems from linear algebra. For example, suppose we want to solve the matrix equation $Bx = c$, where B is a symmetric matrix. Now consider the corresponding adjacency matrix A where $A_{ij} = 1$ if and only if $B_{ij} \neq 0$. If an algorithm for computing connected components finds that the undirected graph represented by A contains two distinct connected components, this information can be used to reorder the rows and columns of B such that we obtain an equivalent equation of the form

$$\begin{pmatrix} B_1 & 0 \\ 0 & B_2 \end{pmatrix} \begin{pmatrix} x_1 \\ x_2 \end{pmatrix} = \begin{pmatrix} c_1 \\ c_2 \end{pmatrix}.$$

This equation can now be solved by solving $B_1 x_1 = c_1$ and $B_2 x_2 = c_2$ separately. In practice, the situation is more complicated, since we rarely have matrices whose corresponding graphs are disconnected. Still, more sophisticated graph-theoretic concepts such as cuts can help to discover structure in the matrix which can then be exploited in solving problems in linear algebra.

8.5 Implicit Representations

Many applications work with graphs of special structure. Frequently, this structure can be exploited to obtain simpler and more efficient representations. We shall give two examples.

The *grid graph* $G_{k\ell}$ with node set $V = [0..k-1] \times [0..\ell-1]$ and edge set

$$E = \left\{ ((i,j),(i,j')) \in V^2 : |j-j'| = 1 \right\} \cup \left\{ ((i,j),(i',j)) \in V^2 : |i-i'| = 1 \right\}$$

is completely defined by the two parameters k and ℓ. Figure 8.2 shows $G_{3,4}$. Edge weights could be stored in two two-dimensional arrays, one for the vertical edges and one for the horizontal edges.

An *interval graph* is defined by a set of intervals. For each interval, we have a node in the graph, and two nodes are adjacent if the corresponding intervals overlap.

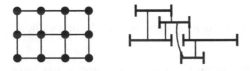

Fig. 8.2. The grid graph G_{34} (*left*) and an interval graph with five nodes and six edges (*right*)

Exercise 8.6 (representation of interval graphs).

(a) Show that for any set of n intervals there is a set of intervals whose endpoints are integers in $[1..2n]$ and that defines the same graph.
(b) Devise an algorithm that decides whether the graph defined by a set of n intervals is connected. Hint: sort the endpoints of the intervals and then scan over the endpoints in sorted order. Keep track of the number of intervals that have started but not ended.
(c*) Devise a representation for interval graphs that needs $O(n)$ space and supports efficient navigation. Given an interval I, you need to find all intervals I' intersecting it; I' intersects I if I contains an endpoint of I' or $I \subseteq I'$. How can you find the former and the latter kinds of interval?

8.6 Implementation Notes

We have seen several representations of graphs in this chapter. They are suitable for different sets of operations on graphs, and can be tuned further for maximum performance in any particular application. The edge sequence representation is good only in specialized situations. Adjacency matrices are good for rather dense graphs. Adjacency lists are good if the graph changes frequently. Very often, some variant of adjacency arrays is fastest. This may be true even if the graph changes, because often there are only a few changes, or all changes happen in an initialization phase of a graph algorithm, or changes can be agglomerated into occasional rebuildings of the graph, or changes can be simulated by building several related graphs.

There are many variants of the adjacency array representation. Information associated with nodes and edges may be stored together with these objects or in separate arrays. A rule of thumb is that information that is frequently accessed should be stored with the nodes and edges. Rarely used data should be kept in separate arrays, because otherwise it would often be moved to the cache without being used. However, there can be other, more complicated reasons why separate arrays may be faster. For example, if both adjacency information and edge weights are read but only the weights are changed, then separate arrays may be faster because the amount of data written back to the main memory is reduced.

Unfortunately, no graph representation is best for all purposes. How can one cope with the zoo of graph representations? First, libraries such as LEDA and the Boost graph library offer several different graph data types, and one of them may suit your purposes. Second, if your application is not particularly time- or space-critical, several representations might do and there is no need to devise a custom-built representation for the particular application. Third, we recommend that graph algorithms should be written in the style of generic programming [71]. The algorithms should access the graph data structure only through a small set of operations, such as iterating over the edges out of a node, accessing information associated with an edge, and proceeding to the target node of an edge. The interface can be captured in an interface description, and a graph algorithm can be run on any representation that realizes the interface. In this way, one can experiment with different representations. Fourth, if you have to build a custom representation for your application, make it available to others.

8.6.1 C++

LEDA [131, 118, 145] offers a powerful graph data type that supports a large variety of operations in constant time and is convenient to use, but is also space-consuming. Therefore LEDA also implements several more space-efficient adjacency array representations.

The Boost graph library [27, 119] emphasizes a strict separation of representation and interface. In particular, Boost graph algorithms run on any representation that realizes the Boost interface. Boost also offers its own graph representation class *adjacency_list*. A large number of parameters allow one to choose between variants of graphs (directed and undirected graphs and multigraphs[2]), types of navigation available (in-edges, out-edges, ...), and representations of vertex and edge sequences

---

[2] Multigraphs allow multiple parallel edges.

(arrays, linked lists, sorted sequences, ...). However, it should be noted that the array representation uses a separate array for the edges adjacent to each vertex.

8.6.2 Java

JDSL [78] offers rich support for graphs in *jdsl.graph*. It has a clear separation between interfaces, algorithms, and representation. It offers an adjacency list representation of graphs that supports directed and undirected edges.

8.7 Historical Notes and Further Findings

Special classes of graphs may result in additional requirements for their representation. An important example is *planar graphs* – graphs that can be drawn in the plane without edges crossing. Here, the ordering of the edges adjacent to a node should be in counterclockwise order with respect to a planar drawing of the graph. In addition, the graph data structure should efficiently support iterating over the edges along a *face* of the graph, a cycle that does not enclose any other node. LEDA offers representations for planar graphs.

Recall that *bipartite graphs* are special graphs where the node set $V = L \cup R$ can be decomposed into two disjoint subsets L and R such that the edges are only between nodes in L and R. All representations discussed here also apply to bipartite graphs. In addition, one may want to store the two sides L and R of the graph.

Hypergraphs $H = (V, E)$ are generalizations of graphs, where edges can connect more than two nodes. Hypergraphs are conveniently represented as the corresponding bipartite graph $B_H = (E \cup V, \{(e, v) : e \in E, v \in V, v \in e\})$.

Cayley graphs are an interesting example of implicitly defined graphs. Recall that a set V is a *group* if it has an associative multiplication operation $*$, a neutral element, and a multiplicative inverse operation. The *Cayley graph* (V, E) with respect to a set $S \subseteq V$ has the edge set $\{(u, u * s) : u \in V, s \in S\}$. Cayley graphs are useful because graph-theoretic concepts can be useful in group theory. On the other hand, group theory yields concise definitions of many graphs with interesting properties. For example, Cayley graphs have been proposed as interconnection networks for parallel computers [12].

In this book, we have concentrated on convenient data structures for *processing* graphs. There is also a lot of work on *storing* graphs in a flexible, portable, space-efficient way. Significant compression is possible if we have a priori information about the graphs. For example, the edges of a triangulation of n points in the plane can be represented with about $6n$ bits [42, 168].

9

Graph Traversal

Suppose you are working in the traffic planning department of a town with a nice medieval center[1]. An unholy coalition of shop owners, who want more street-side parking, and the Green Party, which wants to discourage car traffic altogether, has decided to turn most streets into one-way streets. You want to avoid the worst by checking whether the current plan maintains the minimal requirement that one can still drive from every point in town to every other point.

In the language of graphs (see Sect. 2.9), the question is whether the directed graph formed by the streets is strongly connected. The same problem comes up in other applications. For example, in the case of a communication network with unidirectional channels (e.g., radio transmitters), we want to know who can communicate with whom. Bidirectional communication is possible within the strongly connected components of the graph.

We shall present a simple, efficient algorithm for computing strongly connected components (SCCs) in Sect. 9.2.2. Computing SCCs and many other fundamental problems on graphs can be reduced to systematic graph exploration, inspecting each edge exactly once. We shall present the two most important exploration strategies: *breadth-first search* , in Sect. 9.1, and *depth-first search*, in Sect. 9.2. Both strategies construct forests and partition the edges into four classes: *tree* edges comprising the forest, *forward* edges running parallel to paths of tree edges, *backward* edges running antiparallel to paths of tree edges, and *cross* edges that connect two different branches of a tree in the forest. Figure 9.1 illustrates the classification of edges.

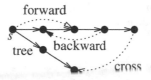

Fig. 9.1. Graph edges classified as tree edges, forward edges, backward edges, and cross edges

---

[1] The copper engraving above shows a part of Frankfurt around 1628 (M. Merian).

9.1 Breadth-First Search

A simple way to explore all nodes reachable from some node s is *breadth-first search* (BFS). BFS explores the graph *layer by layer*. The starting node s forms layer 0. The direct neighbors of s form layer 1. In general, all nodes that are neighbors of a node in layer i but not neighbors of nodes in layers 0 to $i-1$ form layer $i+1$.

The algorithm in Fig. 9.2 takes a node s and constructs the BFS tree rooted at s. For each node v in the tree, the algorithm records its distance $d(v)$ from s, and the parent node *parent*(v) from which v was first reached. The algorithm returns the pair $(d, parent)$. Initially, s has been reached and all other nodes store some special value $\perp$ to indicate that they have not been reached yet. Also, the depth of s is zero. The main loop of the algorithm builds the BFS tree layer by layer. We maintain two sets Q and Q'; Q contains the nodes in the current layer, and we construct the next layer in Q'. The inner loops inspect all edges (u, v) leaving nodes u in the current layer Q. Whenever v has no parent pointer yet, we put it into the next layer Q' and set its parent pointer and distance appropriately. Figure 9.3 gives an example of a BFS tree and the resulting backward and cross edges.

BFS has the useful feature that its tree edges define paths from s that have a minimum number of edges. For example, you could use such paths to find railway connections that minimize the number of times you have to change trains or to find paths in communication networks with a minimal number of hops. An actual path from s to a node v can be found by following the parent references from v backwards.

Exercise 9.1. Show that BFS will never classify an edge as forward, i.e., there are no edges (u, v) with $d(v) > d(u) + 1$.

Function *bfs*$(s : NodeId) : (NodeArray \text{ of } NodeId) \times (NodeArray \text{ of } 0..n)$
    $d = \langle \infty, \ldots, \infty \rangle \; : NodeArray \text{ of } NodeId$ // distance from root
    parent $= \langle \perp, \ldots, \perp \rangle \; : NodeArray \text{ of } NodeId$
    $d[s] := 0$
    parent$[s] := s$ // self-loop signals root
    $Q = \langle s \rangle \; : Set \text{ of } NodeId$ // current layer of BFS tree
    $Q' = \langle \rangle \; : Set \text{ of } NodeId$ // next layer of BFS tree
    for $\ell := 0$ **to** ∞ **while** $Q \neq \langle \rangle$ **do**   // explore layer by layer
        invariant Q contains all nodes with distance ℓ from s
        foreach $u \in Q$ **do**
            foreach $(u, v) \in E$ **do**   // *scan* edges out of u
               if *parent*$(v) = \perp$ **then**   // found an unexplored node
                    $Q' := Q' \cup \{v\}$ // remember for next layer
                    $d[v] := \ell + 1$
                    parent$(v) := u$ // update BFS tree
    $(Q, Q') := (Q', \langle \rangle)$ // switch to next layer
    return $(d, parent)$ // the BFS tree is now $\{(v, w) : w \in V, v = parent(w)\}$

Fig. 9.2. Breadth-first search starting at a node s

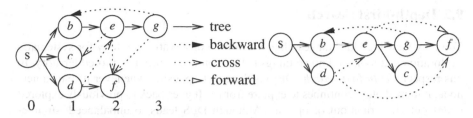

Fig. 9.3. An example of how BFS (*left*) and DFS (*right*) classify edges into tree edges, backward edges, cross edges, and forward edges. BFS visits the nodes in the order s, b, c, d, e, f, g. DFS visits the nodes in the order s, b, e, g, f, c, d

Exercise 9.2. What can go wrong with our implementation of BFS if $parent[s]$ is initialized to $\perp$ rather than s? Give an example of an erroneous computation.

Exercise 9.3. BFS trees are not necessarily unique. In particular, we have not specified in which order nodes are removed from the current layer. Give the BFS tree that is produced when d is removed before b when one performs a BFS from node s in the graph in Fig. 9.3.

Exercise 9.4 (FIFO BFS). Explain how to implement BFS using a single FIFO queue of nodes whose outgoing edges still have to be scanned. Prove that the resulting algorithm and our two-queue algorithm compute exactly the same tree if the two-queue algorithm traverses the queues in an appropriate order. Compare the FIFO version of BFS with Dijkstra's algorithm described in Sect. 10.3, and the Jarník–Prim algorithm described in Sect. 11.2. What do they have in common? What are the main differences?

Exercise 9.5 (graph representation for BFS). Give a more detailed description of BFS. In particular, make explicit how to implement it using the adjacency array representation described in Sect. 8.2. Your algorithm should run in time $O(n+m)$.

Exercise 9.6 (connected components). Explain how to modify BFS so that it computes a spanning forest of an undirected graph in time $O(m+n)$. In addition, your algorithm should select a *representative* node r for each connected component of the graph and assign it to $component[v]$ for each node v in the same component as r. Hint: scan all nodes $s \in V$ and start BFS from any node s that it still unreached when it is scanned. Do not reset the parent array between different runs of BFS. Note that isolated nodes are simply connected components of size one.

Exercise 9.7 (transitive closure). The *transitive closure* $G^+ = (V, E^+)$ of a graph $G = (V, E)$ has an edge $(u, v) \in E^+$ whenever there is a path from u to v in E. Design an algorithm for computing transitive closures. Hint: run $bfs(v)$ for each node v to find all nodes reachable from v. Try to avoid a full reinitialization of the arrays d and $parent$ at the beginning of each call. What is the running time of your algorithm?

9.2 Depth-First Search

You may view breadth-first search as a careful, conservative strategy for systematic exploration that looks at known things before venturing into unexplored territory. In this respect, *depth-first search* (DFS) is the exact opposite: whenever it finds a new node, it immediately continues to explore from it. It goes back to previously explored nodes only if it runs out of options. Although DFS leads to unbalanced, strange-looking exploration trees compared with the orderly layers generated by BFS, the combination of eager exploration with the perfect memory of a computer makes DFS very useful. Figure 9.4 gives an algorithm template for DFS. We can derive specific algorithms from it by specifying the subroutines *init*, *root*, *traverseTreeEdge*, *traverseNonTreeEdge*, and *backtrack*.

DFS marks a node when it first discovers it; initially, all nodes are unmarked. The main loop of DFS looks for unmarked nodes s and calls $DFS(s,s)$ to grow a tree rooted at s. The recursive call $DFS(u,v)$ explores all edges (v,w) out of v. The argument (u,v) indicates that v was reached via the edge (u,v) into v. For root nodes s, we use the "dummy" argument (s,s). We write $DFS(*,v)$ if the specific nature of the incoming edge is irrelevant to the discussion at hand. Assume now that we are exploring edge (v,w) within the call $DFS(*,v)$.

If w has been seen before, w is already a node of the DFS forest. So (v,w) is not a tree edge, and hence we call *traverseNonTreeEdge*(v,w) and make no recursive call of *DFS*.

If w has not been seen before, (v,w) becomes a tree edge. We therefore call *traverseTreeEdge*(v,w), mark w, and make the recursive call $DFS(v,w)$. When we return from this call, we explore the next edge out of v. Once all edges out of v have been explored, we call *backtrack* on the incoming edge (u,v) to perform any summarizing or cleanup operations needed and return.

At any point in time during the execution of *DFS*, there are a number of active calls. More precisely, there are nodes $v_1, v_2, \ldots v_k$ such that we are currently exploring edges out of v_k, and the active calls are $DFS(v_1,v_1)$, $DFS(v_1,v_2)$, $\ldots$, $DFS(v_{k-1},v_k)$. In this situation, we say that the nodes $v_1, v_2, \ldots, v_k$ are *active* and form the DFS recursion stack. The node v_k is called the *current node*. We say that a node v has been reached when $DFS(*,v)$ is called, and is finished when the call $DFS(*,v)$ terminates.

Exercise 9.8. Give a nonrecursive formulation of DFS. You need to maintain a stack of active nodes and, for each active node, the set of unexplored edges.

9.2.1 DFS Numbering, Finishing Times, and Topological Sorting

DFS has numerous applications. In this section, we use it to number the nodes in two ways. As a by-product, we see how to detect cycles. We number the nodes in the order in which they are reached (array *dfsNum*) and in the order in which they are finished (array *finishTime*). We have two counters *dfsPos* and *finishingTime*, both initialized to one. When we encounter a new root or traverse a tree edge, we set the

Depth-first search of a directed graph $G = (V, E)$
unmark all nodes
init
foreach $s \in V$ **do**
   if s is not marked **then**
      mark s // make s a root and grow
      root(s) // a new DFS tree rooted at it.
      DFS(s, s)

Procedure *DFS*$(u, v : NodeId)$ // Explore v coming from u.
   foreach $(v, w) \in E$ **do**
      if w is marked **then** *traverseNonTreeEdge*(v, w) // w was reached before
      else   *traverseTreeEdge*(v, w) // w was not reached before
          mark w
          DFS(v, w)
   backtrack(u, v) // return from v along the incoming edge

Fig. 9.4. A template for depth-first search of a graph $G = (V, E)$. We say that a call $DFS(*, v)$ explores v. The exploration is complete when we return from this call

dfsNum of the newly encountered node and increment *dfsPos*. When we backtrack from a node, we set its *finishTime* and increment *finishingTime*. We use the following subroutines:

   init: $dfsPos = 1 : 1..n; \quad finishingTime = 1 : 1..n$
   root(s): $dfsNum[s] := dfsPos++$
   traverseTreeEdge(v, w): $dfsNum[w] := dfsPos++$
   backtrack(u, v): $finishTime[v] := finishingTime++$

The ordering by *dfsNum* is so useful that we introduce a special notation '$\prec$' for it. For any two nodes u and v, we define

$$u \prec v \Leftrightarrow dfsNum[u] < dfsNum[v] .$$

The numberings *dfsNum* and *finishTime* encode important information about the execution of *DFS*, as we shall show next. We shall first show that the DFS numbers increase along any path of the DFS tree, and then show that the numberings together classify the edges according to their type.

Lemma 9.1. *The nodes on the DFS recursion stack are sorted with respect to* $\prec$.

Proof. *dfsPos* is incremented after every assignment to *dfsNum*. Thus, when a node v becomes active by a call $DFS(u, v)$, it has just been assigned the largest *dfsNum* so far. $\square$

dfsNums and *finishTimes* classify edges according to their type, as shown in Table 9.1. The argument is as follows. Two calls of DFS are either nested within each other, i.e., when the second call starts, the first is still active, or disjoint, i.e., when the

Table 9.1. The classification of an edge (v, w). Tree and forward edges are also easily distinguished. Tree edges lead to recursive calls, and forward edges do not

Type	$dfsNum[v] < dfsNum[w]$	$finishTime[w] < FinishTime[v]$
Tree	Yes	Yes
Forward	Yes	Yes
Backward	No	No
Cross	No	Yes

second starts, the first is already completed. If $DFS(*, w)$ is nested in $DFS(*, v)$, the former call starts after the latter and finishes before it, i.e., $dfsNum[v] < dfsNum[w]$ and $finishTime[w] < finishTime[v]$. If $DFS(*, w)$ and $DFS(*, v)$ are disjoint and the former call starts before the latter, it also ends before the latter, i.e., $dfsNum[w] < dfsNum[v]$ and $finishTime[w] < finishTime[v]$. The tree edges record the nesting structure of recursive calls. When a tree edge (v, w) is explored within $DFS(*, v)$, the call $DFS(v, w)$ is made and hence is nested within $DFS(*, v)$. Thus w has a larger DFS number and a smaller finishing time than v. A forward edge (v, w) runs parallel to a path of tree edges and hence w has a larger DFS number and a smaller finishing time than v. A backward edge (v, w) runs antiparallel to a path of tree edges, and hence w has a smaller DFS number and a larger finishing time than v. Let us look, finally, at a cross edge (v, w). Since (v, w) is not a tree, forward, or backward edge, the calls $DFS(*, v)$ and $DFS(*, w)$ cannot be nested within each other. Thus they are disjoint. So w is marked either before $DFS(*, v)$ starts or after it ends. The latter case is impossible, since, in this case, w would be unmarked when the edge (v, w) was explored, and the edge would become a tree edge. So w is marked before $DFS(*, v)$ starts and hence $DFS(*, w)$ starts and ends before $DFS(*, v)$. Thus $dfsNum[w] < dfsNum[v]$ and $finishTime[w] < finishTime[v]$. The following Lemma summarizes the discussion.

Lemma 9.2. *Table 9.1 shows the characterization of edge types in terms of dfsNum and finishTime.*

Exercise 9.9. Modify DFS such that it labels the edges with their type. What is the type of an edge (v, w) when w is on the recursion stack when the edge is explored?

Finishing times have an interesting property for directed acyclic graphs.

Lemma 9.3. *The following properties are equivalent: (i) G is an acyclic directed graph (DAG); (ii) DFS on G produces no backward edges; (iii) all edges of G go from larger to smaller finishing times.*

Proof. Backward edges run antiparallel to paths of tree edges and hence create cycles. Thus DFS on an acyclic graph cannot create any backward edges. All other types of edge run from larger to smaller finishing times according to Table 9.1. Assume now that all edges run from larger to smaller finishing times. In this case the graph is clearly acyclic. □

An order of the nodes of a DAG in which all edges go from left to right is called a *topological sorting*. By Lemma 9.3, the ordering by decreasing finishing time is a topological ordering. Many problems on DAGs can be solved efficiently by iterating over the nodes in a topological order. For example, in Sect. 10.2 we shall see a fast, simple algorithm for computing shortest paths in acyclic graphs.

Exercise 9.10 (topological sorting). Design a DFS-based algorithm that outputs the nodes in topological order if G is a DAG. Otherwise, it should output a cycle.

Exercise 9.11. Design a BFS-based algorithm for topological sorting.

Exercise 9.12. Show that DFS on an undirected graph does not produce any cross edges.

9.2.2 Strongly Connected Components

We now come back to the problem posed at the beginning of this chapter. Recall that two nodes belong to the same strongly connected component (SCC) of a graph iff they are reachable from each other. In undirected graphs, the relation "being reachable" is symmetric, and hence strongly connected components are the same as connected components. Exercise 9.6 outlines how to compute connected components using BFS, and adapting this idea to DFS is equally simple. For directed graphs, the situation is more interesting; see Fig. 9.5 for an example. We shall show that an extension of DFS computes the strongly connected components of a digraph G in linear time $O(n+m)$. More precisely, the algorithm will output an array *component* indexed by nodes such that $component[v] = component[w]$ iff v and w belong to the same SCC. Alternatively, it could output the node set of each SCC.

Exercise 9.13. Show that the node sets of distinct SCCs are disjoint. Hint: assume that SCCs C and D have a common node v. Show that any node in C can reach any node in D and vice versa.

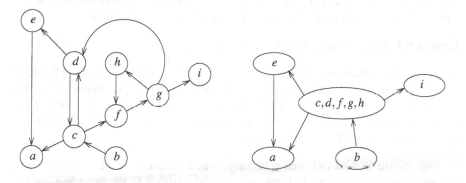

Fig. 9.5. A digraph G and the corresponding shrunken graph G_s. The SCCs of G have node sets $\{a\}$, $\{b\}$, $\{c,d,f,g,h\}$, $\{e\}$, and $\{i\}$

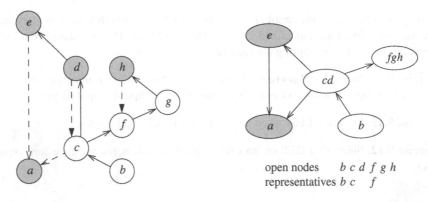

open nodes $b\ c\ d\ f\ g\ h$
representatives $b\ c\quad f$

Fig. 9.6. A snapshot of DFS on the graph of Fig. 9.5 and the corresponding shrunken graph. The first DFS was started at node a and a second DFS was started at node b, the current node is g, and the recursion stack contains b, c, f, g. The edges (g, i) and (g, d) have not been explored yet. Edges (h, f) and (d, c) are back edges, (e, a) is a cross edge, and all other edges are tree edges. Finished nodes and closed components are shaded. There are closed components $\{a\}$ and $\{e\}$ and open components $\{b\}$, $\{c, d\}$, and $\{f, g, h\}$. The open components form a path in the shrunken graph with the current node g belonging to the last component. The representatives of the open components are the nodes b, c, and f, respectively. DFS has reached the open nodes in the order b, c, d, f, g, h. The representatives partition the sequence of open nodes into the SCCs of G_c

The idea underlying the algorithm is simple. We imagine that the edges of G are added one by one to an initially edgeless graph. We use $G_c = (V, E_c)$ to denote the current graph, and keep track of how the SCCs of G_c evolve as edges are added. Initially, there are no edges and each node forms an SCC of its own. For the addition step, it is helpful to introduce the notion of a *shrunken graph*. We use G_c^s to denote the shrunken graph corresponding to G_c. The nodes of G_c^s are the SCCs of G_c. If C and D are distinct SCCs of G_c, we have an edge (C, D) in G_c^s iff there are nodes $u \in C$ and $v \in D$ where (u, v) is an edge of G_c. Figure 9.5 shows an example.

Lemma 9.4. *The shrunken graph G_c^s is acyclic.*

Proof. Assume otherwise, and let $C_1, C_2, \ldots, C_{k-1}, C_k$ with $C_k = C_1$ be a cycle in G_c^s. Recall that the C_i are SCCs of G_c. By the definition of G_c^s, G_c contains an edge (v_i, w_{i+1}) with $v_i \in C_i$ and $w_{i+1} \in C_{i+1}$ for $0 \le i < k$. Define $v_k = v_1$. Since C_i is strongly connected, G_c contains a path from w_{i+1} to v_{i+1}, $0 \le i < k$. Thus all the v_i's belong to the same SCC, a contradiction.   □

How do the SCCs of G_c and G_c^s change when we add an edge e to G_c? There are three cases to consider. (1) Both endpoints of e belong to the same SCC of G_c. The shrunken graph and the SCCs do not change. (2) e connects nodes in different SCCs but does not close a cycle. The SCCs do not change, and an edge is added to the shrunken graph. (3) e connects nodes in different SCCs and closes one or more cycles. In this case, all SCCs lying on one of the newly formed cycles are merged into a single SCC, and the shrunken graph changes accordingly.

In order to arrive at an efficient algorithm, we need to describe how we maintain the SCCs as the graph evolves. If the edges are added in arbitrary order, no efficient simple method is known. However, if we use DFS to explore the graph, an efficient solution is fairly simple to obtain. Consider a depth-first search on G and let E_c be the set of edges already explored by DFS. A subset V_c of the nodes is already marked. We distinguish between three kinds of SCC of G_c: unreached, open, and closed. Unmarked nodes have indegree and outdegree zero in G_c and hence form SCCs consisting of a single node. This node is isolated in the shrunken graph. We call these SCCs *unreached*. The other SCCs consist of marked nodes only. We call an SCC consisting of marked nodes *open* if it contains an active node, and *closed* if it contains only finished nodes. We call a marked node "open" if it belongs to an open component and "closed" if it belongs to a closed component. Observe that a closed node is always finished and that an open node may be either active or finished. For every SCC, we call the node with the smallest DFS number in the SCC the *representative* of the SCC. Figure 9.6 illustrates these concepts. We state next some important invariant properties of G_c; see also Fig. 9.7:

(1) All edges in G (not just G_c) out of closed nodes lead to closed nodes. In our example, the nodes a and e are closed.
(2) The tree path to the current node contains the representatives of all open components. Let S_1 to S_k be the open components as they are traversed by the tree path to the current node. There is then a tree edge from a node in S_{i-1} to the representative of S_i, and this is the only edge into S_i, $2 \leq i \leq k$. Also, there is no edge from an S_j to an S_i with $i < j$. Finally, all nodes in S_j are reachable from the representative r_i of S_i for $1 \leq i \leq j \leq k$. In short, the open components form a path in the shrunken graph. In our example, the current node is g. The tree path $\langle b, c, f, g \rangle$ to the current node contains the open representatives b, c, and f.
(3) Consider the nodes in open components ordered by their DFS numbers. The representatives partition the sequence into the open components. In our example, the sequence of open nodes is $\langle b, c, d, f, g, h \rangle$ and the representatives partition this sequence into the open components $\{b\}$, $\{c, d\}$, and $\{f, g, h\}$.

We shall show below that all three properties hold true generally, and not only for our example. The three properties will be invariants of the algorithm to be developed. The first invariant implies that the closed SCCs of G_c are actually SCCs of G, i.e., it is justified to call them closed. This observation is so important that it deserves to be stated as a lemma.

Lemma 9.5. *A closed SCC of G_c is an SCC of G.*

Proof. Let v be a closed vertex, let S be the SCC of G containing v, and let S_c be the SCC of G_c containing v. We need to show that $S = S_c$. Since G_c is a subgraph of G, we have $S_c \subseteq S$. So, it suffices to show that $S \subseteq S_c$. Let w be any vertex in S. There is then a cycle C in G passing through v and w. The first invariant implies that all vertices of C are closed. Since closed vertices are finished, all edges out of them have been explored. Thus C is contained in G_c, and hence $w \in S_c$.   □

The Invariants (2) and (3) suggest a simple method to represent the open SCCs of G_c. We simply keep a sequence *oNodes* of all open nodes in increasing order of DFS numbers, and the subsequence *oReps* of open representatives. In our example, we have *oNodes* $= \langle b, c, d, f, g, h \rangle$ and *oReps* $= \langle b, c, f \rangle$. We shall later see that the type *Stack* **of** *NodeId* is appropriate for both sequences.

Let us next see how the SCCs of G_c develop during DFS. We shall discuss the various actions of DFS one by one and show that the invariants are maintained. We shall also discuss how to update our representation of the open components.

When DFS starts, the invariants clearly hold: no node is marked, no edge has been traversed, G_c is empty, and hence there are neither open nor closed components yet. Our sequences *oNodes* and *oReps* are empty.

Just before a new root will be marked, all marked nodes are finished and hence there cannot be any open component. Therefore, both of the sequences *oNodes* and *oReps* are empty, and marking a new root s produces the open component $\{s\}$. The invariants are clearly maintained. We obtain the correct representation by adding s to both sequences.

If a tree edge $e = (v, w)$ is traversed and hence w becomes marked, $\{w\}$ becomes an open component on its own. All other open components are unchanged. The first invariant is clearly maintained, since v is active and hence open. The old current node is v and the new current node is w. The sequence of open components is extended by $\{w\}$. The open representatives are the old open representatives plus the node w. Thus the second invariant is maintained. Also, w becomes the open node with the largest DFS number and hence *oNodes* and *oReps* are both extended by w. Thus the third invariant is maintained.

Now suppose that a nontree edge $e = (v, w)$ out of the current node v is explored. If w is closed, the SCCs of G_c do not change when e is added to G_c since, by Lemma 9.5, the SCC of G_c containing w is already an SCC of G *before* e is traversed. So, assume that w is open. Then w lies in some open SCC S_i of G_c. We claim

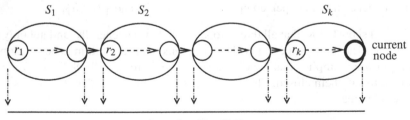

open nodes ordered by dfsNum

Fig. 9.7. The open SCCs are shown as ovals, and the current node is shown as a **bold** circle. The tree path to the current node is indicated. It enters each component at its representative. The horizontal line below represents the open nodes, ordered by *dfsNum*. Each open SCC forms a contiguous subsequence, with its representative as its leftmost element

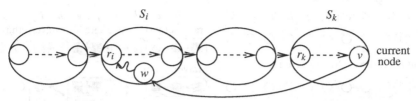

Fig. 9.8. The open SCCs are shown as ovals and their representatives as circles to the left of an oval. All representatives lie on the tree path to the current node v. The nontree edge $e = (v, w)$ ends in an open SCC S_i with representative r_i. There is a path from w to r_i since w belongs to the SCC with representative r_i. Thus the edge (v, w) merges S_i to S_k into a single SCC

that the SCCs S_i to S_k are merged into a single component and all other components are unchanged; see Fig. 9.8. Let r_i be the representative of S_i. We can then go from r_i to v along a tree path by invariant (2), then follow the edge (v, w), and finally return to r_i. The path from w to r_i exists, since w and r_i lie in the same SCC of G_c. We conclude that any node in an S_j with $i \leq j \leq k$ can be reached from r_i and can reach r_i. Thus the SCCs S_i to S_k become one SCC, and r_i is their representative. The S_j with $j < i$ are unaffected by the addition of the edge.

The third invariant tells us how to find r_i, the representative of the component containing w. The sequence *oNodes* is ordered by *dfsNum*, and the representative of an SCC has the smallest *dfsNum* of any node in that component. Thus $dfsNum[r_i] \leq dfsNum[w]$ and $dfsNum[w] < dfsNum[r_j]$ for all $j > i$. It is therefore easy to update our representation. We simply delete all representatives r with $dfsNum[r] > dfsNum[w]$ from *oReps*.

Finally, we need to consider finishing a node v. When will this close an SCC? By invariant (2), all nodes in a component are tree descendants of the representative of the component, and hence the representative of a component is the last node to be finished in the component. In other words, we close a component iff we finish a representative. Since *oReps* is ordered by *dfsNum*, we close a component iff the last node of *oReps* finishes. So, assume that we finish a representative v. Then, by invariant (3), the component S_k with representative $v = r_k$ consists of v and all nodes in *oNodes* following v. Finishing v closes S_k. By invariant (2), there is no edge out of S_k into an open component. Thus invariant (1) holds after S_k is closed. The new current node is the parent of v. By invariant (2), the parent of v lies in S_{k-1}. Thus invariant (2) holds after S_k is closed. Invariant (3) holds after v is removed from *oReps*, and v and all nodes following it are removed from *oNodes*.

It is now easy to instantiate the DFS template. Fig. 9.10 shows the pseudocode, and Fig. 9.9 illustrates a complete run. We use an array *component* indexed by nodes to record the result, and two stacks *oReps* and *oNodes*. When a new root is marked or a tree edge is explored, a new open component consisting of a single node is created by pushing this node onto both stacks. When a cycle of open components is created, these components are merged by popping representatives from *oReps* as long as the top representative is not to the left of the node w closing the cycle. An SCC S is closed when its representative v finishes. At that point, all nodes of S are stored

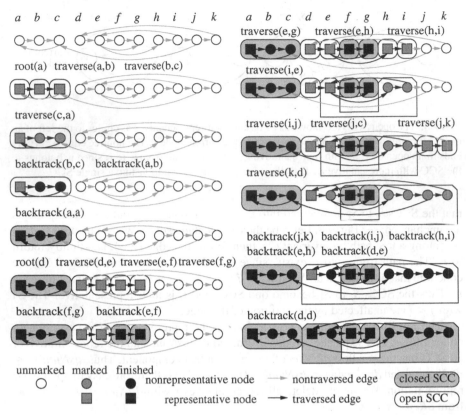

Fig. 9.9. An example of the development of open and closed SCCs during DFS. Unmarked nodes are shown as empty circles, marked nodes are shown in gray, and finished nodes are shown in black. Nontraversed edges are shown in gray, and traversed edges are shown in black. Open SCCs are shown as empty ovals, and closed SCCs are shown as gray ovals. We start in the situation shown at the upper left. We make a a root and traverse the edges (a, b) and (b, c). This creates three open SSCs. The traversal of edge (c, a) merges these components into one. Next, we backtrack to b, then to a, and finally from a. At this point, the component becomes closed. Please complete the description

above v in *oNodes*. The operation *backtrack* therefore closes S by popping v from *oReps*, and by popping the nodes $w \in S$ from *oNodes* and setting their *component* to the representative v.

Note that the test $w \in oNodes$ in *traverseNonTreeEdge* can be done in constant time by storing information with each node that indicates whether the node is open or not. This indicator is set when a node v is first marked, and reset when the component of v is closed. We give implementation details in Sect. 9.3. Furthermore, the while loop and the repeat loop can make at most n iterations during the entire execution of the algorithm, since each node is pushed onto the stacks exactly once. Hence, the execution time of the algorithm is $O(m + n)$. We have the following theorem.

init:
    component : NodeArray **of** *NodeId*   // SCC representatives
    oReps = ⟨⟩ *: Stack* **of** *NodeId*   // representatives of open SCCs
    oNodes = ⟨⟩ *: Stack* **of** *NodeId*   // all nodes in open SCCs

root(w) or traverseTreeEdge(v,w):
    oReps.push(w)   // new open
    oNodes.push(w)   // component

traverseNonTreeEdge(v,w):
    if *w* ∈ *oNodes* **then**
        while *w* ≺ *oReps.top* **do** *oReps.pop*   // collapse components on cycle

backtrack(u,v):
    if *v* = *oReps.top* **then**
        oReps.pop   // close
        repeat   // component
            w := *oNodes.pop*
            component[w] := *v*
        until *w* = *v*

Fig. 9.10. An instantiation of the DFS template that computes strongly connected components of a graph $G = (V, E)$

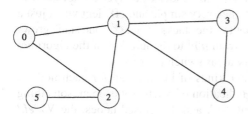

Fig. 9.11. The graph has two 2-edge con-nected components, namely $\{0,1,2,3,4\}$ and $\{5\}$. The graph has three bicon-nected components, namely the subgraphs spanned by the sets $\{0,1,2\}$, $\{1,3,4\}$ and $\{2,5\}$. The vertices 1 and 2 are articulation points

Theorem 9.6. *The algorithm in Fig. 9.10 computes strongly connected components in time* $O(m + n)$.

Exercise 9.14 (certificates). Let G be a strongly connected graph and let s be a node of G. Show how to construct two trees rooted at s. The first tree proves that all nodes can be reached from s, and the second tree proves than s can be reached from all nodes.

Exercise 9.15 (2-edge-connected components). An undirected graph is 2-edge-connected if its edges can be oriented so that the graph becomes strongly connected. The 2-edge-connected components are the maximal 2-edge-connected subgraphs; see Fig. 9.11. Modify the SCC algorithm shown in Fig. 9.10 so that it computes 2-edge-connected components. Hint: show first that DFS of an undirected graph never produces any cross edges.

Exercise 9.16 (biconnected components). Two nodes of an *undirected* graph belong to the same *biconnected component* (BCC) iff they are connected by an edge or there are two edge-disjoint paths connecting them; see Fig. 9.11. A node is an *articulation point* if it belongs to more than one BCC. Design an algorithm that computes biconnected components using a single pass of DFS. Hint: adapt the strongly-connected-components algorithm. Define the representative of a BCC as the node with the second smallest *dfsNum* in the BCC. Prove that a BCC consists of the parent of the representative and all tree descendants of the representative that can be reached without passing through another representative. Modify *backtrack*. When you return from a representative *v*, output *v*, all nodes above *v* in *oNodes*, and the parent of *v*.

9.3 Implementation Notes

BFS is usually implemented by keeping unexplored nodes (with depths d and $d+1$) in a FIFO queue. We chose a formulation using two separate sets for nodes at depth d and nodes at depth $d+1$ mainly because it allows a simple loop invariant that makes correctness immediately evident. However, our formulation might also turn out to be somewhat more efficient. If Q and Q' are organized as stacks, we will have fewer cache faults than with a queue, in particular if the nodes of a layer do not quite fit into the cache. Memory management becomes very simple and efficient when just a single array a of n nodes is allocated for both of the stacks Q and Q'. One stack grows from $a[1]$ to the right and the other grows from $a[n]$ to the left. When the algorithm switches to the next layer, the two memory areas switch their roles.

Our SCC algorithm needs to store four kinds of information for each node v: an indication of whether v is marked, an indication of whether v is open, something like a DFS number in order to implement "$\prec$", and, for closed nodes, the *NodeId* of the representative of its component. The array *component* suffices to keep this information. For example, if *NodeId*s are integers in $1..n$, $component[v] = 0$ could indicate an unmarked node. Negative numbers can indicate negated DFS numbers, so that $u \prec v$ iff $component[u] > component[v]$. This works because "$\prec$" is never applied to closed nodes. Finally, the test $w \in oNodes$ simply becomes $component[v] < 0$. With these simplifications in place, additional tuning is possible. We make *oReps* store *component* numbers of representatives rather than their IDs, and save an access to $component[oReps.top]$. Finally, the array *component* should be stored with the node data as a single array of records. The effect of these optimization on the performance of our SCC algorithm is discussed in [132].

9.3.1 C++

LEDA [118] has implementations for topological sorting, reachability from a node (*DFS*), DFS numbering, BFS, strongly connected components, biconnected components, and transitive closure. BFS, DFS, topological sorting, and strongly connected components are also available in a very flexible implementation that separates representation and implementation, supports incremental execution, and allows various other adaptations.

The Boost graph library [27] uses the *visitor concept* to support graph traversal. A visitor class has user-definable methods that are called at *event points* during the execution of a graph traversal algorithm. For example, the DFS visitor defines event points similar to the operations *init*, *root*, *traverse*∗, and *backtrack* used in our DFS template; there are more event points in Boost.

9.3.2 Java

The JDSL [78] library [78] supports DFS in a very flexible way, not very much different from the visitor concept described for Boost. There are also more specialized algorithms for topological sorting and finding cycles.

9.4 Historical Notes and Further Findings

BFS and DFS were known before the age of computers. Tarjan [185] discovered the power of DFS and provided linear-time algorithms for many basic problems related to graphs, in particular biconnected and strongly connected components. Our SCC algorithm was invented by Cheriyan and Mehlhorn [39] and later rediscovered by Gabow [70]. Yet another linear-time SCC algorithm is that due to Kosaraju and Sharir [178]. It is very simple, but needs two passes of DFS. DFS can be used to solve many other graph problems in linear time, for example ear decomposition, planarity testing, planar embeddings, and triconnected components.

It may seem that problems solvable by graph traversal are so simple that little further research is needed on them. However, the bad news is that graph traversal itself is very difficult on advanced models of computation. In particular, DFS is a nightmare for both parallel processing [161] and memory hierarchies [141, 128]. Therefore alternative ways to solve seemingly simple problems are an interesting area of research. For example, in Sect. 11.8 we describe an approach to constructing minimum spanning trees using *edge contraction* that also works for finding connected components. Furthermore, the problem of finding biconnected components can be reduced to finding connected components [189]. The DFS-based algorithms for biconnected components and strongly connected components are almost identical. But this analogy completely disappears for advanced models of computation, so that algorithms for strongly connected components remain an area of intensive (and sometimes frustrating) research. More generally, it seems that problems for undirected graphs (such as finding biconnected components) are often easier to solve than analogous problems for directed graphs (such as finding strongly connected components).

10

Shortest Paths

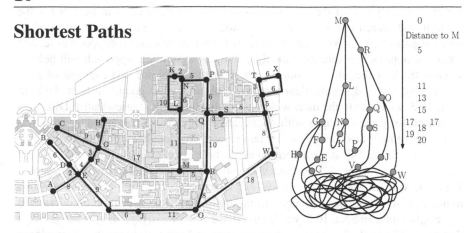

The problem of the shortest, quickest or cheapest path is ubiquitous. You solve it daily. When you are in a location s and want to move to a location t, you ask for the quickest path from s to t. The fire department may want to compute the quickest routes from a fire station s to all locations in town – the single-source problem. Sometimes we may even want a complete distance table from everywhere to everywhere – the all-pairs problem. In a road atlas, you will usually find an all-pairs distance table for the most important cities.

Here is a route-planning algorithm that requires a city map and a lot of dexterity but no computer. Lay thin threads along the roads on the city map. Make a knot wherever roads meet, and at your starting position. Now lift the starting knot until the entire net dangles below it. If you have successfully avoided any tangles and the threads and your knots are thin enough so that only tight threads hinder a knot from moving down, the tight threads define the shortest paths. The introductory figure of this chapter shows the campus map of the University of Karlsruhe[1] and illustrates the route-planning algorithm for the source node M.

Route planning in road networks is one of the many applications of shortest-path computations. When an appropriate graph model is defined, many problems turn out to profit from shortest-path computations. For example, Ahuja et al. [8] mentioned such diverse applications as planning flows in networks, urban housing, inventory planning, DNA sequencing, the knapsack problem (see also Chap. 12), production planning, telephone operator scheduling, vehicle fleet planning, approximating piecewise linear functions, and allocating inspection effort on a production line.

The most general formulation of the shortest-path problem looks at a directed graph $G = (V, E)$ and a cost function c that maps edges to arbitrary real-number

---

[1] (c) Universität Karlsruhe (TH), Institut für Photogrammetrie und Fernerkundung.

costs. It turns out that the most general problem is fairly expensive to solve. So we are also interested in various restrictions that allow simpler and more efficient algorithms: nonnegative edge costs, integer edge costs, and acyclic graphs. Note that we have already solved the very special case of unit edge costs in Sect. 9.1 – the breadth-first search (BFS) tree rooted at node s is a concise representation of all shortest paths from s. We begin in Sect. 10.1 with some basic concepts that lead to a generic approach to shortest-path algorithms. A systematic approach will help us to keep track of the zoo of shortest-path algorithms. As our first example of a restricted but fast and simple algorithm, we look at acyclic graphs in Sect. 10.2. In Sect. 10.3, we come to the most widely used algorithm for shortest paths: Dijkstra's algorithm for general graphs with nonnegative edge costs. The efficiency of Dijkstra's algorithm relies heavily on efficient priority queues. In an introductory course or at first reading, Dijkstra's algorithm might be a good place to stop. But there are many more interesting things about shortest paths in the remainder of the chapter. We begin with an average-case analysis of Dijkstra's algorithm in Sect. 10.4 which indicates that priority queue operations might dominate the execution time less than one might think. In Sect. 10.5, we discuss *monotone priority queues for integer keys* that take additional advantage of the properties of Dijkstra's algorithm. Combining this with average-case analysis leads even to a linear expected execution time. Section 10.6 deals with arbitrary edge costs, and Sect. 10.7 treats the all-pairs problem. We show that the all-pairs problem for general edge costs reduces to one general single-source problem plus n single-source problems with nonnegative edge costs. This reduction introduces the generally useful concept of node potentials. We close with a discussion of shortest path queries in Sect. 10.8.

10.1 From Basic Concepts to a Generic Algorithm

We extend the cost function to paths in the natural way. The cost of a path is the sum of the costs of its constituent edges, i.e., if $p = \langle e_1, e_2, \ldots, e_k \rangle$, then $c(p) = \sum_{1 \le i \le k} c(e_i)$. The empty path has cost zero.

For a pair s and v of nodes, we are interested in a shortest path from s to v. We avoid the use of the definite article "the" here, since there may be more than one shortest path. Does a shortest path always exist? Observe that the number of paths from s to v may be infinite. For example, if $r = pCq$ is a path from s to v containing a cycle C, then we may go around the cycle an arbitrary number of times and still have a path from s to v; see Fig. 10.1. More precisely, p is a path leading from s to u, C is a path leading from u to u, and q is a path from u to v. Consider the path $r^{(i)} = pC^i q$ which first uses p to go from s to u, then goes around the cycle i times, and finally follows q from u to v. The cost of $r^{(i)}$ is $c(p) + i \cdot c(C) + c(q)$. If C is a *negative cycle*, i.e., $c(C) < 0$, then $c(r^{(i+1)}) < c(r^{(i)})$. In this situation, there is no shortest path from s to v. Assume otherwise: say, P is a shortest path from s to v. Then $c(r^{(i)}) < c(P)$ for i large enough[2], and so P is not a shortest path from s to v. We shall show next that shortest paths exist if there are no negative cycles.

---

[2] $i > (c(p) + c(q) - c(P))/|c(C)|$ will do.

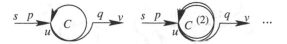

Fig. 10.1. A nonsimple path pCq from s to v

Lemma 10.1. *If G contains no negative cycles and v is reachable from s, then a shortest path P from s to v exists. Moreover P can be chosen to be simple.*

Proof. Let x be a shortest *simple* path from s to v. If x is not a shortest path from s to v, there is a shorter nonsimple path r from s to v. Since r is nonsimple we can, as in Fig. 10.1, write r as pCq, where C is a cycle and pq is a simple path. Then $c(x) \leq c(pq)$, and hence $c(pq) + c(C) = c(r) < c(x) \leq c(pq)$. So $c(C) < 0$ and we have shown the existence of a negative cycle. $\qquad\square$

Exercise 10.1. Strengthen the lemma above and show that if v is reachable from s, then a shortest path from s to v exists iff there is no negative cycle that is reachable from s and from which one can reach v.

For two nodes s and v, we define the shortest-path distance $\mu(s,v)$ from s to v as

$$\mu(s,v) := \begin{cases} +\infty & \text{if there is no path from } s \text{ to } v, \\ -\infty & \text{if there is no shortest path from } s \text{ to } v, \\ c\,(\text{a shortest path from } s \text{ to } v) & \text{otherwise.} \end{cases}$$

Since we use s to denote the source vertex most of the time, we also use the shorthand $\mu(v) := \mu(s,v)$. Observe that if v is reachable from s but there is no shortest path from s to v, then there are paths of arbitrarily large negative cost. Thus it makes sense to define $\mu(v) = -\infty$ in this case. Shortest paths have further nice properties, which we state as exercises.

Exercise 10.2 (subpaths of shortest paths). Show that subpaths of shortest paths are themselves shortest paths, i.e., if a path of the form pqr is a shortest path, then q is also a shortest path.

Exercise 10.3 (shortest-path trees). Assume that all nodes are reachable from s and that there are no negative cycles. Show that there is an n-node tree T rooted at s such that all tree paths are shortest paths. Hint: assume first that shortest paths are unique, and consider the subgraph T consisting of all shortest paths starting at s. Use the preceding exercise to prove that T is a tree. Extend this result to the case where shortest paths are not unique.

Our strategy for finding shortest paths from a source node s is a generalization of the BFS algorithm shown in Fig. 9.3. We maintain two *NodeArrays* d and *parent*. Here, $d[v]$ contains our current knowledge about the distance from s to v, and *parent*$[v]$ stores the predecessor of v on the current shortest path to v. We usually

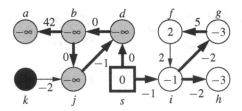

Fig. 10.2. A graph with shortest-path distances $\mu(v)$. Edge costs are shown as edge labels, and the distances are shown inside the nodes. The thick edges indicate shortest paths

refer to $d[v]$ as the *tentative distance* of v. Initially, $d[s] = 0$ and $parent[s] = s$. All other nodes have infinite distance and no parent.

The natural way to improve distance values is to propagate distance information across edges. If there is a path from s to u of cost $d[u]$, and $e = (u,v)$ is an edge out of u, then there is a path from s to v of cost $d[u] + c(e)$. If this cost is smaller than the best previously known distance $d[v]$, we update d and *parent* accordingly. This process is called *edge relaxation*:

Procedure *relax*($e = (u,v)$: *Edge*)
    if $d[u] + c(e) < d[v]$ **then** $d[v] := d[u] + c(e);$ $parent[v] := u$

Lemma 10.2. *After any sequence of edge relaxations, if $d[v] < \infty$, then there is a path of length $d[v]$ from s to v.*

Proof. We use induction on the number of edge relaxations. The claim is certainly true before the first relaxation. The empty path is a path of length zero from s to s, and all other nodes have infinite distance. Consider next a relaxation of an edge $e = (u,v)$. By the induction hypothesis, there is a path p of length $d[u]$ from s to u and a path of length $d[v]$ from s to v. If $d[u] + c(e) \geq d[v]$, there is nothing to show. Otherwise, pe is a path of length $d[u] + c(e)$ from s to v.   □

The common strategy of the algorithms in this chapter is to relax edges until either all shortest paths have been found or a negative cycle is discovered. For example, the (reversed) thick edges in Fig. 10.2 give us the *parent* information obtained after a sufficient number of edge relaxations: nodes f, g, i, and h are reachable from s using these edges and have reached their respective $\mu(\cdot)$ values 2, -3, -1, and -3. Nodes b, j, and d form a negative-cost cycle so that their shortest-path cost is $-\infty$. Node a is attached to this cycle, and thus $\mu(a) = -\infty$.

What is a good sequence of edge relaxations? Let $p = \langle e_1, \ldots, e_k \rangle$ be a path from s to v. If we relax the edges in the order e_1 to e_k, we have $d[v] \leq c(p)$ after the sequence of relaxations. If p is a shortest path from s to v, then $d[v]$ cannot drop below $c(p)$, by the preceding lemma, and hence $d[v] = c(p)$ after the sequence of relaxations.

Lemma 10.3 (correctness criterion). *After performing a sequence R of edge relaxations, we have $d[v] = \mu(v)$ if, for some shortest path $p = \langle e_1, e_2, \ldots, e_k \rangle$ from* *s to v, p is a subsequence of R, i.e., there are indices $t_1 < t_2 < \cdots < t_k$ such that $R[t_1] = e_1, R[t_2] = e_2, \ldots, R[t_k] = e_k$. Moreover, the parent information defines a path of length $\mu(v)$ from s to v.*

Proof. The following is a schematic view of R and p: the first row indicates the time. At time t_1, the edge e_1 is relaxed, at time t_2, the edge e_2 is relaxed, and so on:

$$1, 2, \ldots, \quad t_1, \quad \ldots, \quad t_2, \quad \ldots \ldots \quad , t_k, \quad \ldots$$
$$R := \langle \quad \ldots \quad , e_1, \quad \ldots, \quad e_2, \quad \ldots \ldots \quad , e_k, \quad \ldots \rangle$$
$$p := \qquad \langle e_1, \qquad e_2, \quad \ldots \quad , e_k \rangle$$

We have $\mu(v) = \sum_{1 \le j \le k} c(e_j)$. For $i \in 1..k$, let v_i be the target node of e_i, and we define $t_0 = 0$ and $v_0 = s$. Then $d[v_i] \le \sum_{1 \le j \le i} c(e_j)$ after time t_i, as a simple induction shows. This is clear for $i = 0$, since $d[s]$ is initialized to zero and d-values are only decreased. After the relaxation of $e_i = R[t_i]$ for $i > 0$, we have $d[v_i] \le d[v_{i-1}] + c(e_i) \le \sum_{1 \le j \le i} c(e_j)$. Thus, after time t_k, we have $d[v] \le \mu(v)$. Since $d[v]$ cannot go below $\mu(v)$, by Lemma 10.2, we have $d[v] = \mu(v)$ after time t_k and hence after performing all relaxations in R.

Let us prove next that the *parent* information traces out shortest paths. We shall do so under the additional assumption that shortest paths are unique, and leave the general case to the reader. After the relaxations in R, we have $d[v_i] = \mu(v_i)$ for $1 \le i \le k$. When $d[v_i]$ was set to $\mu(v_i)$ by an operation $relax(u, v_i)$, the existence of a path of length $\mu(v_i)$ from s to v_i was established. Since, by assumption, the shortest path from s to v_i is unique, we must have $u = v_{i-1}$, and hence $parent[v_i] = v_{i-1}$. □

Exercise 10.4. Redo the second paragraph in the proof above, but without the assumption that shortest paths are unique.

Exercise 10.5. Let S be the edges of G in some arbitrary order and let $S^{(n-1)}$ be $n - 1$ copies of S. Show that $\mu(v) = d[v]$ for all nodes v with $\mu(v) \ne -\infty$ after the relaxations $S^{(n-1)}$ have been performed.

In the following sections, we shall exhibit more efficient sequences of relaxations for acyclic graphs and for graphs with nonnegative edge weights. We come back to general graphs in Sect. 10.6.

10.2 Directed Acyclic Graphs

In a directed acyclic graph (DAG), there are no directed cycles and hence no negative cycles. Moreover, we have learned in Sect. 9.2.1 that the nodes of a DAG can be topologically sorted into a sequence $\langle v_1, v_2, \ldots, v_n \rangle$ such that $(v_i, v_j) \in E$ implies $i < j$. A topological order can be computed in linear time $O(m + n)$ using either depth-first search or breadth-first search. The nodes on any path in a DAG increase in topological order. Thus, by Lemma 10.3, we can compute correct shortest-path distances if we first relax the edges out of v_1, then the edges out of v_2, etc.; see Fig. 10.3 for an example. In this way, each edge is relaxed only once. Since every edge relaxation takes constant time, we obtain a total execution time of $O(m + n)$.

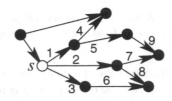

Fig. 10.3. Order of edge relaxations for the computation of the shortest paths from node s in a DAG. The topological order of the nodes is given by their x-coordinates

Theorem 10.4. *Shortest paths in acyclic graphs can be computed in time* $O(m+n)$.

Exercise 10.6 (route planning for public transportation). Finding the quickest routes in public transportation systems can be modeled as a shortest-path problem for an acyclic graph. Consider a bus or train leaving a place p at time t and reaching its next stop p' at time t'. This connection is viewed as an edge connecting nodes (p,t) and (p',t'). Also, for each stop p and subsequent events (arrival and/or departure) at p, say at times t and t' with $t < t'$, we have the *waiting link* from (p,t) to (p,t'). (a) Show that the graph obtained in this way is a DAG. (b) You need an additional node that models your starting point in space and time. There should also be one edge connecting it to the transportation network. What should this edge be? (c) Suppose you have computed the shortest-path tree from your starting node to all nodes in the public transportation graph reachable from it. How do you actually find the route you are interested in?

10.3 Nonnegative Edge Costs (Dijkstra's Algorithm)

We now assume that all edge costs are nonnegative. Thus there are no negative cycles, and shortest paths exist for all nodes reachable from s. We shall show that if the edges are relaxed in a judicious order, every edge needs to be relaxed only once.

What is the right order? Along any shortest path, the shortest-path distances increase (more precisely, do not decrease). This suggests that we should scan nodes (to scan a node means to relax all edges out of the node) in order of increasing shortest-path distance. Lemma 10.3 tells us that this relaxation order ensures the computation of shortest paths. Of course, in the algorithm, we do not know the shortest-path distances; we only know the *tentative distances* $d[v]$. Fortunately, for an unscanned node with minimal tentative distance, the true and tentative distances agree. We shall prove this in Theorem 10.5. We obtain the algorithm shown in Fig. 10.4. This algorithm is known as Dijkstra's shortest-path algorithm. Figure 10.5 shows an example run.

Note that Dijkstra's algorithm is basically the thread-and-knot algorithm we saw in the introduction to this chapter. Suppose we put all threads and knots on a table and then lift the starting node. The other knots will leave the surface of the table in the order of their shortest-path distances.

Theorem 10.5. *Dijkstra's algorithm solves the single-source shortest-path problem for graphs with nonnegative edge costs.*

Dijkstra's Algorithm

declare all nodes unscanned and initialize d and *parent*

while there is an unscanned node with tentative distance $< +\infty$ **do**

    $u :=$ the unscanned node with minimal tentative distance

    relax all edges (u,v) out of u and declare u scanned

Fig. 10.4. Dijkstra's shortest-path algorithm for nonnegative edge weights

Operation	Queue
insert(s)	$\langle (s,0) \rangle$
deleteMin↝ $(s,0)$	$\langle \rangle$
relax $s \xrightarrow{2} a$	$\langle (a,2) \rangle$
relax $s \xrightarrow{10} d$	$\langle (a,2),(d,10) \rangle$
deleteMin↝ $(a,2)$	$\langle (d,10) \rangle$
relax $a \xrightarrow{3} b$	$\langle (b,5),(d,10) \rangle$
deleteMin↝ $(b,5)$	$\langle (d,10) \rangle$
relax $b \xrightarrow{2} c$	$\langle (c,7),(d,10) \rangle$
relax $b \xrightarrow{1} e$	$\langle (e,6),(c,7),(d,10) \rangle$
deleteMin↝ $(e,6)$	$\langle (c,7),(d,10) \rangle$
relax $e \xrightarrow{9} b$	$\langle (c,7),(d,10) \rangle$
relax $e \xrightarrow{8} c$	$\langle (c,7),(d,10) \rangle$
relax $e \xrightarrow{0} d$	$\langle (d,6),(c,7) \rangle$
deleteMin↝ $(d,6)$	$\langle (c,7) \rangle$
relax $d \xrightarrow{4} s$	$\langle (c,7) \rangle$
relax $d \xrightarrow{5} b$	$\langle (c,7) \rangle$
deleteMin↝ $(c,7)$	$\langle \rangle$

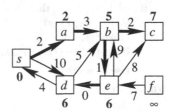

Fig. 10.5. Example run of Dijkstra's algorithm on the graph given on the *right*. The bold edges form the shortest-path tree, and the numbers in bold indicate shortest-path distances. The table on the *left* illustrates the execution. The *queue* contains all pairs $(v,d[v])$ with v reached and unscanned. A node is called *reached* if its tentative distance is less than $+\infty$. Initially, s is reached and unscanned. The actions of the algorithm are given in the first column. The second column shows the state of the queue after the action

Proof. We proceed in two steps. In the first step, we show that all nodes reachable from s are scanned. In the second step, we show that the tentative and true distances agree when a node is scanned. In both steps, we argue by contradiction.

For the first step, assume the existence of a node v that is reachable from s, but never scanned. Consider a shortest path $p = \langle s = v_1, v_2, \ldots, v_k = v \rangle$ from s to v, and let i be minimal such that v_i is not scanned. Then $i > 1$, since s is the first node scanned (in the first iteration, s is the only node whose tentative distance is less than $+\infty$) . By the definition of i, v_{i-1} has been scanned. When v_{i-1} is scanned, $d[v_i]$ is set to $d[v_{i-1}] + c(v_{i-1}, v_i)$, a value less than $+\infty$. So v_i must be scanned at some point during the execution, since the only nodes that stay unscanned are nodes u with $d[u] = +\infty$ at termination.

For the second step, consider the first point in time t, when a node v is scanned with $\mu[v] < d(v)$. As above, consider a shortest path $p = \langle s = v_1, v_2, \ldots, v_k = v \rangle$ from s to v, and let i be minimal such that v_i is not scanned before time t. Then $i > 1$, since s is the first node scanned and $\mu(s) = 0 = d[s]$ when s is scanned. By the definition of i,

Function *Dijkstra(s : NodeId) : NodeArray×NodeArray*   // returns (*d*,*parent*)
  $d = \langle \infty, \ldots, \infty \rangle$: *NodeArray* **of** $\mathbb{R} \cup \{\infty\}$ // tentative distance from root
  parent = $\langle \bot, \ldots, \bot \rangle$: *NodeArray* **of** *NodeId*
  parent[*s*] := *s*   // self-loop signals root
  Q : *NodePQ*   // unscanned reached nodes
  d[*s*] := 0;   *Q.insert*(*s*)
  while $Q \neq \emptyset$ **do**
    u := *Q.deleteMin*   // we have *d*[*u*] = $\mu(u)$
    foreach *edge* $e = (u,v) \in E$ **do**
      if *d*[*u*] + *c*(*e*) < *d*[*v*] **then**   // relax
        d[*v*] := *d*[*u*] + *c*(*e*)
        parent[*v*] := *u*   // update tree
        if $v \in Q$ **then** *Q.decreaseKey*(*v*)
        else *Q.insert*(*v*)
  return (*d*,*parent*)

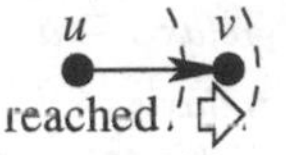

scanned

reached

Fig. 10.6. Pseudocode for Dijkstra's algorithm

v_{i-1} was scanned before time t. Hence $d[v_{i-1}] = \mu(v_{i-1})$ when v_{i-1} is scanned. When v_{i-1} is scanned, $d[v_i]$ is set to $d[v_{i-1}] + c(v_{i-1}, v_i) = \mu(v_{i-1}) + c(v_{i-1}, v_i) = \mu(v_i)$. So, at time t, we have $d[v_i] = \mu(v_i) \leq \mu(v_k) < d[v_k]$ and hence v_i is scanned instead of v_k, a contradiction.   □

Exercise 10.7. Let v_1, v_2, ... be the order in which the nodes are scanned. Show that $\mu(v_1) \leq \mu(v_2) \leq \ldots$, i.e., the nodes are scanned in order of increasing shortest-path distance.

Exercise 10.8 (checking of shortest-path distances). Assume that all edge costs are positive, that all nodes are reachable from s, and that d is a node array of nonnegative reals satisfying $d[s] = 0$ and $d[v] = \min_{(u,v) \in E} d[u] + c(u,v)$ for $v \neq s$. Show that $d[v] = \mu(v)$ for all v. Does the claim still hold in the presence of edges of cost zero?

We come now to the implementation of Dijkstra's algorithm. We store all unscanned reached nodes in an addressable priority queue (see Sect. 6.2) using their tentative-distance values as keys. Thus, we can extract the next node to be scanned using the queue operation *deleteMin*. We need a variant of a priority queue where the operation *decreaseKey* addresses queue items using nodes rather than handles. Given an ordinary priority queue, such a *NodePQ* can be implemented using an additional *NodeArray* translating nodes into handles. We can also store the priority queue items directly in a *NodeArray*. We obtain the algorithm given in Fig. 10.6. Next, we analyze its running time in terms of the running times for the queue operations. Initializing the arrays d and *parent* and setting up a priority queue $Q = \{s\}$ takes time O(n). Checking for $Q = \emptyset$ and loop control takes constant time per iteration of the while loop, i.e., O(n) time in total. Every node reachable from s is removed from the queue exactly once. Every reachable node is also *insert*ed exactly once. Thus we have at most n *deleteMin* and *insert* operations. Since each node is scanned at most once, each edge is relaxed at most once, and hence there can be at most m *decreaseKey* operations. We obtain a total execution time of

$$T_{\text{Dijkstra}} = O\left(m \cdot T_{decreaseKey}(n) + n \cdot (T_{deleteMin}(n) + T_{insert}(n))\right),$$

where $T_{deleteMin}$, T_{insert}, and $T_{decreaseKey}$ denote the execution times for *deleteMin*, *insert*, and *decreaseKey*, respectively. Note that these execution times are a function of the queue size $|Q| = O(n)$.

Exercise 10.9. Design a graph and a nonnegative cost function such that the relaxation of $m - (n-1)$ edges causes a *decreaseKey* operation.

In his original 1959 paper, Dijkstra proposed the following implementation of the priority queue: maintain the number of reached unscanned nodes, and two arrays indexed by nodes – an array d storing the tentative distances and an array storing, for each node, whether it is unscanned or reached. Then *insert* and *decreaseKey* take time $O(1)$. A *deleteMin* takes time $O(n)$, since it has to scan the arrays in order to find the minimum tentative distance of any reached unscanned node. Thus the total running time becomes

$$T_{Dijkstra59} = O\left(m + n^2\right).$$

Much better priority queue implementations have been invented since Dijkstra's original paper. Using the binary heap and Fibonacci heap priority queues described in Sect. 6.2, we obtain

$$T_{DijkstraBHeap} = O((m+n)\log n)$$

and

$$T_{DijkstraFibonacci} = O(m + n\log n),$$

respectively. Asymptotically, the Fibonacci heap implementation is superior except for sparse graphs with $m = O(n)$. In practice, Fibonacci heaps are usually not the fastest implementation, because they involve larger constant factors and the actual number of *decreaseKey* operations tends to be much smaller than what the worst case predicts. This experimental observation will be supported by theoretical analysis in the next section.

10.4 *Average-Case Analysis of Dijkstra's Algorithm

We shall show that the expected number of *decreaseKey* operations is $O(n\log(m/n))$.

Our model of randomness is as follows. The graph G and the source node s are arbitrary. Also, for each node v, we have an arbitrary set $C(v)$ of $indegree(v)$ nonnegative real numbers. So far, everything is arbitrary. The randomness comes now: we assume that, for each v, the costs in $C(v)$ are assigned randomly to the edges *into* v, i.e., our probability space consists of $\prod_{v \in V} indegree(v)!$ assignments of edge costs to edges. We want to stress that this model is quite general. In particular, it covers the situation where edge costs are drawn independently from a common distribution.

Theorem 10.6. *Under the assumptions above, the expected number of decreaseKey operations is* $O(n \log(m/n))$.

Proof. We present a proof due to Noshita [151]. Consider a particular node v. In any run of Dijkstra's algorithm, the edges whose relaxation can cause *decreaseKey* operations for v have the form $e_i := (u_i, v)$, where $\mu(u_i) \le \mu(v)$. Say there are k such edges $e_1, \ldots, e_k$. We number them in the order in which their source nodes u_i are scanned. We then have $\mu(u_1) \le \mu(u_2) \le \ldots \le \mu(u_k) \le \mu(v)$. These edges are relaxed in the order $e_1, \ldots, e_k$, no matter how the costs in $C(v)$ are assigned to them. If e_i causes a *decreaseKey* operation, then

$$\mu(u_i) + c(e_i) < \min_{j<i} \mu(u_j) + c(e_j) .$$

Since $\mu(u_j) \le \mu(u_i)$, this implies

$$c(e_i) < \min_{j<i} c(e_j),$$

i.e., only left-to-right minima of the sequence $c(e_1), \ldots, c(e_k)$ can cause *decreaseKey* operations. We conclude that the number of *decreaseKey* operations on v is bounded by the number of left-to-right minima in the sequence $c(e_1), \ldots, c(e_k)$ minus one; the "-1" accounts for the fact that the first element in the sequence counts as a left-to-right minimum but causes an *insert* and no *decreaseKey*. In Sect. 2.8, we have shown that the expected number of left-to-right maxima in a permutation of size k is bounded by H_k. The same bound holds for minima. Thus the expected number of *decreaseKey* operations is bounded by $H_k - 1$, which in turn is bounded by $\ln k$. Also, $k \le indegree(v)$. Summing over all nodes, we obtain the following bound for the expected number of *decreaseKey* operations:

$$\sum_{v \in V} \ln indegree(v) \le n \ln \frac{m}{n} ,$$

where the last inequality follows from the concavity of the ln function (see (A.15)).

$\square$

We conclude that the expected running time is $O(m + n \log(m/n) \log n)$ with the binary heap implementation of priority queues. For sufficiently dense graphs ($m > n \log n \log \log n$), we obtain an execution time linear in the size of the input.

Exercise 10.10. Show that $E[T_{DijkstraBHeap}] = O(m)$ if $m = \Omega(n \log n \log \log n)$.

10.5 Monotone Integer Priority Queues

Dijkstra's algorithm is designed to scan nodes in order of nondecreasing distance values. Hence, a monotone priority queue (see Chapter 6) suffices for its implementation. It is not known whether monotonicity can be exploited in the case of general real edge costs. However, for integer edge costs, significant savings are possible. We therefore assume in this section that edge costs are integers in the range $0..C$ for some integer C. C is assumed to be known when the queue is initialized.

Since a shortest path can consist of at most $n-1$ edges, the shortest-path distances are at most $(n-1)C$. The range of values in the queue at any one time is even smaller. Let min be the last value deleted from the queue (zero before the first deletion). Dijkstra's algorithm maintains the invariant that all values in the queue are contained in $min..min+C$. The invariant certainly holds after the first insertion. A $deleteMin$ may increase min. Since all values in the queue are bounded by C plus the old value of min, this is certainly true for the new value of min. Edge relaxations insert priorities of the form $d[u] + c(e) = min + c(e) \in min..min+C$.

10.5.1 Bucket Queues

A bucket queue is a circular array B of $C+1$ doubly linked lists (see Figs. 10.7 and 3.8). We view the natural numbers as being wrapped around the circular array; all integers of the form $i + (C+1)j$ map to the index i. A node $v \in Q$ with tentative distance $d[v]$ is stored in $B[d[v] \bmod (C+1)]$. Since the priorities in the queue are always in $min..min+C$, all nodes in a bucket have the *same* distance value.

Initialization creates $C+1$ empty lists. An $insert(v)$ inserts v into $B[d[v] \bmod C+1]$. A $decreaseKey(v)$ removes v from the list containing it and inserts v into $B[d[v] \bmod C+1]$. Thus $insert$ and $decreaseKey$ take constant time if buckets are implemented as doubly linked lists.

A $deleteMin$ first looks at bucket $B[min \bmod C+1]$. If this bucket is empty, it increments min and repeats. In this way, the total cost of all $deleteMin$ operations is $O(n+nC) = O(nC)$, since min is incremented at most nC times and at most n elements are deleted from the queue. Plugging the operation costs for the bucket queue implementation with integer edge costs in $0..C$ into our general bound for the cost of Dijkstra's algorithm, we obtain

$$T_{\text{DijkstraBucket}} = O(m+nC).$$

*Exercise 10.11 (Dinic's refinement of bucket queues [57]). Assume that the edge costs are positive real numbers in $[c_{min}, c_{max}]$. Explain how to find shortest paths in time $O(m + nc_{max}/c_{min})$. Hint: use buckets of width c_{min}. Show that all nodes in the smallest nonempty bucket have $d[v] = \mu(v)$.

10.5.2 *Radix Heaps

Radix heaps [9] improve on the bucket queue implementation by using buckets of different widths. Narrow buckets are used for tentative distances close to min, and

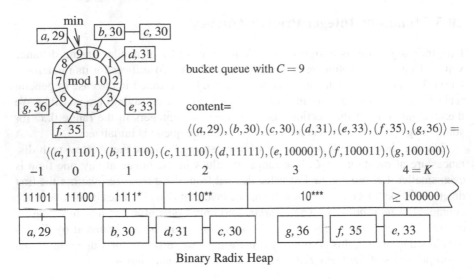

Binary Radix Heap

Fig. 10.7. Example of a bucket queue (*upper part*) and a radix heap (*lower part*). Since $C = 9$, we have $K = 1 + \lfloor \log C \rfloor = 4$. The bit patterns in the buckets of the radix heap indicate the set of keys they can accommodate

wide buckets are used for tentative distances far away from *min*. In this subsection, we shall show how this approach leads to a version of Dijkstra's algorithm with running time

$$T_{\text{DijkstraRadix}} := O(m + n \log C).$$

Radix heaps exploit the binary representation of tentative distances. We need the concept of the *most significant distinguishing index* of two numbers. This is the largest index where the binary representations differ, i.e., for numbers a and b with binary representations $a = \sum_{i \geq 0} \alpha_i 2^i$ and $b = \sum_{i \geq 0} \beta_i 2^i$, we define the most significant distinguishing index $msd(a, b)$ as the largest i with $\alpha_i \neq \beta_i$, and let it be -1 if $a = b$. If $a < b$, then a has a zero bit in position $i = msd(a, b)$ and b has a one bit.

A radix heap consists of an array of buckets $B[-1]$, $B[0]$, ..., $B[K]$, where $K = 1 + \lfloor \log C \rfloor$. The queue elements are distributed over the buckets according to the following rule:

any queue element v is stored in bucket $B[i]$, where $i = \min(msd(min, d[v]), K)$.

We refer to this rule as the bucket queue invariant. Figure 10.7 gives an example. We remark that if *min* has a one bit in position i for $0 \leq i < K$, the corresponding bucket $B[i]$ is empty. This holds since any $d[v]$ with $i = msd(min, d[v])$ would have a zero bit in position i and hence be smaller than *min*. But all keys in the queue are at least as large as *min*.

How can we compute $i := msd(a, b)$? We first observe that for $a \neq b$, the bitwise exclusive OR $a \oplus b$ of a and b has its most significant one in position i and hence represents an integer whose value is at least 2^i and less than 2^{i+1}. Thus $msd(a, b) =$

$\lfloor \log(a \oplus b) \rfloor$, since $\log(a \oplus b)$ is a real number with its integer part equal to i and the floor function extracts the integer part. Many processors support the computation of *msd* by machine instructions.[3] Alternatively, we can use lookup tables or yet other solutions. From now on, we shall assume that *msd* can be evaluated in constant time.

We turn now to the queue operations. Initialization, *insert*, and *decreaseKey* work completely analogously to bucket queues. The only difference is that bucket indices are computed using the bucket queue invariant.

A *deleteMin* first finds the minimum i such that $B[i]$ is nonempty. If $i = -1$, an arbitrary element in $B[-1]$ is removed and returned. If $i \geq 0$, the bucket $B[i]$ is scanned and *min* is set to the smallest tentative distance contained in the bucket. Since *min* has changed, the bucket queue invariant needs to be restored. A crucial observation for the efficiency of radix heaps is that only the nodes in bucket i are affected. We shall discuss below how they are affected. Let us consider first the buckets $B[j]$ with $j \neq i$. The buckets $B[j]$ with $j < i$ are empty. If $i - K$, there are no j's with $j > K$. If $i < K$, any key a in bucket $B[j]$ with $j > i$ will still have $msd(a, min) = j$, because the old and new values of *min* agree at bit positions greater than i.

What happens to the elements in $B[i]$? Its elements are moved to the appropriate new bucket. Thus a *deleteMin* takes constant time if $i = -1$ and takes time $O(i + |B[i]|) = O(K + |B[i]|)$ if $i \geq 0$. Lemma 10.7 below shows that every node in bucket $B[i]$ is moved to a bucket with a smaller index. This observation allows us to account for the cost of a *deleteMin* using amortized analysis. As our unit of cost (one token), we shall use the time required to move one node between buckets.

We charge $K + 1$ tokens for operation *insert*(v) and associate these $K + 1$ tokens with v. These tokens pay for the moves of v to lower-numbered buckets in *deleteMin* operations. A node starts in some bucket j with $j \leq K$, ends in bucket -1, and in between never moves back to a higher-numbered bucket. Observe that a *decreaseKey*(v) operation will also never move a node to a higher-numbered bucket. Hence, the $K + 1$ tokens can pay for all the node moves of *deleteMin* operations. The remaining cost of a *deleteMin* is $O(K)$ for finding a nonempty bucket. With amortized costs $K + 1 + O(1) = O(K)$ for an *insert* and $O(1)$ for a *decreaseKey*, we obtain a total execution time of $O(m + n \cdot (K + K)) = O(m + n \log C)$ for Dijkstra's algorithm, as claimed.

It remains to prove that *deleteMin* operations move nodes to lower-numbered buckets.

Lemma 10.7. *Let i be minimal such that $B[i]$ is nonempty and assume $i \geq 0$. Let min be the smallest element in $B[i]$. Then $msd(min, x) < i$ for all $x \in B[i]$.*

---

[3] $\oplus$ is a direct machine instruction, and $\lfloor \log x \rfloor$ is the exponent in the floating-point representation of x.

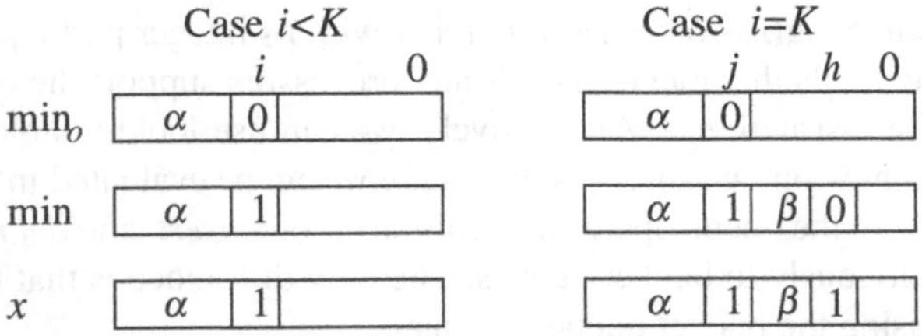

Case $i<K$ Case $i=K$

Fig. 10.8. The structure of the keys relevant to the proof of Lemma 10.7. In the proof, it is shown that β starts with $j-K$ zeros

Proof. Observe first that the case $x = min$ is easy, since $msd(x,x) = -1 < i$. For the nontrivial case $x \neq min$, we distinguish the subcases $i < K$ and $i = K$. Let min_o be the old value of min. Figure 10.8 shows the structure of the relevant keys.

Case $i < K$. The most significant distinguishing index of min_o and any $x \in B[i]$ is i, i.e., min_o has a zero in bit position i, and all $x \in B[i]$ have a one in bit position i. They agree in all positions with an index larger than i. Thus the most significant distinguishing index for min and x is smaller than i.

Case $i = K$. Consider any $x \in B[K]$. Let $j = msd(min_o, min)$. Then $j \geq K$, since $min \in B[K]$. Let $h = msd(min, x)$. We want to show that $h < K$. Let α comprise the bits in positions larger than j in min_o, and let A be the number obtained from min_o by setting the bits in positions 0 to j to zero. Then α followed by $j+1$ zeros is the binary representation of A. Since the j-th bit of min_o is zero and that of min is one, we have $min_o < A + 2^j$ and $A + 2^j \leq min$. Also, $x \leq min_o + C < A + 2^j + C \leq A + 2^j + 2^K$. So

$$A + 2^j \leq min \leq x < A + 2^j + 2^K,$$

and hence the binary representations of min and x consist of α followed by a 1, followed by $j - K$ zeros, followed by some bit string of length K. Thus min and x agree in all bits with index K or larger, and hence $h < K$.

In order to aid intuition, we give a second proof for the case $i = K$. We first observe that the binary representation of min starts with α followed by a one. We next observe that x can be obtained from min_o by adding some K-bit number. Since $min \leq x$, the final carry in this addition must run into position j. Otherwise, the j-th bit of x would be zero and hence $x < min$. Since min_o has a zero in position j, the carry stops at position j. We conclude that the binary representation of x is equal to α followed by a 1, followed by $j - K$ zeros, followed by some K-bit string. Since $min \leq x$, the $j - K$ zeros must also be present in the binary representation of min.   □

*Exercise 10.12. Radix heaps can also be based on number representations with base b for any $b \geq 2$. In this situation we have buckets $B[i, j]$ for $i = -1, 0, 1, \ldots, K$ and $0 \leq j \leq b$, where $K = 1 + \lfloor \log C / \log b \rfloor$. An unscanned reached node x is stored in bucket $B[i, j]$ if $msd(min, d[x]) = i$ and the i-th digit of $d[x]$ is equal to j. We also store, for each i, the number of nodes contained in the buckets $\cup_j B[i, j]$. Discuss the implementation of the priority queue operations and show that a shortest-path algorithm with running time $O(m + n(b + \log C / \log b))$ results. What is the optimal choice of b?

If the edge costs are random integers in the range $0..C$, a small change to Dijkstra's algorithm with radix heaps guarantees linear running time [139, 76]. For every node v, let $c^{in}_{min}(v)$ denote the minimum cost of an incoming edge. We divide Q into two parts, a set F which contains unscanned nodes whose tentative-distance label is known to be equal to their exact distance from s, and a part B which contains all other reached unscanned nodes. B is organized as a radix heap. We also maintain a value min. We scan nodes as follows.

When F is nonempty, an arbitrary node in F is removed and the outgoing edges are relaxed. When F is empty, the minimum node is selected from B and min is set to its distance label. When a node is selected from B, the nodes in the first nonempty bucket $B[i]$ are redistributed if $i \geq 0$. There is a small change in the redistribution process. When a node v is to be moved, and $d[v] \leq min + c^{in}_{min}(v)$, we move v to F. Observe that any future relaxation of an edge into v cannot decrease $d[v]$, and hence $d[v]$ is known to be exact at this point.

We call this algorithm ALD (average-case linear Dijkstra). The algorithm ALD is correct, since it is still true that $d[v] = \mu(v)$ when v is scanned. For nodes removed from F, this was argued in the previous paragraph, and for nodes removed from B, this follows from the fact that they have the smallest tentative distance among all unscanned reached nodes.

Theorem 10.8. *Let G be an arbitrary graph and let c be a random function from E to $0..C$. The algorithm ALD then solves the single-source problem in expected time $O(m + n)$.*

Proof. We still need to argue the bound on the running time. To do this, we modify the amortized analysis of plain radix heaps. As before, nodes start out in $B[K]$. When a node v has been moved to a new bucket but not yet to F, $d[v] > min + c^{in}_{min}(v)$, and hence v is moved to a bucket $B[i]$ with $i \geq \log c^{in}_{min}(v)$. Hence, it suffices if *insert* pays $K - \log c^{in}_{min}(v) + 1$ tokens into the account for node v in order to cover all costs due to *decreaseKey* and *deleteMin* operations operating on v. Summing over all nodes, we obtain a total payment of

$$\sum_v (K - \log c^{in}_{min}(v) + 1) = n + \sum_v (K - \log c^{in}_{min}(v)) \ .$$

We need to estimate this sum. For each vertex, we have one incoming edge contributing to this sum. We therefore bound the sum from above if we sum over all edges, i.e.,

$$\sum_v (K - \log c^{in}_{min}(v)) \leq \sum_e (K - \log c(e))$$

$K - \log c(e)$ is the number of leading zeros in the binary representation of $c(e)$ when written as a K-bit number. Our edge costs are uniform random numbers in $0..C$, and $K = 1 + \lfloor \log C \rfloor$. Thus $prob(K - \log c(e) = i) = 2^{-i}$. Using (A.14), we conclude that

$$E\left[\sum_e (k - \log c(e))\right] = \sum_e \sum_{i \geq 0} i2^{-i} = O(m).$$

Thus the total expected cost of the *deleteMin* and *decreaseKey* operations is $O(m+n)$. The time spent outside these operations is also $O(m+n)$.   □

It is a little odd that the maximum edge cost C appears in the premise but not in the conclusion of Theorem 10.8. Indeed, it can be shown that a similar result holds for random real-valued edge costs.

**Exercise 10.13. Explain how to adapt the algorithm ALD to the case where c is a random function from E to the real interval $(0, 1]$. The expected time should still be $O(m+n)$. What assumptions do you need about the representation of edge costs and about the machine instructions available? Hint: you may first want to solve Exercise 10.11. The narrowest bucket should have a width of $\min_{e \in E} c(e)$. Subsequent buckets have geometrically growing widths.

10.6 Arbitrary Edge Costs (Bellman–Ford Algorithm)

For acyclic graphs and for nonnegative edge costs, we got away with m edge relaxations. For arbitrary edge costs, no such result is known. However, it is easy to guarantee the correctness criterion of Lemma 10.3 using $O(n \cdot m)$ edge relaxations: the Bellman–Ford algorithm [18, 63] given in Fig. 10.9 performs $n - 1$ rounds. In each round, it relaxes all edges. Since simple paths consist of at most $n - 1$ edges, every shortest path is a subsequence of this sequence of relaxations. Thus, after the relaxations are completed, we have $d[v] = \mu(v)$ for all v with $-\infty < d[v] < \infty$, by Lemma 10.3. Moreover, *parent* encodes the shortest paths to these nodes. Nodes v unreachable from s will still have $d[v] = \infty$, as desired.

It is not so obvious how to find the nodes v with $\mu(v) = -\infty$. Consider any edge $e = (u, v)$ with $d[u] + c(e) < d[v]$ after the relaxations are completed. We can set $d[v] := -\infty$ because if there were a shortest path from s to v, we would have found it by now and relaxing e would not lead to shorter distances anymore. We can now also set $d[w] = -\infty$ for all nodes w reachable from v. The pseudocode implements this approach using a recursive function *infect*(v). It sets the d-value of v and all nodes reachable from it to $-\infty$. If *infect* reaches a node w that already has $d[w] = -\infty$, it breaks the recursion because previous executions of *infect* have already explored all nodes reachable from w. If $d[v]$ is not set to $-\infty$ during postprocessing, we have $d[x] + c(e) \geq d[y]$ for any edge $e = (x, y)$ on any path p from s to v. Thus $d[s] + c(p) \geq d[v]$ for any path p from s to v, and hence $d[v] \leq \mu(v)$. We conclude that $d[v] = \mu(v)$.

Exercise 10.14. Show that the postprocessing runs in time $O(m)$. Hint: relate *infect* to *DFS*.

Exercise 10.15. Someone proposes an alternative postprocessing algorithm: set $d[v]$ to $-\infty$ for all nodes v for which following parents does not lead to s. Give an example where this method overlooks a node with $\mu(v) = -\infty$.

Function *BellmanFord*(s : *NodeId*) : *NodeArray* × *NodeArray*
    $d = \langle \infty, \ldots, \infty \rangle$: *NodeArray* **of** $\mathbb{R} \cup \{-\infty, \infty\}$ // distance from root
    parent = $\langle \bot, \ldots, \bot \rangle$: *NodeArray* **of** *NodeId*
    $d[s] := 0;$ *parent*[s] := s   // self-loop signals root
    for $i := 1$ **to** $n - 1$ **do**
        forall $e \in E$ **do** *relax*(e)   // round i
    forall $e = (u, v) \in E$ **do**   // postprocessing
        if $d[u] + c(e) < d[v]$ **then** *infect*(v)
    return (d, *parent*)

Procedure *infect*(v)
    if $d[v] > -\infty$ **then**
        $d[v] := -\infty$
        foreach $(v, w) \in E$ **do** *infect*(w)

Fig. 10.9. The Bellman–Ford algorithm for shortest paths in arbitrary graphs

Exercise 10.16 (arbitrage). Consider a set of currencies C with an exchange rate of r_{ij} between currencies i and j (you obtain r_{ij} units of currency j for one unit of currency i). A *currency arbitrage* is possible if there is a sequence of elementary currency exchange actions (*transactions*) that starts with one unit of a currency and ends with more than one unit of the same currency. (a) Show how to find out whether a matrix of exchange rates admits currency arbitrage. Hint: $\log(xy) = \log x + \log y$. (b) Refine your algorithm so that it outputs a sequence of exchange steps that maximizes the average profit *per transaction*.

Section 10.10 outlines further refinements of the Bellman–Ford algorithm that are necessary for good performance in practice.

10.7 All-Pairs Shortest Paths and Node Potentials

The all-pairs problem is tantamount to n single-source problems and hence can be solved in time $O(n^2 m)$. A considerable improvement is possible. We shall show that it suffices to solve one general single-source problem plus n single-source problems with nonnegative edge costs. In this way, we obtain a running time of $O(nm + n(m + n \log n)) = O(nm + n^2 \log n)$. We need the concept of node potentials.

A *(node) potential function* assigns a number $pot(v)$ to each node v. For an edge $e = (v, w)$, we define its *reduced cost* $\bar{c}(e)$ as

$$\bar{c}(e) = pot(v) + c(e) - pot(w) .$$

Lemma 10.9. *Let p and q be paths from v to w. Then $\bar{c}(p) = pot(v) + c(p) - pot(w)$ and $\bar{c}(p) \leq \bar{c}(q)$ iff $c(p) \leq c(q)$. In particular, the shortest paths with respect to $\bar{c}$ are the same as those with respect to c.*

All-Pairs Shortest Paths in the Absence of Negative Cycles
add a new node s and zero length edges (s,v) for all v // no new cycles, time $O(m)$
compute $\mu(v)$ for all v with Bellman–Ford   // time $O(nm)$
set $pot(v) = \mu(v)$ and compute reduced costs $\bar{c}(e)$ for $e \in E$ // time $O(m)$
forall nodes x **do**   // time $O(n(m+n\log n))$
     use Dijkstra's algorithm to compute the reduced shortest-path distances $\bar{\mu}(x,v)$
     using source x and the reduced edge costs $\bar{c}$
// translate distances back to original cost function   // time $O(m)$
forall $e = (v,w) \in V \times V$ **do** $\mu(v,w) := \bar{\mu}(v,w) + pot(w) - pot(v)$ // use Lemma 10.9

Fig. 10.10. Algorithm for all-pairs shortest paths in the absence of negative cycles

Proof. The second and the third claim follow from the first. For the first claim, let $p = \langle e_0, \ldots, e_{k-1} \rangle$, where $e_i = (v_i, v_{i+1})$, $v = v_0$, and $w = v_k$. Then

$$\bar{c}(p) = \sum_{i=0}^{k-1} \bar{c}(e_i) = \sum_{0 \le i < k} (pot(v_i) + c(e_i) - pot(v_{i+1}))$$

$$= pot(v_0) + \sum_{0 \le i < k} c(e_i) - pot(v_k) = pot(v_0) + c(p) - pot(v_k) . \qquad \square$$

Exercise 10.17. Node potentials can be used to generate graphs with negative edge costs but no negative cycles: generate a (random) graph, assign to every edge e a (random) nonnegative cost $c(e)$, assign to every node v a (random) potential $pot(v)$, and set the cost of $e = (u,v)$ to $\bar{c}(e) = pot(u) + c(e) - pot(v)$. Show that this rule does not generate negative cycles.

Lemma 10.10. *Assume that G has no negative cycles and that all nodes can be reached from s. Let $pot(v) = \mu(v)$ for $v \in V$. With these node potentials, the reduced edge costs are nonnegative.*

Proof. Since all nodes are reachable from s and since there are no negative cycles, $\mu(v) \in \mathbb{R}$ for all v. Thus the reduced costs are well defined. Consider an arbitrary edge $e = (v,w)$. We have $\mu(v) + c(e) \ge \mu(w)$, and thus $\bar{c}(e) = \mu(v) + c(e) - \mu(w) \ge 0$. $\quad\square$

Theorem 10.11. *The all-pairs shortest-path problem for a graph without negative cycles can be solved in time $O(nm + n^2 \log n)$.*

Proof. The algorithm is shown in Fig. 10.10. We add an auxiliary node s and zero-cost edges (s,v) for all nodes of the graph. This does not create negative cycles and does not change $\mu(v,w)$ for any of the existing nodes. Then we solve the single-source problem for the source s, and set $pot(v) = \mu(v)$ for all v. Next we compute the reduced costs and then solve the single-source problem for each node x by means of Dijkstra's algorithm. Finally, we translate the computed distances back to the original cost function. The computation of the potentials takes time $O(nm)$, and the n shortest-path calculations take time $O(n(m + n\log n))$. The preprocessing and postprocessing take linear time. $\quad\square$

The assumption that G has no negative cycles can be removed [133].

Exercise 10.18. The *diameter* D of a graph G is defined as the largest distance between any two of its nodes. We can easily compute it using an all-pairs computation. Now we want to consider ways to *approximate* the diameter of a strongly connected graph using a constant number of single-source computations. (a) For any starting node s, let $D'(s) := \max_{u \in V} \mu(u)$. Show that $D'(s) \le D \le 2D'(s)$ for undirected graphs. Also, show that no such relation holds for directed graphs. Let $D''(s) := \max_{u \in V} \mu(u, s)$. Show that $\max(D'(s), D''(s)) \le D \le D'(s) + D''(s)$ for both undirected and directed graphs. (b) How should a graph be represented to support both forward and backward search? (c) Can you improve the approximation by considering more than one node s?

10.8 Shortest-Path Queries

We are often interested in the shortest path from a specific source node s to a specific target node t; route planning in a traffic network is one such scenario. We shall explain some techniques for solving such *shortest-path queries* efficiently and argue for their usefulness for the route-planning application.

We start with a technique called *early stopping*. We run Dijkstra's algorithm to find shortest paths starting at s. We stop the search as soon as t is removed from the priority queue, because at this point in time the shortest path to t is known. This helps except in the unfortunate case where t is the node farthest from s. On average, early stopping saves a factor of two in scanned nodes in any application. In practical route planning, early stopping saves much more because modern car navigation systems have a map of an entire continent but are mostly used for distances up to a few hundred kilometers.

Another simple and general heuristic is *bidirectional search*, from s forward and from t backward until the search frontiers meet. More precisely, we run two copies of Dijkstra's algorithm side by side, one starting from s and one starting from t (and running on the reversed graph). The two copies have their own queues, say Q_s and Q_t, respectively. We grow the search regions at about the same speed, for example by removing a node from Q_s if $\min Q_s \le \min Q_t$ and a node from Q_t otherwise.

It is tempting to stop the search once the first node u has been removed from both queues, and to claim that $\mu(t) = \mu(s, u) + \mu(u, t)$. Observe that execution of Dijkstra's algorithm on the reversed graph with a starting node t determines $\mu(u, t)$. This is not quite correct, but almost so.

Exercise 10.19. Give an example where u is *not* on the shortest path from s to t.

However, we have collected enough information once some node u has been removed from both queues. Let d_s and d_t denote the tentative-distance labels at the time of termination in the runs with source s and source t, respectively. We show that $\mu(t) < \mu(s, u) + \mu(u, t)$ implies the existence of a node $v \in Q_s$ with $\mu(t) = d_s[v] + d_t[v]$.

Let $p = \langle s = v_0, \ldots, v_i, v_{i+1}, \ldots, v_k = t \rangle$ be a shortest path from s to t. Let i be maximal such that v_i has been removed from Q_s. Then $d_s[v_{i+1}] = \mu(s, v_{i+1})$ and $v_{i+1} \in Q_s$ when the search stops. Also, $\mu(s, u) \leq \mu(s, v_{i+1})$, since u has already been removed from Q_s, but v_{i+1} has not. Next, observe that

$$\mu(s, v_{i+1}) + \mu(v_{i+1}, t) = c(p) < \mu(s, u) + \mu(u, t) \,,$$

since p is a shortest path from s to t. By subtracting $\mu(s, v_{i+1})$, we obtain

$$\mu(v_{i+1}, t) < \underbrace{\mu(s, u) - \mu(s, v_{i+1})}_{\leq 0} + \mu(u, t) \leq \mu(u, t)$$

and hence, since u has been scanned from t, v_{i+1} must also have been scanned from t, i.e., $d_t[v_{i+1}] = \mu(v_{i+1}, t)$ when the search stops. So we can determine the shortest distance from s to t by inspecting not only the first node removed from both queues, but also all nodes in, say, Q_s. We iterate over all such nodes v and determine the minimum value of $d_s[v] + d_t[v]$.

Dijkstra's algorithm scans nodes in order of increasing distance from the source. In other words, it grows a circle centered on the source node. The circle is defined by the shortest-path metric in the graph. In the route-planning application for a road network, we may also consider geometric circles centered on the source and argue that shortest-path circles and geometric circles are about the same. We can then estimate the speedup obtained by bidirectional search using the following heuristic argument: a circle of a certain diameter has twice the area of two circles of half the diameter. We could thus hope that bidirectional search will save a factor of two compared with unidirectional search.

Exercise 10.20 (bidirectional search). (a) Consider bidirectional search in a grid graph with unit edge weights. How much does it save over unidirectional search? (*b) Try to find a family of graphs where bidirectional search visits exponentially fewer nodes on average than does unidirectional search. Hint: consider random graphs or hypercubes. (c) Give an example where bidirectional search in a real road network takes *longer* than unidirectional search. Hint: consider a densely inhabited city with sparsely populated surroundings. (d) Design a strategy for switching between forward and backward search such that bidirectional search will *never* inspect more than twice as many nodes as unidirectional search.

We shall next describe two techniques that are more complex and less generally applicable: however, if they are applicable, they usually result in larger savings. Both techniques mimic human behavior in route planning.

10.8.1 Goal-Directed Search

The idea is to bias the search space such that Dijkstra's algorithm does not grow a disk but a region protruding toward the target; see Fig. 10.11. Assume we know a function $f : V \to \mathbb{R}$ that estimates the distance to the target, i.e., $f(v)$ estimates

$\mu(v,t)$ for all nodes v. We use the estimates to modify the distance function. For each $e = (u,v)$, let[4] $\bar{c}(e) = c(e) + f(v) - f(u)$. We run Dijkstra's algorithm with the modified distance function. We know already that node potentials do not change shortest paths, and hence correctness is preserved. Tentative distances are related via $\bar{d}[v] = d[v] + f(v) - f(s)$. An alternative view of this modification is that we run Dijkstra's algorithm with the original distance function but remove the node with minimal value $d[v] + f(v)$ from the queue. The algorithm just described is known as *A*-search*.

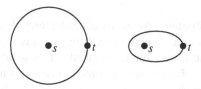

Fig. 10.11. The standard Dijkstra search grows a circular region centered on the source; goal-directed search grows a region protruding toward the target

Before we state requirements on the estimate f, let us see one specific example. Assume, in a thought experiment, that $f(v) = \mu(v,t)$. Then $\bar{c}(e) = c(e) + \mu(v,t) - \mu(u,t)$ and hence edges on a shortest path from s to t have a modified cost equal to zero and all other edges have a positive cost. Thus Dijkstra's algorithm only follows shortest paths, without looking left or right.

The function f must have certain properties to be useful. First, we want the modified distances to be nonnegative. So, we need $c(e) + f(v) \geq f(u)$ for all edges $e = (u,v)$. In other words, our estimate of the distance from u should be at most our estimate of the distance from v plus the cost of going from u to v. This property is called consistency of estimates. We also want to be able to stop the search when t is removed from the queue. This works if f is a lower bound on the distance to the target, i.e., $f(v) \leq \mu(v,t)$ for all $v \in V$. Then $f(t) = 0$. Consider the point in time when t is removed from the queue, and let p be any path from s to t. If all edges of p have been relaxed at termination, $d[t] \leq c(p)$. If not all edges of p have been relaxed at termination, there is a node v on p that is contained in the queue at termination. Then $d(t) + f(t) \leq d(v) + f(v)$, since t was removed from the queue but v was not, and hence

$$d[t] = d[t] + f(t) \leq d[v] + f(v) \leq d[v] + \mu(v,t) \leq c(p) .$$

In either case, we have $d[t] \leq c(p)$, and hence the shortest distance from s to t is known as soon as t is removed from the queue.

What is a good heuristic function for route planning in a road network? Route planners often give a choice between *shortest* and *fastest* connections. In the case

---

[4] In Sect. 10.7, we added the potential of the source and subtracted the potential of the target. We do exactly the opposite now. The reason for changing the sign convention is that in Lemma 10.10, we used $\mu(s,v)$ as the node potential. Now, f estimates $\mu(v,t)$.

of shortest paths, a feasible lower bound $f(v)$ is the straight-line distance between v and t. Speedups by a factor of roughly four are reported in the literature. For fastest paths, we may use the geometric distance divided by the speed assumed for the best kind of road. This estimate is extremely optimistic, since targets are frequently in the center of a town, and hence no good speedups have been reported. More sophisticated methods for computing lower bounds are known; we refer the reader to [77] for a thorough discussion.

10.8.2 Hierarchy

Road networks usually contain a hierarchy of roads: throughways, state roads, county roads, city roads, and so on. Average speeds are usually higher on roads of higher status, and therefore the fastest routes frequently follow the pattern that one starts on a road of low status, changes several times to roads of higher status, drives the largest fraction of the path on a road of high status, and finally changes down to lower-status roads near the target. A heuristic approach may therefore restrict the search to high-status roads except for suitably chosen neighborhoods of the source and target. Observe, however, that the choice of neighborhood is nonobvious, and that this heuristic sacrifices optimality. You may be able to think of an example from your driving experience where shortcuts over small roads are required even far away from the source and target. Exactness can be combined with the idea of hierarchies if the hierarchy is defined algorithmically and is not taken from the official classification of roads. We now outline one such approach [165], called *highway hierarchies*. It first defines a notion of locality, say anything within a distance of 10 km from either the source or the target. An edge $(u, v) \in E$ is a *highway edge* with respect to this notion of locality if there is a source node s and a target node t such that (u, v) is on the fastest path from s to t, v is not within the local search radius of s, and u is not within the local (backward) search radius of t. The resulting network is called the *highway network*. It usually has many vertices of degree two. Think of a fast road to which a slow road connects. The slow road is not used on any fastest path outside the local region of a nearby source or nearby target, and hence will not be in the highway network. Thus the intersection will have degree three in the original road network, but will have degree two in the highway network. Two edges joined by a degree-two node may be collapsed into a single edge. In this way, the *core* of the highway network is determined. Iterating this procedure of finding a highway network and contracting degree-two nodes leads to a hierarchy of roads. For example, in the case of the road networks of Europe and North America, a hierarchy of up to ten levels resulted. Route planning using the resulting highway hierarchy can be several thousand times faster than Dijkstra's algorithm.

10.8.3 Transit Node Routing

Using another observation from daily life, we can get even faster [15]. When you drive to somewhere "far away", you will leave your current location via one of only a few "important" traffic junctions. It turns out that in real-world road networks about

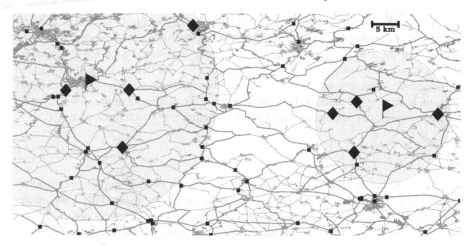

Fig. 10.12. Finding the optimal travel time between two points (the flags) somewhere between Saarbrücken and Karlsruhe amounts to retrieving the 2×4 *access nodes* (diamonds), performing 16 table lookups between all pairs of access nodes, and checking that the two disks defining the *locality filter* do not overlap. The small squares indicate further transit nodes

99% of all quickest paths go through about $O(\sqrt{n})$ important *transit nodes* that can be automatically selected, for example using highway hierarchies. Moreover, for each particular source or target node, all long-distance connections go through one of about ten of these transit nodes – the *access nodes*. During preprocessing, we compute a complete distance table between the transit nodes, and the distances from all nodes to their access nodes. Now, suppose we have a way to tell that a source s and a target t are sufficiently far apart.[5] There must then be access nodes a_s and a_t such that $\mu(t) = \mu(a_s) + \mu(a_s, a_t) + \mu(a_t, t)$. All these distances have been precomputed and there are only about ten candidates for a_s and for a_t, respectively, i.e., we need (only) about 100 accesses to the distance table. This can be more than 1 000 000 times faster than Dijkstra's algorithm. Local queries can be answered using some other technique that will profit from the closeness of the source and target. We can also cover local queries using additional precomputed tables with more local information. Figure 10.12 from [15] gives an example.

10.9 Implementation Notes

Shortest-path algorithms work over the set of extended reals $\mathbb{R} \cup \{+\infty, -\infty\}$. We may ignore $-\infty$, since it is needed only in the presence of negative cycles and, even there, it is needed only for the output; see Sect. 10.6. We can also get rid of $+\infty$ by noting that $parent(v) = \bot$ iff $d[v] = +\infty$, i.e., when $parent(v) = \bot$, we assume that $d[v] = +\infty$ and ignore the number stored in $d[v]$.

---

[5] We may need additional preprocessing to decide this.

A refined implementation of the Bellman–Ford algorithm [187, 131] explicitly maintains a current approximation T of the shortest-path tree. Nodes still to be scanned in the current iteration of the main loop are stored in a set Q. Consider the relaxation of an edge $e = (u, v)$ that reduces $d[v]$. All descendants of v in T will subsequently receive a new d-value. Hence, there is no reason to scan these nodes with their current d-values and one may remove them from Q and T. Furthermore, negative cycles can be detected by checking whether v is an ancestor of u in T.

10.9.1 C++

LEDA [118] has a special priority queue class *node_pq* that implements priority queues of graph nodes. Both LEDA and the Boost graph library [27] have implementations of the Dijkstra and Bellman–Ford algorithms and of the algorithms for acyclic graphs and the all-pairs problem. There is a graph iterator based on Dijkstra's algorithm that allows more flexible control of the search process. For example, one can use it to search until a given set of target nodes has been found. LEDA also provides a function that verifies the correctness of distance functions (see Exercise 10.8).

10.9.2 Java

JDSL [78] provides Dijkstra's algorithm for integer edge costs. This implementation allows detailed control over the search similarly to the graph iterators of LEDA and Boost.

10.10 Historical Notes and Further Findings

Dijkstra [56], Bellman [18], and Ford [63] found their algorithms in the 1950s. The original version of Dijkstra's algorithm had a running time $O(m + n^2)$ and there is a long history of improvements. Most of these improvements result from better data structures for priority queues. We have discussed binary heaps [208], Fibonacci heaps [68], bucket heaps [52], and radix heaps [9]. Experimental comparisons can be found in [40, 131]. For integer keys, radix heaps are not the end of the story. The best theoretical result is $O(m + n \log \log n)$ time [194]. Interestingly, for *undirected* graphs, linear time can be achieved [190]. The latter algorithm still scans nodes one after the other, but not in the same order as in Dijkstra's algorithm.

Meyer [139] gave the first shortest-path algorithm with linear average-case running time. The algorithm ALD was found by Goldberg [76]. For graphs with bounded degree, the Δ-stepping algorithm [140] is even simpler. This uses bucket queues and also yields a good parallel algorithm for graphs with bounded degree and small diameter.

Integrality of edge costs is also of use when negative edge costs are allowed. If all edge costs are integers greater than $-N$, a *scaling algorithm* achieves a time $O(m\sqrt{n}\log N)$ [75].

In Sect. 10.8, we outlined a small number of speedup techniques for route planning. Many other techniques exist. In particular, we have not done justice to advanced goal-directed techniques, combinations of different techniques, etc. Recent overviews can be found in [166, 173]. Theoretical performance guarantees beyond Dijkstra's algorithm are more difficult to achieve. Positive results exist for special families of graphs such as planar graphs and when approximate shortest paths suffice [60, 195, 192].

There is a generalization of the shortest-path problem that considers several cost functions at once. For example, your grandfather might want to know the fastest route for visiting you but he only wants routes where he does not need to refuel his car, or you may want to know the fastest route subject to the condition that the road toll does not exceed a certain limit. Constrained shortest-path problems are discussed in [86, 135].

Shortest paths can also be computed in geometric settings. In particular, there is an interesting connection to optics. Different materials have different refractive indices, which are related to the speed of light in the material. Astonishingly, the laws of optics dictate that a ray of light always travels along a shortest path.

Exercise 10.21. An ordered semigroup is a set S together with an associative and commutative operation $+$, a neutral element 0, and a linear ordering $\leq$ such that for all x, y, and z, $x \leq y$ implies $x + z \leq y + z$. Which of the algorithms of this chapter work when the edge weights are from an ordered semigroup? Which of them work under the additional assumption that $0 \leq x$ for all x?

11

Minimum Spanning Trees

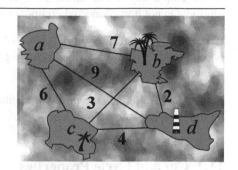

The atoll of Taka-Tuka-Land in the South Seas asks you for help.[1] The people want to connect their islands by ferry lines. Since money is scarce, the total cost of the connections is to be minimized. It needs to be possible to travel between any two islands; direct connections are not necessary. You are given a list of possible connections together with their estimated costs. Which connections should be opened?

More generally, we want to solve the following problem. Consider a connected undirected graph $G = (V, E)$ with real edge costs $c : E \to \mathbb{R}_+$. A *minimum spanning tree* (MST) of G is defined by a set $T \subseteq E$ of edges such that the graph (V, T) is a tree where $c(T) := \sum_{e \in T} c(e)$ is minimized. In our example, the nodes are islands, the edges are possible ferry connections, and the costs are the costs of opening a connection. Throughout this chapter, G denotes an undirected connected graph.

Minimum spanning trees are perhaps the simplest variant of an important family of problems known as *network design problems*. Because MSTs are such a simple concept, they also show up in many seemingly unrelated problems such as clustering, finding paths that minimize the maximum edge cost used, and finding approximations for harder problems. Sections 11.6 and 11.8 discuss this further. An equally good reason to discuss MSTs in a textbook on algorithms is that there are simple, elegant, fast algorithms to find them. We shall derive two simple properties of MSTs in Sect. 11.1. These properties form the basis of most MST algorithms. The Jarník–Prim algorithm grows an MST starting from a single node and will be discussed in Sect. 11.2. Kruskal's algorithm grows many trees in unrelated parts of the graph at once and merges them into larger and larger trees. This will be discussed in Sect. 11.3. An efficient implementation of the algorithm requires a data structure for maintaining partitions of a set of elements under two operations: "determine whether two elements are in the same subset" and "join two subsets". We shall discuss the union–find data structure in Sect. 11.4. This has many applications besides the construction of minimum spanning trees.

---

[1] The figure was drawn by A. Blancani.

Exercise 11.1. If the input graph is not connected, we may ask for a *minimum spanning forest* – a set of edges that defines an MST for each connected component of G. Develop a way to find minimum spanning forests using a single call of an MST routine. Do not find connected components first. Hint: insert $n-1$ additional edges.

Exercise 11.2 (spanning sets). A set T of edges spans a connected graph G if (V,T) is connected. Is a minimum-cost spanning set of edges necessarily a tree? Is it a tree if all edge costs are positive?

Exercise 11.3. Reduce the problem of finding *maximum*-cost spanning trees to the minimum-spanning-tree problem.

11.1 Cut and Cycle Properties

We shall prove two simple Lemmas which allow one to add edges to an MST and to exclude edges from consideration for an MST. We need the concept of a cut in a graph. A *cut* in a connected graph is a subset E' of edges such that $G \setminus E'$ is not connected. Here, $G \setminus E'$ is an abbreviation for $(V, E \setminus E')$. If S is a set of nodes with $\emptyset \neq S \neq V$, the set of edges with exactly one endpoint in S forms a cut. Figure 11.1 illustrates the proofs of the following lemmas.

Lemma 11.1 (cut property). *Let E' be a cut and let e be a minimal-cost edge in E'. There is then an MST T of G that contains e. Moreover, if T' is a set of edges that is contained in some MST and T' contains no edge from E', then $T' \cup \{e\}$ is also contained in some MST.*

Proof. We shall prove the second claim. The first claim follows by setting $T' = \emptyset$. Consider any MST T of G with $T' \subseteq T$. Let u and v be the endpoints of e. Since T is a spanning tree, it contains a path from u to v, say p. Since E' is a cut separating u and

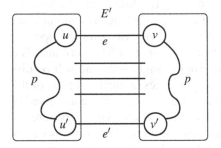
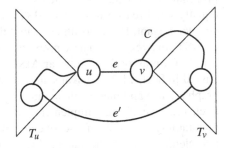

Fig. 11.1. Cut and cycle properties. The *left* part illustrates the proof of the cut property. e is an edge of minimum cost in the cut E', and p is a path in the MST connecting the endpoints of e. p must contain an edge in E'. The figure on the *right* illustrates the proof of the cycle property. C is a cycle in G, e is an edge of C of maximal weight, and T is an MST containing e. T_u and T_v are the components of $T \setminus e$; and e' is an edge in C connecting T_u and T_v

v, p must contain an edge from E', say e'. Now, $T'' := (T \setminus e') \cup e$ is also a spanning tree, because removal of e' splits T into two subtrees, which are then joined together by e. Since $c(e) \leq c(e')$, we have $c(T'') \leq c(T)$, and hence T'' is also an MST.   □

Lemma 11.2 (cycle property). *Consider any cycle $C \subseteq E$ and an edge $e \in C$ with maximal cost among all edges of C. Then any MST of $G' = (V, E \setminus \{e\})$ is also an MST of G.*

Proof. Consider any MST T of G. Suppose T contains $e = (u, v)$. Edge e splits T into two subtrees T_u and T_v. There must be another edge $e' = (u', v')$ from C such that $u' \in T_u$ and $v' \in T_v$. $T' := (T \setminus \{e\}) \cup \{e'\}$ is a spanning tree which does not contain e. Since $c(e') \leq c(e)$, T' is also an MST.   □

The cut property yields a simple greedy algorithm for finding an MST. Start with an empty set T of edges. As long as T is not a spanning tree, let E' be a cut not containing any edge from T. Add a minimal-cost edge from E' to T.

Different choices of E' lead to different specific algorithms. We discuss two approaches in detail in the following sections and outline a third approach in Sect. 11.8. Also, we need to explain how to find a minimum cost edge in the cut.

The cycle property also leads to a simple algorithm for finding an MST. Set T to the set of all edges. As long as T is not a spanning tree, find a cycle in T and delete an edge of maximal cost from T. No efficient implementation of this approach is known, and we shall not discuss it further.

Exercise 11.4. Show that the MST is uniquely defined if all edge costs are different. Show that in this case the MST does not change if each edge cost is replaced by its rank among all edge costs.

11.2 The Jarník–Prim Algorithm

The Jarník–Prim (JP) algorithm [98, 158, 56] for MSTs is very similar to Dijkstra's algorithm for shortest paths.[2] Starting from an (arbitrary) source node s, the JP algorithm grows an MST by adding one node after another. At any iteration, S is the set of nodes already added to the tree, and the cut E' is the set of edges with exactly one endpoint in S. A minimum-cost edge leaving S is added to the tree in every iteration. The main challenge is to find this edge efficiently. To this end, the algorithm maintains the shortest connection between any node $v \in V \setminus S$ and S in a priority queue Q. The smallest element in Q gives the desired edge. When a node is added to S, its incident edges are checked to see whether they yield improved connections to nodes in $V \setminus S$. Fig. 11.2 illustrates the operation of the JP algorithm, and Figure 11.3 shows the pseudocode. When node u is added to S and an incident edge $e = (u, v)$ is inspected, the algorithm needs to know whether $v \in S$. A bitvector could be used to

---

[2] Actually, Dijkstra also described this algorithm in his seminal 1959 paper on shortest paths [56]. Since Prim described the same algorithm two years earlier, it is usually named after him. However, the algorithm actually goes back to a 1930 paper by Jarník [98].

encode this information. If all edge costs are positive, we can reuse the d-array for this purpose. For any node v, $d[v] = 0$ indicates $v \in S$ and $d[v] > 0$ encodes $v \notin S$.

In addition to the space savings, this trick also avoids a comparison in the innermost loop. Observe that $c(e) < d[v]$ is only true if $d[v] > 0$, i.e., $v \notin S$, and e is an improved connection from v to S.

The only important difference from Dijkstra's algorithm is that the priority queue stores edge costs rather than path lengths. The analysis of Dijkstra's algorithm carries over to the JP algorithm, i.e., the use of a Fibonacci heap priority queue yields a running time $O(n \log n + m)$.

Exercise 11.5. Dijkstra's algorithm for shortest paths can use monotone priority queues. Show that monotone priority queues do *not* suffice for the JP algorithm.

*Exercise 11.6 (average-case analysis of the JP algorithm). Assume that the edge costs $1, \ldots, m$ are assigned randomly to the edges of G. Show that the expected number of *decreaseKey* operations performed by the JP algorithm is then bounded by $O(n \log(m/n))$. Hint: the analysis is very similar to the average-case analysis of Dijkstra's algorithm in Theorem 10.6.

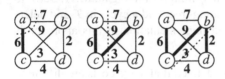

Fig. 11.2. A sequence of cuts (dotted lines) corresponding to the steps carried out by the Jarník–Prim algorithm with starting node a. The edges (a,c), (c,b), and (b,d) are added to the MST

Function *jpMST* : **Set of** *Edge*
   $d = \langle \infty, \ldots, \infty \rangle$: *NodeArray*[1..n] **of** $\mathbb{R} \cup \{\infty\}$ // $d[v]$ is the distance of v from the tree
   parent : *NodeArray* **of** *NodeId*   // *parent*[v] is shortest edge between S and v
   Q : *NodePQ*   // uses $d[\cdot]$ as priority
   $Q.insert(s)$ for some arbitrary $s \in V$
   while $Q \neq \emptyset$ **do**
      $u := Q.deleteMin$
      $d[u] := 0$ // $d[u] = 0$ encodes $u \in S$
      foreach *edge* $e = (u,v) \in E$ **do**
         if $c(e) < d[v]$ **then**   // $c(e) < d[v]$ implies $d[v] > 0$ and hence $v \notin S$
            $d[v] := c(e)$
            parent[v] := u
         if $v \in Q$ **then** $Q.decreaseKey(v)$ **else** $Q.insert(v)$
      invariant $\forall v \in Q : d[v] = \min \{c((u,v)) : (u,v) \in E \wedge u \in S\}$
   return $\{(v, parent[v]) : v \in V \setminus \{s\}\}$

Fig. 11.3. The Jarník–Prim MST algorithm. Positive edge costs are assumed

11.3 Kruskal's Algorithm

The JP algorithm is probably the best general-purpose MST algorithm. Nevertheless, we shall now present an alternative algorithm, Kruskal's algorithm [116]. It also has its merits. In particular, it does not need a sophisticated graph representation, but works even when the graph is represented by its sequence of edges. Also, for sparse graphs with $m = O(n)$, its running time is competitive with the JP algorithm.

The pseudocode given in Fig. 11.4 is extremely compact. The algorithm scans over the edges of G in order of increasing cost and maintains a partial MST T; T is initially empty. The algorithm maintains the invariant that T can be extended to an MST. When an edge e is considered, it is either discarded or added to the MST. The decision is made on the basis of the cycle or cut property. The endpoints of e either belong to the same connected component of (V, T) or do not. In the former case, $T \cup e$ contains a cycle and e is an edge of maximum cost in this cycle. Since edges are considered in order of increasing cost, e can be discarded, by the cycle property. If e connects distinct components, e is a minimum-cost edge in the cut E' consisting of all edges connecting distinct components of (V, T); again, it is essential that edges are considered in order of increasing cost. We may therefore add e to T, by the cut property. The invariant is maintained. Figure 11.5 gives an example.

In an implementation of Kruskal's algorithm, we have to find out whether an edge connects two components of (V, T). In the next section, we shall see that this can be done so efficiently that the main cost factor is sorting the edges. This takes time $O(m \log m)$ if we use an efficient comparison-based sorting algorithm. The constant factor involved is rather small, so that for $m = O(n)$ we can hope to do better than the $O(m + n \log n)$ JP algorithm.

Function *kruskalMST(V, E, c)* : *Set* **of** *Edge*
   $T := \emptyset$
   invariant T *is a subforest of an MST*
   foreach $(u, v) \in E$ in ascending order of cost **do**
      if u and v are in different subtrees of T **then**
         $T := T \cup \{(u, v)\}$ // join two subtrees
   return T

Fig. 11.4. Kruskal's MST algorithm

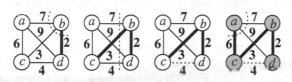

Fig. 11.5. In this example, Kruskal's algorithm first proves that (b, d) and (b, c) are MST edges using the cut property. Then (c, d) is excluded because it is the heaviest edge on the cycle $\langle b, c, d \rangle$, and, finally, (a, c) completes the MST

Exercise 11.7 (streaming MST). Suppose the edges of a graph are presented to you only once (for example over a network connection) and you do not have enough memory to store all of them. The edges do *not* necessarily arrive in sorted order.

(a) Outline an algorithm that nevertheless computes an MST using space $O(V)$.
(*b) Refine your algorithm to run in time $O(m \log n)$. Hint: process batches of $O(n)$
  edges (or use the *dynamic tree* data structure described by Sleator and Tarjan
  [182]).

11.4 The Union–Find Data Structure

A *partition* of a set M is a collection $M_1, \ldots, M_k$ of subsets of M with the property that the subsets are disjoint and cover M, i.e., $M_i \cap M_j = \emptyset$ for $i \neq j$ and $M = M_1 \cup \cdots \cup M_k$. The subsets M_i are called the *blocks* of the partition. For example, in Kruskal's algorithm, the forest T partitions V. The blocks of the partition are the connected components of (V, T). Some components may be trivial and consist of a single isolated node. Kruskal's algorithm performs two operations on the partition: testing whether two elements are in the same subset (subtree) and joining two subsets into one (inserting an edge into T).

The *union–find data structure* maintains a partition of the set $1..n$ and supports these two operations. Initially, each element is a block on its own. Each block chooses one of its elements as its representative; the choice is made by the data structure and not by the user. The function *find*(i) returns the representative of the block containing i. Thus, testing whether two elements are in the same block amounts to comparing their respective representatives. An operation *link*(i, j) applied to representatives of different blocks joins the blocks.

A simple solution is as follows. Each block is represented as a rooted tree[3], with the root being the representative of the block. Each element stores its parent in this tree (the array *parent*). We have self-loops at the roots.

The implementation of *find*(i) is trivial. We follow parent pointers until we encounter a self-loop. The self-loop is located at the representative of i. The implementation of *link*(i, j) is equally simple. We simply make one representative the parent of the other. The latter has ceded its role to the former, which is now the representative of the combined block. What we have described so far yields a correct but inefficient union–find data structure. The *parent* references could form long chains that are traversed again and again during *find* operations. In the worst case, each operation may take linear time.

Exercise 11.8. Give an example of an n-node graph with $O(n)$ edges where a naive implementation of the union–find data structure without union by rank and path compression would lead to quadratic execution time for Kruskal's algorithm.

---

[3] Note that this tree may have a structure very different from the corresponding subtree in
  Kruskal's algorithm.

Class *UnionFind*($n : \mathbb{N}$)   // Maintain a partition of 1..n

   parent = $\langle 1, 2, \ldots, n \rangle$: *Array* $[1..n]$ **of** 1..n

   rank = $\langle 0, \ldots, 0 \rangle$: *Array* $[1..n]$ **of** 0..$\log n$ // rank of representatives

Function *find*($i : 1..n$) : 1..n
   if *parent*$[i] = i$ **then return** i
   else $i' := find(parent[i])$ // path compression
      parent$[i] := i'$
      return i'

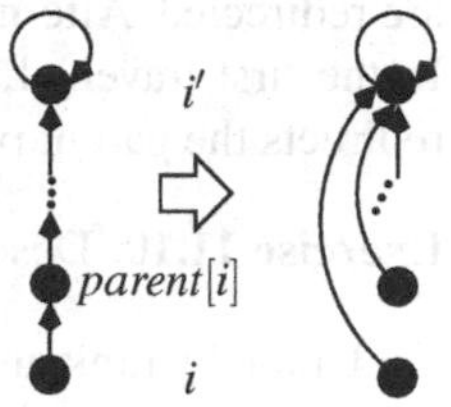

Procedure *link*($i, j : 1..n$)
   assert i and j are representatives of different blocks
   if *rank*$[i] < rank[j]$ **then** *parent*$[i] := j$
   else
      parent$[j] := i$
      if *rank*$[i] = rank[j]$ **then** *rank*$[i]$++

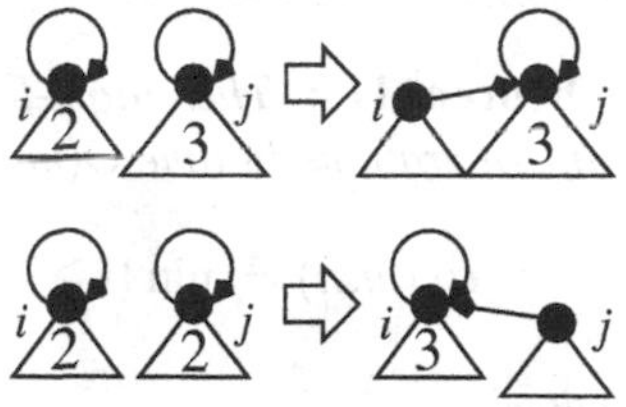

Procedure *union*($i, j : 1..n$)
   if *find*(i) $\neq$ *find*(j) **then** *link*(*find*(i), *find*(j))

Fig. 11.6. An efficient union–find data structure that maintains a partition of the set $\{1, \ldots, n\}$

Therefore, Figure 11.6 introduces two optimizations. The first optimization limits the maximal depth of the trees representing blocks. Every representative stores a nonnegative integer, which we call its *rank*. Initially, every element is a representative and has rank zero. When we link two representatives and their ranks are different, we make the representative of smaller rank a child of the representative of larger rank. When their ranks are the same, the choice of the parent is arbitrary; however, we increase the rank of the new root. We refer to the first optimization as *union by rank*.

Exercise 11.9. Assume that the second optimization (described below) is not used. Show that the rank of a representative is the height of the tree rooted at it.

Theorem 11.3. *Union by rank ensures that the depth of no tree exceeds* $\log n$.

Proof. Without path compression, the rank of a representative is equal to the height of the tree rooted at it. Path compression does not increase heights. It therefore suffices to prove that the rank is bounded by $\log n$. We shall show that a tree whose root has rank k contains at least 2^k elements. This is certainly true for $k = 0$. The rank of a root grows from $k - 1$ to k when it receives a child of rank $k - 1$. Thus the root had at least 2^{k-1} descendants before the link operation and it receives a child which also had at least 2^{k-1} descendants. So the root has at least 2^k descendants after the link operation.   □

The second optimization is called *path compression*. This ensures that a chain of parent references is never traversed twice. Rather, all nodes visited during an operation $find(i)$ redirect their parent pointers directly to the representative of i. In Fig. 11.6, we have formulated this rule as a recursive procedure. This procedure first traverses the path from i to its representative and then uses the recursion stack to traverse the path back to i. When the recursion stack is unwound, the parent pointers are redirected. Alternatively, one can traverse the path twice in the forward direction. In the first traversal, one finds the representative, and in the second traversal, one redirects the parent pointers.

Exercise 11.10. Describe a nonrecursive implementation of *find*.

Union by rank and path compression make the union–find data structure "breathtakingly" efficient – the amortized cost of any operation is almost constant.

Theorem 11.4. *The union–find data structure of Fig. 11.6 performs m find and $n-1$ link operations in time $O(m\alpha_T(m,n))$. Here,*

$$\alpha_T(m,n) = \min\{i \geq 1 : A(i, \lceil m/n \rceil) \geq \log n\},$$

where

$$
\begin{aligned}
A(1,j) &= 2^j & \text{for } j \geq 1, \\
A(i,1) &= A(i-1,2) & \text{for } i \geq 2, \\
A(i,j) &= A(i-1,A(i,j-1)) & \text{for } i \geq 2 \text{ and } j \geq 2.
\end{aligned}
$$

Proof. The proof of this theorem is beyond the scope of this introductory text. We refer the reader to [186, 177]. ☐

You will probably find the formulae overwhelming. The function[4] A grows extremely rapidly. We have $A(1,j) = 2^j$, $A(2,1) = A(1,2) = 2^2 = 4$, $A(2,2) = A(1,A(2,1)) = 2^4 = 16$, $A(2,3) = A(1,A(2,2)) = 2^{16}$, $A(2,4) = 2^{2^{16}}$, $A(2,5) = 2^{2^{2^{16}}}$, $A(3,1) = A(2,2) = 16$, $A(3,2) = A(2,A(3,1)) = A(2,16)$, and so on.

Exercise 11.11. Estimate $A(5,1)$.

For all practical n, we have $\alpha_T(m,n) \leq 5$, and union–find with union by rank and path compression essentially guarantees constant amortized cost per operation.

We close this section with an analysis of union–find with path compression but without union by rank. The analysis illustrates the power of path compression and also gives a glimpse of how Theorem 11.4 can be proved.

Theorem 11.5. *The union–find data structure with path compression but without union by rank processes m find and $n-1$ link operations in time $O((m+n)\log n)$.*

---

[4] The usage of the letter A is a reference to the logician Ackermann [3], who first studied a variant of this function in the late 1920s.

Proof. A link operation has cost one and adds one edge to the data structure. The total cost of all links is $O(n)$. The difficult part is to bound the cost of the finds. Note that the cost of a *find* is $O(1 + \text{number of edges constructed in path compression})$. So our task is to bound the total number of edges constructed.

In order to do so, every node v is assigned a weight $w(v)$ that is defined as the maximum number of descendants of v (including v) during the evolution of the data structure. Observe that $w(v)$ may increase as long as v is a representative, $w(v)$ reaches its maximal value when v ceases to be a representative (because it is linked to another representative), and $w(v)$ may decrease afterwards (because path compression removes a child of v to link it to a higher node). The weights are integers in the range $1..n$.

All edges that ever exist in our data structure go from nodes of smaller weight to nodes of larger weight. We define the span of an edge as the difference between the weights of its endpoints. We say that an edge has a class i if its span lies in the range $2^i..2^{i+1} - 1$. The class of any edge lies between 0 and $\lceil \log n \rceil$.

Consider a particular node x. The first edge out of x is created when x ceases to be a representative. Also, x receives a new parent whenever a find operation passes through the edge $(x, parent(x))$ and this edge is not the last edge traversed by the find. The new edge out of x has a larger span.

We account for the edges out of x as follows. The first edge is charged to the union operation. Consider now any edge $e = (x, y)$ and the find operation which destroys it. Let e have class i. The find operation traverses a path of edges. If e is the last (= topmost) edge of class i traversed by the find, we charge the construction of the new edge out of x to the find operation; otherwise, we charge it to x. Observe that in this way, at most $1 + \lceil \log n \rceil$ edges are charged to any find operation (because there are only $1 + \lceil \log n \rceil$ different classes of edges). If the construction of the new edge out of x is charged to x, there is another edge $e' = (x', y')$ in class i following e on the find path. Also, the new edge out of x has a span at least as large as the sum of the spans of e and e', since it goes to an ancestor (not necessarily proper) of y'. Thus the new edge out of x has a span of at least $2^i + 2^i = 2^{i+1}$ and hence is in class $i+1$ or higher. We conclude that at most one edge in each class is charged to each node x. Thus the total number of edges constructed is at most $n + (n + m)(1 + \lceil \log n \rceil)$, and the time bound follows. $\square$

11.5 *External Memory

The MST problem is one of the very few graph problems that are known to have an efficient external-memory algorithm. We shall give a simple, elegant algorithm that exemplifies many interesting techniques that are also useful for other external-memory algorithms and for computing MSTs in other models of computation. Our algorithm is a composition of techniques that we have already seen: external sorting, priority queues, and internal union–find. More details can be found in [50].

11.5.1 A Semiexternal Kruskal Algorithm

We begin with an easy case. Suppose we have enough internal memory to store the union–find data structure of Sect. 11.4 for n nodes. This is enough to implement Kruskal's algorithm in the external-memory model. We first sort the edges using the external-memory sorting algorithm described in Sect. 5.7. Then we scan the edges in order of increasing weight, and process them as described by Kruskal's algorithm. If an edge connects two subtrees, it is an MST edge and can be output; otherwise, it is discarded. External-memory graph algorithms that require $\Theta(n)$ internal memory are called *semiexternal* algorithms.

11.5.2 Edge Contraction

If the graph has too many nodes for the semiexternal algorithm of the preceding subsection, we can try to reduce the number of nodes. This can be done using *edge contraction*. Suppose we know that $e = (u, v)$ is an MST edge, for example because e is the least-weight edge incident on v. We add e, and somehow need to remember that u and v are already connected in the MST under construction. Above, we used the union–find data structure to record this fact; now we use edge contraction to encode the information into the graph itself. We identify u and v and replace them by a single node. For simplicity, we again call this node u. In other words, we delete v and *relink* all edges incident on v to u, i.e., any edge (v, w) now becomes an edge (u, w). Figure 11.7 gives an example. In order to keep track of the origin of relinked edges, we associate an additional attribute with each edge that indicates its *original* endpoints. With this additional information, the MST of the contracted graph is easily translated back to the original graph. We simply replace each edge by its original.

We now have a blueprint for an external MST algorithm: repeatedly find MST edges and contract them. Once the number of nodes is small enough, switch to a semiexternal algorithm. The following subsection gives a particularly simple implementation of this idea.

11.5.3 Sibeyn's Algorithm

Suppose $V = 1..n$. Consider the following simple strategy for reducing the number of nodes from n to n' [50]:

> **for** $v := 1$ **to** $n - n'$ **do**
> *find the lightest edge (u, v) incident on v and contract it*

Figure 11.7 gives an example, with $n = 4$ and $n' = 2$. The strategy looks deceptively simple. We need to discuss how we find the cheapest edge incident on v and how we relink the other edges incident on v, i.e., how we inform the neighbors of v that they are receiving additional incident edges. We can use a priority queue for both purposes. For each edge $e = (u, v)$, we store the item

$$(\min(u, v), \max(u, v), \text{weight of } e, \text{origin of } e)$$

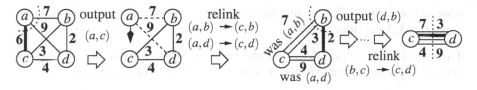

Fig. 11.7. An execution of Sibeyn's algorithm with $n' = 2$. The edge $(c,a,6)$ is the cheapest edge incident on a. We add it to the MST and merge a into c. The edge $(a,b,7)$ becomes an edge $(c,b,7)$ and $(a,d,9)$ becomes $(c,d,9)$. In the new graph, $(d,b,2)$ is the cheapest edge incident on b. We add it to the spanning tree and merge b into d. The edges $(b,c,3)$ and $(b,c,7)$ become $(d,c,3)$ and $(d,c,7)$, respectively. The resulting graph has two nodes that are connected by four parallel edges of weight 3, 4, 7, and 9, respectively

Function *sibeynMST*(V, E, c) : *Set* **of** *Edge*
  let π be a random permutation of $1..n$
  Q: *priority queue*   // Order: *min node*, then *min edge weight*
  foreach $e = (u,v) \in E$ **do**
    $Q.insert(\min\{\pi(u),\pi(v)\},\max\{\pi(u),\pi(v)\},c(e),u,v)$
  $current := 0$ // we are just before processing node 1
  loop
    $(u,v,c,u_0,v_0) := \min Q$ // next edge
    if $current \neq u$ **then**   // new node
      if $u = n - n' + 1$ **then** *break loop*   // node reduction completed
      $Q.deleteMin$
      output (u_0,v_0) // the original endpoints define an MST edge
      $(current, relinkTo) := (u,v)$ // prepare for relinking remaining u-edges
    else if $v \neq relinkTo$ **then**
      $Q.insert((\min\{v,relinkTo\},\max\{v,relinkTo\},c,u_0,v_0))$ // relink
  $S := sort(Q)$ // sort by increasing edge weight
  apply semiexternal Kruskal to S

Fig. 11.8. Sibeyn's MST algorithm

in the priority queue. The ordering is lexicographic by the first and third components, i.e., edges are first ordered by the lower-numbered endpoint and then according to weight. The algorithm operates in phases. In each phase, we select all edges incident on the *current* node. The lightest edge (= first edge delivered by the queue), say $(current, relinkTo)$, is added to the MST, and all others are relinked. In order to relink an edge $(current, z, c, u_0, v_0)$ with $z \neq RelinkTo$, we add $(\min(z, RelinkTo), \max(z, RelinkTo), c, u_0, v_0)$ to the queue.

Figure 11.8 gives the details. For reasons that will become clear in the analysis, we renumber the nodes randomly before starting the algorithm, i.e., we chose a random permutation of the integers 1 to n and rename node v as $\pi(v)$. For any edge $e = (u,v)$ we store $(\min\{\pi(u),\pi(v)\}, \max\{\pi(u),\pi(v)\}, c(e), u, v)$ in the queue. The main loop stops when the number of nodes is reduced to n'. We complete the construction of the MST by sorting the remaining edges and then running the semiexternal Kruskal algorithm on them.

Theorem 11.6. *Let* sort(x) *denote the I/O complexity of sorting x items. The expected number of I/O steps needed by the algorithm sibeynMST is* $O(\text{sort}(m\ln(n/n')))$.

Proof. From Sect. 6.3, we know that an external-memory priority queue can execute K queue operations using $O(\text{sort}(K))$ I/Os. Also, the semiexternal Kruskal step requires $O(\text{sort}(m))$ I/Os. Hence, it suffices to count the number of operations in the reduction phases. Besides the m insertions during initialization, the number of queue operations is proportional to the sum of the degrees of the nodes encountered. Let the random variable X_i denote the degree of node i when it is processed. By the linearity of expectations, we have $E[\sum_{1 \le i \le n-n'} X_i] = \sum_{1 \le i \le n-n'} E[X_i]$. The number of edges in the contracted graph is at most m, so that the average degree of a graph with $n-i+1$ remaining nodes is at most $2m/(n-i+1)$. We obtain.

$$
E\left[\sum_{1 \le i \le n-n'} X_i\right] = \sum_{1 \le i \le n-n'} E[X_i] \le \sum_{1 \le i \le n-n'} \frac{2m}{n-i+1}
$$

$$
= 2m\left(\sum_{1 \le i \le n} \frac{1}{i} - \sum_{1 \le i \le n'} \frac{1}{i}\right) = 2m(H_n - H_{n'})
$$

$$
= 2m(\ln n - \ln n') + O(1) = 2m\ln\frac{n}{n'} + O(1) \;,
$$

where $H_n := \sum_{1 \le i \le n} 1/i = \ln n + \Theta(1)$ is the n-th harmonic number (see (A.12)).   □

Note that we could do without switching to the semiexternal Kruskal algorithm. However, then the logarithmic factor in the I/O complexity would become $\ln n$ rather than $\ln(n/n')$ and the practical performance would be much worse. Observe that $n' = \Theta(M)$ is a large number, say 10^8. For $n = 10^{12}$, $\ln n$ is three times $\ln(n/n')$.

Exercise 11.12. For any n, give a graph with n nodes and $O(n)$ edges where Sibeyn's algorithm *without random renumbering* would need $\Omega(n^2)$ relink operations.

11.6 Applications

The MST problem is useful in attacking many other graph problems. We shall discuss the Steiner tree problem and the traveling salesman problem.

11.6.1 The Steiner Tree Problem

We are given a nonnegatively weighted undirected graph $G = (V, E)$ and a set S of nodes. The goal is to find a minimum-cost subset T of the edges that connects the nodes in S. Such a T is called a minimum Steiner tree. It is a tree connecting a set U with $S \subseteq U \subseteq V$. The challenge is to choose U so as to minimize the cost of the tree. The minimum-spanning-tree problem is the special case where S consists of all nodes. The Steiner tree problem arises naturally in our introductory example. Assume that some of the islands in Taka-Tuka-Land are uninhabited. The goal is to connect all the inhabited islands. The optimal solution will, in general, have some of the uninhabited islands in the solution.

The Steiner tree problem is **NP**-complete (see Sect. 2.10). We shall show how to construct a solution which is within a factor of two of the optimum. We construct an auxiliary complete graph with node set S: for any pair u and v of nodes in S, the cost of the edge (u, v) in the auxiliary graph is their shortest-path distance in G. Let T_A be an MST of the auxiliary graph. We obtain a Steiner tree of G by replacing every edge of T_A by the path it represents in G. The resulting subgraph of G may contain cycles. We delete edges from cycles until the remaining subgraph is cycle-free. The cost of the resulting Steiner tree is at most the cost of T_A.

Theorem 11.7. *The algorithm above constructs a Steiner tree which has at most twice the cost of an optimal Steiner tree.*

Proof. The algorithm constructs a Steiner tree of cost at most $c(T_A)$. It therefore suffices to show that $c(T_A) \le 2c(T_{opt})$, where T_{opt} is a minimum Steiner tree for S in G. To this end, it suffices to show that the auxiliary graph has a spanning tree of cost $2c(T_{opt})$. Figure 11.9 indicates how to construct such a spanning tree. "Walking once around the Steiner tree" defines a cycle in G of cost $2c(T_{opt})$; observe that every edge in T_{opt} occurs exactly twice in this path. Deleting the nodes outside S in this path gives us a cycle in the auxiliary graph. The cost of this path is at most $2c(T_{opt})$, because edge costs in the auxiliary graph are shortest-path distances in G. The cycle in the auxiliary graph spans S, and therefore the auxiliary graph has a spanning tree of cost at most $2c(T_{opt})$. □

Exercise 11.13. Improve the above bound to $2(1 - 1/|S|)$ times the optimum.

The algorithm can be implemented to run in time $O(m + n \log n)$ [126]. Algorithms with better approximation ratios exist [163].

Exercise 11.14. Outline an implementation of the algorithm above and analyze its running time.

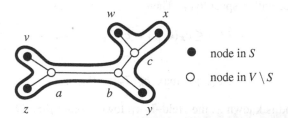

Fig. 11.9. Once around the tree. We have $S = \{v, w, x, y, z\}$, and the minimum Steiner tree is shown. The Steiner tree also involves the nodes a, b, and c in $V \setminus S$. Walking once around the tree yields the cycle $\langle v, a, b, c, w, c, x, c, b, y, b, a, z, a, v \rangle$. It maps into the cycle $\langle v, w, x, y, z, v \rangle$ in the auxiliary graph

11.6.2 Traveling Salesman Tours

The traveling salesman problem is one of the most intensively studied optimization problems [197, 117, 13]: given an undirected complete graph on a node set V with edge weights $c(e)$, the goal is to find the minimum-weight simple cycle passing through all nodes. This is the path a traveling salesman would want to take whose goal it is to visit all nodes of the graph. We assume in this section that the edge weights satisfy the triangle inequality, i.e., $c(u,v) + c(v,w) \geq c(u,w)$ for all nodes u, v, and w. There is then always an optimal round trip which visits no node twice (because leaving it out would not increase the cost).

Theorem 11.8. *Let C_{opt} and C_{MST} be the cost of an optimal tour and of an MST, respectively. Then*

$$C_{MST} \leq C_{opt} \leq 2C_{MST} .$$

Proof. Let C be an optimal tour. Deleting any edge from C yields a spanning tree. Thus $C_{MST} \leq C_{opt}$. Conversely, let T be an MST. Walking once around the tree as shown in Fig. 11.9 gives us a cycle of cost at most $2C_{MST}$, passing through all nodes. It may visit nodes several times. Deleting an extra visit to a node does not increase the cost, owing to the triangle inequality.   □

In the remainder of this section, we shall briefly outline a technique for improving the lower bound of Theorem 11.8. We need two additional concepts: 2-trees and node potentials. Let G' be obtained from G by deleting node 1 and the edges incident on it. A minimum 2-tree consists of the two cheapest edges incident on node 1 and an MST of G'. Since deleting the two edges incident on node 1 from a tour C yields a spanning tree of G', we have $C_2 \leq C_{opt}$, where C_2 is the minimum cost of a 2-tree. A node potential is any real-valued function π defined on the nodes of G. Any node potential yields a modified cost function c_π by defining

$$c_\pi(u,v) = c(u,v) + \pi(v) + \pi(u)$$

for any pair u and v of nodes. For any tour C, the costs under c and c_π differ by $2S_\pi := 2\sum_v \pi(v)$, since a tour uses exactly two edges incident on any node. Let T_π be a minimum 2-tree with respect to c_π. Then

$$c_\pi(T_\pi) \leq c_\pi(C_{opt}) = c(C_{opt}) + 2S_\pi,$$

and hence

$$c(C_{opt}) \geq \max_\pi \left(c_\pi(T_\pi) - 2S_\pi \right) .$$

This lower bound is known as the Held–Karp lower bound [88, 89]. The maximum is over all node potential functions π. It is hard to compute the lower bound exactly. However, there are fast iterative algorithms for approximating it. The idea is as follows, and we refer the reader to the original papers for details. Assume we have a potential function π and the optimal 2-tree T_π with respect to it. If all nodes of T_π have degree two, we have a traveling salesman tour and stop. Otherwise, we make the edges incident on nodes of degree larger than two a little more expensive and the edges incident on nodes of degree one a little cheaper. This can be done by modifying the node potential of v as follows. We define a new node potential π' by

$$\pi'(v) = \pi(v) + \varepsilon \cdot (\deg(v, T_\pi) - 2)$$

where ε is a parameter which goes to zero with increasing iteration number, and $\deg(v, T_\pi)$ is the degree of v in T_π. We next compute an optimal 2-tree with respect to π' and hope that it will yield a better lower bound.

11.7 Implementation Notes

The minimum-spanning-tree algorithms discussed in this chapter are so fast that the running time is usually dominated by the time required to generate the graphs and appropriate representations. The JP algorithm works well for all m and n if an adjacency array representation (see Sect. 8.2) of the graph is available. Pairing heaps [142] are a robust choice for the priority queue. Kruskal's algorithm may be faster for sparse graphs, in particular if only a list or array of edges is available or if we know how to sort the edges very efficiently.

The union–find data structure can be implemented more space-efficiently by exploiting the observation that only representatives need a rank, whereas only nonrepresentatives need a parent. We can therefore omit the array *rank* in Fig. 11.4. Instead, a root of rank g stores the value $n + 1 + g$ in *parent*. Thus, instead of two arrays, only one array with values in the range $1..n + 1 + \lceil \log n \rceil$ is needed. This is particularly useful for the semiexternal algorithm.

11.7.1 C++

LEDA [118] uses Kruskal's algorithm for computing MSTs. The union–find data structure is called *partition* in LEDA. The Boost graph library [27] gives a choice between Kruskal's algorithm and the JP algorithm. Boost offers no public access to the union–find data structure.

11.7.2 Java

JDSL [78] uses the JP algorithm.

11.8 Historical Notes and Further Findings

The oldest MST algorithm is based on the cut property and uses edge contractions. *Boruvka's algorithm* [28, 148] goes back to 1926 and hence represents one of the oldest graph algorithms. The algorithm operates in phases, and identifies many MST edges in each phase. In a phase, each node identifies the lightest incident edge. These edges are added to the MST (here it is assumed that the edge costs are pairwise distinct) and then contracted. Each phase can be implemented to run in time $O(m)$. Since a phase at least halves the number of remaining nodes, only a single node is left after $O(\log n)$ phases, and hence the total running time is $O(m \log n)$. Boruvka's algorithm is not often used, because it is somewhat complicated to implement. It is nevertheless important as a basis for parallel MST algorithms.

There is a randomized linear-time MST algorithm that uses phases of Boruvka's algorithm to reduce the number of nodes [105, 111]. The second building block of this algorithm reduces the number of edges to about $2n$: we sample $O(m/2)$ edges randomly, find an MST T' of the sample, and remove edges $e \in E$ that are the heaviest edge in a cycle in $e \cup T'$. The last step is rather difficult to implement efficiently. But, at least for rather dense graphs, this approach can yield a practical improvement [108]. The linear-time algorithm can also be parallelized [84]. An adaptation to the external-memory model [2] saves a factor $\ln(n/n')$ in the asymptotic I/O complexity compared with Sibeyn's algorithm but is impractical for currently interesting values of n owing to its much larger constant factor in the O-notation.

The theoretically best *deterministic* MST algorithm [35, 155] has the interesting property that it has optimal worst-case complexity, although it is not exactly known what this complexity is. Hence, if you come up with a completely different deterministic MST algorithm and prove that your algorithm runs in linear time, then we would know that the old algorithm also runs in linear time.

Minimum spanning trees define a single path between any pair of nodes. Interestingly, this path is a *bottleneck shortest path* [8, Application 13.3], i.e., it minimizes the maximum edge cost for all paths connecting the nodes in the original graph. Hence, finding an MST amounts to solving the all-pairs bottleneck-shortest-path problem in much less time than that for solving the all-pairs shortest-path problem.

A related and even more frequently used application is clustering based on the MST [8, Application 13.5]: by dropping $k-1$ edges from the MST, it can be split into k subtrees. The nodes in a subtree T' are far away from the other nodes in the sense that all paths to nodes in other subtrees use edges that are at least as heavy as the edges used to cut T' out of the MST.

Many applications lead to MST problems on complete graphs. Frequently, these graphs have a compact description, for example if the nodes represent points in the plane and the edge costs are Euclidean distances (these MSTs are called Euclidean minimum spanning trees). In these situations, it is an important concern whether one can rule out most of the edges as too heavy without actually looking at them. This is the case for Euclidean MSTs. It can be shown that Euclidean MSTs are contained in the Delaunay triangulation [46] of the point set. This triangulation has linear size and can be computed in time $O(n \log n)$. This leads to an algorithm of the same time complexity for Euclidean MSTs.

We discussed the application of MSTs to the Steiner tree and the traveling salesman problem. We refer the reader to the books [8, 13, 117, 115, 200] for more information about these and related problems.

12

Generic Approaches to Optimization

A smuggler in the mountainous region of Profitania has n items in his cellar. If he sells an item i across the border, he makes a profit p_i. However, the smuggler's trade union only allows him to carry knapsacks with a maximum weight of M. If item i has weight w_i, what items should he pack into the knapsack to maximize the profit from his next trip?

This problem, usually called the *knapsack problem*, has many other applications. The books [122, 109] describe many of them. For example, an investment bank might have an amount M of capital to invest and a set of possible investments. Each investment i has an expected profit p_i for an investment of cost w_i. In this chapter, we use the knapsack problem as an example to illustrate several generic approaches to optimization. These approaches are quite flexible and can be adapted to complicated situations that are ubiquitous in practical applications.

In the previous chapters we have considered very efficient specific solutions for frequently occurring simple problems such as finding shortest paths or minimum spanning trees. Now we look at generic solution methods that work for a much larger range of applications. Of course, the generic methods do not usually achieve the same efficiency as specific solutions. However, they save development time.

Formally, an optimization problem can be described by a set $\mathcal{U}$ of *potential* solutions, a set $\mathcal{L}$ of *feasible* solutions, and an *objective function* $f : \mathcal{L} \to \mathbb{R}$. In a *maximization* problem, we are looking for a feasible solution $x^* \in \mathcal{L}$ that maximizes the value of the objective function over all feasible solutions. In a *minimization* problem, we look for a solution that minimizes the value of the objective. In an *existence problem*, f is arbitrary and the question is whether the set of feasible solutions is nonempty.

For example, in the case of the knapsack problem with n items, a potential solution is simply a vector $x = (x_1, \ldots, x_n)$ with $x_i \in \{0, 1\}$. Here $x_i = 1$ indicates that "element i is put into the knapsack" and $x_i = 0$ indicates that "element i is left out". Thus $\mathcal{U} = \{0, 1\}^n$. The profits and weights are specified by vectors $p = (p_1, \ldots, p_n)$ and $w = (w_1, \ldots, w_n)$. A potential solution x is feasible if its weight does not exceed

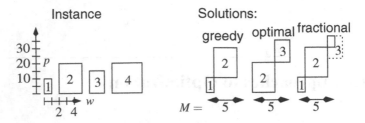

Fig. 12.1. The *left part* shows a knapsack instance with $p = (10, 20, 15, 20)$, $w = (1, 3, 2, 4)$, and $M = 5$. The items are indicated as rectangles whose width and height correspond to weight and profit, respectively. The *right part* shows three solutions: the one computed by the greedy algorithm from Sect. 12.2, an optimal solution computed by the dynamic programming algorithm from Sect. 12.3, and the solution of the linear relaxation (Sect. 12.1.1). The optimal solution has weight 5 and profit 35

the capacity of the knapsack, i.e., $\sum_{1 \le i \le n} w_i x_i \le M$. The dot product $w \cdot x$ is a convenient shorthand for $\sum_{1 \le i \le n} w_i x_i$. We can then say that $\mathcal{L} = \{x \in \mathcal{U} : w \cdot x \le M\}$ is the set of feasible solutions and $f(x) = p \cdot x$ is the objective function.

The distinction between minimization and maximization problems is not essential because setting $f := -f$ converts a maximization problem into a minimization problem and vice versa. We shall use maximization as our default simply because our example problem is more naturally viewed as a maximization problem.[1]

We shall present seven generic approaches. We start out with black-box solvers that can be applied to any problem that can be formulated in the problem specification language of the solver. In this case, the only task of the user is to formulate the given problem in the language of the black-box solver. Section 12.1 introduces this approach using *linear programming* and *integer linear programming* as examples. The *greedy approach* that we have already seen in Chap. 11 is reviewed in Sect. 12.2. The approach of *dynamic programming* discussed in Sect. 12.3 is a more flexible way to construct solutions. We can also systematically explore the entire set of potential solutions, as described in Sect. 12.4. *Constraint programming*, *SAT solvers*, and *ILP solvers* are special cases of *systematic search*. Finally, we discuss two very flexible approaches to exploring only a subset of the solution space. *Local search*, discussed in Sect. 12.5, modifies a single solution until it has the desired quality. *Evolutionary algorithms*, described in Sect. 12.6, simulate a population of candidate solutions.

12.1 Linear Programming – a Black-Box Solver

The easiest way to solve an optimization problem is to write down a specification of the space of feasible solutions and of the objective function and then use an existing software package to find an optimal solution. Of course, the question is, for what

---

[1] Be aware that most of the literature uses minimization as the default.

kinds of specification are general solvers available? Here, we introduce a particularly large class of problems for which efficient black-box solvers are available.

Definition 12.1. *A* linear program *(LP)*[2] *with n* variables *and m* constraints *is a maximization problem defined on a vector* $x = (x_1, \ldots, x_n)$ *of real-valued variables. The objective function is a linear function f of x, i.e.,* $f : \mathbb{R}^n \to \mathbb{R}$ *with* $f(x) = c \cdot x$*, where* $c = (c_1, \ldots, c_n)$ *is called* cost *or* profit[3] *vector. The variables are constrained by m linear constraints of the form* $a_i \cdot x \bowtie_i b_i$*, where* $\bowtie_i \in \{\leq, \geq, =\}$*,* $a_i = (a_{i1}, \ldots, a_{in}) \in \mathbb{R}^n$*, and* $b_i \in \mathbb{R}$ *for* $i \in 1..m$*. The set of feasible solutions is given by*

$$\mathscr{L} = \left\{ x \in \mathbb{R}^n : \forall i \in 1..m \text{ and } j \in 1..n : x_j \geq 0 \wedge a_i \cdot x \bowtie_i b_i \right\}.$$

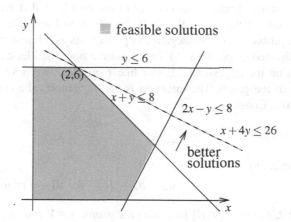

Fig. 12.2. A simple two-dimensional linear program in variables x and y, with three constraints and the objective "maximize $x + 4y$". The feasible region is shaded, and $(x, y) = (2, 6)$ is the optimal solution. Its objective value is 26. The vertex $(2, 6)$ is optimal because the half-plane $x + 4y \leq 26$ contains the entire feasible region and has $(2, 6)$ in its boundary

Figure 12.2 shows a simple example. A classical application of linear programming is the *diet problem*. A farmer wants to mix food for his cows. There are n different kinds of food on the market, say, corn, soya, fish meal, ... One kilogram of a food j costs c_j euros. There are m requirements for healthy nutrition; for example the cows should get enough calories, protein, vitamin C, and so on. One kilogram of food j contains a_{ij} percent of a cow's daily requirement with respect to requirement i. A solution to the following linear program gives a cost-optimal diet that satisfies the health constraints. Let x_j denote the amount (in kilogram) of food j used by the

---

[2] The term "linear program" stems from the 1940s [45] and has nothing to do with the modern meaning of "program" as in "computer program".

[3] It is common to use the term "profit" in maximization problems and "cost" in minimization problems.

farmer. The i-th nutritional requirement is modeled by the inequality $\sum_j a_{ij} x_j \geq 100$. The cost of the diet is given by $\sum_j c_j x_j$. The goal is to minimize the cost of the diet.

Exercise 12.1. How do you model supplies that are available only in limited amounts, for example food produced by the farmer himself? Also, explain how to specify additional constraints such as "no more than 0.01mg cadmium contamination per cow per day".

Can the knapsack problem be formulated as a linear program? Probably not. Each item either goes into the knapsack or it does not. There is no possibility of adding an item partially. In contrast, it is assumed in the diet problem that any arbitrary amount of any food can be purchased, for example 3.7245 kg and not just 3 kg or 4 kg. Integer linear programs (see Sect. 12.1.1) are the right tool for the knapsack problem.

We next connect linear programming to the problems that we have studied in previous chapters of the book. We shall show how to formulate the single-source shortest-path problem with nonnegative edge weights as a linear program. Let $G = (V, E)$ be a directed graph, let $s \in V$ be the source node, and let $c : E \to \mathbb{R}_{\geq 0}$ be the cost function on the edges of G. In our linear program, we have a variable d_v for every vertex of the graph. The intention is that d_v denotes the cost of the shortest path from s to v. Consider

$$\text{maximize} \quad \sum_{v \in V} d_v$$

$$\text{subject to} \quad d_s = 0$$

$$d_w \leq d_v + c(e) \quad \text{for all } e = (v, w) \in E .$$

Theorem 12.2. *Let $G = (V, E)$ be a directed graph, $s \in V$ a designated vertex, and $c : E \to \mathbb{R}_{\geq 0}$ a nonnegative cost function. If all vertices of G are reachable from s, the shortest-path distances in G are the unique optimal solution to the linear program above.*

Proof. Let $\mu(v)$ be the length of the shortest path from s to v. Then $\mu(v) \in \mathbb{R}_{\geq 0}$, since all nodes are reachable from s, and hence no vertex can have a distance $+\infty$ from s. We observe first that $d_v := \mu(v)$ for all v satisfies the constraints of the LP. Indeed, $\mu(s) = 0$ and $\mu(w) \leq \mu(v) + c(e)$ for any edge $e = (v, w)$.

We next show that if $(d_v)_{v \in V}$ satisfies all constraints of the LP above, then $d_v \leq \mu(v)$ for all v. Consider any v, and let $s = v_0, v_1, \ldots, v_k = v$ be a shortest path from s to v. Then $\mu(v) = \sum_{0 \leq i < k} c(v_i, v_{i+1})$. We shall show that $d_{v_j} \leq \sum_{0 \leq i < j} c(v_i, v_{i+1})$ by induction on j. For $j = 0$, this follows from $d_s = 0$ by the first constraint. For $j > 0$, we have

$$d_{v_j} \leq d_{v_{j-1}} + c(v_{j-1}, v_j) \leq \sum_{0 \leq i < j-1} c(v_i, v_{i+1}) + c(v_{j-1}, v_j) = \sum_{0 \leq i < j} c(v_i, v_{i+1}) ,$$

where the first inequality follows from the second set of constraints of the LP and the second inequality comes from the induction hypothesis.

We have now shown that $(\mu(v))_{v \in V}$ is a feasible solution, and that $d_v \leq \mu(v)$ for all v for any feasible solution $(d_v)_{v \in V}$. Since the objective of the LP is to maximize the sum of the d_v's, we must have $d_v = \mu(v)$ for all v in the optimal solution to the LP. $\square$

Exercise 12.2. Where does the proof above fail when not all nodes are reachable from s or when there are negative weights? Does it still work in the absence of negative cycles?

The proof that the LP above actually captures the shortest-path problem is nontrivial. When you formulate a problem as an LP, you should always prove that the LP is indeed a correct description of the problem that you are trying to solve.

Exercise 12.3. Let $G = (V, E)$ be a directed graph and let s and t be two nodes. Let $cap : E \to \mathbb{R}_{\geq 0}$ and $c : E \to \mathbb{R}_{\geq 0}$ be nonnegative functions on the edges of G. For an edge e, we call $cap(e)$ and $c(e)$ the capacity and cost, respectively, of e. A flow is a function $f : E \to \mathbb{R}_{\geq 0}$ with $0 \leq f(e) \leq cap(e)$ for all e and flow conservation at all nodes except s and t, i.e., for all $v \neq s, t$, we have

$$\text{flow into } v = \sum_{e=(u,v)} f(e) = \sum_{e=(v,w)} f(e) = \text{flow out of } v .$$

The value of the flow is the net flow out of s, i.e., $\sum_{e=(s,v)} f(e) - \sum_{e=(u,s)} f(e)$. The *maximum-flow problem* asks for a flow of maximum value. Show that this problem can be formulated as an LP.

The cost of a flow is $\sum_e f(e)c(e)$. The *minimum-cost maximum-flow problem* asks for a maximum flow of minimum cost. Show how to formulate this problem as an LP.

Linear programs are so important because they combine expressive power with efficient solution algorithms.

Theorem 12.3. *Linear programs can be solved in polynomial time [110, 106].*

The worst-case running time of the best algorithm known is $O(\max(m,n)^{7/2}L)$. In this bound, it is assumed that all coefficients c_j, a_{ij}, and b_i are integers with absolute value bounded by 2^L; n and m are the numbers of variables and constraints, respectively. Fortunately, the worst case rarely arises. Most linear programs can be solved relatively quickly by several procedures. One, the simplex algorithm, is briefly outlined in Sect. 12.5.1. For now, we should remember two facts: first, many problems can be formulated as linear programs, and second, there are efficient linear-program solvers that can be used as black boxes. In fact, although LP solvers are used on a routine basis, very few people in the world know exactly how to implement a highly efficient LP solver.

12.1.1 Integer Linear Programming

The expressive power of linear programming grows when some or all of the variables can be designated to be integral. Such variables can then take on only integer values, and not arbitrary real values. If all variables are constrained to be integral, the formulation of the problem is called an *integer linear program* (ILP). If some but not all variables are constrained to be integral, the formulation is called a *mixed integer linear program* (MILP). For example, our knapsack problem is tantamount to the following $0-1$ integer linear program:

$$\text{maximize } p \cdot x$$

subject to

$$w \cdot x \le M, \quad \text{and} \quad x_i \in \{0, 1\} \text{ for } i \in 1..n \, .$$

In a $0-1$ integer linear program, the variables are constrained to the values 0 and 1.

Exercise 12.4. Explain how to replace any ILP by a $0-1$ ILP, assuming that you know an upper bound U on the value of any variable in the optimal solution. Hint: replace any variable of the original ILP by a set of $O(\log U)$ $0-1$ variables.

Unfortunately, solving ILPs and MILPs is **NP**-hard. Indeed, even the knapsack problem is **NP**-hard. Nevertheless, ILPs can often be solved in practice using linear-programming packages. In Sect. 12.4, we shall outline how this is done. When an exact solution would be too time-consuming, linear programming can help to find approximate solutions. The *linear-program relaxation* of an ILP is the LP obtained by omitting the integrality constraints on the variables. For example, in the knapsack problem we would replace the constraint $x_i \in \{0, 1\}$ by the constraint $x_i \in [0, 1]$.

An LP relaxation can be solved by an LP solver. In many cases, the solution to the relaxation teaches us something about the underlying ILP. One observation always holds true (for maximization problems): the objective value of the relaxation is at least as large as the objective value of the underlying ILP. This claim is trivial, because any feasible solution to the ILP is also a feasible solution to the relaxation. The optimal solution to the LP relaxation will in general be *fractional*, i.e., variables will take on rational values that are not integral. However, it might be the case that only a few variables have nonintegral values. By appropriate rounding of fractional variables to integer values, we can often obtain good integer feasible solutions.

We shall give an example. The linear relaxation of the knapsack problem is given by

$$\text{maximize } p \cdot x$$

subject to

$$w \cdot x \le M, \quad \text{and} \quad x_i \in [0, 1] \text{ for } i \in 1..n \, .$$

This has a natural interpretation. It is no longer required to add items completely to the knapsack; one can now take any fraction of an item. In our smuggling scenario, the *fractional knapsack problem* corresponds to a situation involving divisible goods such as liquids or powders.

The fractional knapsack problem is easy to solve in time $O(n\log n)$; there is no need to use a general-purpose LP solver. We renumber (sort) the items by *profit density* such that

$$\frac{p_1}{w_1} \geq \frac{p_2}{w_2} \geq \cdots \geq \frac{p_n}{w_n} .$$

We find the smallest index j such that $\sum_{i=1}^{j} w_i > M$ (if there is no such index, we can take all knapsack items). Now we set

$$x_1 = \cdots = x_{j-1} = 1, x_j = \left(M - \sum_{i=1}^{j-1} w_i \right) / w_j, \text{ and } x_{j+1} = \cdots = x_n = 0 .$$

Figure 12.1 gives an example. The fractional solution above is the starting point for many good algorithms for the knapsack problem. We shall see more of this later.

Exercise 12.5 (linear relaxation of the knapsack problem).

(a) Prove that the above routine computes an optimal solution. Hint: you might want to use an *exchange argument* similar to the one used to prove the cut property of minimum spanning trees in Sect. 11.1.
(b) Outline an algorithm that computes an optimal solution in linear expected time. Hint: use a variant of *quickSelect*, described in Sect. 5.5.

A solution to the fractional knapsack problem is easily converted to a feasible solution to the knapsack problem. We simply take the fractional solution and round the sole fractional variable x_j to zero. We call this algorithm *roundDown*.

Exercise 12.6. Formulate the following *set-covering* problem as an ILP. Given a set M, subsets $M_i \subseteq M$ for $i \in 1..n$ with $\bigcup_{i=1}^{n} M_i = M$, and a cost c_i for each M_i, select $F \subseteq 1..n$ such that $\bigcup_{i \in F} M_i = M$ and $\sum_{i \in F} c_i$ is minimized.

12.2 Greedy Algorithms – Never Look Back

The term *greedy algorithm* is used for a problem-solving strategy where the items under consideration are inspected in some order, usually some carefully chosen order, and a decision about an item, for example, whether to include it in the solution or not, is made when the item is considered. Decisions are never reversed. The algorithm for the fractional knapsack problem given in the preceding section follows the greedy strategy; we consider the items in decreasing order of profit density. The algorithms for shortest paths in Chap. 10 and for minimum spanning trees in Chap. 11 also follow the greedy strategy. For the single-source shortest-path problem with nonnegative weights, we considered the edges in order of the tentative distance of their source nodes. For these problems, the greedy approach led to an optimal solution.

Usually, greedy algorithms yield only suboptimal solutions. Let us consider the knapsack problem again. A typical greedy approach would be to scan the items in

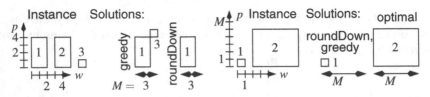

Fig. 12.3. Two instances of the knapsack problem. *Left*: for $p = (4,4,1)$, $w = (2,2,1)$, and $M = 3$, *greedy* performs better than *roundDown*. *Right*: for $p = (1, M-1)$ and $w = (1, M)$, both *greedy* and *roundDown* are far from optimal

order of decreasing profit density and to include items that still fit into the knapsack. We shall give this algorithm the name *greedy*. Figures 12.1 and 12.3 give examples. Observe that *greedy* always gives solutions at least as good as *roundDown* gives. Once *roundDown* encounters an item that it cannot include, it stops. However, *greedy* keeps on looking and often succeeds in including additional items of less weight. Although the example in Fig. 12.1 gives the same result for both *greedy* and *roundDown*, the results generally *are* different. For example, with profits $p = (4,4,1)$, weights $w = (2,2,1)$, and $M = 3$, *greedy* includes the first and third items yielding a profit of 5, whereas *roundDown* includes just the first item and obtains only a profit of 4. Both algorithms may produce solutions that are far from optimum. For example, for any capacity M, consider the two-item instance with profits $p = (1, M-1)$ and weights $w = (1, M)$. Both *greedy* and *roundDown* include only the first item, which has a high profit density but a very small absolute profit. In this case it would be much better to include just the second item.

We can turn this observation into an algorithm, which we call *round*. This computes two solutions: the solution x^d proposed by *roundDown* and the solution x^c obtained by choosing exactly the critical item x_j of the fractional solution.[4] It then returns the better of the two.

We can give an interesting performance guarantee. The algorithm *round* always achieves at least 50% of the profit of the optimal solution. More generally, we say that an algorithm achieves an *approximation ratio* of α if for all inputs, its solution is at most a factor α worse than the optimal solution.

Theorem 12.4. *The algorithm round achieves an approximation ratio of 2.*

Proof. Let x^* denote any optimal solution, and let x^f be the optimal solution to the fractional knapsack problem. Then $p \cdot x^* \leq p \cdot x^f$. The value of the objective function is increased further by setting $x_j = 1$ in the fractional solution. We obtain

$$p \cdot x^* \leq p \cdot x^f \leq p \cdot x^d + p \cdot x^c \leq 2 \max \left\{ p \cdot x^d, p \cdot x^c \right\} .$$

$\square$

---

[4] We assume here that "unreasonably large" items with $w_i > M$ have been removed from the problem in a preprocessing step.

There are many ways to refine the algorithm *round* without sacrificing this approximation guarantee. We can replace x^d by the greedy solution. We can similarly augment x^c with any greedy solution for a smaller instance where item j is removed and the capacity is reduced by w_j.

We now come to another important class of optimization problems, called *scheduling problems*. Consider the following scenario, known as the *scheduling problem for independent weighted jobs on identical machines*. We are given m identical machines on which we want to process n jobs; the execution of job j takes t_j time units. An assignment $x : 1..n \rightarrow 1..m$ of jobs to machines is called a *schedule*. Thus the *load* ℓ_j assigned to machine j is $\sum_{\{i:x(i)=j\}} t_i$. The goal is to minimize the *makespan* $L_{\max} = \max_{1 \leq j \leq m} \ell_j$ of the schedule.

One application scenario is as follows. We have a video game processor with several identical processor cores. The jobs would be the tasks executed in a video game such as audio processing, preparing graphics objects for the image processing unit, simulating physical effects, and simulating the intelligence of the game.

We give next a simple greedy algorithm for the problem above [80] that has the additional property that it does not need to know the sizes of the jobs in advance. We assign jobs in the order they arrive. Algorithms with this property ("unknown future") are called *online* algorithms. When job i arrives, we assign it to the machine with the smallest load. Formally, we compute the loads $\ell_j = \sum_{h<i \wedge x(h)=j} t_h$ of all machines j, and assign the new job to the least loaded machine, i.e., $x(i) := j_i$, where j_i is such that $\ell_{j_i} = \min_{1 \leq j \leq m} \ell_j$. This algorithm is frequently referred to as the *shortest-queue algorithm*. It does not guarantee optimal solutions, but always computes nearly optimal solutions.

Theorem 12.5. *The shortest-queue algorithm ensures that*

$$L_{\max} \leq \frac{1}{m} \sum_{i=1}^{n} t_i + \frac{m-1}{m} \max_{1 \leq i \leq n} t_i .$$

Proof. In the schedule generated by the shortest-queue algorithm, some machine has a load $L_{\max}$. We focus on the job $\hat{\imath}$ that is the last job that has been assigned to the machine with the maximum load. When job $\hat{\imath}$ is scheduled, all m machines have a load of at least $L_{\max} - t_{\hat{\imath}}$, i.e.,

$$\sum_{i \neq \hat{\imath}} t_i \geq (L_{\max} - t_{\hat{\imath}}) \cdot m .$$

Solving this for $L_{\max}$ yields

$$L_{\max} \leq \frac{1}{m} \sum_{i \neq \hat{\imath}} t_i + t_{\hat{\imath}} = \frac{1}{m} \sum_i t_i + \frac{m-1}{m} t_{\hat{\imath}} \leq \frac{1}{m} \sum_{i=1}^{n} t_i + \frac{m-1}{m} \max_{1 \leq i \leq n} t_i .$$

$\square$

We are almost finished. We now observe that $\sum_i t_i / m$ and $\max_i t_i$ are lower bounds on the makespan of any schedule and hence also the optimal schedule. We obtain the following corollary.

Corollary 12.6. *The approximation ratio of the shortest-queue algorithm is* $2 - 1/m$.

Proof. Let $L_1 = \sum_i t_i/m$ and $L_2 = \max_i t_i$. The makespan of the optimal solution is at least $\max(L_1, L_2)$. The makespan of the shortest-queue solution is bounded by

$$L_1 + \frac{m-1}{m}L_2 \leq \frac{mL_1 + (m-1)L_2}{m} \leq \frac{(2m-1)\max(L_1,L_2)}{m}$$

$$= (2 - \frac{1}{m}) \cdot \max(L_1, L_2) .$$

$\square$

The shortest-queue algorithm is no better than claimed above. Consider an instance with $n = m(m-1) + 1$, $t_n = m$, and $t_i = 1$ for $i < n$. The optimal solution has a makespan $L_{\max}^{opt} = m$, whereas the shortest-queue algorithm produces a solution with a makespan $L_{\max} = 2m - 1$. The shortest-queue algorithm is an online algorithm. It produces a solution which is at most a factor $2 - 1/m$ worse than the solution produced by an algorithm that knows the entire input. In such a situation, we say that the online algorithm has a *competitive ratio* of $\alpha = 2 - 1/m$.

*Exercise 12.7. Show that the shortest-queue algorithm achieves an approximation ratio of $4/3$ if the jobs are sorted by decreasing size.

*Exercise 12.8 (bin packing). Suppose a smuggler boss has perishable goods in her cellar. She has to hire enough porters to ship all items tonight. Develop a greedy algorithm that tries to minimize the number of people she needs to hire, assuming that they can all carry a weight M. Try to obtain an approximation ratio for your *bin-packing* algorithm.

Boolean formulae provide another powerful description language. Here, variables range over the Boolean values 1 and 0, and the connectors $\wedge$, $\vee$, and $\neg$ are used to build formulae. A Boolean formula is *satisfiable* if there is an assignment of Boolean values to the variables such that the formula evaluates to 1. As an example, we now formulate the *pigeonhole principle* as a satisfiability problem: it is impossible to pack $n+1$ items into n bins such that every bin contains one item at most. We have variables x_{ij} for $1 \leq i \leq n+1$ and $1 \leq j \leq n$. So i ranges over items and j ranges over bins. Every item must be put into (at least) one bin, i.e., $x_{i1} \vee \ldots \vee x_{in}$ for $1 \leq i \leq n+1$. No bin should receive more than one item, i.e., $\neg(\vee_{1 \leq i < h \leq n+1} x_{ij} x_{hj})$ for $1 \leq j \leq n$. The conjunction of these formulae is unsatisfiable. SAT solvers decide the satisfiability of Boolean formulae. Although the satisfiability problem is **NP**-complete, there are now solvers that can solve real-world problems that involve hundreds of thousands of variables.[5]

Exercise 12.9. Formulate the pigeonhole principle as an integer linear program.

---

[5] See http://www.satcompetition.org/.

12.3 Dynamic Programming – Building It Piece by Piece

For many optimization problems, the following *principle of optimality* holds: *an optimal solution is composed of optimal solutions to subproblems. If a subproblem has several optimal solutions, it does not matter which one is used.*

The idea behind dynamic programming is to build an exhaustive table of optimal solutions. We start with trivial subproblems. We build optimal solutions for increasingly larger problems by constructing them from the tabulated solutions to smaller problems.

Again, we shall use the knapsack problem as an example. We define $P(i,C)$ as the maximum profit possible when only items 1 to i can be put in the knapsack and the total weight is at most C. Our goal is to compute $P(n,M)$. We start with trivial cases and work our way up. The trivial cases are "no items" and "total weight zero". In both of these cases, the maximum profit is zero. So

$$P(0,C) = 0 \text{ for all } C \quad \text{and} \quad P(i,0) = 0 .$$

Consider next the case $i > 0$ and $C > 0$. In the solution that maximizes the profit, we either use item i or do not use it. In the latter case, the maximum achievable profit is $P(i-1,C)$. In the former case, the maximum achievable profit is $P(i-1,C-w_i)+p_i$, since we obtain a profit of p_i for item i and must use a solution of total weight at most $C - w_i$ for the first $i - 1$ items. Of course, the former alternative is only feasible if $C \geq w_i$. We summarize this discussion in the following recurrence for $P(i,C)$:

$$P(i,C) = \begin{cases} \max(P(i-1,C), P(i-1,C-w_i)+p_i) & \text{if } w_i \leq C \\ P(i-1,C) & \text{if } w_i > C \end{cases}$$

Exercise 12.10. Show that the case distinction in the definition of $P(i,C)$ can be avoided by defining $P(i,C) = -\infty$ for $C < 0$.

Using the above recurrence, we can compute $P(n,M)$ by filling a table $P(i,C)$ with one column for each possible capacity C and one row for each item i. Table 12.1 gives an example. There are many ways to fill this table, for example row by row. In order to reconstruct a solution from this table, we work our way backwards, starting at the bottom right-hand corner of the table. We set $i = n$ and $C = M$. If $P(i,C) = P(i-1,C)$, we set $x_i = 0$ and continue to row $i-1$ and column C. Otherwise, we set $x_i = 1$. We have $P(i,C) = P(i-1,C-w_i) + p_i$, and therefore continue to row $i-1$ and column $C - w_i$. We continue with this procedure until we arrive at row 0, by which time the solution $(x_1, \ldots, x_n)$ has been completed.

Exercise 12.11. Dynamic programming, as described above, needs to store a table containing $\Theta(nM)$ integers. Give a more space-efficient solution that stores only a single bit in each table entry except for two rows of $P(i,C)$ values at any given time. What information is stored in this bit? How is it used to reconstruct a solution? How can you get down to *one* row of stored values? Hint: exploit your freedom in the order of filling in table values.

Table 12.1. A dynamic-programming table for the knapsack instance with $p = (10,20,15,20)$, $w = (1,3,2,4)$, and $M = 5$. **Bold-face** entries contribute to the optimal solution

$i \backslash C$	0	1	2	3	4	5
0	0	0	0	0	0	0
1	**0**	10	10	10	10	10
2	0	10	10	**20**	30	30
3	0	10	15	25	30	**35**
4	0	10	15	25	30	35

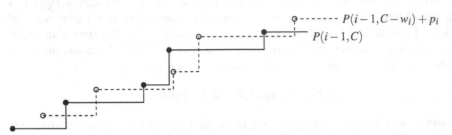

Fig. 12.4. The solid step function shows $C \mapsto P(i-1,C)$, and the dashed step function shows $C \mapsto P(i-1,C-w_i) + p_i$. $P(i,C)$ is the pointwise maximum of the two functions. The solid step function is stored as the sequence of solid points. The representation of the dashed step function is obtained by adding (w_i, p_i) to every solid point. The representation of $C \mapsto P(i,C)$ is obtained by merging the two representations and deleting all dominated elements

We shall next describe an important improvement with respect to space consumption and speed. Instead of computing $P(i,C)$ for all i and all C, the *Nemhauser–Ullmann algorithm* [146, 17] computes only *Pareto-optimal* solutions. A solution x is Pareto-optimal if there is no solution that *dominates* it, i.e., has a greater profit and no greater cost or the same profit and less cost. In other words, since $P(i,C)$ is an increasing function of C, only the pairs $(C, P(i,C))$ with $P(i,C) > P(i,C-1)$ are needed for an optimal solution. We store these pairs in a list L_i sorted by C value. So $L_0 = \langle (0,0) \rangle$, indicating that $P(0,C) = 0$ for all $C \geq 0$, and $L_1 = \langle (0,0), (w_1, p_1) \rangle$, indicating that $P(1,C) = 0$ for $0 \leq C < w_1$ and $P(i,C) = p_1$ for $C \geq w_1$.

How can we go from L_{i-1} to L_i? The recurrence for $P(i,C)$ paves the way; see Fig. 12.4. We have the list representation L_{i-1} for the function $C \mapsto P(i-1,C)$. We obtain the representation L'_{i-1} for $C \mapsto P(i-1,C-w_i) + p_i$ by shifting every point in L_{i-1} by (w_i, p_i). We merge L_{i-1} and L'_{i-1} into a single list by order of first component and delete all elements that are dominated by another value, i.e., we delete all elements that are preceded by an element with a higher second component, and, for each fixed value of C, we keep only the element with the largest second component.

Exercise 12.12. Give pseudocode for the above merge. Show that the merge can be carried out in time $|L_{i-1}|$. Conclude that the running time of the algorithm is proportional to the number of Pareto-optimal solutions.

The basic dynamic-programming algorithm for the knapsack problem and also its optimization require $\Theta(nM)$ worst-case time. This is quite good if M is not too large. Since the running time is polynomial in n and M, the algorithm is called *pseudo-polynomial*. The "pseudo" means that it is not necessarily polynomial in the *input size* measured in bits; however, it is polynomial in the natural parameters n and M. There is, however, an important difference between the basic and the refined approach. The basic approach has best-case running time $\Theta(nM)$. The best case for the refined approach is $O(n)$. The *average-case* complexity of the refined algorithm is polynomial in n, independent of M. This holds even if the averaging is done only over perturbations of an arbitrary instance by a small amount of random noise. We refer the reader to [17] for details.

Exercise 12.13 (dynamic programming by profit). Define $W(i,P)$ to be the smallest weight needed to achieve a profit of at least P using knapsack items $1..i$.

(a) Show that $W(i,P) = \min\{W(i-1,P), W(i-1,P-p_i)+w_i\}$.
(b) Develop a table-based dynamic-programming algorithm using the above recurrence that computes optimal solutions to the knapsack problem in time $O(np^*)$, where p^* is the profit of the optimal solution. Hint: assume first that p^*, or at least a good upper bound for it, is known. Then remove this assumption.

Exercise 12.14 (making change). Suppose you have to program a vending machine that should give exact change using a minimum number of coins.

(a) Develop an optimal greedy algorithm that works in the euro zone with coins worth 1, 2, 5, 10, 20, 50, 100, and 200 cents and in the dollar zone with coins worth 1, 5, 10, 25, 50, and 100 cents.
(b) Show that this algorithm would not be optimal if there were also a 4 cent coin.
(c) Develop a dynamic-programming algorithm that gives optimal change for any currency system.

Exercise 12.15 (chained matrix products). We want to compute the matrix product $M_1M_2\cdots M_n$, where M_i is a $k_{i-1} \times k_i$ matrix. Assume that a pairwise matrix product is computed in the straightforward way using mks element multiplications to obtain the product of an $m \times k$ matrix with a $k \times s$ matrix. Exploit the associativity of matrix products to minimize the number of element multiplications needed. Use dynamic programming to find an optimal evaluation order in time $O(n^3)$. For example, the product of a 4×5 matrix M_1, a 5×2 matrix M_2, and a 2×8 matrix M_3 can be computed in two ways. Computing $M_1(M_2M_3)$ takes $5\cdot2\cdot8+4\cdot5\cdot8 = 240$ multiplications, whereas computing $(M_1M_2)M_3$ takes only $4\cdot5\cdot2+4\cdot2\cdot8 = 104$ multiplications.

Exercise 12.16 (minimum edit distance). The *minimum edit distance* (or *Levenshtein distance*) $L(s,t)$ between two strings s and t is the minimum number of character deletions, insertions, and replacements applied to s that produces the string t. For example, $L(\text{graph},\text{group}) = 3$ (delete h, replace a by o, insert u before p). Define $d(i,j) = L(\langle s_1,\ldots,s_i\rangle, \langle t_1,\ldots,t_j\rangle)$. Show that

$$d(i,j) = \min\left\{d(i-1,j)+1, d(i,j-1)+1, d(i-1,j-1)+[s_i \neq t_j]\right\}$$

where $[s_i \neq t_j]$ is one if s_i and t_j are different and is zero otherwise.

Exercise 12.17. Does the principle of optimality hold for minimum spanning trees? Check the following three possibilities for definitions of subproblems: subsets of nodes, arbitrary subsets of edges, and prefixes of the sorted sequence of edges.

Exercise 12.18 (constrained shortest path). Consider a directed graph $G = (V,E)$ where edges $e \in E$ have a *length* $\ell(e)$ and a *cost* $c(e)$. We want to find a path from node s to node t that minimizes the total length subject to the constraint that the total cost of the path is at most C. Show that subpaths $\langle s', t' \rangle$ of optimal solutions are *not* necessarily shortest paths from s' to t'.

12.4 Systematic Search – When in Doubt, Use Brute Force

In many optimization problems, the universe $\mathcal{U}$ of possible solutions is finite, so that we can in principle solve the optimization problem by trying all possibilities. Naive application of this idea does not lead very far, however, but we can frequently restrict the search to *promising* candidates, and then the concept carries a lot further.

We shall explain the concept of systematic search using the knapsack problem and a specific approach to systematic search known as *branch-and-bound*. In Exercises 12.20 and 12.21, we outline systematic-search routines following a somewhat different pattern.

Figure 12.5 gives pseudocode for a systematic-search routine *bbKnapsack* for the knapsack problem and Figure 12.6 shows a sample run. *Branching* is the most fundamental ingredient of systematic-search routines. All sensible values for some piece of the solution are tried. For each of these values, the resulting problem is solved recursively. Within the recursive call, the chosen value is fixed. The routine *bbKnapsack* first tries including an item by setting $x_i := 1$, and then excluding it by setting $x_i := 0$. The variables are fixed one after another in order of decreasing profit density. The assignment $x_i := 1$ is not tried if this would exceed the remaining knapsack capacity M'. With these definitions, after all variables have been set, in the n-th level of recursion, *bbKnapsack* will have found a feasible solution. Indeed, without the bounding rule below, the algorithm would systematically explore *all* possible solutions and the *first* feasible solution encountered would be the solution found by the algorithm *greedy*. The (partial) solutions explored by the algorithm form a tree. Branching happens at internal nodes of this tree.

Bounding is a method for pruning subtrees that cannot contain optimal solutions. A branch-and-bound algorithm keeps the best feasible solution found in a global variable $\hat{x}$; this solution is often called the *incumbent* solution. It is initialized to a solution determined by a heuristic routine and, at all times, provides a lower bound $p \cdot \hat{x}$ on the value of the objective function that can be obtained. This lower bound is complemented by an upper bound u for the value of the objective function obtainable by extending the current partial solution x to a full feasible solution. In our example,

Function $bbKnapsack((p_1,\ldots,p_n),(w_1,\ldots,w_n),M) : \mathscr{L}$
   assert $p_1/w_1 \geq p_2/w_2 \geq \cdots \geq p_n/w_n$ // assume input sorted by profit density
   $\hat{x} = heuristicKnapsack((p_1,\ldots,p_n),(w_1,\ldots,w_n),M) : \mathscr{L}$ // best solution so far
   $x : \mathscr{L}$ // current partial solution
   $recurse(1,M,0)$
   return $\hat{x}$

   // Find solutions assuming $x_1,\ldots,x_{i-1}$ are fixed, $M' = M - \sum_{k<i} x_k w_k$, $P = \sum_{k<i} x_k p_k$.
   Procedure $recurse(i,M',P : \mathbb{N})$
     $u := P + upperBound((p_i,\ldots,p_n),(w_i,\ldots,w_n),M')$
     if $u > p \cdot \hat{x}$ **then**   // not bounded
       if $i > n$ **then** $\hat{x} := x$
       else   // branch on variable x_i
         if $w_i \leq M'$ **then** $x_i := 1;\ recurse(i+1,M'-w_i,P+p_i)$
         if $u > p \cdot \hat{x}$ **then** $x_i := 0;\ recurse(i+1,M',P)$

Fig. 12.5. A branch-and-bound algorithm for the knapsack problem. An initial feasible solution is constructed by the function *heuristicKnapsack* using some heuristic algorithm. The function *upperBound* computes an upper bound for the possible profit

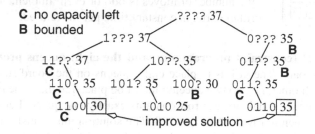

Fig. 12.6. The search space explored by *knapsackBB* for a knapsack instance with $p = (10,20,15,20)$, $w = (1,3,2,4)$, and $M = 5$, and an empty initial solution $\hat{x} = (0,0,0,0)$. The function *upperBound* is computed by rounding down the optimal value of the objective function for the fractional knapsack problem. The nodes of the search tree contain $x_1 \cdots x_{i-1}$ and the upper bound u. Left children are explored first and correspond to setting $x_i := 1$. There are two reasons for not exploring a child: either there is not enough capacity left to include an element (indicated by C), or a feasible solution with a profit equal to the upper bound is already known (indicated by B)

the upper bound could be the profit for the fractional knapsack problem with items $i..n$ and capacity $M' = M - \sum_{j<i} x_j w_j$.

    Branch-and-bound stops expanding the current branch of the search tree when $u \leq p \cdot \hat{x}$, i.e., when there is no hope of an improved solution in the current subtree of the search space. We test $u > p \cdot \hat{x}$ again before exploring the case $x_i = 0$ because $\hat{x}$ might change when the case $x_i = 1$ is explored.

Exercise 12.19. Explain how to implement the function *upperBound* in Fig. 12.5 so that it runs in time $O(\log n)$. Hint: precompute the prefix sums $\sum_{k \leq i} w_i$ and $\sum_{k \leq i} p_i$ and use binary search.

Exercise 12.20 (the 15-puzzle). The 15-puzzle is a popular sliding-block puzzle. You have to move 15 square tiles in a 4×4 frame into the right order. Define a move as the action of interchanging a square and the hole in the array of tiles.

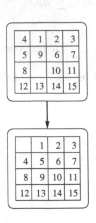

Design an algorithm that finds a shortest-move sequence from a given starting configuration to the ordered configuration shown at the bottom of the figure on the left. Use *iterative deepening depth-first search* [114]: try all one-move sequences first, then all two-move sequences, and so on. This should work for the simpler 8-puzzle. For the 15-puzzle, use the following optimizations. Never undo the immediately preceding move. Use the number of moves that would be needed if all pieces could be moved freely as a lower bound and stop exploring a subtree if this bound proves that the current search depth is too small. Decide beforehand whether the number of moves is odd or even. Implement your algorithm to run in constant time per move tried.

Exercise 12.21 (constraint programming and the eight-queens problem). Consider a chessboard. The task is to place eight queens on the board so that they do not attack each other, i.e., no two queens should be placed in the same row, column, diagonal, or antidiagonal. So each row contains exactly one queen. Let x_i be the position of the queen in row i. Then $x_i \in 1..8$. The solution must satisfy the following constraints: $x_i \neq x_j$, $i + x_i \neq j + x_j$, and $x_i - i \neq x_j - j$ for $1 \leq i < j \leq 8$. What do these conditions express? Show that they are sufficient. A systematic search can use the following optimization. When a variable x_i is fixed at some value, this excludes some values for variables that are still free. Modify the systematic search so that it keeps track of the values that are still available for free variables. Stop exploration as soon as there is a free variable that has no value available to it anymore. This technique of eliminating values is basic to *constraint programming*.

12.4.1 Solving Integer Linear Programs

In Sect. 12.1.1, we have seen how to formulate the knapsack problem as a $0-1$ integer linear program. We shall now indicate how the branch-and-bound procedure developed for the knapsack problem can be applied to any $0-1$ integer linear program. Recall that in a $0-1$ integer linear program the values of the variables are constrained to 0 and 1. Our discussion will be brief, and we refer the reader to a textbook on integer linear programming [147, 172] for more information.

The main change is that the function *upperBound* now solves a general linear program that has variables $x_i, \dots, x_n$ with range $[0, 1]$. The constraints for this LP come from the input ILP, with the variables x_1 to x_{i-1} replaced by their values. In the remainder of this section, we shall simply refer to this linear program as "the LP".

If the LP has a feasible solution, *upperBound* returns the optimal value for the LP. If the LP has no feasible solution, *upperBound* returns $-\infty$ so that the ILP solver will stop exploring this branch of the search space. We shall describe next several generalizations of the basic branch-and-bound procedure that sometimes lead to considerable improvements.

Branch Selection: We may pick any unfixed variable x_j for branching. In particular, we can make the choice depend on the solution of the LP. A commonly used rule is to branch on a variable whose fractional value in the LP is closest to $1/2$.

Order of Search Tree Traversal: In the knapsack example, the search tree was traversed depth-first, and the 1-branch was tried first. In general, we are free to choose any order of tree traversal. There are at least two considerations influencing the choice of strategy. If no good feasible solution is known, it is good to use a depth-first strategy so that complete solutions are explored quickly. Otherwise, it is better to use a *best-first* strategy that explores those search tree nodes that are most likely to contain good solutions. Search tree nodes are kept in a priority queue, and the next node to be explored is the most promising node in the queue. The priority could be the upper bound returned by the LP. However, since the LP is expensive to evaluate, one sometimes settles for an approximation.

Finding Solutions: We may be lucky in that the solution of the LP turns out to assign integer values to all variables. In this case there is no need for further branching. Application-specific heuristics can additionally help to find good solutions quickly.

Branch-and-Cut: When an ILP solver branches too often, the size of the search tree explodes and it becomes too expensive to find an optimal solution. One way to avoid branching is to add constraints to the linear program that *cut* away solutions with fractional values for the variables without changing the solutions with integer values.

12.5 Local Search – Think Globally, Act Locally

The optimization algorithms we have seen so far are applicable only in special circumstances. Dynamic programming needs a special structure of the problem and may require a lot of space and time. Systematic search is usually too slow for large inputs. Greedy algorithms are fast but often yield only low-quality solutions. *Local search* is a widely applicable iterative procedure. It starts with some feasible solution and then moves from feasible solution to feasible solution by local modifications. Figure 12.7 gives the basic framework. We shall refine it later.

Local search maintains a current feasible solution x and the best solution $\hat{x}$ seen so far. In each step, local search moves from the current solution to a neighboring solution. What are neighboring solutions? Any solution that can be obtained from the current solution by making small changes to it. For example, in the case of the knapsack problem, we might remove up to two items from the knapsack and replace them by up to two other items. The precise definition of the neighborhood depends on the application and the algorithm designer. We use $\mathcal{N}(x)$ to denote the *neighborhood* of x. The second important design decision is which solution from the neighborhood is chosen. Finally, some heuristic decides when to stop.

In the rest of this section, we shall tell you more about local search.

12.5.1 Hill Climbing

Hill climbing is the greedy version of local search. It moves only to neighbors that are better than the currently best solution. This restriction further simplifies the local search. The variables $\hat{x}$ and x are the same, and we stop when there are no improved solutions in the neighborhood $\mathcal{N}$. The only nontrivial aspect of hill climbing is the choice of the neighborhood. We shall give two examples where hill climbing works quite well, followed by an example where it fails badly.

Our first example is the traveling salesman problem described in Sect. 11.6.2. Given an undirected graph and a distance function on the edges satisfying the triangle inequality, the goal is to find a shortest tour that visits all nodes of the graph. We define the neighbors of a tour as follows. Let (u,v) and (w,y) be two edges of the tour, i.e., the tour has the form $(u,v), p, (w,y), q$, where p is a path from v to w and q is a path from y to u. We remove these two edges from the tour, and replace them by the edges (u,w) and (v,y). The new tour first traverses (u,w), then uses the reversal of p back to v, then uses (v,y), and finally traverses q back to u. This move is known as a 2-exchange, and a tour that cannot be improved by a 2-exchange is said to be 2-optimal. In many instances of the traveling salesman problem, 2-optimal tours come quite close to optimal tours.

Exercise 12.22. Describe a scheme where three edges are removed and replaced by new edges.

An interesting example of hill climbing with a clever choice of the neighborhood function is the *simplex algorithm* for linear programming (see Sect. 12.1). This is the most widely used algorithm for linear programming. The set of feasible solutions $\mathcal{L}$ of a linear program is defined by a set of linear equalities and inequalities $a_i \cdot x \bowtie b_i$, $1 \leq i \leq m$. The points satisfying a linear equality $a_i \cdot x = b_i$ form a *hyperplane* in R^n, and the points satisfying a linear inequality $a_i \cdot x \leq b_i$ or $a_i \cdot x \geq b_i$ form a

find some feasible solution $x \in \mathcal{L}$
$\hat{x} := x$ // $\hat{x}$ is best solution found so far
while not satisfied with $\hat{x}$ **do**
    $x :=$ some heuristically chosen element from $\mathcal{N}(x) \cap \mathcal{L}$
    if $f(x) > f(\hat{x})$ **then** $\hat{x} := x$

Fig. 12.7. Local search

half-space. Hyperplanes are the n-dimensional analogues of planes and half-spaces are the analogues of half-planes. The set of feasible solutions is an intersection of m half-spaces and hyperplanes and forms a *convex polytope.* We have already seen an example in two-dimensional space in Fig. 12.2. Figure 12.8 shows an example in three-dimensional space. Convex polytopes are the n-dimensional analogues of convex polygons. In the interior of the polytope, all inequalities are strict (= satisfied with inequality); on the boundary some inequalities are tight (= satisfied with equality). The vertices and edges of the polytope are particularly important parts of the boundary. We shall now sketch how the simplex algorithm works. We assume that there are no equality constraints. Observe that an equality constraint c can be solved for any one of its variables; this variable can then be removed by substituting into the other equalities and inequalities. Afterwards, the constraint c is redundant and can be dropped.

The simplex algorithm starts at an arbitrary vertex of the feasible region. In each step, it moves to a neighboring vertex, i.e., a vertex reachable via an edge, with a larger objective value. If there is more than one such neighbor, a common strategy is to move to the neighbor with the largest objective value. If there is no neighbor with a larger objective value, the algorithm stops. *At this point, the algorithm has found the vertex with the maximal objective value.* In the examples in Figs. 12.2 and 12.8, the captions argue why this is true. The general argument is as follows. Let x^* be the vertex at which the simplex algorithm stops. The feasible region is contained in a cone with apex x^* and spanned by the edges incident on x^*. All these edges go to vertices with smaller objective values and hence the entire cone is contained in the half-space $\{x : c \cdot x \leq c \cdot x^*\}$. Thus no feasible point can have an objective value

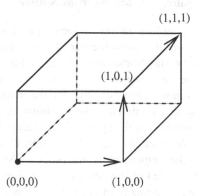

(1,1,1)

(1,0,1)

(0,0,0)   (1,0,0)

Fig. 12.8. The three-dimensional unit cube is defined by the inequalities $x \geq 0$, $x \leq 1$, $y \geq 0$, $y \leq 1$, $z \geq 0$, and $z \leq 1$. At the vertices $(1,1,1)$ and $(1,0,1)$, three inequalities are tight, and on the edge connecting these vertices, the inequalities $x \leq 1$ and $z \leq 1$ are tight. For the objective "maximize $x + y + z$", the simplex algorithm starting at $(0,0,0)$ may move along the path indicated by arrows. The vertex $(1,1,1)$ is optimal, since the half-space $x + y + z \leq 3$ contains the entire feasible region and has $(1,1,1)$ in its boundary

larger than x^*. We have described the simplex algorithm as a walk on the boundary of a convex polytope, i.e., in geometric language. It can be described equivalently using the language of linear algebra. Actual implementations use the linear-algebra description.

In the case of linear programming, hill climbing leads to an optimal solution. In general, however, hill climbing will not find an optimal solution. In fact, it will not even find a near-optimal solution. Consider the following example. Our task is to find the highest point on earth, i.e., Mount Everest. A feasible solution is any point on earth. The local neighborhood of a point is any point within a distance of 10 km. So the algorithm would start at some point on earth, then go to the highest point within a distance of 10 km, then go again to the highest point within a distance of 10 km, and so on. If one were to start from the first author's home (altitude 206 meters), the first step would lead to an altitude of 350 m, and there the algorithm would stop, because there is no higher hill within 10 km of that point. There are very few places in the world where the algorithm would continue for long, and even fewer places where it would find Mount Everest.

Why does hill climbing work so nicely for linear programming, but fail to find Mount Everest? The reason is that the earth has many local optima, hills that are the highest point within a range of 10 km. In contrast, a linear program has only one local optimum (which then, of course, is also a global optimum). For a problem with many local optima, we should expect *any* generic method to have difficulties. Observe that increasing the size of the neighborhoods in the search for Mount Everest does not really solve the problem, except if the neighborhoods are made to cover the entire earth. But finding the optimum in a neighborhood is then as hard as the full problem.

12.5.2 Simulated Annealing – Learning from Nature

If we want to ban the bane of local optima in local search, we must find a way to escape from them. This means that we sometimes have to accept moves that decrease the objective value. What could "sometimes" mean in this context? We have contradictory goals. On the one hand, we must be willing to make many downhill steps so that we can escape from wide local optima. On the other hand, we must be sufficiently target-oriented so that we find a global optimum at the end of a long narrow ridge. A very popular and successful approach for reconciling these contradictory goals is *simulated annealing*; see Fig. 12.9. This works in phases that are controlled by a parameter T, called the *temperature* of the process. We shall explain below why the language of physics is used in the description of simulated annealing. In each phase, a number of moves are made. In each move, a neighbor $x' \in \mathcal{N}(x) \cap \mathcal{L}$ is chosen uniformly at random, and the move from x to x' is made with a certain probability. This probability is one if x' improves upon x. It is less than one if the move is to an inferior solution. The trick is to make the probability depend on T. If T is large, we make the move to an inferior solution relatively likely; if T is close to zero, we make such a move relatively unlikely. The hope is that, in this way, the process zeros in on a region containing a good local optimum in phases of high temperature and then actually finds a near-optimal solution in the phases of low temperature.

find some feasible solution $x \in \mathcal{L}$
$T :=$ some positive value   // initial temperature of the system
while T is still sufficiently large **do**
   perform a number of steps of the following form
     pick x' from $\mathcal{N}(x) \cap \mathcal{L}$ uniformly at random
     with probability $\min(1, \exp(\frac{f(x') - f(x)}{T}))$ **do** $x := x'$
   decrease T // make moves to inferior solutions less likely

Fig. 12.9. Simulated annealing

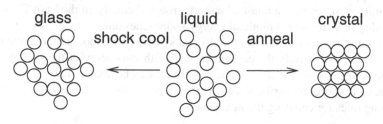

Fig. 12.10. Annealing versus shock cooling

The exact choice of the transition probability in the case where x' is an inferior solution is given by $\exp((f(x') - f(x))/T)$. Observe that T is in the denominator and
that $f(x') - f(x)$ is negative. So the probability decreases with T and also with the
absolute loss in objective value.

Why is the language of physics used, and why this apparently strange choice of
transition probabilities? Simulated annealing is inspired by the physical process of
annealing, which can be used to minimize[6] the global energy of a physical system.
For example, consider a pot of molten silica (SiO_2); see Fig. 12.10. If we cool it very
quickly, we obtain a glass – an amorphous substance in which every molecule is in
a local minimum of energy. This process of shock cooling has a certain similarity to
hill climbing. Every molecule simply drops into a state of locally minimal energy;
in hill climbing, we accept a local modification of the state if it leads to a smaller
value of the objective function. However, a glass is not a state of global minimum
energy. A state of much lower energy is reached by a quartz crystal, in which all
molecules are arranged in a regular way. This state can be reached (or approximated)
by cooling the melt very slowly. This process is called *annealing*. How can it be
that molecules arrange themselves into a perfect shape over a distance of billions
of molecular diameters although they feel only local forces extending over a few
molecular diameters?

Qualitatively, the explanation is that local energy minima have enough time to
dissolve in favor of globally more efficient structures. For example, assume that a
cluster of a dozen molecules approaches a small perfect crystal that already consists
of thousands of molecules. Then, with enough time, the cluster will dissolve and

---

[6] Note that we are talking about *minimization* now.

its molecules can attach to the crystal. Here is a more formal description of this process, which can be shown to hold for a reasonable model of the system: if cooling is sufficiently slow, the system reaches *thermal equilibrium* at every temperature. Equilibrium at temperature T means that a state x of the system with energy E_x is assumed with probability

$$\frac{\exp(-E_x/T)}{\sum_{y\in\mathscr{L}}\exp(-E_y/T)}$$

where T is the temperature of the system and $\mathscr{L}$ is the set of states of the system. This energy distribution is called the *Boltzmann distribution*. When T decreases, the probability of states with a minimal energy grows. Actually, in the limit $T \to 0$, the probability of states with a minimal energy approaches one.

The same mathematics works for abstract systems corresponding to a maximization problem. We identify the cost function f with the energy of the system, and a feasible solution with the state of the system. It can be shown that the system approaches a Boltzmann distribution for a quite general class of neighborhoods and the following rules for choosing the next state:

> pick x' from $\mathscr{N}(x)\cap\mathscr{L}$ uniformly at random
> with probability $\min(1,\exp((f(x') - f(x))/T))$ **do** $x := x'$.

The physical analogy gives some idea of why simulated annealing might work,[7] but it does not provide an implementable algorithm. We have to get rid of two infinities: for every temperature, we wait infinitely long to reach equilibrium, and do that for infinitely many temperatures. Simulated-annealing algorithms therefore have to decide on a *cooling schedule*, i.e., how the temperature T should be varied over time. A simple schedule chooses a starting temperature T_0 that is supposed to be just large enough so that all neighbors are accepted. Furthermore, for a given problem instance, there is a fixed number N of iterations to be used at each temperature. The idea is that N should be as small as possible but still allow the system to get close to equilibrium. After every N iterations, T is decreased by multiplying it by a constant α less than one. Typically, α is between 0.8 and 0.99. When T has become so small that moves to inferior solutions have become highly unlikely (this is the case when T is comparable to the smallest difference in objective value between any two feasible solutions), T is finally set to 0, i.e., the annealing process concludes with a hill-climbing search.

Better performance can be obtained with *dynamic schedules*. For example, the initial temperature can be determined by starting with a low temperature and increasing it quickly until the fraction of transitions accepted approaches one. Dynamic schedules base their decision about how much T should be lowered on the actually observed variation in $f(x)$ during the local search. If the temperature change is tiny compared with the variation, it has too little effect. If the change is too close to or even larger than the variation observed, there is a danger that the system will be prematurely forced into a local optimum. The number of steps to be made until the temperature is lowered can be made dependent on the actual number of moves

---

[7] Note that we have written "might work" and not "works".

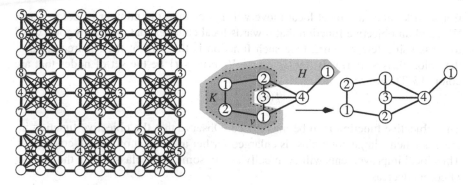

Fig. 12.11. The figure on the *left* shows a partial coloring of the graph underlying sudoku puzzles. The **bold** straight-line segments indicate cliques consisting of all nodes touched by the line. The figure on the *right* shows a step of Kempe chain annealing using colors 1 and 2 and a node v

accepted. Furthermore, one can use a simplified statistical model of the process to estimate when the system is approaching equilibrium. The details of dynamic schedules are beyond the scope of this exposition. Readers are referred to [1] for more details on simulated annealing.

Exercise 12.23. Design a simulated-annealing algorithm for the knapsack problem. The local neighborhood of a feasible solution is all solutions that can be obtained by removing up to two elements and then adding up to two elements.

Graph Coloring

We shall now exemplify simulated annealing on the *graph-coloring problem* already mentioned in Sect. 2.10. Recall that we are given an undirected graph $G = (V, E)$ and are looking for an assignment $c : V \to 1..k$ such that no two adjacent nodes are given the same color, i.e., $c(u) \neq c(v)$ for all edges $\{u, v\} \in E$. There is always a solution with $k = |V|$ colors; we simply give each node its own color. The goal is to minimize k. There are many applications of graph coloring and related problems. The most "classical" one is map coloring – the nodes are countries and edges indicate that these countries have a common border, and thus these countries should not be rendered in the same color. A famous theorem of graph theory states that all maps (i.e. planar graphs) can be colored with at most four colors [162]. Sudoku puzzles are a well-known instance of the graph-coloring problem, where the player is asked to complete a partial coloring of the graph shown in Fig. 12.11 with the digits 1..9. We shall present two simulated-annealing approaches to graph coloring; many more have been tried.

Kempe Chain Annealing

Of course, the obvious objective function for graph coloring is the number of colors used. However, this choice of objective function is too simplistic in a local-search framework, since a typical local move will not change the number of colors used. We need an objective function that rewards local changes that are "on a good way" towards using fewer colors. One such function is the sum of the squared sizes of the color classes. Formally, let $C_i = \{v \in V : c(v) = i\}$ be the set of nodes that are colored i. Then

$$f(c) = \sum_i |C_i|^2 .$$

This objective function is to be maximized. Observe that the objective function increases when a large color class is enlarged further at the cost of a small color class. Thus local improvements will eventually empty some color classes, i.e., the number of colors decreases.

Having settled the objective function, we come to the definition of a local change or a neighborhood. A trivial definition is as follows: a local change consists in recoloring a single vertex; it can be given any color not used on one of its neighbors. Kempe chain annealing uses a more liberal definition of "local recoloring". Alfred Bray Kempe (1849–1922) was one of the early investigators of the four-color problem; he invented Kempe chains in his futile attempts at a proof. Suppose that we want to change the color $c(v)$ of node v from i to j. In order to maintain feasibility, we have to change some other node colors too: node v might be connected to nodes currently colored j. So we color these nodes with color i. These nodes might, in turn, be connected to other nodes of color j, and so on. More formally, consider the node-induced subgraph H of G which contains all nodes with colors i and j. The connected component of H that contains v is the *Kempe chain* K we are interested in. We maintain feasibility by swapping colors i and j in K. Figure 12.11 gives an example. Kempe chain annealing starts with any feasible coloring.

*Exercise 12.24. Use Kempe chains to prove that any planar graph G can be colored with five colors. Hint: use the fact that a planar graph is guaranteed to have a node of degree five or less. Let v be any such node. Remove it from G, and color $G - v$ recursively. Put v back in. If at most four different colors are used on the neighbors of v, there is a free color for v. So assume otherwise. Assume, without loss of generality, that the neighbors of v are colored with colors 1 to 5 in clockwise order. Consider the subgraph of nodes colored 1 and 3. If the neighbors of v with colors 1 and 3 are in distinct connected components of this subgraph, a Kempe chain can be used to recolor the node colored 1 with color 3. If they are in the same component, consider the subgraph of nodes colored 2 and 4. Argue that the neighbors of v with colors 2 and 4 must be in distinct components of this subgraph.

The Penalty Function Approach

A generally useful idea for local search is to relax some of the constraints on feasible solutions in order to make the search more flexible and to ease the discovery of a starting solution. Observe that we have assumed so far that we somehow have a feasible solution available to us. However, in some situations, finding any feasible solution is already a hard problem; the eight-queens problem of Exercise 12.21 is an example. In order to obtain a feasible solution at the end of the process, the objective function is modified to penalize infeasible solutions. The constraints are effectively moved into the objective function.

In the graph-coloring example, we now also allow illegal colorings, i.e., colorings in which neighboring nodes may have the same color. An initial solution is generated by guessing the number of colors needed and coloring the nodes randomly. A neighbor of the current coloring c is generated by picking a random color j and a random node v colored j, i.e., $x(v) = j$. Then, a random new color for node v is chosen from all the colors already in use plus one fresh, previously unused color.

As above, let C_i be the set of nodes colored i and let $E_i = E \cap C_i \times C_i$ be the set of edges connecting two nodes in C_i. The objective is to minimize

$$f(c) = 2 \sum_i |C_i| \cdot |E_i| - \sum_i |C_i|^2 .$$

The first term penalizes illegal edges; each illegal edge connecting two nodes of color i contributes the size of the i-th color class. The second term favors large color classes, as we have already seen above. The objective function does not necessarily have its global minimum at an optimal coloring, however, local minima are legal colorings. Hence, the penalty version of simulated annealing is guaranteed to find a legal coloring even if it starts with an illegal coloring.

Exercise 12.25. Show that the objective function above has its local minima at legal colorings. Hint: consider the change in $f(c)$ if one end of a legally colored edge is recolored with a fresh color. Prove that the objective function above does not necessarily have its global optimum at a solution using the minimal number of colors.

Experimental Results

Johnson et al. [101] performed a detailed study of algorithms for graph coloring, with particular emphasis on simulated annealing. We shall briefly report on their findings and then draw some conclusions. Most of their experiments were performed on random graphs in the $G_{n,p}$-model or on random geometric graphs.

In the $G_{n,p}$-model, where p is a parameter in $[0,1]$, an undirected random graph with n nodes is built by adding each of the $n(n-1)/2$ candidate edges with probability p. The random choices for distinct edges are independent. In this way, the expected degree of every node is $p(n-1)$ and the expected number of edges is $pn(n-1)/2$. For random graphs with 1 000 nodes and edge probability 0.5, Kempe chain annealing produced very good colorings, given enough time. However, a sophisticated and expensive greedy algorithm, XRLF, produced even better solutions in less time. For very dense random graphs with $p = 0.9$, Kempe chain annealing performed better than XRLF. For sparser random graphs with edge probability 0.1, penalty function annealing outperformed Kempe chain annealing and could sometimes compete with XRLF.

Another interesting class of random inputs is *random geometric graphs*. Here, we choose n random, uniformly distributed points in the unit square $[0,1] \times [0,1]$. These points represent the nodes of the graph. We connect two points by an edge if their Euclidean distance is less than or equal to some given range r. Figure 12.12

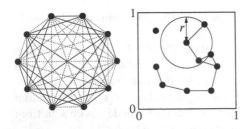

Fig. 12.12. *Left*: a random graph with 10 nodes and $p = 0.5$. The edges chosen are drawn solid, and the edges rejected are drawn dashed. *Right*: a random geometric graph with 10 nodes and range $r = 0.27$

gives an example. Such instances are frequently used to model situations where the nodes represent radio transmitters and colors represent frequency bands. Nodes that lie within a distance r from one another must not use the same frequency, to avoid interference. For this model, Kempe chain annealing performed well, but was out-performed by a third annealing strategy, called *fixed-K annealing*.

What should we learn from this? The relative performance of the simulated-annealing approaches depends strongly on the class of inputs and the available computing time. Moreover, it is impossible to make predictions about their performance on any given instance class on the basis of experience from other instance classes. So be warned. Simulated annealing is a heuristic and, as for any other heuristic, you should not make claims about its performance on an instance class before you have tested it extensively on that class.

12.5.3 More on Local Search

We close our treatment of local search with a discussion of three refinements that can be used to modify or replace the approaches presented so far.

Threshold Acceptance

There seems to be nothing magic about the particular form of the acceptance rule used in simulated annealing. For example, a simpler yet also successful rule uses the parameter T as a threshold. New states with a value $f(x)$ below the threshold are accepted, whereas others are not.

Tabu Lists

Local-search algorithms sometimes return to the same suboptimal solution again and again – they cycle. For example, simulated annealing might have reached the top of a steep hill. Randomization will steer the search away from the optimum, but the state may remain on the hill for a long time. *Tabu search* steers the search away from local optima by keeping a *tabu list* of "solution elements" that should be "avoided" in new solutions for the time being. For example, in graph coloring, a search step could change the color of a node v from i to j and then store the tuple (v, i) in the tabu list to indicate that color i is forbidden for v as long as (v, i) is in the tabu list. Usually, this tabu condition is not applied if an improved solution is obtained by coloring node v

with color i. Tabu lists are so successful that they can be used as the core technique of an independent variant of local search called *tabu search*.

Restarts

The typical behavior of a well-tuned local-search algorithm is that it moves to an area with good feasible solutions and then explores this area, trying to find better and better local optima. However, it might be that there are other, far away areas with much better solutions. The search for Mount Everest illustrates this point. If we start in Australia, the best we can hope for is to end up at Mount Kosciusko (altitude 2229 m), a solution far from optimum. It therefore makes sense to run the algorithm multiple times with different random starting solutions because it is likely that different starting points will explore different areas of good solutions. Starting the search for Mount Everest at multiple locations and in all continents will certainly lead to a better solution than just starting in Australia. Even if these restarts do not improve the average performance of the algorithm, they may make it more robust in the sense that it will be less likely to produce grossly suboptimal solutions. Several independent runs are also an easy source of parallelism: just run the program on several different workstations concurrently.

12.6 Evolutionary Algorithms

Living beings are ingeniously adaptive to their environment, and master the problems encountered in daily life with great ease. Can we somehow use the principles of life for developing good algorithms? The theory of evolution tells us that the mechanisms leading to this performance are *mutation, recombination,* and *survival of the fittest*. What could an evolutionary approach mean for optimization problems?

The genome describing an individual corresponds to the description of a feasible solution. We can also interpret infeasible solutions as dead or ill individuals. In nature, it is important that there is a sufficiently large *population* of genomes; otherwise, recombination deteriorates to incest, and survival of the fittest cannot demonstrate its benefits. So, instead of one solution as in local search, we now work with a pool of feasible solutions.

The individuals in a population produce offspring. Because resources are limited, individuals better adapted to the environment are more likely to survive and to produce more offspring. In analogy, feasible solutions are evaluated using a fitness function f, and fitter solutions are more likely to survive and to produce offspring. Evolutionary algorithms usually work with a solution pool of limited size, say N. Survival of the fittest can then be implemented as keeping only the N best solutions.

Even in bacteria, which reproduce by cell division, no offspring is identical to its parent. The reason is *mutation*. When a genome is copied, small errors happen. Although mutations usually have an adverse effect on fitness, some also improve fitness. Local changes in a solution are the analogy of mutations.

Create an initial population $population = \{x^1, \ldots, x^N\}$
while not finished **do**
    if matingStep **then**
        select individuals x^1, x^2 with high fitness and produce $x' := mate(x^1, x^2)$
        else select an individual x^1 with high fitness and produce $x' = mutate(x^1)$
        $population := population \cup \{x'\}$
        $population := \{x \in population : x \text{ is sufficiently fit}\}$

Fig. 12.13. A generic evolutionary algorithm

An even more important ingredient in evolution is *recombination*. Offspring contain genetic information from both parents. The importance of recombination is easy to understand if one considers how rare useful mutations are. Therefore it takes much longer to obtain an individual with two new useful mutations than it takes to combine two individuals with two different useful mutations.

We now have all the ingredients needed for a generic evolutionary algorithm; see Fig. 12.13. As with the other approaches presented in this chapter, many details need to be filled in before one can obtain an algorithm for a specific problem. The algorithm starts by creating an initial population of size N. This process should involve randomness, but it is also useful to use heuristics that produce good initial solutions.

In the loop, it is first decided whether an offspring should be produced by mutation or by recombination. This is a probabilistic decision. Then, one or two individuals are chosen for reproduction. To put selection pressure on the population, it is important to base reproductive success on the fitness of the individuals. However, it is usually not desirable to draw a hard line and use only the fittest individuals, because this might lead to too uniform a population and incest. For example, one can instead choose reproduction candidates randomly, giving a higher selection probability to fitter individuals. An important design decision is how to fix these probabilities. One choice is to sort the individuals by fitness and then to define the reproduction probability as some decreasing function of rank. This indirect approach has the advantage that it is independent of the objective function f and the absolute fitness differences between individuals, which are likely to decrease during the course of evolution.

The most critical operation is *mate*, which produces new offspring from two ancestors. The "canonical" mating operation is called *crossover*. Here, individuals are assumed to be represented by a string of n bits. An integer k is chosen. The new individual takes its first k bits from one parent and its last $n - k$ bits from the other parent. Figure 12.14 shows this procedure. Alternatively, one may choose k random positions from the first parent and the remaining bits from the other parent. For our knapsack example, crossover is a quite natural choice. Each bit decides whether the corresponding item is in the knapsack or not. In other cases, crossover is less natural or would require a very careful encoding. For example, for graph coloring, it would seem more natural to cut the graph into two pieces such that only a few edges are cut. Now one piece inherits its colors from the first parent, and the other piece inherits its colors from the other parent. Some of the edges running between the pieces might

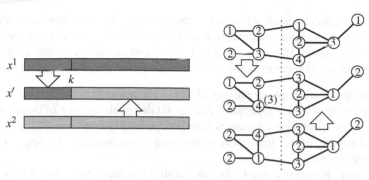

Fig. 12.14. Mating using crossover (*left*) and by stitching together pieces of a graph coloring (*right*)

now connect nodes with the same color. This could be repaired using some heuristics, for example choosing the smallest legal color for miscolored nodes in the part corresponding to the first parent. Figure 12.14 gives an example.

Mutations are realized as in local search. In fact, local search is nothing but an evolutionary algorithm with population size one.

The simplest way to limit the size of the population is to keep it fixed by removing the least fit individual in each iteration. Other approaches that provide room for different "ecological niches" can also be used. For example, for the knapsack problem, one could keep all Pareto-optimal solutions. The evolutionary algorithm would then resemble the optimized dynamic-programming algorithm.

12.7 Implementation Notes

We have seen several generic approaches to optimization that are applicable to a wide variety of problems. When you face a new application, you are therefore likely to have a choice from among more approaches than you can realistically implement. In a commercial environment, you may even have to home in on a single approach quickly. Here are some rules of thumb that may help.

- Study the problem, relate it to problems you are familiar with, and search for it on the Web.
- Look for approaches that have worked on related problems.
- Consider blackbox solvers.
- If the problem instances are small, systematic search or dynamic programming may allow you to find optimal solutions.
- If none of the above looks promising, implement a simple prototype solver using a greedy approach or some other simple, fast heuristic; the prototype will help you to understand the problem and might be useful as a component of a more sophisticated algorithm.

- Develop a local-search algorithm. Focus on a good representation of solutions and how to incorporate application-specific knowledge into the searcher. If you have a promising idea for a mating operator, you can also consider evolutionary algorithms. Use randomization and restarts to make the results more robust.

There are many implementations of linear-programming solvers. Since a good implementation is *very* complicated, you should definitely use one of these packages except in very special circumstances. The Wikipedia page on "linear programming" is a good starting point. Some systems for linear programming also support integer linear programming.

There are also many frameworks that simplify the implementation of local-search or evolutionary algorithms. Since these algorithms are fairly simple, the use of these frameworks is not as widespread as for linear programming. Nevertheless, the implementations available might have nontrivial built-in algorithms for dynamic setting of search parameters, and they might support parallel processing. The Wikipedia page on "evolutionary algorithm" contains pointers.

12.8 Historical Notes and Further Findings

We have only scratched the surface of (integer) linear programming. Implementing solvers, clever modeling of problems, and handling huge input instances have led to thousands of scientific papers. In the late 1940s, Dantzig invented the simplex algorithm [45]. Although this algorithm works well in practice, some of its variants take exponential time in the worst case. It is a famous open problem whether some variant runs in polynomial time in the worst case. It is known, though, that even slightly perturbing the coefficients of the constraints leads to polynomial expected execution time [184]. Sometimes, even problem instances with an exponential number of constraints or variables can be solved efficiently. The trick is to handle explicitly only those constraints that may be violated and those variables that may be nonzero in an optimal solution. This works if we can efficiently find violated constraints or possibly nonzero variables and if the total number of constraints and variables generated remains small. Khachiyan [110] and Karmakar [106] found polynomial-time algorithms for linear programming. There are many good textbooks on linear programming (e.g. [23, 58, 73, 147, 172, 199]).

Another interesting blackbox solver is *constraint programming* [90, 121]. We hinted at the technique in Exercise 12.21. Here, we are again dealing with variables and constraints. However, now the variables come from discrete sets (usually small finite sets). Constraints come in a much wider variety. There are equalities and inequalities, possibly involving arithmetic expressions, but also higher-level constraints. For example, *allDifferent*$(x_1, \ldots, x_k)$ requires that $x_1, \ldots, x_k$ all receive different values. Constraint programs are solved using a cleverly pruned systematic search. Constraint programming is more flexible than linear programming, but restricted to smaller problem instances. Wikipedia is a good starting point for learning more about constraint programming.

A

Appendix

A.1 Mathematical Symbols

$\{e_0, \ldots, e_{n-1}\}$: set containing elements $e_0, \ldots, e_{n-1}$.

$\{e : P(e)\}$: set of all elements that fulfill the predicate P.

$\langle e_0, \ldots, e_{n-1}\rangle$: sequence consisting of elements $e_0, \ldots, e_{n-1}$.

$\langle e \in S : P(e)\rangle$: subsequence of all elements of sequence S that fulfill the predicate P.

$|x|$: the absolute value of x.

$\lfloor x \rfloor$: the largest integer $\leq x$.

$\lceil x \rceil$: the smallest integer $\geq x$.

$[a,b] := \{x \in \mathbb{R} : a \leq x \leq b\}$.

$i..j$: abbreviation for $\{i, i+1, \ldots, j\}$.

A^B: when A and B are sets, this is the set of all functions that map B to A.

$A \times B$: the set of pairs (a,b) with $a \in A$ and $b \in B$.

$\perp$: an undefined value.

$(-)\infty$: (minus) infinity.

$\forall x : P(x)$: for *all* values of x, the proposition $P(x)$ is true.

$\exists x : P(x)$: there *exists* a value of x such that the proposition $P(x)$ is true.

$\mathbb{N}$: nonnegative integers; $\mathbb{N} = \{0, 1, 2, \ldots\}$.

$\mathbb{N}_+$: positive integers; $\mathbb{N}_+ = \{1, 2, \ldots\}$.

$\mathbb{Z}$: integers.

$\mathbb{R}$: real numbers.

$\mathbb{Q}$: rational numbers.

$|$, $\&$, $\ll$, $\gg$, $\oplus$: bitwise OR, bitwise AND, leftshift, rightshift, and exclusive OR respectively.

$\sum_{i=1}^{n} a_i = \sum_{1 \leq i \leq n} a_i = \sum_{i \in \{1,\dots,n\}} a_i := a_1 + a_2 + \cdots + a_n$.

$\prod_{i=1}^{n} a_i = \prod_{1 \leq i \leq n} a_i = \prod_{i \in \{1,\dots,n\}} a_i := a_1 \cdot a_2 \cdots a_n$.

$n! := \prod_{i=1}^{n} i$, the *factorial* of n.

$H_n := \sum_{i=1}^{n} 1/i$, the n-th *harmonic number* (Equation (A.12)).

$\log x$: The logarithm to base two of x, $\log_2 x$.

$\mu(s,t)$: the shortest-path distance from s to t; $\mu(t) := \mu(s,t)$.

div: integer division; $m \operatorname{div} n := \lfloor m/n \rfloor$.

mod: modular arithmetic; $m \bmod n = m - n(m \operatorname{div} n)$.

$a \equiv b (\bmod m)$: a and b are congruent modulo m, i.e., $a + im = b$ for some integer i.

$\prec$: some ordering relation. In Sect. 9.2, it denotes the order in which nodes are marked during depth-first search.

1, 0: the boolean values "true" and "false".

A.2 Mathematical Concepts

antisymmetric: a relation $\sim$ is *antisymmetric* if for all a and b, $a \sim b$ and $b \sim a$ implies $a = b$.

asymptotic notation:

$$O(f(n)) := \{g(n) : \exists c > 0 : \exists n_0 \in \mathbb{N}_+ : \forall n \geq n_0 : g(n) \leq c \cdot f(n)\}.$$
$$\Omega(f(n)) := \{g(n) : \exists c > 0 : \exists n_0 \in \mathbb{N}_+ : \forall n \geq n_0 : g(n) \geq c \cdot f(n)\}.$$
$$\Theta(f(n)) := O(f(n)) \cap \Omega(f(n)).$$
$$o(f(n)) := \{g(n) : \forall c > 0 : \exists n_0 \in \mathbb{N}_+ : \forall n \geq n_0 : g(n) \leq c \cdot f(n)\}.$$
$$\omega(f(n)) := \{g(n) : \forall c > 0 : \exists n_0 \in \mathbb{N}_+ : \forall n \geq n_0 : g(n) \geq c \cdot f(n)\}.$$

See also Sect. 2.1.

concave: a function f is concave on an interval $[a,b]$ if

$$\forall x,y \in [a,b] : \forall t \in [0,1] : f(tx+(1-t)y) \geq tf(x)+(1-t)f(y).$$

convex: a function f is convex on an interval $[a,b]$ if

$$\forall x,y \in [a,b] : \forall t \in [0,1] : f(tx+(1-t)y) \leq tf(x)+(1-t)f(y).$$

equivalence relation: a transitive, reflexive, symmetric relation.

field: a set of elements that support addition, subtraction, multiplication, and division by nonzero elements. Addition and multiplication are associative and commutative, and have neutral elements analogous to zero and one for the real numbers. The prime examples are $\mathbb{R}$, the real numbers; $\mathbb{Q}$, the rational numbers; and $\mathbb{Z}_p$, the integers modulo a prime p.

iff: abbreviation for "if and only if".

lexicographic order: the canonical way of extending a total order on a set of elements to tuples, strings, or sequences over that set. We have $\langle a_1, a_2, \ldots, a_k \rangle < \langle b_1, b_2, \ldots, b_k \rangle$ if and only if $a_1 < b_1$ or $a_1 = b_1$ and $\langle a_2, \ldots, a_k \rangle < \langle b_2, \ldots, b_k \rangle$.

linear order: a reflexive, transitive, weakly antisymmetric relation.

median: an element with rank $\lceil n/2 \rceil$ among n elements.

multiplicative inverse: if an object x is multiplied by a *multiplicative inverse x^{-1}* of x, we obtain $x \cdot x^{-1} = 1$ – the neutral element of multiplication. In particular, in a *field*, every element except zero (the neutral element of addition) has a unique multiplicative inverse.

prime number: an integer n, $n \geq 2$, is a prime iff there are no integers $a, b > 1$ such that $n = a \cdot b$.

rank: a one-to-one mapping $r : S \rightarrow 1..n$ is a ranking function for the elements of a set $S = \{e_1, \ldots, e_n\}$ if $r(x) < r(y)$ whenever $x < y$.

reflexive: a relation $\sim \subseteq A \times A$ is reflexive if $\forall a \in A : (a,a) \in R$.

relation: a set of pairs R. Often, we write relations as operators; for example, if $\sim$ is a relation, $a \sim b$ means $(a,b) \in \sim$.

symmetric relation: a relation $\sim$ is *symmetric* if for all a and b, $a \sim b$ implies $b \sim a$.

total order: a reflexive, transitive, antisymmetric relation.

transitive: a relation $\sim$ is *transitive* if for all a, b, c, $a \sim b$ and $b \sim c$ imply $a \sim c$.

weakly antisymmetric: a relation $\leq$ is *weakly antisymmetric* if for all a, b, $a \leq b$ or $b \leq a$. If $a \leq b$ and $b \leq a$, we write $a \equiv b$. Otherwise, we write $a < b$ or $b < a$.

A.3 Basic Probability Theory

Probability theory rests on the concept of a *sample space* $\mathscr{S}$. For example, to describe the rolls of two dice, we would use the 36-element sample space $\{1,\ldots,6\} \times \{1,\ldots,6\}$, i.e., the elements of the sample space are the pairs (x,y) with $1 \leq x,y \leq 6$ and $x,y \in \mathbb{N}$. Generally, a sample space is any set. In this book, all sample spaces are finite. In a *random experiment*, any element of $s \in \mathscr{S}$ is chosen with some elementary *probability* p_s, where $\sum_{s \in \mathscr{S}} p_s = 1$. A sample space together with a probability distribution is called a *probability space*. In this book, we use *uniform probabilities* almost exclusively; in this case $p_s = p = 1/|\mathscr{S}|$. Subsets $\mathscr{E}$ of the sample space are called *events*. The probability of an *event* $\mathscr{E} \subseteq \mathscr{S}$ is the sum of the probabilities of its elements, i.e., $\mathrm{prob}(\mathscr{E}) = |\mathscr{E}|/|\mathscr{S}|$ in the uniform case. So the probability of the event $\{(x,y) : x+y = 7\} = \{(1,6),(2,5),\ldots,(6,1)\}$ is equal to $6/36 = 1/6$, and the probability of the event $\{(x,y) : x+y \geq 8\}$ is equal to $15/36 = 5/12$.

A *random variable* is a mapping from the sample space to the real numbers. Random variables are usually denoted by capital letters to distinguish them from plain values. For example, the random variable X could give the number shown by the first die, the random variable Y could give the number shown by the second die, and the random variable S could give the sum of the two numbers. Formally, if $(x,y) \in \mathscr{S}$, then $X((x,y)) = x$, $Y((x,y)) = y$, and $S((x,y)) = x+y = X((x,y)) + Y((x,y))$.

We can define new random variables as expressions involving other random variables and ordinary values. For example, if V and W are random variables, then $(V+W)(s) = V(s) + W(s)$, $(V \cdot W)(s) = V(s) \cdot W(s)$, and $(V+3)(s) = V(s) + 3$.

Events are often specified by predicates involving random variables. For example, $X \leq 2$ denotes the event $\{(1,y),(2,y) : 1 \leq y \leq 6\}$, and hence $\mathrm{prob}(X \leq 2) = 1/3$. Similarly, $\mathrm{prob}(X+Y = 11) = \mathrm{prob}(\{(5,6),(6,5)\}) = 1/18$.

Indicator random variables are random variables that take only the values zero and one. Indicator variables are an extremely useful tool for the probabilistic analysis of algorithms because they allow us to encode the behavior of complex algorithms into simple mathematical objects. We frequently use the letters I and J for indicator variables.

The *expected value* of a random variable $Z : \mathscr{S} \to \mathbb{R}$ is

$$E[Z] = \sum_{s \in \mathscr{S}} p_s \cdot Z(s) = \sum_{z \in \mathbb{R}} z \cdot \mathrm{prob}(Z = z) , \qquad (A.1)$$

i.e., every sample s contributes the value of Z at s times its probability. Alternatively, we can group all s with $Z(s) = z$ into the event $Z = z$ and then sum over the $z \in \mathbb{R}$.

In our example, $E[X] = (1+2+3+4+5+6)/6 = 21/6 = 3.5$, i.e., the expected value of the first die is 3.5. Of course, the expected value of the second die is also 3.5. For an indicator random variable I, we have

$$E[I] = 0 \cdot \mathrm{prob}(I = 0) + 1 \cdot \mathrm{prob}(I = 1) = \mathrm{prob}(I = 1) .$$

Often, we are interested in the expectation of a random variable that is defined in terms of other random variables. This is easy for sums owing to the *linearity of expectations* of random variables: for any two random variables V and W,

$$E[V + W] = E[V] + E[W] .$$ (A.2)

This equation is easy to prove and extremely useful. Let us prove it. It amounts essentially to an application of the distributive law of arithmetic. We have

$$E[V + W] = \sum_{s \in \mathscr{S}} p_s \cdot (V(s) + W(s))$$
$$= \sum_{s \in \mathscr{S}} p_s \cdot V(s) + \sum_{s \in \mathscr{S}} p_s \cdot W(s)$$
$$= E[V] + E[W] .$$

As our first application, let us compute the expected sum of two dice. We have

$$E[S] = E[X + Y] = E[X] + E[Y] = 3.5 + 3.5 = 7 .$$

Observe that we obtain the result with almost no computation. Without knowing about the linearity of expectations, we would have to go through a tedious calculation:

$$E[S] = 2 \cdot \tfrac{1}{36} + 3 \cdot \tfrac{2}{36} + 4 \cdot \tfrac{3}{36} + 5 \cdot \tfrac{4}{36} + 6 \cdot \tfrac{5}{36} + 7 \cdot \tfrac{6}{36} + 8 \cdot \tfrac{5}{36} + 9 \cdot \tfrac{4}{36} + \ldots + 12 \cdot \tfrac{1}{36}$$
$$= \frac{2 \cdot 1 + 3 \cdot 2 + 4 \cdot 3 + 5 \cdot 4 + 6 \cdot 5 + 7 \cdot 6 + 8 \cdot 5 + \ldots + 12 \cdot 1}{36} = 7 .$$

Exercise A.1. What is the expected sum of three dice?

We shall now give another example with a more complex sample space. We consider the experiment of throwing n balls into m bins. The balls are thrown at random and distinct balls do not influence each other. Formally, our sample space is the set of all functions f from $1..n$ to $1..m$. This sample space has size m^n, and $f(i)$, $1 \le i \le n$, indicates the bin into which the ball i is thrown. All elements of the sample space are equally likely. How many balls should we expect in bin 1? We use I to denote the number of balls in bin 1. To determine $E[I]$, we introduce indicator variables I_i, $1 \le i \le n$. The variable I_i is 1, if ball i is thrown into bin 1, and is 0 otherwise. Formally, $I_i(f) = 0$ iff $f(i) \ne 1$. Then $I = \sum_i I_i$. We have

$$E[I] = E[\sum_i I_i] = \sum_i E[I_i] = \sum_i \text{prob}(I_i = 1) ,$$

where the first equality is the linearity of expectations and the second equality follows from the I_i's being indicator variables. It remains to determine the probability that $I_i = 1$. Since the balls are thrown at random, ball i ends up in any bin[1] with the same probability. Thus $\text{prob}(I_i = 1) = 1/m$, and hence

$$E[I] = \sum_i \text{prob}(I_i = 1) = \sum_i \frac{1}{m} = \frac{n}{m} .$$

---

[1] Formally, there are exactly m^{n-1} functions f with $f(i) = 1$.

Products of random variables behave differently. In general, we have $E[X \cdot Y] \neq E[X] \cdot E[Y]$. There is one important exception: if X and Y are *independent*, equality holds. Random variables $X_1, \ldots, X_k$ are independent if and only if

$$\forall x_1, \ldots, x_k : \text{prob}(X_1 = x_1 \wedge \cdots \wedge X_k = x_k) = \prod_{1 \leq i \leq k} \text{prob}(X_i = x_i) . \quad \text{(A.3)}$$

As an example, when we roll two dice, the value of the first die and the value of the second die are independent random variables. However, the value of the first die and the sum of the two dice are not independent random variables.

Exercise A.2. Let I and J be independent indicator variables and let $X = (I + J) \mod 2$, i.e., X is one iff I and J are different. Show that I and X are independent, but that I, J, and X are dependent.

Assume now that X and Y are independent. Then

$$E[X] \cdot E[Y] = \left(\sum_x x \cdot \text{prob}(X = x) \right) \cdot \left(\sum_y y \cdot \text{prob}(X = y) \right)$$
$$= \sum_{x,y} x \cdot y \cdot \text{prob}(X = x) \cdot \text{prob}(X = y)$$
$$= \sum_{x,y} x \cdot y \cdot \text{prob}(X = x \wedge Y = y)$$
$$= \sum_z \sum_{x,y \text{ with } z = x \cdot y} z \cdot \text{prob}(X = x \wedge Y = y)$$
$$= \sum_z z \cdot \sum_{x,y \text{ with } z = x \cdot y} \text{prob}(X = x \wedge Y = y)$$
$$= \sum_z z \cdot \text{prob}(X \cdot Y = z)$$
$$= E[X \cdot Y] .$$

How likely is it that a random variable will deviate substantially from its expected value? *Markov's inequality* gives a useful bound. Let X be a nonnegative random variable and let c be any constant. Then

$$\text{prob}(X \geq c \cdot E[X]) \leq \frac{1}{c} . \quad \text{(A.4)}$$

The proof is simple. We have

$$E[X] = \sum_{z \in \mathbb{R}} z \cdot \text{prob}(X = z)$$
$$\geq \sum_{z \geq c \cdot E[X]} z \cdot \text{prob}(X = z)$$
$$\geq c \cdot E[X] \cdot \text{prob}(X \geq c \cdot E[X]) ,$$

where the first inequality follows from the fact that we sum over a subset of the possible values and X is nonnegative, and the second inequality follows from the fact that the sum in the second line ranges only over z such that $z \geq cE[X]$.

Much tighter bounds are possible for some special cases of random variables. The following situation arises several times, in the book. We have a sum $X = X_1 + \cdots + X_n$ of n independent indicator random variables $X_1, \ldots, X_n$ and want to bound the probability that X deviates substantially from its expected value. In this situation, the following variant of the *Chernoff bound* is useful. For any $\varepsilon > 0$, we have

$$\text{prob}(X < (1 - \varepsilon)E[X]) \leq e^{-\varepsilon^2 E[X]/2} , \tag{A.5}$$

$$\text{prob}(X > (1 + \varepsilon)E[X]) \leq \left(\frac{e^\varepsilon}{(1+\varepsilon)^{(1+\varepsilon)}} \right)^{E[X]} . \tag{A.6}$$

A bound of the form above is called a *tail bound* because it estimates the "tail" of the probability distribution, i.e., the part for which X deviates considerably from its expected value.

Let us see an example. If we throw n coins and let X_i be the indicator variable for the i-th coin coming up heads, $X = X_1 + \cdots + X_n$ is the total number of heads. Clearly, $E[X] = n/2$. The bound above tells us that $\text{prob}(X \leq (1 - \varepsilon)n/2) \leq e^{-\varepsilon^2 n/4}$. In particular, for $\varepsilon = 0.1$, we have $\text{prob}(X \leq 0.9 \cdot n/2) \leq e^{-0.01 \cdot n/4}$. So, for $n = 10\,000$, the expected number of heads is $5\,000$ and the probability that the sum is less than $4\,500$ is smaller than e^{-25}, a very small number.

Exercise A.3. Estimate the probability that X in the above example is larger than $5\,050$.

If the indicator random variables are independent and identically distributed with $\text{prob}(X_i = 1) = p$, X is *binomially distributed*, i.e.,

$$\text{prob}(X = k) = \binom{n}{k} p^k (1 - p)^{(n-k)} . \tag{A.7}$$

Exercise A.4 (balls and bins continued). Let, as above, I denote the number of balls in bin 1. Show

$$\text{prob}(I = k) = \binom{n}{k} \left(\frac{1}{m} \right)^k \left(1 - \frac{1}{m} \right)^{(n-k)} ,$$

and then attempt to compute $E[I]$ as $\sum_k \text{prob}(I = k)k$.

A.4 Useful Formulae

We shall first list some useful formulae and then prove some of them.

- A simple approximation to the factorial:

$$\left(\frac{n}{e}\right)^n \leq n! \leq n^n. \tag{A.8}$$

- Stirling's approximation to the factorial:

$$n! = \left(1 + O\left(\frac{1}{n}\right)\right) \sqrt{2\pi n} \left(\frac{n}{e}\right)^n. \tag{A.9}$$

- An approximation to the binomial coefficients:

$$\binom{n}{k} \leq \left(\frac{n \cdot e}{k}\right)^k. \tag{A.10}$$

- The sum of the first n integers:

$$\sum_{i=1}^{n} i = \frac{n(n+1)}{2}. \tag{A.11}$$

- The harmonic numbers:

$$\ln n \leq H_n = \sum_{i=1}^{n} \frac{1}{i} \leq \ln n + 1. \tag{A.12}$$

- The geometric series:

$$\sum_{i=0}^{n-1} q^i = \frac{1-q^n}{1-q} \quad \text{for } q \neq 1 \text{ and } \quad \sum_{i\geq 0} q^i = \frac{1}{1-q} \quad \text{for } 0 \leq q < 1. \tag{A.13}$$

$$\sum_{i\geq 0} 2^{-i} = 2 \quad \text{and} \quad \sum_{i\geq 0} i \cdot 2^{-i} = \sum_{i\geq 1} i \cdot 2^{-i} = 2. \tag{A.14}$$

- Jensen's inequality:

$$\sum_{i=1}^{n} f(x_i) \leq n \cdot f\left(\frac{\sum_{i=1}^{n} x_i}{n}\right) \tag{A.15}$$

for any concave function f. Similarly, for any convex function f,

$$\sum_{i=1}^{n} f(x_i) \geq n \cdot f\left(\frac{\sum_{i=1}^{n} x_i}{n}\right). \tag{A.16}$$

A.4.1 Proofs

For (A.8), we first observe that $n! = n(n-1)\cdots 1 \leq n^n$. Also, for all $i \geq 2$, $\ln i \geq \int_{i-1}^{i} \ln x\, dx$, and therefore

$$\ln n! = \sum_{2 \leq i \leq n} \ln i \geq \int_1^n \ln x\, dx = \Big[x(\ln x - 1) \Big]_{x=1}^{x=n} \geq n(\ln n - 1) \,.$$

Thus

$$n! \geq e^{n(\ln n - 1)} = (e^{\ln n - 1})^n = \left(\frac{n}{e} \right)^n \,.$$

Equation (A.10) follows almost immediately from (A.8). We have

$$\binom{n}{k} = \frac{n(n-1)\cdots(n-k+1)}{k!} \leq \frac{n^k}{(k/e)^k} = \left(\frac{n \cdot e}{k} \right)^k \,.$$

Equation (A.11) can be computed by a simple trick:

$$1 + 2 + \ldots + n = \frac{1}{2} \big((1 + 2 + \ldots + n - 1 + n) + (n + n - 1 + \ldots + 2 + 1) \big)$$

$$= \frac{1}{2} \big((n+1) + (2 + n - 1) + \ldots + (n - 1 + 2) + (n+1) \big)$$

$$= \frac{n(n+1)}{2} \,.$$

The sums of higher powers are estimated easily; exact summation formulae are also available. For example, $\int_{i-1}^{i} x^2\, dx \leq i^2 \leq \int_{i}^{i+1} x^2\, dx$, and hence

$$\sum_{1 \leq i \leq n} i^2 \leq \int_1^{n+1} x^2\, dx = \left[\frac{x^3}{3} \right]_{x=1}^{x=n+1} = \frac{(n+1)^3 - 1}{3}$$

and

$$\sum_{1 \leq i \leq n} i^2 \geq \int_0^n x^2\, dx = \left[\frac{x^3}{3} \right]_{x=0}^{x=n} = \frac{n^3}{3} \,.$$

For (A.12), we also use estimation by integral. We have $\int_{i}^{i+1} (1/x)\, dx \leq 1/i \leq \int_{i-1}^{i} (1/x)\, dx$, and hence

$$\ln n = \int_1^n \frac{1}{x}\, dx \leq \sum_{1 \leq i \leq n} \frac{1}{i} \leq 1 + \int_1^n \frac{1}{x}\, dx = 1 + \ln n \,.$$

Equation (A.13) follows from

$$(1 - q) \cdot \sum_{0 \leq i \leq n-1} q^i = \sum_{0 \leq i \leq n-1} q^i - \sum_{1 \leq i \leq n} q^i = 1 - q^n \,.$$

Letting n pass to infinity yields $\sum_{i\geq 0} q^i = 1/(1-q)$ for $0 \leq q < 1$. For $q = 1/2$, we obtain $\sum_{i\geq 0} 2^{-i} = 2$. Also,

$$\sum_{i\geq 1} i \cdot 2^{-i} = \sum_{i\geq 1} 2^{-i} + \sum_{i\geq 2} 2^{-i} + \sum_{i\geq 3} 2^{-i} + \ldots$$

$$= (1 + 1/2 + 1/4 + 1/8 + \ldots) \cdot \sum_{i\geq 1} 2^{-i}$$

$$= 2 \cdot 1 = 2 .$$

For the first equality, observe that the term 2^{-i} occurs in exactly the first i sums of the right-hand side.

Equation (A.15) can be shown by induction on n. For $n = 1$, there is nothing to show. So assume $n \geq 2$. Let $x^* = \sum_{1\leq i\leq n} x_i/n$ and $\bar{x} = \sum_{1\leq i\leq n-1} x_i/(n-1)$. Then $x^* = ((n-1)\bar{x} + x_n)/n$, and hence

$$\sum_{1\leq i\leq n} f(x_i) = f(x_n) + \sum_{1\leq i\leq n-1} f(x_i)$$

$$\leq f(x_n) + (n-1) \cdot f(\bar{x}) = n \cdot \left(\frac{1}{n} \cdot f(x_n) + \frac{n-1}{n} \cdot f(\bar{x}) \right)$$

$$\leq n \cdot f(x^*) ,$$

where the first inequality uses the induction hypothesis and the second inequality uses the definition of concavity with $x = x_n$, $y = \bar{x}$, and $t = 1/n$. The extension to convex functions is immediate, since convexity of f implies concavity of $-f$.

References

[1] E. H. L. Aarts and J. Korst. *Simulated Annealing and Boltzmann Machines.* Wiley, 1989.

[2] J. Abello, A. Buchsbaum, and J. Westbrook. A functional approach to external graph algorithms. *Algorithmica*, 32(3):437–458, 2002.

[3] W. Ackermann. Zum hilbertschen Aufbau der reellen Zahlen. *Mathematische Annalen*, 99:118–133, 1928.

[4] G. M. Adel'son-Vel'skii and E. M. Landis. An algorithm for the organization of information. *Soviet Mathematics Doklady*, 3:1259–1263, 1962.

[5] A. Aggarwal and J. S. Vitter. The input/output complexity of sorting and related problems. *Communications of the ACM*, 31(9):1116–1127, 1988.

[6] A. V. Aho, J. E. Hopcroft, and J. D. Ullman. *The Design and Analysis of Computer Algorithms.* Addison-Wesley, 1974.

[7] A. V. Aho, B. W. Kernighan, and P. J. Weinberger. *The AWK Programming Language.* Addison-Wesley, 1988.

[8] R. K. Ahuja, R. L. Magnanti, and J. B. Orlin. *Network Flows.* Prentice Hall, 1993.

[9] R. K. Ahuja, K. Mehlhorn, J. B. Orlin, and R. E. Tarjan. Faster algorithms for the shortest path problem. *Journal of the ACM*, 3(2):213–223, 1990.

[10] N. Alon, M. Dietzfelbinger, P. B. Miltersen, E. Petrank, and E. Tardos. Linear hash functions. *Journal of the ACM*, 46(5):667–683, 1999.

[11] A. Andersson, T. Hagerup, S. Nilsson, and R. Raman Sorting in linear time? *Journal of Computer and System Sciences*, 57(1):74–93, 1998.

[12] F. Annexstein, M. Baumslag, and A. Rosenberg. Group action graphs and parallel architectures. *SIAM Journal on Computing*, 19(3):544–569, 1990.

[13] D. L. Applegate, R. E. Bixby, V. Chvátal, and W. J. Cook. *The Traveling Salesman Problem: A Computational Study.* Princeton University Press, 2007.

[14] G. Ausiello, P. Crescenzi, G. Gambosi, V. Kann, A. Murchetti-Spaccamela, and M. Protasi. *Complexity and Approximation: Combinatorial Optimization Problems and Their Approximability Properties.* Springer, 1999.

[15] H. Bast, S. Funke, P. Sanders, and D. Schultes. Fast routing in road networks with transit nodes. *Science*, 316(5824):566, 2007.

[16] R. Bayer and E. M. McCreight. Organization and maintenance of large ordered indexes. *Acta Informatica*, 1(3):173–189, 1972.

[17] R. Beier and B. Vöcking. Random knapsack in expected polynomial time. *Journal of Computer and System Sciences*, 69(3):306–329, 2004.

[18] R. Bellman. On a routing problem. *Quarterly of Applied Mathematics*, 16(1):87–90, 1958.

[19] M. A. Bender, E. D. Demaine, and M. Farach-Colton. Cache-oblivious B-trees. In *41st Annual Symposium on Foundations of Computer Science*, pages 399–409, 2000.

[20] J. L. Bentley and M. D. McIlroy. Engineering a sort function. *Software Practice and Experience*, 23(11):1249–1265, 1993.

[21] J. L. Bentley and T. A. Ottmann. Algorithms for reporting and counting geometric intersections. *IEEE Transactions on Computers*, pages 643–647, 1979.

[22] J. L. Bentley and R. Sedgewick. Fast algorithms for sorting and searching strings. In *8th Annual ACM-SIAM Symposium on Discrete Algorithms*, pages 360–369, 1997.

[23] D. Bertsimas and J. N. Tsitsiklis. *Introduction to Linear Optimization*. Athena Scientific, 1997.

[24] G. E. Blelloch, C. E. Leiserson, B. M. Maggs, C. G. Plaxton, S. J. Smith, and M. Zagha. A comparison of sorting algorithms for the connection machine CM-2. In *3rd ACM Symposium on Parallel Algorithms and Architectures*, pages 3–16, 1991.

[25] M. Blum, R. W. Floyd, V. R. Pratt, R. L. Rivest, and R. E. Tarjan. Time bounds for selection. *Journal of Computer and System Sciences*, 7(4):448, 1972.

[26] N. Blum and K. Mehlhorn. On the average number of rebalancing operations in weight-balanced trees. *Theoretical Computer Science*, 11:303–320, 1980.

[27] Boost.org. Boost C++ Libraries. www.boost.org.

[28] O. Boruvka. O jistém problému minimálním. *Pràce, Moravské Prirodovedecké Spolecnosti*, pages 1–58, 1926.

[29] F. C. Botelho, R. Pagh, and N. Ziviani. Simple and space-efficient minimal perfect hash functions. In *10th Workshop on Algorithms and Data Structures*, volume 4619 of Lecture Notes in Computer Science, pages 139–150. Springer, 2007.

[30] G. S. Brodal. Worst-case efficient priority queues. In *7th Annual ACM-SIAM Symposium on Discrete Algorithms*, pages 52–58, 1996.

[31] G. S. Brodal and J. Katajainen. Worst-case efficient external-memory priority queues. In *6th Scandinavian Workshop on Algorithm Theory*, volume 1432 of Lecture Notes in Computer Science, pages 107–118. Springer, 1998.

[32] M. R. Brown and R. E. Tarjan. Design and analysis of a data structure for representing sorted lists. *SIAM Journal of Computing*, 9:594–614, 1980.

[33] R. Brown. Calendar queues: A fast $O(1)$ priority queue implementation for the simulation event set problem. *Communications of the ACM*, 31(10):1220–1227, 1988.

[34] J. L. Carter and M. N. Wegman. Universal classes of hash functions. *Journal of Computer and System Sciences*, 18(2):143–154, Apr. 1979.

[35] B. Chazelle. A minimum spanning tree algorithm with inverse-Ackermann type complexity. *Journal of the ACM*, 47:1028–1047, 2000.

[36] B. Chazelle and L. J. Guibas. Fractional cascading: I. A data structuring technique. *Algorithmica*, 1(2):133–162, 1986.

[37] B. Chazelle and L. J. Guibas. Fractional cascading: II. Applications. *Algorithmica*, 1(2):163–191, 1986.

[38] J.-C. Chen Proportion extend sort. *SIAM Journal on Computing*, 31(1):323–330, 2001.

[39] J. Cheriyan and K. Mehlhorn. Algorithms for dense graphs and networks. *Algorithmica*, 15(6):521–549, 1996.

[40] B. V. Cherkassky, A. V. Goldberg, and T. Radzik. Shortest path algorithms: Theory and experimental evaluation. *Mathematical Programming*, 73:129–174, 1996.

[41] E. G. Coffman, M. R. Garey, and D. S. Johnson. Approximation algorithms for bin packing: A survey. In D. Hochbaum, editor, *Approximation Algorithms for NP-Hard Problems*, pages 46–93. PWS, 1997.

[42] D. Cohen-Or, D. Levin, and O. Remez. Progressive compression of arbitrary triangular meshes. In *IEEE Conference on Visualization*, pages 67–72, 1999.

[43] S. A. Cook. *On the Minimum Computation Time of Functions*. PhD thesis, Harvard University, 1966.

[44] S. A. Cook. The complexity of theorem proving procedures. In *3rd ACM Symposium on Theory of Computing*, pages 151–158, 1971.

[45] G. B. Dantzig. Maximization of a linear function of variables subject to linear inequalities. In T. C. Koopmans, editor, *Activity Analysis of Production and Allocation*, pages 339–347. Wiley, 1951.

[46] M. de Berg, M. van Kreveld, M. Overmars, and O. Schwarzkopf. *Computational Geometry – Algorithms and Applications*. Springer, 2nd edition, 2000.

[47] R. Dementiev, L. Kettner, J. Mehnert, and P. Sanders. Engineering a sorted list data structure for 32 bit keys. In *6th Workshop on Algorithm Engineering & Experiments*, New Orleans, 2004.

[48] R. Dementiev, L. Kettner, and P. Sanders. STXXL: Standard Template Library for XXL data sets. *Software: Practice and Experience*, 2007. To appear, see also http://stxxl.sourceforge.net/.

[49] R. Dementiev and P. Sanders. Asynchronous parallel disk sorting. In *15th ACM Symposium on Parallelism in Algorithms and Architectures*, pages 138–148, San Diego, 2003.

[50] R. Dementiev, P. Sanders, D. Schultes, and J. Sibeyn. Engineering an external memory minimum spanning tree algorithm. In *IFIP TCS*, Toulouse, 2004.

[51] L. Devroye. A note on the height of binary search trees. *Journal of the ACM*, 33:289–498, 1986.

[52] R. B. Dial. Shortest-path forest with topological ordering. *Communications of the ACM*, 12(11):632–633, 1969.

[53] M. Dietzfelbinger, T. Hagerup, J. Katajainen, and M. Penttonen. A reliable randomized algorithm for the closest-pair problem. *Journal of Algorithms*, 1(25):19–51, 1997.

[54] M. Dietzfelbinger, A. Karlin, K. Mehlhorn, F. Meyer auf der Heide, H. Rohnert, and R. E. Tarjan. Dynamic perfect hashing: Upper and lower bounds. *SIAM Journal of Computing*, 23(4):738–761, 1994.

[55] M. Dietzfelbinger and C. Weidling. Balanced allocation and dictionaries with tightly packed constant size bins. *Theoretical Computer Science*, 380(1–2):47–68, 2007.

[56] E. W. Dijkstra. A note on two problems in connexion with graphs. *Numerische Mathematik*, 1:269–271, 1959.

[57] E. A. Dinic. Economical algorithms for finding shortest paths in a network. In *Transportation Modeling Systems*, pages 36–44, 1978.

[58] W. Domschke and A. Drexl. *Einführung in Operations Research*. Springer, 2007.

[59] J. R. Driscoll, N. Sarnak, D. D. Sleator, and R. E. Tarjan. Making data structures persistent. *Journal of Computer and System Sciences*, 38(1):86–124, 1989.

[60] J. Fakcharoenphol and S. Rao. Planar graphs, negative weight edges, shortest paths, and near linear time. *Journal of Computer and System Sciences*, 72(5):868–889, 2006.

[61] R. Fleischer. A tight lower bound for the worst case of Bottom-Up-Heapsort. *Algorithmica*, 11(2):104–115, 1994.

[62] R. Floyd. Assigning meaning to programs. In J. Schwarz, editor, *Mathematical Aspects of Computer Science*, pages 19–32. AMS, 1967.

[63] L. R. Ford. Network flow theory. Technical Report P-923, Rand Corporation, Santa Monica, California, 1956.

[64] E. Fredkin. Trie memory. *Communications of the ACM*, 3:490–499, 1960.

[65] M. L. Fredman. On the efficiency of pairing heaps and related data structures. *Journal of the ACM*, 46(4):473–501, 1999.

[66] M. L. Fredman, J. Komlos, and E. Szemeredi. Storing a sparse table with $O(1)$ worst case access time. *Journal of the ACM*, 31:538–544, 1984.

[67] M. L. Fredman, R. Sedgewick, D. D. Sleator, and R. E. Tarjan. The pairing heap: A new form of self-adjusting heap. *Algorithmica*, 1:111–129, 1986.

[68] M. L. Fredman and R. E. Tarjan. Fibonacci heaps and their uses in improved network optimization algorithms. *Journal of the ACM*, 34:596–615, 1987.

[69] M. Frigo, C. E. Leiserson, H. Prokop, and S. Ramachandran. Cache-oblivious algorithms. In *40th IEEE Symposium on Foundations of Computer Science*, pages 285–298, 1999.

[70] H. N. Gabow. Path-based depth-first search for strong and biconnected components. *Information Processing Letters*, pages 107–114, 2000.

[71] E. Gamma, R. Helm, R. Johnson, and J. Vlissides. *Design Patterns: Elements of Reusable Object-Oriented Software*. Addison-Wesley, 1995.

[72] M. R. Garey and D. S. Johnson. *Computers and Intractability: A Guide to the Theory of NP-Completeness*. W. H. Freeman, 1979.

[73] B. Gärtner and J. Matousek. *Understanding and Using Linear Programming*. Springer, 2006.

[74] GMP (GNU Multiple Precision Arithmetic Library). http://gmplib.org/.

[75] A. V. Goldberg. Scaling algorithms for the shortest path problem. *SIAM Journal on Computing*, 24:494–504, 1995.

[76] A. V. Goldberg. A simple shortest path algorithm with linear average time. In *9th European Symposium on Algorithms*, volume 2161 of Lecture Notes in Computer Science, pages 230–241. Springer, 2001.

[77] A. V. Goldberg and C. Harrelson. Computing the shortest path: A^* meets graph theory. In *16th Annual ACM-SIAM Symposium on Discrete Algorithms*, pages 156–165, 2005.

[78] M. T. Goodrich and R. Tamassia. JDSL – the data structures library in Java. http://www.jdsl.org/.

[79] G. Graefe and P.-A. Larson. B-tree indexes and CPU caches. In *17th International Conference on Data Engineering*, pages 349–358. IEEE, 2001.

[80] R. L. Graham. Bounds for certain multiprocessing anomalies. *Bell System Technical Journal*, 45:1563–1581, 1966.

[81] R. L. Graham, D. E. Knuth, and O. Patashnik. *Concrete Mathematics*. Addison-Wesley, 2nd edition, 1994.

[82] J. F. Grantham and C. Pomerance. Prime numbers. In K. H. Rosen, editor, *Handbook of Discrete and Combinatorial Mathematics*, chapter 4.4, pages 236–254. CRC Press, 2000.

[83] R. Grossi and G. Italiano. Efficient techniques for maintaining multi-dimensional keys in linked data structures. In *26th International Colloquium on Automata, Languages and Programming*, volume 1644 of Lecture Notes in Computer Science, pages 372–381. Springer, 1999.

[84] S. Halperin and U. Zwick. Optimal randomized EREW PRAM algorithms for finding spanning forests and for other basic graph connectivity problems. In *7th Annual ACM-SIAM Symposium on Discrete Algorithms*, pages 438–447, 1996.

[85] Y. Han and M. Thorup. Integer sorting in $O(n\sqrt{\log\log n})$ expected time and linear space. In *42nd IEEE Symposium on Foundations of Computer Science*, pages 135–144, 2002.

[86] G. Handler and I. Zang. A dual algorithm for the constrained shortest path problem. *Networks*, 10:293–309, 1980.

[87] J. Hartmanis and J. Simon. On the power of multiplication in random access machines. In *5th IEEE Symposium on Foundations of Computer Science*, pages 13–23, 1974.

[88] M. Held and R. Karp. The traveling-salesman problem and minimum spanning trees. *Operations Research*, 18:1138–1162, 1970.

[89] M. Held and R. Karp. The traveling-salesman problem and minimum spanning trees, part II. *Mathematical Programming*, 1:6–25, 1971.

[90] P. V. Hentenryck and L. Michel. *Constraint-Based Local Search*. MIT Press, 2005.

[91] C. A. R. Hoare. An axiomatic basis for computer programming. *Communications of the ACM*, 12:576–585, 1969.

278   References

[92] C. A. R. Hoare. Proof of correctness of data representations. *Acta Informatica*, 1:271–281, 1972.

[93] R. D. Hofstadter. Metamagical themas. *Scientific American*, pages 16–22, January 1983.

[94] P. Høyer. A general technique for implementation of efficient priority queues. In *3rd Israeli Symposium on Theory of Computing and Systems*, pages 57–66, 1995.

[95] S. Huddlestone and K. Mehlhorn. A new data structure for representing sorted lists. *Acta Informatica*, 17:157–184, 1982.

[96] J. Iacono. Improved upper bounds for pairing heaps. In *7th Scandinavian Workshop on Algorithm Theory*, volume 1851 of Lecture Notes in Computer Science, pages 32–45. Springer, 2000.

[97] A. Itai, A. G. Konheim, and M. Rodeh. A sparse table implementation of priority queues. In *8th International Colloquium on Automata, Languages and Programming*, volume 115 of Lecture Notes in Computer Science, pages 417–431. Springer, 1981.

[98] V. Jarník. O jistém problému minimálním. *Práca Moravské Přírodovědecké Společnosti*, 6:57–63, 1930.

[99] K. Jensen and N. Wirth. *Pascal User Manual and Report: ISO Pascal Standard*. Springer, 1991.

[100] T. Jiang, M. Li, and P. Vitányi. Average-case complexity of shellsort. In *26th International Colloquium on Automata, Languages and Programming*, volume 1644 of Lecture Notes in Computer Science, pages 453–462. Springer, 1999.

[101] D. S. Johnson, C. R. Aragon, L. A. McGeoch, and C. Schevon. Optimization by simulated annealing: Experimental evaluation; part II, graph coloring and number partitioning. *Operations Research*, 39(3):378–406, 1991.

[102] K. Kaligosi and P. Sanders. How branch mispredictions affect quicksort. In *14th European Symposium on Algorithms*, volume 4168 of Lecture Notes in Computer Science, pages 780–791. Springer, 2006.

[103] H. Kaplan and R. E. Tarjan. New heap data structures. Technical Report TR-597-99, Princeton University, 1999.

[104] A. Karatsuba and Y. Ofman. Multiplication of multidigit numbers on automata. *Soviet Physics Doklady*, 7(7):595–596, 1963.

[105] D. Karger, P. N. Klein, and R. E. Tarjan. A randomized linear-time algorithm for finding minimum spanning trees. *Journal of the ACM*, 42:321–329, 1995.

[106] N. Karmakar. A new polynomial-time algorithm for linear programming. *Combinatorica*, pages 373–395, 1984.

[107] J. Katajainen and B. B. Mortensen. Experiences with the design and implementation of space-efficient deque. In *Workshop on Algorithm Engineering*, volume 2141 of Lecture Notes in Computer Science, pages 39–50. Springer, 2001.

[108] I. Katriel, P. Sanders, and J. L. Träff. A practical minimum spanning tree algorithm using the cycle property. Technical Report MPI-I-2002-1-003, MPI Informatik, Germany, October 2002.

[109] H. Kellerer, U. Pferschy, and D. Pisinger. *Knapsack Problems*. Springer, 2004.

[110] L. Khachiyan. A polynomial time algorithm in linear programming. *Soviet Mathematics Doklady*, 20(1):191–194, 1979.

[111] V. King. A simpler minimum spanning tree verification algorithm. *Algorithmica*, 18:263–270, 1997.

[112] D. E. Knuth. *The Art of Computer Programming: Sorting and Searching*, volume 3. Addison-Wesley, 2nd edition, 1998.

[113] D. E. Knuth. *MMIXware: A RISC Computer for the Third Millennium*, volume 1750 of Lecture Notes in Computer Science. Springer, 1999.

[114] R. E. Korf. Depth-first iterative-deepening: An optimal admissible tree search. *Artificial Intelligence*, 27:97–109, 1985.

[115] B. Korte and J. Vygen. *Combinatorial Optimization: Theory and Algorithms*. Springer, 2000.

[116] J. Kruskal. On the shortest spanning subtree of a graph and the traveling salesman problem. *Proceedings of the American Mathematical Society*, 7:48–50, 1956.

[117] F. L. Lawler, J. K. Lenstra, A. H. G. Rinooy Kan, and D. B. Shmoys. *The Traveling Salesman Problem*. Wiley, 1985.

[118] LEDA (Library of Efficient Data Types and Algorithms). www.algorithmic-solutions.com.

[119] L. Q. Lee, A. Lumsdaine, and J. G. Siek. *The Boost Graph Library: User Guide and Reference Manual*. Addison-Wesley, 2002.

[120] L. Levin. Universal search problems. *Problemy Peredachi Informatsii*, 9(3):265–266, 1973.

[121] I. Lustig and J.-F. Puget. Program does not equal program: Constraint programming and its relationship to mathematical programming. *Interfaces*, 31:29–53, 2001.

[122] S. Martello and P. Toth. *Knapsack Problems: Algorithms and Computer Implementations*. Wiley, 1990.

[123] C. Martínez and S. Roura. Optimal sampling strategies in Quicksort and Quickselect. *SIAM Journal on Computing*, 31(3):683–705, 2002.

[124] C. McGeoch, P. Sanders, R. Fleischer, P. R. Cohen, and D. Precup. Using finite experiments to study asymptotic performance. In *Experimental Algorithmics — From Algorithm Design to Robust and Efficient Software*, volume 2547 of Lecture Notes in Computer Science, pages 1–23. Springer, 2002.

[125] MCSTL: The Multi-Core Standard Template Library. http://algo2.iti.uni-karlsruhe.de/singler/mcstl/.

[126] K. Mehlhorn. A faster approximation algorithm for the Steiner problem in graphs. *Information Processing Letters*, 27(3):125–128, Mar. 1988.

[127] K. Mehlhorn. Amortisierte Analyse. In T. Ottmann, editor, *Prinzipien des Algorithmenentwurfs*, pages 91–102. Spektrum Lehrbuch, 1998.

[128] K. Mehlhorn and U. Meyer. External memory breadth-first search with sublinear I/O. In *10th European Symposium on Algorithms*, volume 2461 of Lecture Notes in Computer Science, pages 723–735. Springer, 2002.

280   References

[129] K. Mehlhorn and S. Näher. Bounded ordered dictionaries in $O(\log\log N)$ time and $O(n)$ space. *Information Processing Letters*, 35(4):183–189, 1990.

[130] K. Mehlhorn and S. Näher. Dynamic fractional cascading. *Algorithmica*, 5:215–241, 1990.

[131] K. Mehlhorn and S. Näher. *The LEDA Platform for Combinatorial and Geometric Computing*. Cambridge University Press, 1999.

[132] K. Mehlhorn, S. Näher, and P. Sanders. Engineering DFS-based graph algorithms. Submitted, 2007.

[133] K. Mehlhorn, V. Priebe, G. Schäfer, and N. Sivadasan. All-pairs shortest-paths computation in the presence of negative cycles. *Information Processing Letters*, 81(6):341–343, 2002.

[134] K. Mehlhorn and P. Sanders. Scanning multiple sequences via cache memory. *Algorithmica*, 35(1):75–93, 2003.

[135] K. Mehlhorn and M. Ziegelmann. Resource constrained shortest paths. In *8th European Symposium on Algorithms*, volume 1879 of Lecture Notes in Computer Science, pages 326–337, 2000.

[136] R. Mendelson, R. E. Tarjan, M. Thorup, and U. Zwick. Melding priority queues. In *9th Scandinavian Workshop on Algorithm Theory*, pages 223–235, 2004.

[137] *Meyers Konversationslexikon*. Bibliographisches Institut, 1888.

[138] B. Meyer. *Object-Oriented Software Construction*. Prentice Hall, 2nd edition, 1997.

[139] U. Meyer. Average-case complexity of single-source shortest-path algorithms: Lower and upper bounds. *Journal of Algorithms*, 48(1):91–134, 2003.

[140] U. Meyer and P. Sanders. Δ-stepping: A parallel shortest path algorithm. In *6th European Symposium on Algorithms*, number 1461 in Lecture Notes in Computer Science, pages 393–404. Springer, 1998.

[141] U. Meyer, P. Sanders, and J. Sibeyn, editors. *Algorithms for Memory Hierarchies*, volume 2625 of Lecture Notes in Computer Science. Springer, 2003.

[142] B. M. E. Moret and H. D. Shapiro. An empirical analysis of algorithms for constructing a minimum spanning tree. In *2nd Workshop on Algorithms and Data Structures*, volume 519 of Lecture Notes in Computer Science, pages 400–411. Springer, 1991.

[143] R. Morris. Scatter storage techniques. *Communications of the ACM*, 11(1):38–44, 1968.

[144] S. S. Muchnick. *Advanced Compiler Design and Implementation*. Morgan Kaufmann, 1997.

[145] S. Näher and O. Zlotowski. Design and implementation of efficient data types for static graphs. In *10th European Symposium on Algorithms*, volume 2461 of Lecture Notes in Computer Science, pages 748–759. Springer, 2002.

[146] G. Nemhauser and Z. Ullmann. Discrete dynamic programming and capital allocation. *Management Science*, 15(9):494–505, 1969.

[147] G. Nemhauser and L. Wolsey. *Integer and Combinatorial Optimization*. Wiley, 1988.

[148] J. Nešetřil, H. Milková, and H. Nešetřilová. Otakar Boruvka on minimum spanning tree problem: Translation of both the 1926 papers, comments, history. *Discrete Mathematics*, 233(1–3):3–36, 2001.

[149] K. S. Neubert. The flashsort1 algorithm. *Dr. Dobb's Journal*, pages 123–125, February 1998.

[150] J. Nievergelt and E. Reingold. Binary search trees of bounded balance. *SIAM Journal of Computing*, 2:33–43, 1973.

[151] K. Noshita. A theorem on the expected complexity of Dijkstra's shortest path algorithm. *Journal of Algorithms*, 6(3):400–408, 1985.

[152] R. Pagh and F. Rodler. Cuckoo hashing. *Journal of Algorithms*, 51:122–144, 2004.

[153] W. W. Peterson. Addressing for random access storage. *IBM Journal of Research and Development*, 1(2), Apr. 1957.

[154] S. Pettie. Towards a final analysis of pairing heaps. In *46th IEEE Symposium on Foundations of Computer Science*, pages 174–183, 2005.

[155] S. Pettie and V. Ramachandran. An optimal minimum spanning tree algorithm. In *27th International Colloquium on Automata, Languages and Programming*, volume 1853 of Lecture Notes in Computer Science, pages 49–60. Springer, 2000.

[156] J. Pinkerton. *Voyages and Travels*, volume 2. 1808.

[157] P. J. Plauger, A. A. Stepanov, M. Lee, and D. R. Musser. *The C++ Standard Template Library*. Prentice Hall, 2000.

[158] R. C. Prim. Shortest connection networks and some generalizations. *Bell Systems Technical Journal*, pages 1389–1401, Nov. 1957.

[159] W. Pugh. Skip lists: A probabilistic alternative to balanced trees. *Communications of the ACM*, 33(6):668–676, 1990.

[160] A. Ranade, S. Kothari, and R. Udupa. Register efficient mergesorting. In *High Performance Computing*, volume 1970 of Lecture Notes in Computer Science, pages 96–103. Springer, 2000.

[161] J. H. Reif. Depth-first search is inherently sequential. *Information Processing Letters*, 20(5):229–234, 1985.

[162] N. Robertson, D. P. Sanders, P. Seymour, and R. Thomas. Efficiently four-coloring planar graphs. In *28th ACM Symposium on Theory of Computing*, pages 571–575, 1996.

[163] G. Robins and A. Zelikwosky. Improved Steiner tree approximation in graphs. In *11th ACM-SIAM Symposium on Discrete Algorithms*, pages 770–779, 2000.

[164] P. Sanders. Fast priority queues for cached memory. *ACM Journal of Experimental Algorithmics*, 5(7), 2000.

[165] P. Sanders and D. Schultes. Highway hierarchies hasten exact shortest path queries. In *13th European Symposium on Algorithms*, volume 3669 of Lecture Notes in Computer Science, pages 568–579. Springer, 2005.

[166] P. Sanders and D. Schultes. Engineering fast route planning algorithms. In *6th Workshop on Experimental Algorithms*, volume 4525 of Lecture Notes in Computer Science, pages 23–36. Springer, 2007.

[167] P. Sanders and S. Winkel. Super scalar sample sort. In *12th European Symposium on Algorithms*, volume 3221 of Lecture Notes in Computer Science, pages 784–796. Springer, 2004.

[168] R. Santos and F. Seidel. A better upper bound on the number of triangulations of a planar point set. *Journal of Combinatorial Theory, Series A*, 102(1):186–193, 2003.

[169] R. Schaffer and R. Sedgewick. The analysis of heapsort. *Journal of Algorithms*, 15:76–100, 1993.

[170] A. Schönhage. Storage modification machines. *SIAM Journal on Computing*, 9:490–508, 1980.

[171] A. Schönhage and V. Strassen. Schnelle Multiplikation großer Zahlen. *Computing*, 7:281–292, 1971.

[172] A. Schrijver. *Theory of Linear and Integer Programming*. Wiley, 1986.

[173] D. Schultes. *Route Planning in Road Networks*. PhD thesis, 2008.

[174] R. Sedgewick. Analysis of shellsort and related algorithms. In *4th European Symposium on Algorithms*, volume 1136 of Lecture Notes in Computer Science, pages 1–11. Springer, 1996.

[175] R. Sedgewick and P. Flajolet. *An Introduction to the Analysis of Algorithms*. Addison-Wesley, 1996.

[176] R. Seidel and C. Aragon. Randomized search trees. *Algorithmica*, 16(4–5):464–497, 1996.

[177] R. Seidel and M. Sharir. Top-down analysis of path compression. *SIAM Journal of Computing*, 34(3):515–525, 2005.

[178] M. Sharir. A strong-connectivity algorithm and its applications in data flow analysis. *Computers and Mathematics with Applications*, 7(1):67–72, 1981.

[179] J. C. Shepherdson and H. E. Sturgis. Computability of recursive functions. *Journal of the ACM*, 10(2):217–255, 1963.

[180] J. Singler, P. Sanders, and F. Putze. MCSTL: The Multi-Core Standard Template Library. In *Euro-Par*, volume 4641 of Lecture Notes in Computer Science, pages 682–694. Springer, 2007.

[181] M. Sipser. *Introduction to the Theory of Computation*. MIT Press, 1998.

[182] D. D. Sleator and R. E. Tarjan. A data structure for dynamic trees. *Journal of Computer and System Sciences*, 26(3):362–391, 1983.

[183] D. D. Sleator and R. E. Tarjan. Self-adjusting binary search trees. *Journal of the ACM*, 32(3):652–686, 1985.

[184] D. Spielman and S.-H. Teng. Smoothed analysis of algorithms: Why the simplex algorithm usually takes polynomial time. *Journal of the ACM*, 51(3):385–463, 2004.

[185] R. E. Tarjan. Depth first search and linear graph algorithms. *SIAM Journal on Computing*, 1:146–160, 1972.

[186] R. E. Tarjan. Efficiency of a good but not linear set union algorithm. *Journal of the ACM*, 22(2):215–225, 1975.

[187] R. E. Tarjan. Shortest paths. Technical report, AT&T Bell Laboratories, 1981.

[188] R. E. Tarjan. Amortized computational complexity. *SIAM Journal on Algebraic and Discrete Methods*, 6(2):306–318, 1985.

[189] R. E. Tarjan and U. Vishkin. An efficient parallel biconnectivity algorithm. *SIAM Journal on Computing*, 14(4):862–874, 1985.

[190] M. Thorup. Undirected single source shortest paths in linear time. *Journal of the ACM*, 46:362–394, 1999.

[191] M. Thorup. Even strongly universal hashing is pretty fast. In *11th Annual ACM-SIAM Symposium on Discrete Algorithms*, pages 496–497, 2000.

[192] M. Thorup. Compact oracles for reachability and approximate distances in planar digraphs. *Journal of the ACM*, 51(6):993–1024, 2004.

[193] M. Thorup. Integer priority queues with decrease key in constant time and the single source shortest paths problem. In *35th ACM Symposium on Theory of Computing*, pages 149–158, 2004.

[194] M. Thorup. Integer priority queues with decrease key in constant time and the single source shortest paths problem. *Journal of Computer and System Sciences*, 69(3):330–353, 2004.

[195] M. Thorup and U. Zwick. Approximate distance oracles. In *33rd ACM Symposium on the Theory of Computing*, pages 183–192, 2001.

[196] A. Toom. The complexity of a scheme of functional elements realizing the multiplication of integers. *Soviet Mathematics Doklady*, 150(3):496–498, 1963.

[197] Unknown. *Der Handlungsreisende – wie er sein soll und was er zu thun hat, um Auftraege zu erhalten und eines gluecklichen Erfolgs in seinen Geschaeften gewiss zu sein – Von einem alten Commis-Voyageur.* 1832.

[198] P. van Emde Boas. Preserving order in a forest in less than logarithmic time. *Information Processing Letters*, 6(3):80–82, 1977.

[199] R. Vanderbei. *Linear Programming: Foundations and Extensions*. Springer, 2001.

[200] V. Vazirani. *Approximation Algorithms*. Springer, 2000.

[201] J. von Neumann. First draft of a report on the EDVAC. Technical report, University of Pennsylvania, 1945.

[202] J. Vuillemin. A data structure for manipulating priority queues. *Communications of the ACM*, 21:309–314, 1978.

[203] L. Wall, T. Christiansen, and J. Orwant. *Programming Perl*. O'Reilly, 3rd edition, 2000.

[204] I. Wegener. BOTTOM-UP-HEAPSORT, a new variant of HEAPSORT beating, on an average, QUICKSORT (if *n* is not very small). *Theoretical Computer Science*, 118(1):81–98, 1993.

[205] I. Wegener. *Complexity Theory: Exploring the Limits of Efficient Algorithms*. Springer, 2005.

[206] R. Wickremesinghe, L. Arge, J. S. Chase, and J. S. Vitter. Efficient sorting using registers and caches. *ACM Journal of Experimental Algorithmics*, 7(9), 2002.

[207] R. Wilhelm and D. Maurer. *Compiler Design*. Addison-Wesley, 1995.

[208] J. W. J. Williams. Algorithm 232: Heapsort. *Communications of the ACM*, 7:347–348, 1964.

Index